REHABILITATION
NURSING
PROCEDURES MANUAL

THE REHABILITATION INSTITUTE OF CHICAGO PUBLICATION SERIES
Don A. Olson, Ph.D., Series Coordinator

Rehabilitation
Institute of
Chicago
PROCEDURE
MANUAL

REHABILITATION
NURSING
PROCEDURES MANUAL

**Rehabilitation Institute of Chicago
Division of Nursing**

AN ASPEN PUBLICATION®
Aspen Publishers, Inc.
Rockville, Maryland
1990

Library of Congress Cataloging-in-Publication Data

Rehabilitation nursing procedures manual/the Nursing Division,
the Rehabilitation Institute of Chicago.
p. cm.--(The Rehabilitation Institute of Chicago series)
"An Aspen publication."
Includes bibliographies and index.
ISBN: 0-8342-0076-7
1. Rehabilitation nursing--Handbooks, manuals, etc.
I. Rehabilitation Institute of Chicago. Nursing Division.
II. Series. [DNLM: 1. Nursing. 2. Rehabilitation--nurses' instruction. WY 150 R3445]
RT120.R4R42   1989   610.73--dc20   DNLM/DLC
for Library of Congress
89-17514
CIP

The authors have made every effort to ensure the accuracy of the information herein,
particularly with regard to drug selection and dose. However, appropriate information
sources should be consulted, especially for new or unfamiliar procedures. It is the
responsibility of every practitioner to evaluate the appropriateness of a particular
opinion in the context of actual clinical situations and with due consideration to new
developments. Authors, editors, and the publisher cannot be held responsible for any
typographical or other errors found in this book.

Editorial Services: Marsha Davies

Library of Congress Catalog Card Number: 89-17514
ISBN: 0-8342-0076-7

Printed in the United States of America

1 2 3 4 5

Table of Contents

Contributors

GENERAL EDITORS

Carolyn E. Carlson, PhD, RN
Associate Director of Nursing for Research and Evaluation
Rehabilitation Institute of Chicago

Winona P. Griggs, MSN, CRRN
Director of Nursing Education
Rehabilitation Institute of Chicago

Rosemarie B. King, MS, RN
Doctoral Candidate, University of Illinois
Clinical Specialist
Rehabilitation Institute of Chicago

CHAPTER EDITORS

Therese T. Alexander, MSN, CRRN
Clinical Educator
Rehabilitation Institute of Chicago

Eileen T. French, BSN, CRRN
Formerly, Clinical Director of Nursing
Rehabilitation Institute of Chicago

Patricia S. Gregor, BSN, RN
Assistant Clinical Director/Nursing
Rehabilitation Institute of Chicago

Winona P. Griggs, MSN, CRRN
Director of Nursing Education
Rehabilitation Institute of Chicago

Nancye B. Holt, MS, RN
Vice President, Nursing and Allied Health
Rehabilitation Institute of Chicago

Rosemarie B. King, MS, RN
Doctoral Candidate, University of Illinois
Clinical Specialist
Rehabilitation Institute of Chicago

Dorothy Kubalanza-Sipp, BSN, CRRN
Staff Nurse
Rehabilitation Institute of Chicago

Mary Ann Pinkowski, BSN, CRRN
Clinical Instructor
Rehabilitation Institute of Chicago

Kathleen A. Stevens, MS, CRRN
Clinical Director of Nursing
Rehabilitation Institute of Chicago

REVIEWERS

Nursing Procedure Committee
Rehabilitation Institute of Chicago

Chairperson

Kathleen A. Stevens, MS, CRRN

Members

Therese T. Alexander, MSN, CRRN
Ruthann Brinkman, BSN, RN
Christine Frost, BSN, CRRN
Betsy Granfeldt, ADN, CRRN
Randy S. Temple, RN, CRRN

GENERAL REVIEWERS

Marikay Kiely-Menard, BSN, RN
Rehabilitation Institute of Chicago

Peggy Matthews Kirk, BSN, CRRN
Rehabilitation Institute of Chicago

Acknowledgments

The procedures that follow are the results of the work of countless members of the nursing staff at the Rehabilitation Institute of Chicago since its establishment. We are grateful for the contributions of each person over the many years. The efforts of Marikay Kiely-Menard deserve special recognition. During her tenure as Clinical Educator, Marikay established a standardized format for procedures and helped the Division of Nursing make great strides in developing and updating procedures. Much of the current work is developed from the foundation that she helped establish.

Several individuals played specific roles in the completion of this book. First, the chapter editors put in many hours in addition to their already heavy schedules to complete their work. The members of the Procedure Committee, under the direction of Kathleen Stevens, reviewed the individual procedures and made helpful suggestions. Mary Davis and Rosa Melendez worked many months typing the multiple drafts required to complete a task of this nature. Peggy Matthews Kirk and Marikay Kiely-Menard reviewed many sections for the editors.

Finally, we thank Nancye B. Holt, Vice President for Nursing and Allied Health, for her unending support and encouragement to the contributors during the many months spent on this book.

Carolyn E. Carlson
Winona P. Griggs
Rosemarie B. King

Introduction

Nursing standards are the foundation for quality patient care. There are many types of standards that contribute to quality outcomes. The Joint Commission on Accreditation of Hospitals (Patterson, Kranz, & Brandt, 1986) identifies three types of nursing standards: standards of care, standards of practice, and standards of performance. Standards of practice focus on the person providing the care and include the plan of care, written policies, and written procedures of the nursing department. Standards of practice reflect the mission and philosophy of the agency and department of nursing. The American Nurses' Association (ANA) and the Association of Rehabilitation Nurses have developed standards for rehabilitation nursing practice (ANA, 1987) that include practice and performance standards. The present text includes procedures that are used commonly by nurses working in rehabilitation and other settings.

The purpose of having a manual of procedures is to provide a foundation for the delivery of safe, effective care. Adherence to procedural standards is imperative for maintaining quality patient care. Advances in knowledge and technology may necessitate changes in procedures; therefore, a regular, systematic process for reviewing, revising, and approving procedures is essential.

SCOPE AND USE

Procedures selected for inclusion are those that are key to rehabilitation. They are commonly used for patients with disabilities such as paraplegia, quadriplegia, and hemiplegia or alterations in function such as mobility, dysphagia, urinary incontinence, actual and potential bowel complications, respiratory problems, and others. The procedures can be used to facilitate the achievement and maintenance of optimal function and to prevent further disability or complication. Although most of the procedures focus on physical needs and functions, these needs and functions are inextricably tied to psychosocial and spiritual needs. Implementation of procedures in a thoughtful and sensitive manner, allowing for individualization of care, can prevent embarrassment and facilitate adaptation to illness and disability. Explanation of procedures to the patient and family before performing them is fundamental to a patient-centered approach.

This book is not exhaustive. We have not included general procedures that are required in all health care institutions, such as procedures for a bed bath, oral hygiene, perineal care, post-mortem care, and administration of medications. These are available in other manuals. Infection control procedures are modified frequently as a result of a changing base of information about disease transmission; therefore, only guidelines that are fundamental to procedures in this manual are included.

The procedures selected for this book are those basic to rehabilitation that may or may not be included in a general nursing procedure book. Lack of inclusion of a particular procedure does not indicate that it is unimportant.

FORMAT

The procedures are presented in chapters that include an introduction, specific procedures, and a bibliography. The introduction to each section provides the reader with a description of the goals to be met through the procedures included in the chapter, a description of the specific procedures that are included, examples of circumstances when the procedures would be used, and factors to consider when doing particular procedures, such as age or developmental level and limiting factors.

Procedures are organized into six chapters that cover feeding, mobility, bowel and bladder elimination, skin care, respiratory care, and safety. In many chapters, specific procedures for home care are included.

LEVEL OF STAFF TO PERFORM

Specification of the level of staff required to perform a procedure (e.g., nursing assistant or registered nurse) is important. The reader will note that the level of staff required to do each procedure is left blank in all the procedures. Because of differences in Nurse Practice Acts from state to state, variations in job descriptions, and institutional preferences, each institution needs to establish standards regarding appropriate personnel to perform specific tasks and procedures.

RATIONALE FOR PROCEDURAL STEPS

The nursing profession is striving to improve its practice through research. Procedures should be developed on the basis of the most current research in nursing and related fields. The authors have attempted to include references to document the rationale for procedures. Research is needed in many areas to determine the most effective, safe, and efficient steps to accomplish the procedural objectives. In the absence of research results, procedures are developed on the basis of clinician experience.

DOCUMENTATION

Documentation is an important part of many procedures. When establishing a bowel program, for example, it is important that the program be part of the nursing care plan and that progress be recorded in the medical record. Each institution has its own procedures and forms for manual or automated documentation. Modifications in documentation procedures will be necessary to meet institutional requirements.

RESOURCES

Each professional or institution that uses these procedures will need to establish resources for obtaining required equipment and determining specific products to use, such as catheters, brands of bed support surfaces, and so forth. These resources can be included as part of the actual procedure. For example, some institutions have a respiratory therapy department as a resource whereas others do not. Respiratory procedures need to be modified to refer to and use appropriate resources.

AUDIENCE

The procedures will be helpful to health care providers in rehabilitation units or facilities, skilled nursing units, nursing homes, home health care agencies, public health agencies, and visiting nurse agencies. Many of the procedures can be adapted for home use by patients and family.

The procedures are intended as guidelines and should be reviewed and adapted as necessary before approval for use in a particular practice setting. Although the authors sincerely hope that the use of the procedures included in this book will benefit all patient populations served, we must expressly disclaim liability for any injury resulting from the improper or negligent use of the procedures. Further, references to and opinions expressed regarding the efficacy of any product or piece of equipment are based on the subjective experience of the staff of the Rehabilitation Institute of Chicago and not on statistical data. Such references and opinions do not constitute an endorsement of any product or equipment.

INFECTION CONTROL

Protection of the patient and caregiver from transmission of infectious diseases and pathogenic organisms is a function of any health care agency. Readers are encouraged to keep up to date on the literature related to infection control.

Procedures for body substance isolation, drug-resistant organism precautions, and strict or respiratory isolation are included in Fundamental Guidelines for Infection Control. All procedures that follow should be viewed within the framework of the steps required to reduce the risk of transmission of disease and pathogenic organisms. For example, handwashing steps as identified in the body substance isolation procedures should be followed as appropriate in all other procedures in the manual.

Fundamental Guidelines for Infection Control

BODY SUBSTANCE ISOLATION

PURPOSE

To reduce the risk of transmission of infectious diseases and pathogenic organisms from a patient or employee to another patient or employee.

GUIDELINES

These guidelines, procedures, and policies reflect, and should be applied within, the limitations imposed by concerns for patient and employee safety, patient clinical status, and product availability.

1. Hands should be washed with the use of appropriate techniques before and after:
   - all direct patient care;
   - all activities involving contact with the excreta or secreta of any patient or self;
   - all activities requiring the handling of any object that may have been contaminated by the excreta or secreta of any patient in any quantity.
2. Gloves are to be worn:
   - for any activity that may involve contact with the excreta, secreta, blood, or blood product of any patient;
   - for any activity requiring the handling of an object that has been contaminated with the excreta or secreta of any patient in any quantity;
   - by any employee who has an exudative dermatitis or open lesion on the hands while providing hands-on care to any patient with nonintact skin or drainage from body orifices;
   - by any employee providing hands-on care to any patient on strict isolation.
3. Moisture-resistant or -impervious gowns are to be worn:
   - for any activity that may involve gross contamination of clothing with the excreta, secreta, blood, or blood product of any patient;
   - for any activity with the probability of direct contact between an object that is likely to be contaminated with the excreta, secreta, blood, or blood product of a patient and an employee's clothing;
   - when splashing of an employee's clothing with patient blood, blood product, excreta, or secreta is likely.
4. Protective masks and eyewear are to be used during any activity that may involve the aerosolization of secreta or blood of any patient. For the employee who wears eyeglasses, the eyeglasses are generally considered sufficient. For the employee who does not wear eyeglasses, protective goggles or a face shield should be used.
5. Needles should be disposed of in puncture-resistant containers at point of use without being recapped, bent, or broken. Needles used to withdraw medications from a

vial may be removed from the syringe before disposal. Needles used for injection with a disposable syringe should be disposed of with the syringe still attached.

DRUG-RESISTANT ORGANISM PRECAUTIONS

PURPOSE

To prevent the transmission of drug-resistant organisms (as defined by current Centers for Disease Control or agency standards) from patient to patient.

RESTRICTIONS

The patient identified as having an infection or colonization caused by an organism defined as drug resistant shall have specific restrictions placed on treatment locale and treatment modality based on site of infection or colonization.

General restrictions applicable to all cases shall be as follows:

1. Such patient may not be treated in the therapeutic pool.
2. Such patient may not share a room with any patient:
   - having an indwelling catheter,
   - with a venous or arterial access device,
   - with a tracheostomy, or
   - who by reason of disease or as a result of other treatment is immunocompromised.
3. Such patient should not share a room with any patient on intermittent catheterization or with a surgical stoma of any type.

These restrictions should be maintained until such time as two consecutive cultures demonstrate no evidence of the resistant organism; cultures shall have been obtained a minimum of 24 hours apart and 48 hours after the patient received any antibiotic therapy.

The need for additional restrictions will be determined on an individual case-by-case basis by the person or persons in charge of infection control at the individual agency.

STRICT OR RESPIRATORY ISOLATION

PURPOSE

To minimize the risks of transmission of airborne pathogens and infectious diseases between a patient and employee or other patient.

GUIDELINES

1. The patient identified as having an airborne infectious disease shall be placed in a private room. The appropriate signage shall be placed outside the door of the patient's room, and all visitors must be screened by means of the appropriate guidelines as determined by the patient's diagnosis.
2. During the period of communicability, all treatment shall be administered in the patient's room unless otherwise authorized by the responsible person or persons at the agency.
3. Visitors to the patient who are not immune should be discouraged from visiting until the period of communicability has passed.
4. Masks shall be worn by all persons entering the room with the following exception: If the patient's diagnosis is one in which immunity may be conferred either by vaccination or previous exposure (i.e., measles [rubeola] or chickenpox [varicella zoster]), immune persons need not wear masks.
5. All other protective garb shall be used as described in the body substance isolation procedures.
6. Employees who are not immune should preferably not be assigned to the routine care of these patients.

REFERENCES

American Nurses' Association. (1987). *Standards of rehabilitation nursing practice*. Kansas City, MO: American Nurses' Association.

Centers for Disease Control. (1975). *Isolation techniques for use in hospitals* (DHEW Publication No. [CDC] 76-8314). Washington, DC: U.S. Government Printing Office.

Patterson, C.H., Kranz, D., & Brandt, B. (1986). *A guide to JCAH nursing service standards*. Chicago: Joint Commission on Accreditation of Hospitals.

chapter 1

Procedures To Establish, Maintain, and Improve Oral and Enteric Intake

INTRODUCTION

The oral and enteral nutritional care of patients in a rehabilitation setting is a shared team responsibility. Medicine and dietary assessments focus on requirements to sustain, supplement, and replenish. Professionals in communicative disorders (speech pathology) focus on oral motor function. The focus of occupational therapy is promoting self-care in feeding skills. All are concerned with the safety and efficiency of the route. Nursing assumes the major responsibility for nutrition, feeding, and ongoing assessment of patients.

Assessment

Although it is beyond the scope of this chapter to address all nutritional parameters, a review of key assessment factors is in order. Somatic parameters used to measure body stores include height, weight, ideal body weight (IBW), external appearance, muscle mass, and condition of the skin, hair, and mucous membranes. Specific measurements such as triceps skin fold and mid-arm circumference have not been standardized for neurologically impaired or immobilized patients; however, they may provide useful data about nutritional status.

Data available on visceral parameters such as oxygenation, hydration, and nutrient requirements vary. Nutrients include calories, proteins, and specific elements such as electrolytes, vitamins, and minerals. Most crucial to the interpretation of these parameters is an accurate appreciation of the patient's recent and present nutritional history, metabolic demands, and medical complications. A baseline assessment should include measurements of serum hemoglobin, hematocrit, white cell differential, chemistries, electrolytes, and protein (usually albumin). Serum levels of zinc, magnesium, and copper are measured intermittently. These are interpreted in relation to metabolic and activity states and expenditure parameters such as urine and body fluids output and content. Visceral parameters measure utilization and production of and demand for nutrients.

Anergy parameters measure immune competence and potential and actual resistance to injury, primarily infection. In an institutional setting, these have an effect not only on nutritional care but also on environmental care. Anergy can be indirectly measured by some of the visceral parameters, namely those that indicate blood cell production, hepatic function, and expenditures that are long term. Direct measures of anergy can be obtained by antigen or antibody tests. The reliability of results and safety in testing compromised patients are controversial, however.

Nurses are in the ideal position to obtain or request measures of nutritional parameters because they observe changes in patient status. They also assess for criteria to begin enteral feeding and to supplement or alter oral feeding. These criteria include:

1. fluctuating or unreliable level of consciousness;
2. cognitive function inconsistent with following commands, attending to, or safely performing oral feeding;
3. endurance or drive inadequate for sufficient intake;
4. oral motor or swallowing dysfunction inadequate for intake or that compromises airway protection;

5. severe metabolic demand; and
6. structural abnormalities or injury of the oral and digestive tracts.

Goal Setting

Major nursing goals to be set for patients requiring enteral nutrition include the following:

1. The patient receives adequate nutrients and fluids to meet requirements and to replenish losses.
2. The patient is free from complications (aspiration, tissue injury, infection, or bowel dysfunction).
3. The patient's nutritional program is adapted to lifestyle and therapeutic demands; it fosters normalcy, is economic, and can be implemented safely by educated caregivers.
4. The patient can be prepared for or upgraded to oral feeding.

Resources

In addition to the skills of the interdisciplinary rehabilitation team, the nurse may also utilize other resources for improved understanding in the care of patients needing specialized feeding approaches. These include:

1. standardized tables for calculating IBW, basal energy requirements, and specific nutrient requirements;
2. comparative product tables, usually available from pharmaceutical companies that produce feeding formulas and supplements (these may not be inclusive of all available, appropriate products);
3. the institution's own dietary manual; and
4. professional consultation services and materials available from gastroenterologists, nutritional support teams, and enterostomal therapists.

Limitations

Because most patients in a rehabilitation setting are presumed to have functional gastrointestinal tracts, the following procedures are limited to the use of the gut as nutritional receptor. Bowel sounds must be present prior to initiating oral or enteric feedings. Tables 1-1, 1-2, and 1-3 offer the enteric tube options related to patient characteristics. It is recognized that additional procedures will be required to supplement patients requiring intravenous or total parenteral nutrition.

Table 1-1 Enteric Tube Options for Patients with Functional Gastrointestinal Tract Who Are Alert and Have Protected Airway and Short-Term Need

Delivery Site	Route	Advantages	Disadvantages	Complications	Management and Prevention
Stomach (distal to esophageal sphincter)	1. Nasogastric (#8 to #16 French red rubber or polyvinyl)	**IN ROUTES 1, 2, 3:** Relative ease in insertion, tube change; placement verified by aspiration; normalized digestive process; wide variety of meal replacement formulas; temporary, noninvasive supplementation; intermittent use with oral feeding.	Gastric distention; small-bore, requires pump or syringe feeding and skilled placement; red rubber not translucent; may not be radiopaque; noxious stimulus in face and visual field.	Gastric reflux; emesis; aspiration rupture. Tube displacement (removal or migration); mucous membrane or tissue trauma.	Gastric residuals; slow upgrading of feeding rate, concentration; patient positioning upright; metoclopramide for motility; prevent bowel stasis. Patient's hands are mitted or restrained; adequate stabilization of tube; nostril care; taping technique.
	2. Gastrostomy (surgical)	Viscous, blenderized diet given as bolus; long-term use; economic; cosmetic and comfortable; no compromise of esophageal sphincter.	Surgical procedure with risks; large stoma.	Infection; gastric leakage or ulceration; hypergranulation of stoma tissue; herniation.	Aseptic wound care; ostomy care; antacids; ulcer prevention; cauterization (silver nitrate or mechanical); abdominal support.
				IN ROUTES 2 AND 3: Tube displacement, removal or migration.	Careful mobility techniques; adequate stabilization techniques; abdominal binder, clothes.
	3. Percutaneous endoscopic gastrostomy (PEG)	Small-bore tube (#10 to #14 French); placement with local anesthesia; few complications; minimal wound at site; economical; easy to care for.	Requires variable healing time for track to develop before tube change; clogs more easily than large tube.		

Table 1-2 Enteric Tube Options for Patients at High Risk for Aspiration

Delivery Site	Route	Advantages	Disadvantages	Complications	Management and Prevention
Duodenum	1. Nasoenteric	Radiopaque; minimal compromise of gastric sphincters; bypasses gastric filling; comfortable oral feeding; little tissue trauma; allows variation in patient position.	Loss of gastric electrolytes, intrinsic factor, and normal digestion; volumetric pump required; lengthy feeding times; requires skilled placement; expensive diet and delivery; easily clogged, kinked tubes; noxious stimulus in face.	Tube displacement, removal, or migration; pulmonary intubation; obstruction; dehydration; diarrhea (three to six loose stools per day); nutrient deficiencies; absorption problems.	Patient restrained; radiograph verification of placement; adequate stabilization; monitor lower bowel sounds and elimination; monitor respiratory function; eliminate lactose and complex nutrients; rule out impaction or obstruction; slow rate of and dilute feeding; antidiarrheal medications; fiber-enriched feeding; rule out electrolyte and endocrine problems and vitamin deficiencies; supplement proteins, vitamins, and minerals.
	2. Gastroenteric (tube may be single or double lumen)	Allows for improvement and upgrading to gastric route from duodenal route; allows gastric drainage while feeding; provides gastric route for bulky medications.	Same as those for nasoenteric and gastrostomy (above), plus: skilled technique required for replacement; expensive; relatively new approach.	Same as those for nasoenteric (above), except: pulmonary intubation.	Same as those for nasoenteric (above); upgrade to gastric feeding as soon as patient meets criteria.

Table 1-3 Enteric Tube Options for Patients at High Risk for Aspiration and Permanent Placement

Delivery Site	Route	Advantages	Disadvantages	Complications	Management and Prevention
		IN ROUTES 1, 2, 3:			
Jejunum	1. Jejunostomy (surgical)	Bypasses all esophageal and gastric sphincters; allows variation in patient position. Permanent, cuffed placement (grows into subcutaneous tissue).	Skilled technique for replacements; surgical risks; limited tolerance to diet preparations.	Same as Table 1-2 plus enhanced problems with absorption, dehydration, bowel regulation, and small bowel obstruction.	Same as Table 1-2 plus free water supplements, flushes, longer infusion times; supplemented by intravenous, parenteral.
	2. PEJ (percutaneous endoscopic jejunostomy)	Reduced surgical risk with local anesthetic; cosmetic.			
	3. Gastrojejunal	Can be converted to gastric feeding route as patient improves.	Relatively new approach.		

Nasoenteric Tube Insertion and Removal

PURPOSES

To establish an enteral route for feeding, fluid, and medication administration; to prevent tissue trauma, discomfort, and nasopulmonary intubation.

STAFF RESPONSIBLE

EQUIPMENT

1. Tubes:
   - Nasoenteric tube of appropriate length and diameter.
     #5 to #8 French (newborn to 2 years of age)
     #8 to #10 French (2 to 5 years of age)
     #8 to #14 French (child to adult; try not to exceed this size)
   - #10 to #16 bore tubes, which are only red rubber or stiffer plastic.
   - Small-diameter tubes, which are available in pediatric lengths, 30 inches (child to small adult), and 43 inches (most adults).
2. Syringe with compatible Luer-lok or catheter tip.
     5 to 10 mL (newborn to 2 years of age)
     20 mL (2 to 5 years of age)
     30 to 60 mL (child to adult with large-bore tube)
3. Water-soluble lubricant or water to moisten the coating of small-bore tubes. Consult manufacturer's recommendation for lubrication.
4. Optional: nonsterile gloves.
5. Ice (only for red rubber tubes to increase rigidity).
6. Adequate lighting (flashlight if possible).
7. Stethoscope.
8. Cup of water.
9. Tape and other anchoring supplies.
10. Soft restraints or blanket wrap if necessary.

GENERAL CONSIDERATIONS

1. It is strongly recommended that insertion of small-diameter flexible polyurethane tubes (e.g., Nutriflex or Dobbhoff) be done by the physician and that radiologic visualization be used initially and thereafter as the only method of confirmation whenever placement is questioned. The small-diameter tubes have unquestioned advantage in reducing trauma and esophageal-gastric sphincter compromise. Nevertheless, they may also present increased risk of asymptomatic pulmonary intubation, especially in poorly responsive patients. Aspiration of gastric contents is not recommended because negative pressure may collapse or kink the tube. Injected air may be audible on auscultation in the epigastric area even with bronchial placement. This technique is unreliable for assessment of placement.
2. A further advantage of flexible tubes is the transpyloric feeding, which bypasses stomach distention and reduces reflux risk for the patient whose airway is unprotected by reflexes or who must remain recumbent. Disadvantages to transpyloric feeding include bypassing the antibacterial barrier of hydrochloric acid and the loss of intrinsic factor, which may lead to pernicious anemia.
3. Feeding the patient with a small-diameter tube requires the use of a volumetric pump and feedings of low osmolality and rate. These present disadvantages of inconvenience in mobility and expense.
4. Gastric reflux and tube displacement are still real possibilities, especially during strong coughing or gagging.
5. Large-bore, stiff nasogastric tubes present a greater risk of irritation and esophageal sphincter compromise. They are used for short periods of time in alert patients who can protect their airways by gag and cough. Placement is more easily confirmed by gastric secretion aspiration. Feedings may be delivered by gravity boluses when tolerated.
6. If enteric feeding is anticipated for more than a few weeks, the patient should be evaluated for a more direct enteric route and more practical management to normalize his or her care.
7. Because aspiration is a major risk, bedside access to suction and airway equipment is a requirement.
8. Modifications in tube placement technique should reflect the individual patient's needs with regard to age, position limits, level of consciousness, and psychological reaction.

PROCEDURE: Nasoenteric Tube Insertion

Steps	*Additional Information*
1. Wash hands.	Use nonsterile gloves if body fluid precautions are indicated.
2. Explain procedure to patient. Elicit cooperation, and provide reassurance (set rubber tube in ice now).	Adequate personnel and gentle restraint should provide comfort and safety but not provoke alarm.
3. Initiate patient positioning.	
• Position patient 45° to 90° with knees bent for comfort and trunk alignment.	
• Stabilize head in midline. Keep head upright to neutral for infants and small children, slightly flexed for older children and adults.	Head position facilitates epiglottis closure and swallowing to guide tube into esophagus. Hyperextension encourages tracheal intubation.
	Infant seats or reclining chairs are useful for positioning, or a caregiver can firmly embrace patient from the side or behind. This assists migration through pylorus.
• Patients with small-bore tubes should be placed in right-side position with elevation.	
4. Use flashlight to examine internal nostrils. Perform hygiene if indicated.	Note inflammation, swelling, or defect. Use the most patent nostril, or alternate nostrils.
5. Estimate length of tube required by measuring from nostril to beyond ear to epigastric area. Add 2 to 3 inches. Mark tube with tape (insert stylet of flexible tubing now).	This ensures placement well into gastric cavity.
6. Lubricate tube along 4 to 6 inches of length or as recommended.	This ensures easy passage and minimal trauma.
7. Insert tube.	
• Stabilize head position, and pass tube through nostril.	Gagging is not uncommon. If coughing or choking occurs or if voice changes or is lost, **STOP** and assess placement. Remove if cough continues. Check mouth for coiled or kinked tubing, and remove tube if present.
• Move quickly past uvula to minimize gag.	
• Verbally cue patient to swallow, or stimulate it by stroking at cricoid cartilage.	
• Continue passage up to tape mark, and anchor tube.	
• Visualize inside of mouth to pharynx.	Recheck to determine whether tubing is coiled or kinked.
8. If placement is suspect, auscultate lungs for equal and full breath sounds.	
9. Gently aspirate for gastric contents. If none, insert tube a little farther and wait, or change patient position. Auscultation of injected air is an adjunct assessment only.	This confirms placement of rubber or stiff plastic tubes. Small-bore tubes must still be radiographed.
10. Anchor tube securely according to procedure. Begin feeding only after placement is confirmed.	

DOCUMENTATION

1. Document tube insertion and observations in the appropriate record.

2. Report unusual events or difficulties to the physician, and discuss modifications.

PROCEDURE: Nasoenteric Tube Removal

Steps	Additional Information
1. Wash hands.	Use nonsterile gloves if body fluid precautions are indicated.
2. Schedule removal well after feeding. Explain procedure to patient, and position him or her upright.	This prevents nausea, emesis, and aspiration.
3. Clamp or stopper tube firmly.	This prevents release of tube contents above gastric sphincters.
4. Loosen tape anchoring tube.	
5. Remove tube gently but swiftly.	This minimizes gag as tube passes through pharynx.
6. Dispose of mercury-weighted tip of tube in designated container.	Mercury cannot be incinerated because of release of toxic fumes. Follow infection control procedures for disposal of other soiled materials.

DOCUMENTATION

1. Document tube removal and observations in the appropriate record.

2. Report unusual events or difficulties to the physician.

Gastrostomy Tube Reinsertion

PURPOSES

To reinsert a gastrostomy tube into the stomach; to prevent trauma or discomfort to the patient.

STAFF RESPONSIBLE

EQUIPMENT

1. Nonsterile gloves (sterile gloves if indicated).
2. Gastrostomy tube or indwelling Foley catheter of specified size.
3. Water-soluble lubricant.
4. Prefilled syringe of water if balloon is to be inflated.
5. Empty syringe to deflate balloon.
6. Soap and water.
7. Other cleansing or antiseptic solution as ordered.
8. Plastic bag for disposal.
9. Tube clamp, stopper, or stopcock.
10. Dressings and tape for anchoring.
11. Irrigation syringe compatible with distal tube end.

GENERAL CONSIDERATIONS

1. Staff should be aware of agency policies regarding the replacement of various types of gastrostomy tubes.
2. The healing time required from original insertion should be specified by the surgeon. Depending on technique, this may be several days to several weeks. During this time, extra precaution is taken to prevent trauma or accidental displacement. Proper stabilization of the tube should be continued. It may be necessary to use a soft binder to protect the site from the patient or accidental traction.
3. An appropriate replacement tube should be kept at the bedside for emergency replacement. Prompt replacement is necessary to prevent the tract from rapid closing or shrinking and to prevent leakage into the abdominal cavity. An emergency replacement should be examined by a physician before use, especially when the original tube has been replaced.
4. It is recommended that the physician order for routine change include type, size of tube, and size of balloon to be used.

PATIENT AND FAMILY EDUCATION

1. The family caregiver and patient are taught the procedure as appropriate before community pass or discharge.
2. Replacement equipment with appropriate instructions/precautions must accompany them.

PROCEDURE

Steps	*Additional Information*
1. Explain procedure to patient and caregiver.	
2. Position patient supine, provide privacy, and drape area.	Choose a quiet time before a feeding to prevent discomfort and spillage.
3. Wash hands.	This is usually a clean procedure unless a fresh or open wound is present.
4. Set up equipment next to patient.	
• Lubricate new tube.	
• Open dressings and tear tape.	
• Apply gloves.	Follow the Centers for Disease Control recommend protection from body fluid contact.
5. Remove old dressings and tape, and cleanse debris from stoma site and skin.	Prevent introduction of debris into stoma. Use plastic bag for disposal.
6. Remove gastrostomy tube.	
• Gently pull on tube to test balloon placement against stomach wall.	
• Mark tube with tape at its exit point from stoma.	This is to mark the length of tube inserted once it is removed.
• Deflate old balloon by aspirating.	
• Pull old tube straight out of stoma.	If resistance is met, seek physician's assistance. Adhesions or sutures may be unseen.
• Examine tube and stoma.	Note marked length of tube and character of drainage and stoma site.
7. Quickly cleanse site, and change gloves if contaminated by debris or discharge.	Avoid introduction of debris into stoma or wound site. Use plastic bag for disposal.
8. Insert new tube.	
• Estimate length to be inserted from marked length on old tube.	Excessive length may pass tube into gastric outlet or duodenum.
• Insert lubricated tube at right angle to stoma.	This prevents undermining or fistula formation at stoma site.
• Pass tube 1 inch or more past referenced length.	This allows room for balloon inflation. If resistance is met, leave tube in place and seek physician's assistance.
• Aspirate stomach contents to verify placement.	
• Inflate balloon with prescribed amount of water. This is a minimum amount to keep tube in place.	Tap water is suitable for a clean procedure. Overinflation may provoke gastric motility or production of secretions because it is perceived as gastric content.
9. Gently pull back on tube until balloon rests against stomach wall.	
10. Clamp, plug, or stopper tube.	
11. Cleanse site as indicated, and dress and anchor.	Use minimum amounts of dressing or tape to prevent irritation to skin but adequate to prevent tube migration or traction.
12. Dress and reposition patient for comfort.	
13. Remove plastic bag for disposal.	Follow infection control procedures to prevent cross-contamination.

DOCUMENTATION

1. Document the gastrostomy tube change. Include the reason for change, type and size of tube and balloon removed and reinserted, condition of stoma, observed condition of tube, drainage characteristics, observed tolerance of patient, and instructions to patient or caregiver.
2. Report to the physician any unusual observations.

Enteric Tube Stabilization and Dressings

PURPOSES

To provide stabilization of the tube; to prevent erosion of the skin around the tube; to prevent tube migration or removal.

STAFF RESPONSIBLE

EQUIPMENT

Equipment options include those appropriate to nasogastric, gastrostomy, and jejunostomy tubes.

1. 1-inch hypoallergenic tape (cloth or paper).
2. 4 × 4 gauze.
3. Fenestrated dressings or 4 × 4 dressings with 2-inch slit.
4. Hydrogen peroxide or other prescribed agents.
5. Normal saline.
6. Tincture of benzoin swabs.
7. Plastic bag for disposal.
8. Optional equipment:
   - Skin barrier.
   - Stoma wafers.
   - Adhesive remover.
   - Nonsterile gloves.

Nasogastric Tube Stabilization (Applicable to Nasoenteric Tubes)

GENERAL CONSIDERATIONS

1. In the rehabilitation setting, nasogastric feedings are utilized for short-term management of nutritional needs or for long-term management of patients in whom gastric or jejunostomy tubes are contraindicated.
2. Displacement or removal can occur with traction on or loosening of the tape. Migration or kinking can occur during reanchoring or with vigorous coughing, gagging, or emesis.
3. Considerations for choice of method 1 or 2 include patient skin tolerance, need for rotation of tape site, patient preference or behavior, and presence of other equipment (e.g., oxygen nasal cannula).
4. Alternate the sites of taping, evaluate skin tolerance to techniques, and avoid direct pressure of tubing against skin or mucous membranes.
5. When anchoring over hair-covered skin other than the face, avoid shaving. Rather, clip the hair short. Remove tape in the direction of hair growth.
6. Adhesive removers must be thoroughly washed off with soap and water to avoid chemical burns.

PATIENT AND FAMILY EDUCATION

Educate the patient and caregivers of the purpose, the method used to anchor tube, and the need to keep the nursing staff informed of problems with the tube or anchoring.

PROCEDURE, METHOD 1

Steps	*Additional Information*
1. Wash hands.	
2. Cut a piece of 2 × 2 hypoallergenic tape.	
3. Secure tube to upper lip or side of nose. (See Figures 1-1A and 1-1B.)	When taping on nose, do not place tape so that it pulls or causes pressure.
4. Use a second piece of tape to secure tube to forehead or cheek.	Do not obstruct vision with tube position and tape (Figures 1-1A and 1-1B).
5. Tape or pin tube to patient's clothing.	Remember to position tube in a way that keeps it out of reach of any patient who might pull it out.

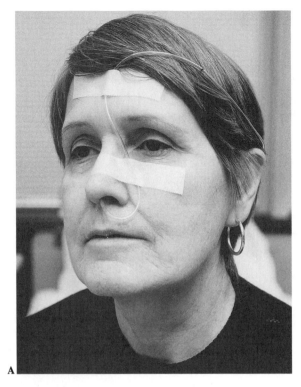

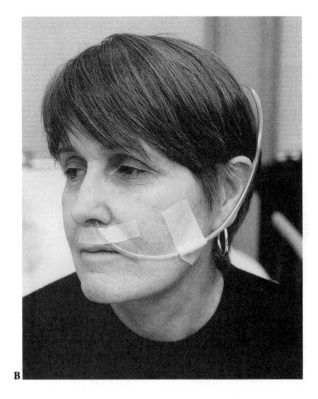

Figure 1-1 Nasogastric Tube Stabilization, Method 1.

PROCEDURE, METHOD 2

Steps	*Additional Information*
1. Wash hands.	
2. Cut a 1½-inch piece of 1-inch wide hypoallergenic tape.	
3. Split tape about 1 inch lengthwise from one end (Figure 1-2A).	
4. Attach unsplit end to patient's nose, then wrap split ends in opposite direction around tube (Figure 1-2, B to E).	
5. If necessary, secure tube to patient's cheek or forehead.	Do not obstruct vision. Keep tube out of reach of patient who may pull it out.
6. With a tincture of benzoin swab, wipe tape on patient's nose or other taped areas.	Tincture of benzoin will absorb through tape and improve adhesion. Use skin barrier as indicated under tape.

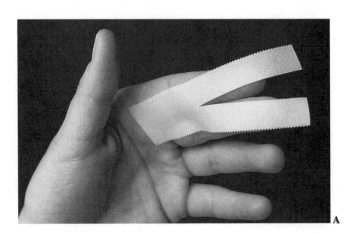

Figure 1-2 Nasogastric Tube Stabilization, Method 2.

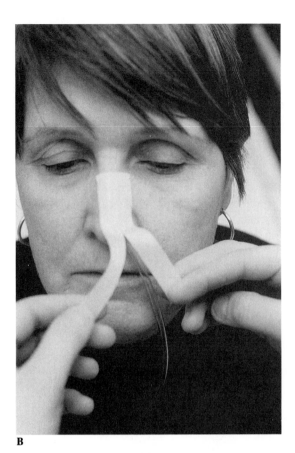

B

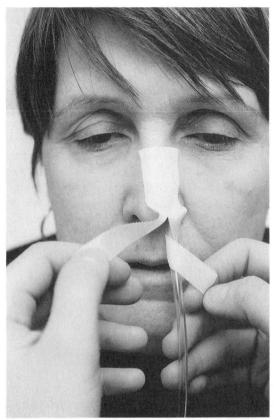

C

D

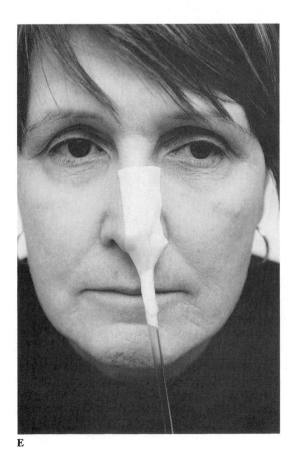

E

Gastric Tube Stabilization and Dressings

GENERAL CONSIDERATIONS

1. Gastrostomy stoma site care for new, infected, or draining wounds requires aseptic cleansing with prescribed agents and rinsing with normal saline. Healed stomas can be cleansed with soap and water and may not need a dressing.
2. One of the problems noted with gastric tube feedings is tube migration. This may cause pyloric or intestinal obstruction, which is prevented by proper anchoring.
3. Excoriation of the stoma edges may occur when lateral traction or taping of the gastric tube is done. Alternate the direction of traction or ease the tension of the traction if this occurs.

4. If gastric tube irrigation or excoriation of stoma edges is a problem, use method 2 for tube stabilization or a similar method that provides vertical traction. If neither of these problems exists, use method 1.

PATIENT AND FAMILY EDUCATION

1. Educate the patient and caregivers of the purpose of the stabilization technique and the care of the stoma site, if appropriate.
2. Inform the patient and caregivers of complications and the need to keep nursing staff informed of problems or anchoring considerations with either method.

PROCEDURE, METHOD 1

Steps	Additional Information
1. Wash hands.	Use nonsterile gloves if body fluid precautions are indicated.
2. Remove old dressing.	Dispose of according to infection control procedures.
3. Cleanse around tube.	
4. Place a fenestrated dressing (4 × 4 dressing with a slit) around gastric tube. Tab the tape ends. Tape down edges window-frame fashion (Figure 1-3A).	This may not be needed if the stoma site is healed.
5. If necessary, tape tube down approximately 4 inches from stoma site. Tape straight across or in a V shape, with the base of the V pointing toward the stoma (Figure 1-3B).	
6. If desired or necessary, swab the tape with tincture of benzoin.	Use skin barrier or stoma wafer under tape if indicated.

PROCEDURE, METHOD 2

Steps	Additional Information
1. Wash hands.	Use nonsterile gloves if body fluid precautions are indicated.
2. Remove old dressing.	Dispose of according to infection control procedures.
3. Cleanse around tube.	
4. Roll two 4 × 4 dressings together to form a cylinder about 4 inches long by 1 inch in diameter.	
5. Place this roll on one side of tube and stoma, and wrap tube completely around roll, going over the cylinder first, then under and back over (Figure 1-4A).	This will provide vertical traction.
6. Place a 4 × 4 dressing over tube and gauze cylinder. Place a piece of tape perpendicular to tube but parallel to gauze roll on opposite side of gauze roll. Then place a piece of tape parallel to and on each side of tube (Figure 1-4B).	
7. Place a piece of tape in a V shape, with the base of the V pointing toward the stoma. Affix this approximately 4 inches from stoma (Figure 1-4C).	This will prevent retraction of the tube into the stoma.
8. If desired, wipe tape with tincture of benzoin swab to improve adhesion.	Use skin barrier or stoma wafer under tape if indicated.

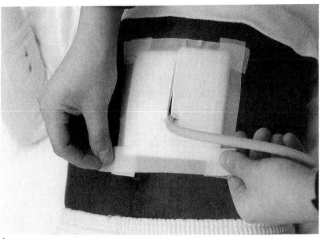 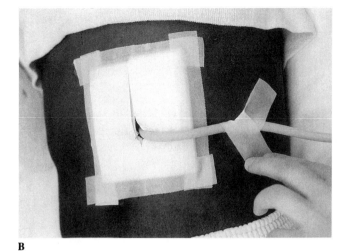

A B

Figure 1-3 Gastric Tube Stabilization Fenestrated Dressing, Method 1.

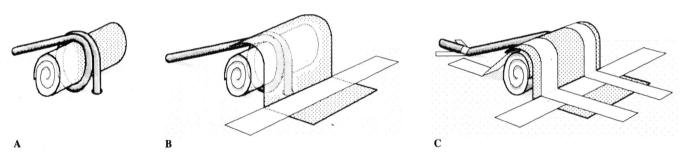

A B C

Figure 1-4 Gastric Tube Stabilization, Method 2. *Source:* From ''A Method for Stabilizing Chronic Gastrostomy or Jejunostomy Tubes'' by S.M. Tuel and Y. Wu, 1986, *Archives of Physical Medicine and Rehabilitation*, 67. Copyright 1986 by American Congress of Rehabilitation Medicine. Reprinted by permission.

Jejunostomy Tube Stabilization

GENERAL CONSIDERATIONS

1. There are various jejunostomy tubes. Some are anchored internally. The ones that are not have the greatest potential to migrate in or to fall out. Physicians may choose to anchor these tubes by suturing them to the patient's abdomen. Sutures may loosen easily, however, which causes an alteration in skin integrity and comfort for the patient. Therefore, appropriate nursing interventions that include jejunostomy tube stabilization are needed.

2. Jejunostomy stoma site care for new, infected, or draining wounds or suture sites may require cleansing with prescribed agents and rinsing with normal saline. Healed stomas can be cleansed with soap and water.

PATIENT AND FAMILY EDUCATION

Educate the patient and caregivers of tube stabilization procedures, purpose, and potential problems or anchoring issues.

PROCEDURE

Steps	*Additional Information*
1. Wash hands.	Use nonsterile gloves if body fluid precautions are indicated.
2. Remove old dressing.	
3. Cleanse around tube.	Discard waste according to infection control procedures. This may not be needed if stoma site is healed.
4. Place fenestrated dressing (4 × 4 dressing with 2-inch slit) around tube. Tape down in window-frame fashion.	
5. Take a 4- to 6-inch piece of hypoallergenic tape and make small tabs on each end.	Tabs make it easier to remove tape when it needs to be changed.
6. Secure tube.	
• Place the piece of tape approximately 4 inches from stoma, perpendicular to tube (Figure 1-5A).	
or	
• Place the piece of tape underneath tube, adhesive side up, approximately 4 inches from stoma. Then cross each end of tape over top of tube and adhere it to patient's abdomen, forming V shape with base of V pointing away from stoma (Figure 1-5B).	This provides stabilization to prevent tube from being pulled out.
7. With a tincture of benzoin swab, wipe taped areas.	Tincture of benzoin will absorb through tape and increase tape adhesion. Use skin barrier or stoma wafer as indicated under tape.

DOCUMENTATION

1. Record any difficulties with stabilization procedures.
2. Document skin or other complications.
3. Record the use of special tape/dressings.

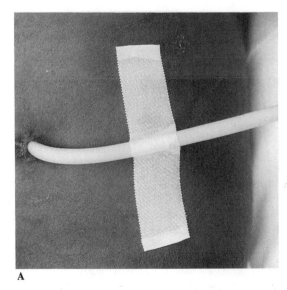
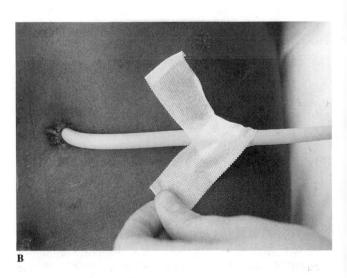

A   B

Figure 1-5 Jejunostomy Tube Stabilization.

Gastric Residual

PURPOSES

To measure gastric contents and, indirectly, gastric motility before, during, or after enteric feeding; to prevent gastroesophageal reflux and potential aspiration.

STAFF RESPONSIBLE

EQUIPMENT

1. Syringe (60-mL catheter or Luer-lok tip compatible with distal tube connection).
2. Clamp, plug, or stopcock.
3. Graduated emesis basin or container.
4. Optional: nonsterile gloves.

GENERAL CONSIDERATIONS

1. Routine measures of gastric residual volume are indicated when:
   - initiating or upgrading volume, rate, or concentration of enteric feeding solution;
   - the patient is identified as high-risk for aspiration;
   - emesis has occurred or is a frequent event;
   - monitoring postoperative recovery from gastrostomy tube insertion or other surgery;
   - the patient is febrile or is under other stress that alters metabolic function or state of responsiveness; or
   - the patient exhibits sudden restlessness, discomfort, or respiratory distress during or after a feeding.
2. Measurement of gastric residual is not always an absolute equivalent of gastric content. The proximal end of the gastric tube may access only the upper portion of the gastric volume. Repositioning the patient may be necessary to aspirate contents fully. Astute clinical judgment must guide the nurse's visualization of this procedure and assessment of the patient.
3. In the event of a medical emergency (e.g., seizure, hypotension, or cardiopulmonary arrest) during feeding or soon after feeding, prompt gastric aspiration may prevent reflux and aspiration. For patients at high risk for crisis or whose feeding tolerance is unknown, suction and airway equipment are kept nearby.

4. Gastric contents are usually returned to the stomach because they contain nutrients, digestive enzymes, and perhaps medications. If the contents exceed the ordered amount or if reflux is imminent, however, the contents may be discarded without serious threat of depletion of enzymes or electrolytes. This should be clarified with a physician order. Obvious loss of medication and discarded volume are reported to the physician.
5. Acceptable residual amounts may vary in physician orders. These are determined by consideration of the individual patient, recovery history, risks, or tube placement protocols. As tolerance is demonstrated, residual amounts are based on hourly rate if feeding is continuous or on percentage of feeding volume if feeding is bolused.
6. Metoclopramide is often used as a short-term adjunct to promote gastric motility:
   - to propel an enteric tube into the duodenum, or
   - to enhance gastric emptying after operative tube placement.

   Occasionally, it is used for more persistent problems.
7. The sudden onset of slowed gastric emptying or reflux requires investigation to rule out:
   - displacement or migration of the gastric tube into the esophageal or pyloric sphincter,
   - severe constipation or other form of intestinal obstruction,
   - a patient position (e.g., flexed or left-sided) that delays emptying, and
   - febrile or less conscious state.
8. Slowed gastric motility may be an anticipated side effect of medications, especially anticholinergics, some antibiotics, preparations in acidic or oil-based solutes, and narcotics. The action of metoclopramide is antagonized by narcotics and anticholinergics. Hypertonic or hypotonic feedings may also slow motility.
9. Jejunostomy tubes and small-diameter polyurethane tubes are not aspirated routinely because the proximal end is located within the intestine, which is emptied by gravity and peristalsis rather than by the sphincters. Aspiration is also likely to clog or kink a small tube. Gastric reflux can still occur but cannot be measured without placement of a gastric tube. On occasion, a gastric tube may be placed for decompression.
10. The following are common interventions that enhance or promote gastric motility:
    - administering metoclopramide;
    - discontinuing medications that decrease gastric motility;
    - emptying the lower bowel;

- positioning the patient upright, with trunk extension or right-side lying (or both);
- diluting the feeding and slowing the rate until tolerance is reestablished;
- correcting metabolic problems; and
- instituting olfactory and oral sensory stimulation.

PATIENT AND FAMILY EDUCATION

1. Educate the patient and caregivers of the complications and risks that may indicate signs of gastric residual problems.
2. Advise that they report these to the appropriate medical or nursing staff (inpatient or outpatient).

PROCEDURE

Steps	*Additional Information*
1. Wash hands.	This is a clean procedure. Apply nonsterile gloves if body fluid precautions are indicated.
2. Prepare patient with explanation. Include family or caregiver as appropriate.	Caregivers must be able to evaluate gastric emptying if tube is used long term.
3. Stop feeding at prescribed time. Pinch tube while disconnecting or unclamping.	Introduction of air can increase distention.
4. Insert syringe snugly into tube, and aspirate stomach contents gently.	Vigorous aspiration may traumatize mucosa.
5. If less than or acceptable residual amount is aspirated, return it to stomach.	Check patient position and comfort to verify reliability of gastric residual.
6. If residual is more than acceptable amount, return only the limit, according to physician's order.	Observe patient closely for increased distress. Report to physician.
7. Pinch tube, withdraw syringe, and clamp or reconnect tubing.	
8. Resume feeding only when residual amount is acceptable or when modifications are made in feeding program as ordered.	

DOCUMENTATION

1. Document the amount of residual, any unusual appearance, and subsequent actions or interventions.

2. Note whether the physician was notified and the reasons for notification.

Enteric Feeding Administration

PURPOSES

To meet nutritional and hydration requirements by delivery through nasogastric, gastric, or intestinal routes; to prevent enteral or respiratory complications.

STAFF RESPONSIBLE

EQUIPMENT

1. Gastric feeding unit.
2. Bottle, bag, or syringe compatible with tubing and pump.
3. Volumetric pump as indicated.
4. Prescribed feeding.
5. Flush solution (usually water).
6. IV pole or hook.
7. Clamp or stopper.
8. Optional equipment:
   - Blue food coloring (yellow, green, or red colors may be mistaken for or mask secretions).
   - Nonsterile gloves.

PATIENT AND FAMILY EDUCATION

1. Educate the patient and caregivers of the proper procedure.
2. Apprise the patient and caregivers of the potential problems and risks of this procedure that are to be reported to available medical or nursing staff (inpatient or outpatient).

PROCEDURE

Steps	*Additional Information*
1. Position patient sitting or at inclined angle of 30° or more.	The supine position is to be avoided for patients at high risk for emesis and aspiration. Gastric emptying is facilitated by upright or right-side lying.
2. Place patient in environment that promotes optimal relaxation and contains tolerable stimulation. Support or cradle infants and small children.	Feeding is normally a social activity. Olfactory, visual, and auditory stimulation are regular components of feeding and may aid gastric motility.
3. Complete oral hygiene, toileting, and suctioning before feeding.	Relaxation of the stomach antrum is necessary for gastric filling. Patients distressed by nonoral intake may need privacy and decreased distraction during normal mealtimes.
4. Wash hands.	Apply nonsterile gloves if body fluid precautions are indicated.
5. Check for feeding tube placement:	Aspirated gastric contents or radiographs are the only certain methods of verifying placement.
• by aspirating gastric contents with a syringe;	Aspiration is not recommended with small-diameter or jejunostomy tubes.
• by observing length of exposed tubing and security of anchoring; and	Abnormally short or long exposed tubing indicates need for further placement checks by physician.
• by gently pulling gastrostomy tube to ensure balloon or mushroom placement at stomach wall.	
6. Check for feeding tube patency by flushing with water, especially with small-diameter tubes.	
7. Set up gastric feeding unit and related equipment. Label equipment with patient name, date, and time. Change equipment at least every 24 hours. Check pump for operation, cleanliness, and a working manual alarm. Set volume rate as ordered.	Residual food is a culture medium for bacterial growth. Residue may interfere with equipment operation.
8. Pour and measure feeding at patient location. Minimal amounts of food coloring may be added to detect aspiration in high-risk patients. Deliver room-temperature or cool fluids at slow rates until tolerance is well established by checking gastric residuals.	Gastric motility is not affected by fluids at cool temperatures, but subjective discomfort may be reported by patient. Some patients may experience cramping with cold fluids.
9. Deliver feeding at prescribed rate with periodic supervision for: • gastric distention, • restlessness, • respiratory difficulty, • tube displacement, and • pump malfunctioning.	Patients with poor arousal or hyperarousal are at high risk for aspiration. Alternatives are slower rates, smaller amounts, or frequent small feedings by syringe.
10. Check patient positioning for trunk alignment and extension, especially for those in bed.	Patients who slide down in bed or assume a flexed position lose elevation and compress abdominal contents, which may encourage regurgitation.
11. If movement or turning is necessary, do so slowly with feeding turned off.	Vestibular stimulation may trigger emesis.

Steps	Additional Information
12. Maintain patient elevation for at least 30 minutes after feeding. Prolong this period as necessary. Interrupt continuous feedings as necessary for recumbent periods or vestibular activity.	Verify emptying with gastric residuals.
13. Follow feeding with flush solution (usually water). Continuous feedings may be flushed at intervals. Clamp or plug feeding tube.	Tube patency is assured. Free water requirement is met. Saline or electrolyte solutions may be used for replacement instead of water.
14. Rinse gastric feeding unit with cool water. Cover delivery end, or tuck it securely into unit.	Cool water will prevent coagulation of protein material. Soap is avoided because of the uncertainty of its complete removal.

DOCUMENTATION

1. Document the delivery of feeding, including endurance of the patient and difficulties in administration.

2. Record intake and calorie count as indicated.

Administration of Enteral Medications

PURPOSES

To administer precise doses of prescribed medication; to prevent obstruction of an enteral tube.

STAFF RESPONSIBLE

EQUIPMENT

1. Syringes sized to volumes of individual medications.
2. Graduated medicine cups.
3. Mortar and pestle or suitable substitute for crushing medications.
4. Administration syringe with catheter or syringe tip compatible with enteral tube connector.
5. Labeled medication containers.
6. Medication order, record, and flow sheet.

GENERAL CONSIDERATIONS

1. As with oral medication, verify the compatibility of drugs with each other and with feeding components.
2. Obtain liquid forms and dose-volume equivalents by physician order. Discuss with the physician the substitution of drugs with like products available in liquid, chewable, or injectable forms. All solid medications must be finely crushed; chewable forms may be easier to crush.
3. Note the volume-required compatibility with fluid requirements or restrictions.
4. Note the content of liquid solutes for calories, alcohol content, or allergens.
5. Ensure clear labeling of suspensions that require thorough shaking to deliver an accurate dose.
6. Do not instill any capsule or particles of capsules into an enteral tube.
7. Avoid thickened solutions, fiber, or bulk formers because these expand in liquid and may obstruct tubes quickly.
8. Use enteric-coated tablets with precaution and physician awareness. Destroying the coating by crushing may affect patient tolerance of the drug. Enteric coatings are difficult to crush.
9. Administer medications with sufficient liquid (usually water) to:
   - enhance the utilization of the drug as recommended by the product literature,
   - dissolve or finely suspend particles of tablets,
   - flush the tube of residue,
   - reduce the osmolality of concentrated medications, and
   - avoid overdistention of stomach or intestinal contents.
10. Simplify procedures for home and community use for practicality, limitations of the caregiver, and accessibility and economy of the equipment.

PATIENT AND FAMILY EDUCATION

If appropriate, educate the patient and caregivers as to the safe administration of enteral medications including potential problems or risks and side effects.

PROCEDURE

Steps	*Additional Information*
1. Wash hands.	Apply nonsterile gloves if body fluid precautions are indicated.
2. Pour or draw up each liquid medication separately.	This prevents error in measurement and waste if discard is necessary.
3. Crush tablets into fine powder and remove thoroughly from container. Avoid pounding or splattering particles outside container. If this occurs, discard thoroughly and begin again.	Dose may be affected by residue left on pestle or in mortar or spilled.
4. Ensure placement and patency of enteral tube. Check gastric residual if appropriate.	Aspirated gastric secretions may be useful for dissolving some medications; see gastric residual procedure.
5. Fit administration syringe to tube before unclamping tube, and fill syringe partially with water.	Air can cause gastric distention.
6. Administer liquid medications first, and follow them with water. Use gravity flow or minimum pressure by syringe plunger.	Vigorous syringe pressure may rupture tube, expecially small-diameter tubes.
7. Mix crushed medications *in syringe*, which is partially filled with water. Gently agitate mixture while administering quickly.	Premixing in separate container may lose some dosage. Agitation prevents particles from settling or clinging to syringe or plunger.
8. Flush contents of syringe and tube.	
9. Reclamp, plug, or reconnect tube to feeding.	
10. Rinse syringes, mortar, and pestle and wipe free of medication traces.	
11. Syringes may be reused for same patient only. They are labeled, dated, stored, and discarded according to reuse protocol and infection control precautions. A mortar and pestle are usually used for more than one patient unless they must be confined to the patient. They must not be in contact with patients if multiple patient use is common.	

DOCUMENTATION

1. Follow medication documentation protocol.

2. Document and report unusual circumstances or reactions to the administration of enteral medications.

Oral Care

PURPOSES

To clean the teeth, tongue, and oral mucosa of debris and bacteria; to prevent mucosal bleeding and breakdown; to promote patient comfort.

STAFF RESPONSIBLE

EQUIPMENT

1. Warm water.
2. Toothpaste or tooth powder.
3. Emesis basin.
4. Toweling.
5. Adequate lighting.
6. Soft-bristle toothbrush.
7. Optional equipment:
   - Bite block.
   - Half-strength peroxide.
   - Baking soda.

- Mouth swabs.
- Water-pick.
- Moisturizers.
- Suction equipment.
- Dental floss on a handled device.
- Nonsterile gloves and mask.

GENERAL CONSIDERATIONS

1. Thorough oral hygiene is necessary at least twice a day for any dependent patient. For patients who are to receive nothing by mouth, who are mouth breathers, or who keep their mouths closed, frequency is increased to three or four times a day.
2. Dental examination and cleaning should be scheduled in the post-acute period. Patients with dental injury or previous dentition problems require repairs to prevent pain or loss of teeth. Loose teeth present a risk for aspiration. Patients with bruxism require mouth guards to protect their teeth and to inhibit grinding or chewing behaviors.
3. Oral hygiene provides sensory stimulation for arousal and comfort and promotes digestive stimulation and saliva production. It may also induce gagging or coughing. As such, it should precede feedings whenever possible.

4. Oral hygiene is vital to the promotion of personal interactions with staff or family. Poor hygiene can present a real social obstacle that deprives a patient of contact.
5. Avoid the use of acidic preparations, such as lemon, for stimulation or care because they promote deterioration of tooth enamel and can be noxious to tender tissue. Likewise, avoid sweetened or alcohol-based preparations.
6. Cold is also noxious to sensitive teeth and is a stimulant to swallow. Warm water is recommended.
7. Baking soda is an effective cleaner, deodorizer, and antiplaque agent recommended by some dentists. Water-picks are also useful.
8. Mouth moisturizers are used in adjunct to routine hygiene, especially for extreme dryness or accumulations. These include artificial saliva and lip balms. Glycerin and peroxide are drying agents but may be effective for cleansing accumulations; their use should be followed by rinsing and moisturizers.
9. Suction equipment and oral catheters must be available for patients at risk for aspiration or who cooperate poorly.

PATIENT AND FAMILY EDUCATION

Educate the patient and caregivers of the importance of oral hygiene, the procedure as appropriate, and the need for reporting problems or difficulties in performing the procedure.

PROCEDURE

Steps	*Additional Information*
1. Wash hands.	Use nonsterile gloves and mask if body fluid precautions are indicated.
2. Explain procedure to patient. Include family or caregiver as appropriate.	
3. Position patient upright with head flexed or in side-lying position.	This promotes ready drainage of oral contents and prevents aspiration.
4. Arrange emesis basin and sufficient toweling. Set up equipment, suction, and supplies in reach, and ensure adequate lighting.	
5. Open patient's mouth, and visualize teeth, tongue, and mucosa. Mouth opening is elicited by gentle head tilt, chin pressure, and jaw massage. Place bite block between back teeth if necessary. Remove mouth guard if present.	Bite blocks are not to be forced between teeth. It may be necessary to wait for relaxation or to elicit a yawn for mouth opening.
6. Gently brush all surfaces of teeth and top of tongue. Remove debris and excess fluid as it accumulates. If patient bites down on brush or swab, wait for relaxation and then remove.	Brush tongue lightly, and avoid provoking gag if possible. Never put fingers into patient's mouth between teeth! Yanking out brush or swab may cause injury or break handle, leaving a piece of brush in mouth.
7. Rinse with warm water or half-strength peroxide (or both). Wipe or suction excess.	
8. Reexamine mouth and teeth.	Open areas and dental abnormalities may be masked by secretions.
9. Floss teeth if patient is cooperative, or floss can be attached to handled device for patient to use.	Broken floss can become trapped in mouth and aspirated.
10. Apply medication if ordered or moisturizers to oral mucosa and tongue.	

Steps	Additional Information
11. Insert mouth guard, if indicated, after cleansing.	
12. Remove bite block.	
13. Apply lip moisturizer.	

DOCUMENTATION

1. Document care and observations.
2. Report to the physician any signs of breakdown, disrepair, or unstable dentition.

3. Discuss modifications in care as required.

Nostril Care

PURPOSES

To preserve integrity of nasal mucosa by lubricating mucosa, and removing debris; to prevent mucosal bleeding and breakdown; to promote patient comfort; to improve airway patency.

STAFF RESPONSIBLE

EQUIPMENT

1. Soap and water.
2. Wash cloth.
3. Tissues.
4. Cotton swabs.
5. Flashlight.
6. Water-soluble lubricant.
7. Optional equipment:
   - Half-strength peroxide.
   - Adhesive remover.

- Tape (hypoallergenic).
- Tincture of benzoin.
- Skin barrier.
- Saline nasal spray.
- Nonsterile gloves.

GENERAL CONSIDERATIONS

1. Particular attention to nasal mucosa is due when:
   - nasoenteric tubes are in place;
   - nasal breathing is the primary route of respiration (patient keeps mouth tightly closed);
   - decannulation of tracheostomy has occurred, rerouting intake of air; or
   - secretions are obvious and audible and patient cannot clear them on command.
2. Nostril care is performed at least daily and more often as indicated by patient characteristics, as above.
3. Schedule the procedure when the patient is relaxed and in an upright position and before feeding.
4. Do not use petrolatum-based products or ointments. Oil droplet aspiration is possible.

PROCEDURE

Steps	Additional Information
1. Wash hands.	Apply nonsterile gloves if body fluid precautions are indicated.
2. Explain procedure to patient, and elicit cooperation. Include caregiver as indicated.	
3. If nasogastric tube is in place, remove tape and temporarily anchor it close to nose.	Caregiver or other staff can anchor tube and assist.
4. Cleanse external nares of tape, debris, oil, and perspiration.	Adhesive removers must be thoroughly removed by soap and water to avoid irritation.

Steps	*Additional Information*
5. Examine internal nares with flashlight for signs of trauma.	Nasogastric tubes can cause pressure necrosis.
6. Lubricate several swabs, and wipe nostrils clear from back to front while visualizing with light. Use half-strength peroxide sparingly for crusted, adherent secretions. Rinse peroxide with saline or water.	Dried secretions may mask pressure areas, bleeding, or septal defects. Probing with swabs from front to back can drive secretions into pharyngeal airway to become aspirants or obstructions.
7. Avoid probing beyond length of nostril.	Vigorous sneezing or gagging can dislodge a nasogastric tube or provoke emesis. Deep probing cannot be visualized and may cause trauma to pharynx.
8. Minimize procedure if patient is uncooperative or cannot be controlled.	Gentle head control and soft wrist restraint may be required. If so, another person should assist with this.
9. If ordered, use saline nasal spray at this point on dry external areas.	Saline spray used two to four times a day maintains mucosal moisture.
10. Clean and dry nasogastric tube.	
11. Reposition nasogastric tube to avoid contact with nasal mucosa.	Tubing placed against mucosa causes pressure and possible necrosis.
12. Apply tape securely to tube, tab it for easy removal, and apply it to new site on nose, below nostril, or nearby on cheek.	Alternate tape sites to prevent irritation to skin.

DOCUMENTATION

1. Document nasal care, observations, and interventions.

2. Report to the physician any unusual occurrence, and request a change in care as indicated.

Unclogging Enteral Tubes

PURPOSES

To reestablish patency of an enteral feeding tube; to prevent the necessity of tube reinsertion.

STAFF RESPONSIBLE

EQUIPMENT

1. Syringes with compatible Luer-lok or catheter tip.
   - 5 to 20 mL for small-diameter tube.
   - 20 to 60 mL for tubes larger than #10 French.
2. Optional equipment:
   - Warm water.
   - Carbonated beverage.
   - Acidic juice.
   - Meat tenderizer.
   - Nonsterile gloves.

GENERAL CONSIDERATIONS

1. The optimal approach to maintain patency of enteral feeding tubes is to follow procedures for administration of feeding and medications. Nevertheless, obstruction may be anticipated as a common problem when:
   - small-diameter feeding tubes are used (#10 French or smaller);
   - viscous formulas are delivered at a slow rate;
   - gastric retention causes stasis of gastric contents;
   - nonliquid medication or supplements are administered;
   - fluid administration is restricted; or
   - gastric content includes the residue of oral feeding.
2. Attempts to unclog enteral tubes carry risks of tube displacement, tube rupture, and, therefore, patient injury. To minimize the risks:
   - assess the patient's recent history of tube-related complications and their resolutions;
   - use the most conservative, simple approaches first;
   - consult the physician for discussion of options available in unclogging the tube and for eliminating options that are contraindicated; and

- assess the relative risks of unclogging the tube compared to the disadvantages of removing and reinserting the tube.
3. Discuss with the physician modifications in care that minimize the recurrence of clogging:

- choice of feeding formula or delivery method;
- alternate choice of tube;
- form of, or substitute for, medication; and
- frequency, amount, and type of tube flush.

PROCEDURE

Steps	*Additional Information*
1. Wash hands.	Apply nonsterile gloves if body precautions are indicated.
2. Explain procedure to patient, and position him or her as if for feeding.	
3. Examine tube for external signs of displacement: • disturbed stabilization, or • abnormal length of tube (shorter or longer than previously observed).	Attempts to unclog a displaced tube could result in aspiration or tissue trauma. Proximal end of tube may also be located against mucosa or kinked or coiled.
4. Disconnect and unclamp tube.	
5. Gently milk tube from point of insertion to distal end, and allow passive gravity drainage.	Milking may move a small plug and create mild negative pressure.
6. Fill a small syringe with warm water. Inject and withdraw water with gentle plunging action.	Water may dissolve a thin plug of particles. Vigorous plunging may further solidify plug or rupture tube.
7. After a few minutes, wait for water to dissolve plug, then withdraw water from tube.	
8. Gently milk tube again as in step 5.	Milk from proximal to distal end of tube.
9. Instill acidic, strained juice or fresh, cold, carbonated beverage into tube, and clamp for 10 to 15 minutes.	Cranberry and citrus juices approximate acidity of gastric secretions. Carbonated beverages may be acidic or basic. Carbonation is most concentrated from a chilled, freshly opened container. Carbonation may work by loosening particles from a mass or by creating pressure in tube. Acidic solutions may be more effective with plugs of medication. With feedings, acidic solutions coagulate protein and form a more solid plug.
10. Monitor patient for signs of discomfort or distress. Observe abdominal insertion sites.	Tube rupture may or may not be perceived by patient. Fluid in tube will be released at site of rupture and may leak at insertion site or compromise patient's airway.
11. Withdraw juice or carbonated beverage with gentle plunging.	
12. As final approach, mix 1 tablespoon meat tenderizer with 1 ounce water. Draw up in syringe, inject into tube, and clamp tube for 30 minutes.	Papain has been demonstrated as the effective ingredient of tenderizers that are enzymatic in action. Papain is derived from papaya, which is an allergen for some people. Check other ingredients as well for contraindications.
13. Gently aspirate tenderizer solution from tube. Use warm water for gentle plunging as in step 6.	Vigorous plunging may further solidify plug or rupture tube.
14. Discard tenderizer aspirant and any material unclogged from tube.	
15. Flush tube thoroughly with water, and resume feeding as appropriate.	
16. If attempts to unclog tube are unsuccessful, report to physician for further intervention.	

DOCUMENTATION

1. Document the problem, the approaches used, and the outcome.

2. Make any necessary modifications in nursing care to prevent its recurrence.

Transition from Enteric to Oral Feeding

PURPOSES

To determine the patient's readiness for oral feeding and the level of oral feeding needed for the patient with chewing and swallowing difficulties; to determine the appropriate feeding method (enteric or oral) for patients with chewing and swallowing difficulties.

GENERAL CONSIDERATIONS

1. Effective control of swallowing implies the use of the lips, cheeks, tongue, palate, larynx, and respiratory musculature (Figure 1-6).
2. There are no absolute guidelines to determine whether a patient should or should not be given oral feedings.
3. The decision to use oral or enteral feeding is based on the physician's, nurse's, and speech therapist's assessments of oral and pharyngeal transit time and potential for aspiration. Ideally, these can be verified by video fluoroscopy.
4. In general, a patient aspirating more than 10% of every bolus and taking more than 10 seconds to swallow a single bolus, regardless of the consistency of the food, should not be fed orally.
5. The amount of time it takes to swallow a single bolus is an important factor in nutritional management. If the patient cannot consume enough nutrition orally, enteric supplements are necessary.
6. The nursing assessment should include:
   - soft palate reflex;
   - swallow reflex;
   - gag reflex;
   - function of the cranial nerves—trigeminal (V), facial (VII), glossopharyngeal (IX), vagus (X), spinal accessory (XI), and hypoglossal (XII);
   - labial function;
   - lingual function;
   - respiratory status—history of aspiration, requirement for suctioning, tracheostomy, and so forth; and
   - level of responsiveness.
7. Other factors that could inhibit oral feeding are degree of head control, general level of endurance, upper extremity function, general coordination, or specific dietary or dentition problems.
8. The managing physician makes the final decision regarding oral feeding.
9. The following may indicate that the patient is at high risk for aspiration and should remain prohibited from oral intake:
   - reduced alertness;
   - reduced responsiveness to stimulation;
   - absent swallow;
   - absent protective cough;
   - difficulty handling secretions, for example, excessive coughing and choking, copious secretions, and a wet, gurgly voice quality; and
   - significant reductions in the range and strength of oral-motor and laryngeal movements.
10. Functional severity levels for dysphagia are as follows (Cherney, Cantieri, & Pannell, 1986):
    - severe (nonfunctional)
      —all nourishment is received from an alternate feeding method
      —patient is receiving nothing by mouth
      —trial oral feeding, with physician's orders, by a speech pathologist or feeding specialist only

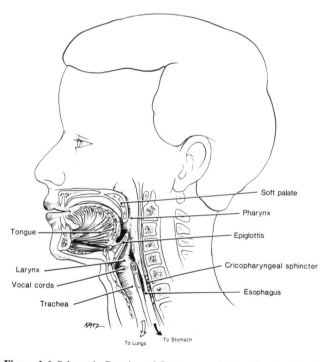

Figure 1-6 Schematic Drawing of Structures and Areas Involved in the Swallowing Process. *Source:* From *Clinical Evaluation of Dysphagia* (p.55) by L.R. Cherney, C.A. Cantieri, and J.J. Pannell, 1986, Rockville, MD: Aspen Publishers, Inc. Copyright 1986 by Aspen Publishers, Inc.

- moderately severe (interferes with function)
  - alternate feeding method is still the primary source of nourishment
  - limited, inconsistent success with oral intake
  - patient requires constant supervision
  - some team involvement is needed, but only the speech pathologist or feeding specialist introduces new items or techniques
- moderate (interferes with function)
  - alternate methods may be withdrawn on a trial basis
  - patient is fairly reliable with a prescribed diet of specific items
  - complete supervision is still needed
  - nursing is most involved and follows the instructions of the speech pathologist or feeding specialist
  - introduction of new items to the patient's diet is being supervised by a speech pathologist or feeding specialist
- mild moderate (interferes with function)
  - patient is fairly reliable with a defined level of food consistency
  - clear liquids or solids may still cause difficulty
  - nursing staff takes primary responsibility for supervision of feeding
  - self-feeding instruction is initiated if upper extremity function permits
- mild (adequate but reduced)
  - patient receives a regular diet with only some foods restricted because of particular difficulty with them
  - patient may still require some special techniques or procedures to achieve successful swallowing
  - less close staff supervision is needed
- minimal (adequate but reduced)
  - patient receives a regular diet without any restrictions
  - no supervision is required
  - occasional episodes of coughing with liquids or solids
- normal (adequate)
  - patient is independent in oral intake of all food consistencies
  - safe and efficient swallowing competency

11. Diet types for solid foods (Steefel, 1981):
- pureed (requires minimal gumming or chewing)
  - eggs (soft boiled or poached)
  - fruit (baby food, ripe mashed bananas)
  - meats, fish, poultry, cheese (baby food, pureed meats, cottage cheese)
  - potatoes (mashed white or sweet)
  - vegetables (baby food)
  - miscellaneous (gravy, cream sauces, nondairy creamers, butter, margarine)
  - sugar and sweets (jelly, plain pudding, boiled custard)
  - breads and cereals (thick, smooth, hot cereals such as Cream of Wheat or Cream of Rice)
  - avoid all other foods
- advanced pureed (added pureed foods that require more active gumming)
  - meat, fish, poultry, cheese, cheese souffle without crust, minced or ground meat
  - breads and cereals (soft breads without crusts or seeds, oatmeal)
  - avoid all other foods
- mechanical soft (soft, textured foods that are easy to chew, swallow, and digest)
  - soft cooked fruits and vegetables, including canned, served whole
  - breads, soft crackers, dry cereals that become soft in milk
  - desserts (cream pies and soft cakes without nuts and coconut)
  - meats, soft sandwiches (no crust), soft casseroles, soft meat salads without raw vegetables
  - potatoes (creamed or baked, without skin), soft noodles, rice
  - sugars and sweets (soft candies, small nuts, small hard ingredients)
  - vegetables (spinach, peas, green beans)
  - avoid toast, coarse cereals, cookies, nuts, bacon, and all other foods not listed above
- soft (foods that are easy to chew, swallow, and digest; slight advancement from mechanical soft)
  - breads and cereals (soft bread with crusts, soft dinner rolls, pancakes, hot breads, coffee cakes with nuts)
  - eggs (scrambled or fried, omelettes)
  - meat, diced steaks, chops, meat casseroles, American cheese
  - vegetables, all cooked (except asparagus) or soft molded, vegetable salads (without lettuce or raw vegetables)
  - avoid hard rolls, nuts, deep fried foods, popcorn

12. Diet types for liquids:
- extra thick liquids
  - thick soups that are strained with mashed potatoes
  - juices thickened with pureed fruit, baby cereal, or gelatin
- thick liquids (all liquids thickened as in extra thick but to a lesser degree)
- minimally thickened liquids
  - strained soups
  - milkshakes and eggnogs that are not too thin
  - thick juices or nectars
  - thick liquids with decreased (or without) thickening agent
- clear and other liquids (unrestricted fluid intake)

13. The length of time that it takes to progress from enteric to oral feeding is determined by the speech pathologist and

the physician. This information will assist in the decision-making process about whether to place a gastrostomy tube or to utilize a nasogastric tube.

14. Nasogastric tube feeding is generally considered a temporary solution and is used with patients whose chewing and swallowing problems are thought to be short term. If swallowing rehabilitation is anticipated to be long, a gastrostomy tube would be more appropriate.

15. Enteric feedings should stabilize a patient's nutritional needs.

DOCUMENTATION

1. Document the patient's progress in any oral intake.
2. Document and report complications.

Management and Safety Measures for Patients with Dysphagia

PURPOSES

To prevent the complications related to swallowing dysfunction (i.e., aspiration, choking, pocketing, dehydration, and malnutrition); to monitor and provide safety measures for the patient with swallowing dysfunction.

STAFF RESPONSIBLE

EQUIPMENT

1. Suction machine and equipment.
2. Feeding utensils (small Teflon-coated spoon, metal spoon, and utensils).
3. Cups (30 to 200 mL).
4. Modified cups with cut-outs.
5. Blue food coloring for patients with tracheostomies.
6. Proper food or liquid for trial feeding.
7. Intake and output and caloric count flow sheets.
8. Pillows for positioning.

GENERAL CONSIDERATIONS

1. Chewing and swallowing dysfunction may be seen in patients with diagnosis of:
   - vascular related disorders
     —cortical involvement
     —brain stem stroke
   - traumatic brain injury
   - degenerative neurological disease
     —parkinsonism
     —amyotrophic lateral sclerosis
     —multiple sclerosis
     —myotonic dystrophy
     —oculopharyngeal muscular dystrophy
     —myasthenia gravis
     —Huntington's chorea

   - other neurological etiologies including
     —poliomyelitis
     —Guillain-Barré syndrome
     —scleroderma
     —systemic lupus erythematosus
   - spinal cord injury
   - debilitation and extreme weakness
   - dementia or confusion

2. Suspect dysphagia if any of the following are noted:
   - uncoordinated chewing and swallowing;
   - presence of dysarthria;
   - drooling;
   - choking;
   - coughing while or immediately after eating or drinking;
   - aspiration of food or saliva;
   - pocketing of food;
   - absence of gag reflex; or
   - moist quality of voice.

3. The major complication associated with dysphagia is aspiration.

4. Assess the patient with dysphagia according to the guidelines in the Dysphagia Assessment Tool (Exhibit 1-1). Assessment is to be done on admission and is ongoing.

5. Incorporate the data obtained from the Dysphagia Assessment Tool into the plan of care.

6. When dysphagia is suspected, initiate contact with the Speech Department to provide a thorough evaluation and guidelines for feeding techniques. Incorporate these techniques into the plan of care.

7. Criteria for food selection to facilitate chewing and swallowing are as follows:
   - Semisolid foods such as purees or foods that hold some shape are the easiest to swallow. Form provides stimulation to initiate the swallow.
   - Foods with texture stimulate chewing. Chewing assists in stimulating the swallow reflex.
   - Liquids, such as water and juices, are difficult to swallow because they are thin and have no texture. Also, water is tasteless.

Exhibit 1-1 Dysphagia Assessment Tool

Obtain data from referral material or referring agency

1. History or etiology of swallowing dysfunction
2. Weight loss
3. Diagnostic testing results
4. Type of diet
5. Results from previous attempts to feed
   - Any problems or difficulties chewing or swallowing
     —solids (pureed, advanced pureed, mechanical soft, soft, regular)
     —liquids (extra thick liquids, thick liquids, minimally thick liquids, clear and other thin liquids)
   - Fatigue
     —with repetition
     —at certain hours of the day
   - Pocketing of food particles, and in what part of mouth
   - Coughing or choking
   - Nasal regurgitation
   - Wet, gurgly voice quality
   - Aspiration
6. Current feeding method
   - Oral
   - Jejunostomy tube
   - Gastrostomy tube
   - Nasogastric tube

Assessment

1. Mobility: Can the patient assume an appropriate feeding position?
   - Head and trunk aligned with midline
   - Good head control
   - Neck slightly flexed
   - Hips flexed
   - Deviations
   - Assistance or assistive devices needed to maintain position
2. Respiratory: Can the patient protect his or her airway?
   - Gag reflex
   - Cough reflex
   - Phonation characteristics
   - Secretions (amount and type)
   - Breath sounds
   - Tracheostomy (type)
   - Suctioning requirements
3. Cognition and behavior
   - Level of responsiveness
   - Lethargy
   - Impulsiveness
   - Memory problems
   - Ability to follow simple commands
   - Attention span
4. Oral sensory and motor
   - Swallow reflex
   - Response to stimuli
   - Mouth posture at rest
   - Oral and facial sensation
   - Voluntary movement
     —opens and closes mouth
     —opens and closes lips
     —moves tongue (in and out, side to side, up and down)
5. Functional
   - Use of empty cup, straw, and spoon
   - Upper extremity function
   - General coordination

- Milk, ice cream, and milkshakes, although they have some form, are difficult to clear rapidly because they form excessive mucus in the mouth and throat.

- Ice cream, ice chips, and Jell-O, although semisolid in form, usually melt to a thin liquid by the time the patient with dysphagia finally swallows the bolus.

- Meats require a great deal of chewing and, therefore, are difficult to manage. Ground meats may crumble and be aspirated. Chicken may be the easiest to chew and holds its form as a bolus.

- Sweet, sour, and salty foods stimulate chewing, which potentiates swallowing.

- Foods at body temperature are not stimulating enough; foods slightly warmer or colder than body temperature are indicated.

8. The patient with dysphagia should be well rested and as calm and undistracted as possible at the time of eating.
9. Criteria to be met before feeding the patient are as follows:
   - patient must be alert and responsive;
   - patient must have control of oral movements;
   - patient must have the ability to protect the airway; and
   - patient must be able to hold and swallow saliva.
10. Other diagnostic tests (i.e., video fluoroscopy) may be ordered by the physician to determine the dynamics of the swallowing sequence and related problems.
11. Before feeding patients with dysphagia or potential chewing and swallowing problems, staff should demonstrate knowledge of and skill in performing Heimlich's maneuver. Family members may need to learn this as well. Recommended approaches are as follows:
    - conscious patient, standing or sitting
      —Stand behind with one foot beside and the other foot behind the patient (this braces you to support the patient and positions you for performing abdominal thrusts).
      —Wrap your arms around the patient's waist.
      —Make a fist with one hand, and grab it with the other. The fist is placed with the thumb side against the patient's abdomen, slightly above the navel and below the rib cage.
      —Press your fist into the patient's abdomen with a quick, forceful, inward and upward thrust. Repeat thrusts in rapid sequence if necessary.

- unconscious patient, lying
  —Position the patient on his or her back.
  —Kneel straddling his or her thighs.
  —With one hand directly over the other, place the heel of the bottom hand in the middle of the patient's abdomen a little above the navel (avoid pressure over or near the xiphoid or rib areas).
  —Press quickly into the abdomen with a forceful upward thrust along the midline of the body. Repeat if necessary.

PATIENT AND FAMILY EDUCATION

1. Educate the patient and caregivers as to the proper method of feeding the individual. Include potential complications, risks, and signs and symptoms indicative of need to discontinue feeding.
2. Record progress.
3. Teach the Heimlich maneuver to family members or caregivers responsible for feeding the patient.

PROCEDURE

Steps	*Additional Information*
1. Initiate intake and output flow sheet.	The patient with dysphagia may not be taking in enough fluids because of difficulty of swallowing; this potentially jeopardizes his or her hydration status. Observation and assessment of intake and output provide information about patient's hydration status and also can indicate cardiac, endocrine, or renal problems. Additional hydration assessment includes observation of skin turgor, condition of mucous membranes, and urine specific gravity.
2. Initiate calorie count.	Foods that are easiest to swallow for the patient with dysphagia may not be the most nutritious. Such patients eat at slow rate and often become fatigued or cannot consume enough at each meal to maintain adequate nutritional intake. Calorie counts provide information about nutritional status. Consult dietitian for appropriate management of nutritional needs.
3. Initiate weights twice a week or on a routine basis.	Patient's weight will assist in determining adequacy of caloric intake.
4. Count number of spoonfuls of food taken at each meal. This may be partial spoonfuls (e.g., ¼-teaspoon amounts).	This is a valuable measure when patient intake is small and progress needs to be monitored or when milliliter measurement is too large.
5. Provide suction setup for patients with severe involvement at risk for aspiration.	A registered nurse and suction equipment must be present for initial feeding evaluation.
6. Maintain proper positioning during feeding:	Appropriate positioning improves patency of esophageal pathway, allows epiglottal closure, and prevents aspiration.
• positioning in bed	
—Lift patient to head of bed.	
—Raise head of bed to 60° to 90°.	
—Align head and trunk with midline with neck slightly flexed.	Flexion also encourages a swallow.
—Support with pillows as necessary to provide trunk and head stability.	
• positioning in chair or wheelchair	
—Seat patient at 90° angle with trunk extended and head aligned with midline.	
—Slightly flex neck.	
—Keep feet flat (preferably on floor).	
—Use lapboard if proper table height is unavailable or if patient has positioning difficulties.	Proper table or lapboard height would allow patient to rest forearms flat on surface with elbows flexed more than 90° and shoulders neutral and symmetrical.
7. Modify environment when appropriate:	Patients who cannot attend to more than one task at a time require environmental modifications.
• decrease distractions;	

Steps	*Additional Information*

- find a quiet, low-stimulus place (e.g., patient's room with curtains drawn, private room, empty part of hallway);
- keep patient focused on task of eating;
- keep conversation to a minimum; and
- focus on one food item at a time.

Place only one food item in front of patient.

8. Reinforce rate and amount of feeding:
   - give ½ to ⅓ teaspoon at a time;
   - put spoon down between portions;
   - check for empty mouth before proceeding; and

   - encourage patient to take a sip of fluid at slow rate.

Teach patient correct rate and amount. If swallowing problem is not severe, promote independence and encourage slower rate.

Give patient enough time to swallow. Teach patient to insert a finger to check oral cavity for food.

The use of cut-out cups or small medicine cups helps limit volume of fluid and amount of neck extension. Slight flexion makes swallowing easier. Straws are difficult to use with facial weakness and paralysis. A short straw may be used because it requires less effort and muscle strength than a long one.

9. Reinforce voluntary swallow:
   - Teach voluntary swallow. Say to patient:
     —"Hold the food in your mouth."
     —"Hold your breath."
     —"Think about swallowing."
     —"Swallow."

   - Place food on intact side or side without sensory or motor loss.
   - Watch for rise of larynx to indicate that swallowing has occurred.
   - Check for clear mouth before proceeding.

10. Ongoing assessment of potential aspiration.

If patient's swallowing problem is severe, emphasize act of swallowing over that of taking food or establishing independence in feeding. Postpone incorporation of feeding into activities of daily living, and focus on swallowing more than task of feeding.

This will heighten patient's awareness of food present in mouth and stimulate swallow reflex.

Look for signs that may indicate aspiration (moist-sounding voice, shortness of breath, difficulty breathing and decreased lung sounds, cyanosis, regurgitation of food particles). Staff and family should be able to perform emergency interventions, such as suctioning or Heimlich's maneuver, as well as call for help.

ADDENDUM: SPECIAL CONSIDERATIONS FOR PATIENTS WITH TRACHEOSTOMY

Follow steps 1 through 10 above. In addition:

1. If patient has cuffed tracheostomy tube, cuff should be inflated during feeding.

Suctioning should be done before deflating in case food has pocketed above cuff. If cuff status is to be deflated, keep inflated for 30 minutes after feeding.

2. Add blue food coloring to food. Show patient food, and let him or her smell it before coloring food.

If patient coughs or is suctioned and substance is blue, aspiration can be determined because food has been dyed a distinct color.

DOCUMENTATION

1. Record the results of assessments.
2. Document safety measures and effectiveness.
3. Record nutritional intake and outcomes.
4. Document patient and family education.

Stimulation Techniques for the Patient with Dysphagia

PURPOSE

To reinforce and initiate the stages and movements of normal chewing and swallowing.

STAFF RESPONSIBLE

EQUIPMENT

1. Ice.
2. Cotton-tipped applicators or stainless-steel spoon.
3. Straw.
4. 1-Ounce medication cup.
5. Laryngeal mirror (size 00).
6. 200-mL Cut-out cup.
7. Optional: nonsterile gloves.

GENERAL CONSIDERATIONS

1. The stages of swallowing are:
   - oral preparatory phase, in which food is manipulated in the mouth;
   - oral phase, in which lingual movement propels the bolus posteriorly;
   - pharyngeal phase, which is the swallowing reflex (involuntary); and
   - esophageal phase, during which peristaltic waves carry food through the esophagus.
2. Feeding techniques deal with the preparatory and oral stages of the swallow, which terminate when the reflexive swallow is triggered.
3. Feeding techniques include:
   - positioning of material (food) in the mouth;
   - manipulating food in the mouth with the tongue;
   - chewing boluses of food of various consistencies;
   - recollecting the bolus into a cohesive mass before initiation of the swallow; and
   - organizing lingual peristalsis to propel the bolus posteriorly.
4. Swallowing techniques deal with the stimulation of the swallowing reflex, improvement of pharyngeal transit time, airway protection, and improvement of the preparatory and oral stages of the swallow.
5. Food is one of the primary facilitators of oral movement because it can stimulate sensations of touch, taste, and temperature as well as provide visual and olfactory input.
6. Direct feeding involves introducing food into the mouth and attempting to reinforce the appropriate behaviors during the stages of swallowing.
7. Therapeutic interventions utilize exercises to improve motor controls that are prerequisites for normal swallowing. Many of these exercises are done by the speech pathologist.
8. Thermal stimulation is a method used to stimulate the swallowing reflex in patients whose swallowing reflex does not trigger or triggers late.
9. It is unlikely that an actual swallow will be triggered with thermal stimulation. The purpose of the exercise is to heighten sensitivity to the swallowing reflex so that, when food or liquid is presented and the patient attempts a voluntary swallow, the reflex will be triggered.
10. The speech-language pathologist will evaluate the patient and make recommendations on the use of thermal stimulation on the nursing unit.
11. Contraindications for thermal stimulation include hypertonicity of the oral musculature and abnormal reflexes. Stimulation may accentuate these problems.
12. The techniques included in this procedure are ones that the nursing staff can utilize as appropriate. There are other techniques that only the speech pathologist should perform.

PROCEDURE

Steps	*Additional Information*
1. Position patient. • In bed —patient at head of bed —head of bed raised 60° to 90° —head and trunk aligned with midline —neck slightly flexed —pillows supporting position if necessary	See Management and Safety Measures for Patients with Dysphagia procedure for more detail.

Steps	*Additional Information*

- In chair
  - —patient sitting at 90° with trunk extended
  - —head aligned with midline
  - —neck slightly flexed
  - —feet flat
  - —table or lapboard at proper height

2. Food temperature should be slightly warmer or colder than body temperature.

This will best stimulate a swallow. Hot foods can burn tongue, cold foods can numb tongue, and foods at room temperature do not provide enough stimulation.

3. Reinforce voluntary swallow. Say to patient:
   - "Hold the food in your mouth."
   - "Hold your breath."
   - "Think about swallowing."
   - "Swallow."

Keep directions short and direct for increased understanding and emphasis. Practice steps with a dry swallow or empty spoon before starting.

4. Hold patient's mouth or lips closed if mouth or lip closure is not adequate.

Mouth and lips must close to initiate and stimulate swallowing. This is the first step in swallowing.

5. Place hand on sagging or drooping facial muscles.

Providing support to drooping facial muscles from facial paralysis will give better control over food particles.

6. Place food on intact side of mouth with patients who have sensory or motor loss.

This will heighten awareness of food and stimulates chewing and swallow reflex.

7. Place food in back of mouth for patients with hyperactive or hypoactive tongues.

This will inhibit hyperactive tongue and assist hypoactive tongue during oral phase of swallowing.

8. Do not combine solid and liquids in same mouthful.

The combination of textures and thicknesses is too confusing and will not enhance swallowing reflex.

9. Assist with swallowing.
   - Apply gentle pressure or massage over larynx.
   - Stroke digastric muscle on either side or both sides.
   - Place ice at sternal notch.

These activities may help stimulate a swallow.

10. Ask patient to wipe his or her lips with napkin.

The automatic response that usually follows is a swallow. Use of napkin also provides pressure on lips and may assist with lip closure.

11. Feeding equipment suggestions are:
    - use cut-out cups or small, 1-ounce medication cups;

These cups will limit volume of fluid and decrease amount of head and neck extension, therefore making it easier for patient to swallow.

    - cut straws shorter, or do not use a straw;

Long straws require effort to use and are difficult for patients with facial weakness or paralysis.

    - do not have patient drink out of cartons; and

It is too difficult to form a seal around the opening, especially when patient has facial weakness or paralysis.

    - use an iced spoon or cold stainless-steel spoon to feed patient.

This will provide more sensory stimulation than a room-temperature or plastic spoon.

12. Thermal stimulation:
    - Wash hands.

Use gloves if body fluid precautions are indicated.

    - Position patient at 80° to 90°.
    - Place cotton-tipped applicator and laryngeal mirror in ice for 10 seconds.
    - Lightly brush base of anterior faucial pillar (Figure 1-7).

If patient begins to gag, stop procedure.

    - Five to ten strokes should be done on each anterior faucial pillar.

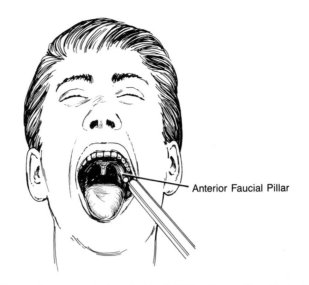

Figure 1-7 Locating the Anterior Faucial Pillar. *Source:* From *Evaluation and Treatment of Swallowing Disorders* by J. Logemann, 1983, Boston, MA: College-Hill Press, Inc. Copyright 1983 by College-Hill Press, Inc. Adapted by permission.

Steps	Additional Information
• If procedure does not produce an involuntary swallow, instruct patient to swallow voluntarily. • Stimulation will need to be repeated four or five times daily for 5 to 10 minutes each time for several weeks to 1 month.	This may help elicit a swallow.

DOCUMENTATION

1. Document the stimulation techniques used.
2. Record the results and any unusual occurrences during the procedures.
3. Document the recommended changes in the procedure based on patient responses.

BIBLIOGRAPHY

Broom, J., & Jones, K. (1981). Causes and prevention of diarrhea in patients receiving enteral nutritional support. *Journal of Human Nutrition, 35,* 123–127.

Cataldi-Betcher, E.L., Seltzer, M.H., Slocum, B.A., & Jones, K.W. (1983). Complications occurring during enteral nutrition support: A prospective study. *Journal of Parenteral and Enteral Nutrition, 7,* 546–552.

Cherney, L.R., Cantieri, C.A., & Pannell, J.J. (1986). *Clinical evaluation of dysphagia.* Rockville, MD: Aspen.

Daeffler, R.J. (1986). Oral care. *The Hospice Journal, 2,* 81–103.

DeBear, K. (1986). Sham feeding, another kind of nourishment. *American Journal of Nursing, 86,* 1142–1143.

DelRio, D., Williams, K., & Esvelt, B.M. (1982). *Handbook of enteral nutrition: A practical guide to tube feeding.* El Segundo, CA: Medical Specifics.

Flynn, K.T., Norton, L.C., and Fisher, R.L. (1987). Enteral tube feeding: Indications, practices, and outcomes. *Image: Journal of Nursing Scholarship, 11*(2), 16–19.

Griggs, B.A., & Hoppe, M.C. (1979). Nasogastric tube feeding. *American Journal of Nursing, 79,* 481–485.

Hargrove, R. (1980). Feeding the severely dysphagic patient. *Journal of Neurosurgical Nursing, 12,* 102–107.

Holtz, L., Milton, J., & Sturek, J.K. (1987). Compatibility of medications with enteral feedings. *Journal of Parenteral and Enteral Nutrition, 11,* 183–186.

Kaminski, M.V., & Freed, B.A. (1981). Enteral hyperalimentation: Prevention and treatment of complications. *Nutritional Support Services, 1,* 29–40.

Lipman, T.O. (1987). Nasopulmonary intubation with feeding tubes, therapeutic misadventure or accepted complication? *Nutrition in Clinical Practice, 2,* 45–48.

Logemann, J. (1983). *Evaluation and treatment of swallowing disorders.* Boston, MA: College-Hill Press.

Mamel, J.J. (1987). Percutaneous endoscopic gastrostomy, a review. *Nutrition in Clinical Practice, 2,* 65–75.

McGee, L. (1987). Feeding gastrostomy: Part I: Indications and complications. *Journal of Enterostomal Therapy, 14,* 73–78.

Metheny, N. (1988). Measures to test placement of nasogastric and nasointestinal feeding tubes: A review. *Nursing Research, 37,* 324–329.

Newmark, S.R., Simpson, M.S., Beskitt, M.P., Black, J., & Subleth, D. (1981). Home tube feeding for long-term nutritional support. *Journal of Parenteral and Enteral Nutrition, 5,* 76–79.

Newmark, S.R., Sublett, D., Black, J., & Geller, R. (1981). Nutritional assessment in a rehabilitation unit. *Archives of Physical Medicine and Rehabilitation, 62,* 279–282.

Nicholson, L.J. (1987). Declogging small-bore feeding tubes. *Journal of Parenteral and Enteral Nutrition, 11,* 594–597.

Rombeau, J.L., & Caldwell, M.D. (1984). *Clinical nutrition: Vol. 1. Enteral and tube feeding.* Philadelphia, PA: Saunders.

Ryan, J.A., & McFadden, M.C. (1982). Practical aspects of jejunal feeding. Silver Spring, MD: American Society for Parenteral and Enteral Nutrition (ASPEN); 1–6. Monograph.

Starkey, J.F., Jefferson, P.A., & Kirby, D.F. (1988). Taking care of percutaneous endoscopic gastrostomy. *American Journal of Nursing, 88,* 42–45.

Steefel, J.S. (1981). *Dysphagia rehabilitation for neurologically impaired adults.* Springfield, IL: Thomas.

Tuel, S.M., & Wu, Y. (1986). A method for stabilizing chronic gastrostomy or jejunostomy tubes. *Archives of Physical Medicine and Rehabilitation, 67,* 175–176.

Umphred, D.A. (Ed.). (1985). *Neurological rehabilitation: Vol. 3.* St. Louis, MO: Mosby.

chapter 2

Procedures To Maintain Mobility

INTRODUCTION

Mobility, or moving easily and freely without restrictions, is an integral part of life. Throughout our lives, we develop skills to learn to control our mobility. A loss in mobility results in both physical and psychological effects. Jacobs and Geels (1984) identify problems that may result in impaired mobility (Table 2-1).

Table 2-1 Problems That May Result in Impaired Mobility

Problem	Condition
1. Activity intolerance, diminished strength or endurance	Acute conditions: myocardial infarctions, gastrointestinal disorders. Chronic conditions: cancer, congestive heart failure, chronic obstructive pulmonary disease, autoimmune deficiency syndrome.
2. Pain or discomfort	Burns, chronic pain, postoperative pain.
3. Perceptual impairment	Visual disorders, tumor, cerebral vascular accident (CVA), brain injury or trauma.
4. Cognitive impairment	Brain injury or trauma, CVA, tumor.
5. Neuromuscular impairment	Multiple sclerosis, Parkinson's disease, spinal cord injury, myelitis.
6. Musculoskeletal impairment	Arthritis, fractures, scoliosis, muscular dystrophy.
7. Psychological impairment	Neurosis, schizophrenia.

The effects of immobility on the human body are well documented (Browse, 1965; Olson, 1967; Carnevali & Brueckner, 1970; Hart, Reese, & Fearing, 1981). Other sections of this book present specific interventions to prevent or minimize the effects of immobility on other body systems. For example, Chapter 4 includes procedures to prevent pressure sores, and Chapter 3 includes procedures to prevent constipation or impaction.

In using the procedures in this chapter, basic patient safety should be the first concern. Therefore, with any newly admitted patient with potential or actual spinal instability, it must first be ensured that the entire spine is stable. Stability is generally determined by the physician on the basis of radiological and neurological examinations. If stability of the spine in the patient with potential or actual spinal injuries has not been determined, the patient must be placed on spinal precautions.

Stabilization of the spine can be accomplished through surgery or with the use of orthoses. If orthoses are used, it is imperative that those who apply them or work with patients who have them know exactly how they are applied, how they are to fit, how to adjust the orthosis, and who may make such adjustments. If a spinal orthosis is used, the patient must be placed on spinal precautions when the orthosis is removed or adjusted. Clarification of roles of various health workers in regard to maintaining spinal stability is vital.

The second area of concern is positioning. Some patients may be prone to or actually have contractures as a result of abnormal muscle tone or improper posturing. Appropriate positioning and frequent range of motion (ROM) can help prevent further limitations or promote functional ROM. To ensure optimal positioning in some patients, splints can be

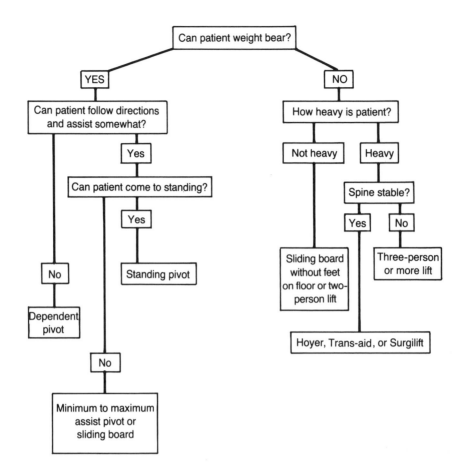

Figure 2-1 Steps for Determining Best Transfer Method.

used. Casts (dropout, serial, and so forth) may be prescribed to stretch out contractures already present. The physical or occupational therapist should be consulted when planning interventions to minimize abnormal tone or to stretch out contractures.

Pain relief can improve mobility skills. Timely administration of pain medications; slow, rhythmic movements; transcutaneous electrical nerve stimulation (TENS); and the like may provide relief and relaxation so that maximum mobility can be achieved. Nevertheless, pain should be considered an important sign when intervening—ROM should only be done to the point of pain that can be detected by the patient's comments and behaviors.

Transfer techniques built on neurodevelopmental techniques as taught by Bobath (1978) and most recently by Gee and Passarella (1985) have been integrated into the procedures

on mobility. When determining how best to transfer any patient, the decision tree in Figure 2-1 will lead to the most appropriate type of transfer.

The nurse should always encourage the patient to assist in the transfer to the extent possible. Patients should never be allowed to put their arms around the nurse's neck. The nurse must use good body mechanics to protect himself or herself from potential back or other injury. Simple one-step commands should be used because these help communicate clearly to the patient what is happening or going to happen in the transfer and establish a routine. When trying new transfer methods, the nurse should practice first on staff members to learn the steps and to identify potential problems. When the nurse is transferring a patient for the first time, someone should stand by for assistance and afterwards give feedback on the performance, use of body mechanics, and so forth.

Assessment and Management of Spinal Cord Instability

PURPOSES

To identify patients at high risk for spinal cord instability; to ensure and maintain spinal stability of all high-risk patients.

STAFF RESPONSIBLE

GENERAL CONSIDERATIONS

1. Any nursing staff member may institute spinal precautions when admitting a patient if the patient meets any of the following criteria:
   - a spinal cord injury within the last 6 months;
   - spinal stabilization surgery within the last 6 months; or
   - an unstable spine due to disease process (cancer, osteoporosis, or the like), spinal surgery (except laminectomy without fracture), or immediately after a fall.
2. Spinal precautions are clarified, further defined, or discontinued only by written physician prescription.
3. Determination of spinal stability is based on examination of full spine roentgenograms to ensure skeletal alignment and stability with or without spinal orthoses and on sensory and motor examination.
4. Spinal orthoses are applied, adjusted, and removed only by nurses, physicians, and certified orthotists in accordance with specific orthosis procedures.
5. Spinal orthoses are to be removed in accordance with the procedure or specific physician order.
6. Whenever an orthosis is removed, spinal precautions will be followed until the orthosis is reapplied.

PATIENT AND FAMILY EDUCATION

1. Initial teaching should include spinal precautions, patient's and family's role in spinal precautions, function of orthosis, and patient's and family's role in orthosis management (cooperation with nursing protocols).
2. If the patient will be discharged or on a pass with an orthosis, obtain written permission from the physician before teaching the application or removal of the orthosis.

DEFINITION OF TERMS

1. Spinal precautions mean that:
   - the patient is to be kept supine, lying flat in bed, with appropriate periodic repositioning by staff;
   - the head and lower section of the bed are not to be elevated;
   - logroll methods are to be used for all turning of the patient; and
   - patient may not be laid prone unless specifically ordered.
2. Stable with orthosis on means that:
   - if prescribed orthosis is fitted securely in place, the patient may engage in the following activities:
     —one- or two-person turns
     —head-of-bed increase to 90°
     —wheelchair to 90° (as tolerated)
     —transfers by Trans-aid, sliding board, Surgilift, dependent pivot
     —long sitting
     —ambulation, if appropriate
     —activities of daily living (as able)
     —weekend passes when medically stable
     —showers (sitting position)
     —pool, only if specifically ordered
     —ROM and manual muscle test of all joints except the spine unless specifically contraindicated
   - if prescribed orthosis is not securely in place, spinal precautions, as described above, are to be observed.
3. Remove brace for hygiene means that orthosis may only be removed for hygiene and skin care and that, while removed, spinal precautions should be observed.
4. D/C spinal orthosis means that the spine is stable and that restrictions to activity are discontinued unless otherwise specifically designated by the physician.
5. Stable without orthosis means that the spine is stable and that activities functionally consistent with the condition or level of the lesion, including those listed in (2), are permitted.

METHODS TO ESTABLISH PRESENCE OF SPINAL STABILITY

All patients with spinal cord injury who are admitted for the first time or who are readmitted within 6 months of injury or spinal stabilization are to be managed with spinal precautions until the status of spinal stability is determined by an attending physician. All prescriptions regarding spinal stability are to be written by an attending physician.

A patient admitted with or without an orthosis is automatically placed on spinal precautions until:

1. appropriate spinal roentgenograms are ordered and examined for evidence of skeletal alignment and stability;
2. appropriate prescriptions are written in established definitions; and
3. prescriptions are changed as indicated to be consistent with determined status of spinal stability and medical or surgical tolerances.

ASSESSING CORRECT BODY ALIGNMENT

Correct body alignment is assessed from the head or foot of the bed when the patient is recumbent (Figure 2-2). First, draw an imaginary line from the patient's chin through the suprasternal notch to the symphysis pubis. This line will be straight if the patient is in correct alignment with the head in midline. If the patient has deformities, such as those caused by scoliosis or contractures, this line may never be straight. Second, draw an imaginary line (from one side of the body to the other) through the shoulders and then through the hips. These two lines will be parallel if the patient is in correct alignment. This ensures that both sides of the body are symmetrical from the midline.

When incorrect body alignment is determined to be present, the nurse must make a judgment as to the degree of misalignment and the effect on the patient. If the misalignment is minute, the patient should be logrolled into correct alignment. If the misalignment is severe or if a change in the patient's level of sensation or motor function results, or if the patient complains of paresthesia, the physician should be called to see the patient. Subsequent prescriptions are carried out and documented.

SPINAL PRECAUTIONS USED IN RADIOLOGY

The Knight-Taylor orthosis is unclipped to place the metal clips aside in the anteroposterior view of the thoracolumbar spine after the patient is positioned supine on the table. For all other views, the orthosis remains intact. A three- or four-person lift is used to transfer the patient from cart to x-ray table. Views such as flexion-extension that necessitate complete removal of any orthosis or any part of a sternal occipital mandibular immobilizer (SOMI) require the presence of a physician. The technologist will remove the orthosis while the physician stabilizes the spine. If a patient is admitted without orthosis, the same precautions as described above are followed.

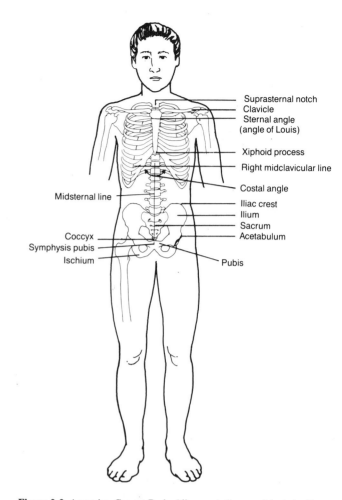

Figure 2-2 Assessing Correct Body Alignment. *Source:* Adapted with permission from *Nurse's Reference Library: Assessment.* Copyright 1982 Springhouse Corporation. All rights reserved.

MEDICAL EMERGENCIES

In the event of life-threatening emergencies, the need for life-support measures transcends spinal stability considerations. Although every reasonable effort to continue spinal stability should be employed, maintaining patency of airway and adequacy of ventilation and circulation are the first priorities. Jaw thrust and other required maneuvers should be carried out with every possible precaution.

DOCUMENTATION

1. Record the need for spinal precautions.
2. Document patient and family education.

Logroll

PURPOSE

To maintain vertebral alignment during position change.

STAFF RESPONSIBLE

EQUIPMENT

1. Three or more regular pillows.
2. One firm head pillow of compact thickness equal to shoulder width or folded sheepskin, rolled sheepskin, rolled towel, or blanket.
3. Bed, cart, or mat.

GENERAL CONSIDERATIONS

1. To logroll is to turn the patient so that the vertebral column moves as one unit.
2. Logrolling is required as follows:
   - for all spinal cord–injured patients who are admitted for the first time or who are readmitted within 6 months of injury or spinal stabilization until physician authorizes spinal stability prescriptions;
   - as prescribed by physician; or
   - for all patients on spinal precautions (see procedure for managing spinal cord instability, above).
3. Spinal precautions mean that the patient is to be kept supine, lying flat in bed, with appropriate periodic repositioning and pressure relief supports. The head and lower foot section of the bed are not to be elevated. Logroll methods are to be used for all turning of the patient.
4. To assess for correct vertebral alignment in supine or side lying, the nurse must ensure that the chin is in line with the suprasternal notch and the symphysis pubis. The head must be in midline, both sides of the body symmetrical from the midline, and the shoulders aligned with the hips.
5. The frequency of turning and positioning is determined by the nurse on assessing:
   - the patient's skin tolerance,
   - the patient's respiratory condition, and
   - the patient's comfort.
6. When the patient is designated by the physician as stable with orthosis on, logrolling is not required while the orthosis is on.

PATIENT AND FAMILY EDUCATION

1. The patient and family are taught the importance of logrolling to gain their cooperation in maintaining vertebral alignment.
2. The family members may participate in the procedure only after proper instruction and supervision by a nurse.

PROCEDURES

Steps	Additional Information
Preparation	
1. Assemble at least three staff members on same side of bed.	If patient's head is unsupported or uncontrolled, an additional staff member is needed to hold head.
2. Wash hands, and remove any watches, bracelets, or rings.	These may scratch patient or cause pain.
3. Remove glasses and neck chains from patient.	
4. Provide privacy.	
5. Have pillows ready and available for final positioning.	
6. All staff stand on same side of bed (Figure 2-3A):	
• Tallest and strongest person (1) stands at head of patient, opposite to side that patient will face after turn.	This person controls head, shoulders, and chest area.
• Second tallest person (2) stands at patient's waist.	This person controls chest to buttocks.
• Third tallest person (3) stands between patient's buttocks and knees.	This person controls buttocks and thighs.

| *Steps* | *Additional Information* |

Supine to Side Lying

1. Each person consecutively places arms under patient by placing palms up and pressing down on mattress (Figure 2-3B).
2. Position of head pillow:
   - Head pillow is placed next to patient's head on side away from positioned staff.
   - Person 1 counts to three. On "three" all lift patient toward them to side of bed. Pillow may need readjustment (Figure 2-3C).

   This is the only lifting that should occur during this procedure.

3. Again, person 1 counts to three. On "three" all roll the patient away from them, onto his or her side in one coordinated movement (Figure 2-3D).

   As patient reaches 90° angle to bed, each person places one arm in front of patient to block further rolling. Patient's head should roll onto head pillow.

4. Persons 1 and 2 stay in position and stabilize patient at head, shoulders, and hips to maintain alignment.

   Chin should be in line with suprasternal notch and symphysis pubis, head in midline, shoulders aligned with hips.

5. Person 3 steps to foot or head of bed and checks alignment.

   If patient is slightly out of alignment, person 3 should return to position, and all should realign patient by logrolling again. If patient is severely out of alignment or exhibiting changes in sensation or motor function, contact physician. Do not move patient.

6. Person 3 adjusts head pillow under patient's head and places one regular pillow behind patient's back and two regular pillows between legs.

   Legs are positioned so that top leg is slightly in front of or in back of bottom leg and ankle, knee and hip of top leg are in same horizontal plane.

7. Person 1 gently pulls own arms out from under patient, one arm at a time. Person 2 then does same.
8. Externally rotate and protract shoulder that patient is lying on, and place arms in functional position (Figure 2-3E).

   Opposite arm of patient is placed in front of hip or back in functional position. If patient has upper extremity edema, support hand and arm on pillows, foam blocks, or patient's hip.

Side Lying to Supine

1. Repeat steps 1 through 6 in preparation.
2. Persons 1 and 2 stabilize patient at shoulders and hips while person 3 removes back and leg pillows and adjusts head pillow.

   Head pillow should be adjusted so that when patient is rolled supine head is flat on bed.

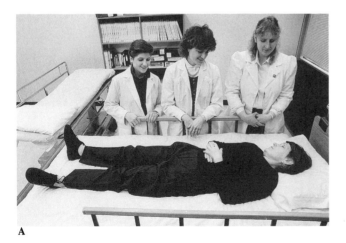

A

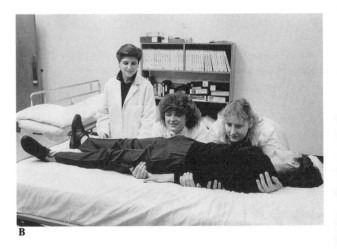

B

Figure 2-3 Logrolling.

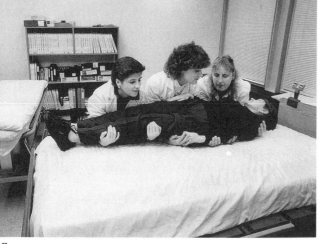

C

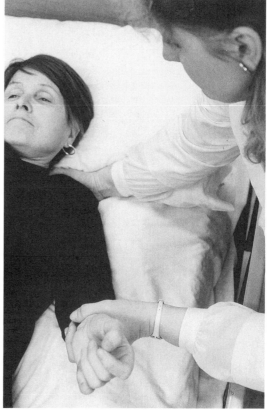

E

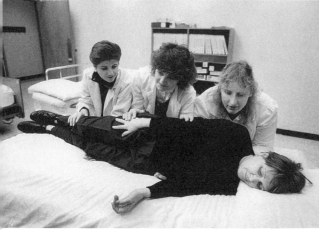

D

Steps	*Additional Information*
3. Person 3 returns to previous position.	
4. All staff place their hands palms up under patient's side and against patient's back.	Consecutively place arms under patient by placing palms up and pressing down on mattress.
5. Person 1 counts to three. On "three" all roll patient toward them onto back in one coordinated movement.	
6. Pull arms gently out from under patient, one arm at a time.	
7. Person 3 checks alignment.	Chin should be in line with suprasternal notch and symphysis pubis, head in midline, shoulders aligned with hips.
8. Put up side rails, move to opposite side of bed, and take up previous positions.	
9. Person 1 counts to three. On "three" all lift patient to middle of bed.	This should be the only lifting of patient.
10. Person 3 moves to foot of bed and checks alignment.	
11. One person places patient's arms at sides in functional position.	If hand edema is a problem, that hand should be propped up on patient's hip or leg or with pillows or foam blocks.

DOCUMENTATION

1. Document routine repositioning.
2. Note any unusual occurrences during the procedure (e.g.,

pain, positioning problems, poor tolerance, signs and symptoms of neurological changes, and so forth).
3. Post "Patient Alert" signs at the bedside.

Application, Removal, and Care of Spinal Orthoses

PURPOSE

To apply, adjust, and remove correctly spinal orthoses to maintain orthotic support of the spinal column.

STAFF RESPONSIBLE

GENERAL CONSIDERATIONS

1. Attending physician will write prescriptions specifying:
   - which orthosis is to be worn,
   - when the orthosis is to be worn,
   - when the orthosis can be removed,
   - how the patient is to be handled with and without the orthosis,
   - sitting angle,
   - positions that may be assumed, and
   - limits to mobility and activities (transfers and exercise). See assessment and management of spinal cord mobility.
2. Orthoses are prescribed depending on factors such as type, extent, and location of injury; patient's general health, healing history, and cooperation; anticipated duration of healing; allowance for maximum mobility; and the desired position for healing to occur.
3. Most orthoses do not provide total immobility (Table 2-2) but rather consist of specific components that limit movement detrimental to healing. A clear understanding of these principles and the position to be maintained (neutral, flexion, or extension) is essential to the type of brace worn, patient assessment, interventions, decision making, and teaching.
4. Maximum orthotic support is provided by applying and maintaining the orthosis position at approximate anatomical landmarks (Figure 2-9) and by molding the orthotic

Table 2-2 Characteristics and Names of Types of Braces Shown in Figures 2-4 to 2-9

	Limitations of ROM				
Type of Brace	Limits Flexion	Limits Flexion and Extension	Limits Flexion, Extension, and Lateral Movements	Limits Flexion, Extension, Lateral Movements, and Rotation	Limits Extension and Lateral Movements
Lumbar sacral orthoses (LSO) (Figures 2-4 and 2-9)		Chairback, Gold Thwait, high-low, low back	Knight, Norton-Brown	Corset, Raney, body jacket, Boston overlap orthosis (BOB)	Williams, Stuttle, hollow back
Thoracolumbar sacral orthoses (TLSO) (Figures 2-5 and 2-9)	Jewett, Cash, Griswold	Taylor, Dorsal-lumbar	Knight-Taylor	Cowhorn, Steindler, high Magnuson, Arnold Baker, corset, body jacket	
Cervical thoracolumbar sacral orthosis (CTLSO) (Figures 2-6 and 2-9)				Halo-hoop, halo-girdle, body jacket	
Cervical thoracic orthosis (CTO) (Figures 2-7 and 2-9)				Halo jacket, long two-poster, Guilford two-poster, Yale, cervicothoracic	
Cervical orthosis (CO) (Figures 2-8 and 2-9)			Soft cervical collar	Sternal occipital mandibular immobilizer (SOMI; four-poster) Nec-Loc, Philadelphia, Thomas	

Source: Adapted from "Clinical Applications in Spinal Orthotics" by D.G. Mueller, 1987, *Topics in Acute Care and Trauma Rehabilitation,* 1(3), p. 49. Copyright January 1987 by Aspen Publishers, Inc. Reprinted by permission of Glenn Case, illustrator.

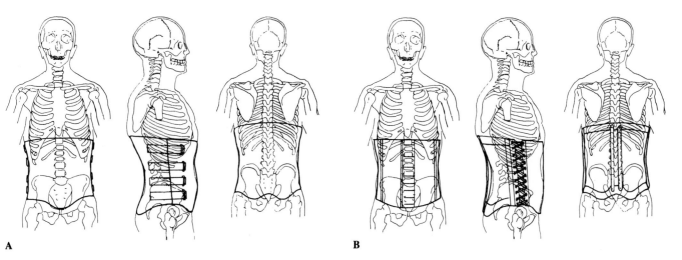

Figure 2-4 Representative Lumbar Sacral Orthoses (LSO). (**A**) Body Jacket, (**B**) Knight. *Source:* From "Clinical Applications in Spinal Orthotics" by D.G. Mueller, 1987, *Topics in Acute Care and Trauma Rehabilitation, 1*(3), p. 52. Copyright January 1987 by Aspen Publishers, Inc. Reprinted by permission of Glenn Case, illustrator.

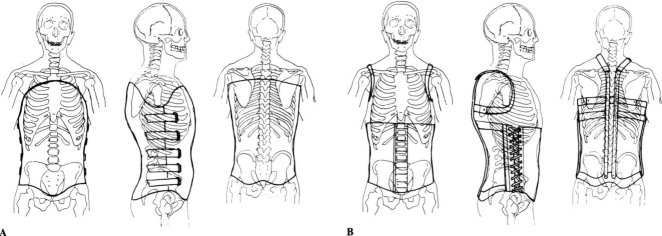

Figure 2-5 Representative Thoracolumbar Sacral Orthoses (TLSO). (**A**) Body Jacket, (**B**) Taylor. *Source:* From "Clinical Applications in Spinal Orthotics" by D.G. Mueller, 1987, *Topics in Acute Care and Trauma Rehabilitation, 1*(3), p. 53. Copyright January 1987 by Aspen Publishers, Inc. Reprinted by permission of Glenn Case, illustrator.

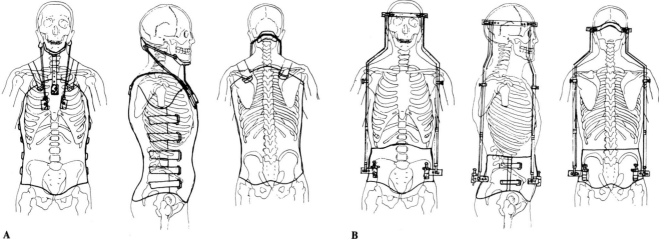

Figure 2-6 Representative Cervical Thoracolumbar Sacral Orthoses (CTLSO). (**A**) Body Jacket, (**B**) Halo-Girdle. *Source:* From "Clinical Applications in Spinal Orthotics" by D.G. Mueller, 1987, *Topics in Acute Care and Trauma Rehabilitation, 1*(3), p. 54. Copyright January 1987 by Aspen Publishers, Inc. Reprinted by permission of Glenn Case, illustrator.

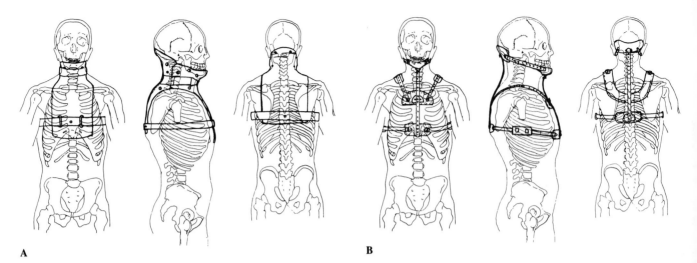

A   **B**

Figure 2-7 Representative Cervical Thoracic Orthoses (CTO). (**A**) Yale, (**B**) Long Two-Poster. *Source:* From "Clinical Applications in Spinal Orthotics" by D.G. Mueller, 1987, *Topics in Acute Care and Trauma Rehabilitation, 1*(3), p. 56. Copyright January 1987 by Aspen Publishers, Inc. Reprinted by permission of Glenn Case, illustrator.

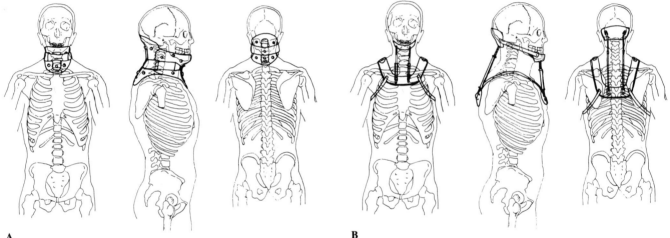

A   **B**

Figure 2-8 Representative Cervical Orthoses (CO). (**A**) Philadelphia, (**B**) Four-Poster. *Source:* From "Clinical Applications in Spinal Orthotics" by D.G. Mueller, 1987, *Topics in Acute Care and Trauma Rehabilitation, 1*(3), p. 57. Copyright January 1987 by Aspen Publishers, Inc. Reprinted by permission of Glenn Case, illustrator.

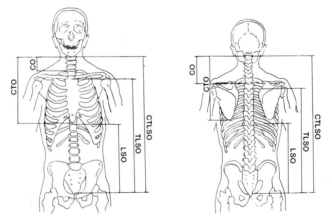

Figure 2-9 Characteristic Fitting Patterns of Spinal Orthoses to Bony Landmarks. *Source:* From "Clinical Applications in Spinal Orthotics" by D.G. Mueller, 1987, *Topics in Acute Care and Trauma Rehabilitation, 1*(3), p. 60. Copyright January 1987 by Aspen Publishers, Inc. Reprinted by permission of Glenn Case, illustrator.

components to the individual patient's body contour. Additional padding to fill contours and to relieve pressure areas is only a temporary measure. No substantial padding (more than ½ inch) is permitted without the physician's prescription.

5. Notify the physician concerning problems with orthotic fit, missing parts, or complaints of pain. If an orthotist is consulted, assist with patient position during adjustment and check for fit and problems in all usual patient positions while orthotist is present. Restrict patient movement and activity until adjustments are made.

6. Major orthotic adjustments (e.g., remolding, affixing pads, and disassembling components) are to be done only by a physician or an orthotist under physician prescription.

7. Minor orthotic adjustments (e.g., tightening or loosening straps and changing the level of the chin piece) are to be performed and anticipated by a nurse whenever a patient's position is changed. The shifting of body mass within some orthoses requires minor adjustments to maintain desired position and support. Other personnel are directed to stabilize the position until the adjustment is completed.

8. Routine skin checks, hygiene, and application or removal of clothing are important adjuncts to the care of a patient in an orthosis and must be planned for in response to individual patient problems and tolerance, in accordance with physician prescription, and with assistance from nursing resource personnel. Patient weight gain or loss must be monitored at least weekly because it can affect orthotic fit.

PATIENT AND FAMILY EDUCATION

1. The patient and family are to be carefully instructed regarding the purpose of the orthosis and mobility restrictions, the importance of full cooperation for maintenance of spinal stability, and the necessity of seeking out the nurse's assistance for needed adjustments.

2. The patient and family may be instructed and supervised in the application, removal, and adjustment of an orthosis by a nurse only with a written prescription by the attending physician.

PROCEDURES, CERVICAL ORTHOSES: SOFT CERVICAL COLLAR

General Considerations for Soft Cervical Collar

1. Soft cervical collars restrict some degree of anterior flexion, posterior extension, and lateral movement of the cervical spine.

2. They are seldom restrictive enough if the injury or condition requires bony immobilization of the cervical spine.

3. They are helpful, after other cervical orthoses have been used, to support weak neck muscles until strength and endurance have developed.

4. Questions regarding adequate spinal stabilization should be discussed with the physician.

Steps	*Additional Information*
To Apply Cervical Collar	
1. Position patient supine.	Observe spinal precautions when collar is off.
2. Position collar so that Velcro closure is posterior and collar rests on inner crest of clavicle.	
3. Fasten Velcro closure.	Collar should fit snugly around patient's neck, yet not so tightly that it restricts respirations or is uncomfortable.
To Remove Soft Cervical Collar	
1. Position patient supine.	Observe spinal precautions when collar is off.
2. Unfasten Velcro closure.	
3. Remove collar.	

Steps   *Additional Information*

Care of Patient Using Soft Cervical Collar

1. Wash patient's neck and chin.
2. Rub in a light layer of cornstarch or powder if collar is dirty or developing an odor.
3. Perform routine skin checks twice a day and as necessary.

4. Tee shirts may be worn under cervical collar.
5. Remove collar to take off tee shirt before hygiene procedures.
6. Shower or bathe patient (on flat-surface cart) without collar.

This minimizes dirt build up.
Powder should be lightly applied and rubbed in thoroughly before applying collar.
Special attention should be given to neck, cervical incision areas, and clavicles. Notify physician regarding problems with collar fit and complaints of pain.
Button-front shirts or V-neck tee shirts are easiest to manage.
A prescription to remove collar for hygiene must be written. Observe spinal precautions with collar off.
Clean and reapply collar after hygiene. Collar should be in place during transfers.

PROCEDURES, CERVICAL ORTHOSES: PHILADELPHIA COLLAR

General Considerations for Philadelphia Collar

1. Philadelphia collars restrict to a moderate degree anterior flexion, posterior extension, and lateral and rotating movements of the cervical spine.
2. They may be used to stabilize the cervical spine to facilitate healing and to prevent further neurological damage.

3. The collar is composed of two pieces of rigid foam reinforced anteriorly and posteriorly. Two Velcro closures are located laterally.

Steps   *Additional Information*

To Apply Philadelphia Collar

1. Position patient supine.
2. Position posterior piece behind patient's head and neck with minimal head and neck movements.
3. Position anterior piece beneath patient's chin, and rest lower edge of collar on inner crest of clavicles.
4. Tuck anterior piece's lateral edges into posterior piece's lateral edges.
5. Secure Velcro closures on both lateral sides.

Observe spinal precautions when collar is off.

Collar should fit snugly around patient's neck, yet not so tightly that it restricts respirations or is uncomfortable.

To Remove Philadelphia Collar

1. Position patient supine.
2. Unfasten Velcro closures.
3. Remove anterior piece of collar.
4. Remove posterior piece of collar by pressing down on bed to minimize head and neck movement.

Observe spinal precautions when collar is off.

Care of Patient Using Philadelphia Collar

Steps	Additional Information
1. Wash patient's neck and chin twice a day and as needed.	This minimizes dirt build up.
2. Routine skin checks are to be performed twice a day and as needed.	Special attention should be given to neck, cervical incision areas, clavicles, and chin. Notify physician regarding problems with collar fit and complaints of pain.
3. Tee shirts may be worn under Philadelphia collar.	Button-front shirts or V-neck tee shirts are easiest to manage.
4. Remove collar to take off tee shirt before hygiene procedures. Remove collar before bathing.	A prescription to remove collar for hygiene must be written. Observe spinal precautions with collar off. Clean collar with damp cloth, dry, and reapply after hygiene.
5. Shower patient on flat surface (cart) without collar.	Collar should be on for transfer to cart for bathing.

PROCEDURES, CERVICAL ORTHOSES: STERNAL OCCIPITAL MANDIBULAR IMMOBILIZER (SOMI) ORTHOSIS

General Considerations for SOMI

1. The SOMI restricts to a moderate degree anterior flexion, posterior extension, and lateral and rotating movements of the cervical spine.
2. Maximum orthotic support is provided by applying and maintaining the SOMI orthosis in the following positions:
   - sternal piece, ½ to 1 inch below the suprasternal notch;
   - occipital piece, just under the projection of the occiput; and
   - mandibular piece, so that the patient can open his or her mouth wide enough to chew but not as wide as possible.
3. The chin piece will need adjustment with position change (sitting, lying, or standing).
4. Tee shirts worn under a SOMI should have a loose neck opening and be one to two sizes larger than usual.

To Apply or Remove SOMI

Steps	Additional Information
1. Position patient supine, head neutral.	Neutral is when a straight plane passing under chin will be perpendicular to plane of bed with patient in supine position and parallel to floor in 90° angle with patient in sitting position.
2. Put on sternal piece with shoulder supports.	Sternal piece should be 1 inch below sternal notch.
3. Feed shoulder straps under neck to opposite side.	Be careful because patient may have increased sensitivity in posterior neck due to healing cervical incision.
4. Pull straps down past scapulae, and fasten to sternal piece.	Lift each shoulder slightly to facilitate movement of strap over scapulae.
5. Turn occipital piece, and slide it under posterior aspect of neck just under projection of occiput.	Put pressure on bed when sliding piece through to avoid pulling hair, touching stitches, and chilling neck from cold metal.
6. Turn occipital piece so that prongs fit in sternal piece, and lock it in place.	
7. Place mandibular support under chin, and set in proper hole.	Position so that patient can open mouth enough to chew but not as wide as possible. Patient should see only distal one-third to one-half of lap when sitting and only toes when supine.
8. Lock mandibular support in place.	
9. Buckle lateral chin straps beneath projection of occipital piece.	
10. Reverse procedure to remove.	

To Apply or Remove Tee Shirt under SOMI

1. Position patient in supine position.
2. Put one arm in tee shirt.
3. Pull tee shirt over patient's head from front to back. Do not move head.
4. Slide tee shirt behind head with minimal head movement.
5. Pull other arm through sleeve.

    If patient has pain or limited range in one shoulder, pull this arm through first.

6. Pull shirt down over chest.
7. Apply brace per above instructions.
8. Remove shirt by reversing procedure.

Care of Patient Using SOMI

1. Perform routine skin checks.

    Special attention should be given to occiput, scapula, chin, and clavicles. Notify physician of reddened areas, and plan for pressure relief.

2. No substantial padding (more than ½ inch) of orthosis is permitted without physician's order.

    Tee shirts should be worn under SOMI brace. These shirts should have a large neck opening and be one to two sizes larger than regularly worn so as to avoid excessive movement of neck during application or removal.

3. Remove brace to take off tee shirt before hygiene procedures.

    A prescription to remove brace for hygiene must be written if patient is to be on spinal precautions when brace is off.

4. Reapply brace before showering.

    Do not transport patient with a mechanical lifter when SOMI brace is off. These devices do not provide enough support.

5. Remove brace, dry, and reapply after showering.
6. Mark horizontal and vertical chin support adjustments.

    Two people are to be available when adjusting chin piece with patient in sitting position (one to hold patient's head).

PROCEDURES, CERVICAL THORACIC ORTHOSES: HALO JACKET

General Considerations for Halo Jacket

1. There are several different types of halo jackets; one such is shown in Figure 2-10. Regardless of type, there are certain common characteristics:

    - The halo is stabilized by pins that are inserted into the patient's skull. This results in maximal limitations in head and neck (cervical spine) flexion, extension, hyperextension, rotation, and lateral movements.

    - The halo is usually applied by a physician in surgery after a fusion or other surgical procedure has been performed.

    - The halo usually remains in place for at least 3 months.

2. Do not use rods, head support bars, or any other metal hardware to turn, lift, or transfer patient.

3. Daily care should include:
    - checking all bolts and skull pins for tightness;
    - inspecting skin surfaces for pressure areas;
    - inspecting skull pins for infection and skin adhesions; and
    - cleaning all pin sites with Betadine solution.
4. Weekly tightening of bolts by means of a torque screwdriver should be performed by a physician.
5. Inform physician of:
    - any pressure areas around or under halo brace;
    - suspected infection at or around pin sites;
    - patient complaints of pin site pain;
    - patient complaints of clicking noises or buzzing;

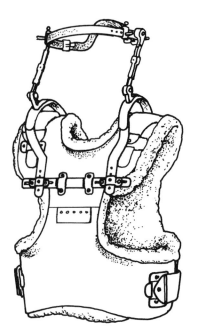

Figure 2-10 Halo Jacket. *Source:* Drawing prepared by Rehabilitation Institute of Chicago from literature distributed by Kirchner Medical Corporation, Timonium, MD. Used with permission.

- slight movement of patient's head or neck (could indicate loose pin);
- patient complaints of paresthesias; and
- changes in patient's motor abilities or sensation.

6. The vest lining should be kept clean and dry. A physician's prescription is necessary to remove the liner to shower the patient. Do not shower the patient with the liner in place, unless a replacement is available. When showering a patient with a halo jacket, protect the liner by removing it. The patient's hair may be washed carefully. After drying the inside and outside of the jacket, replace the liner. If the liner cannot be removed, shower below the vest or jacket and carefully wash by hand above it.

7. The two topmost anterior and posterior bolts (one on each side, which attach the hardware to the anterior and posterior vest plates) should be painted red (nail polish could be used) on admission, if this has not already been done. This provides access for cardiopulmonary resuscitation in emergencies so that the bolts and the straps of the front vest can be unfastened. A cardiac board is not necessary if the patient remains in the posterior shell of the brace. Mark the two anterior and two posterior bolts in some manner (e.g., red nail polish) for ease in removal in an emergency.

8. All patients with a halo brace should have a complete wrench set attached to their wheelchair or nearby (e.g., taped to the front vest plate) at all times. A complete wrench set should be available on the nursing floor for emergency use.

9. The halo ring should ride 1 cm above the patient's eyebrows and ears and 1.5 cm away from the head. Skull pins should be at 90° angles to the skull. All bolts should be tight. The physician may tighten the bolts on a regular basis (every week).

Steps	*Additional Information*

Bathing Patient with Halo Jacket

Steps	Additional Information
1. Position patient supine.	
2. Test anterior vest, hardware bolts, and skull pins with your fingers for tightness.	If bolts are loose, institute spinal precautions and notify physician.
3. Inspect skull pin sites for any sign of infection or adhesions.	Hair surrounding pin sites should be kept short to aid in inspection and to prevent infections.
4. Cleanse skin surrounding skull pins with Betadine solution.	If crusting is present around pin sites, use one-half saline and one-half hydrogen peroxide solution to remove crusting.
5. Open straps at bottom of vest, and inspect skin surface for pressure.	Use flashlight, and feel with your hand.
6. Cleanse skin surface without soap under vest padding.	Use a damp washcloth to clean skin surfaces under vest.
7. Dry skin surfaces thoroughly.	Wet or damp vest padding can lead to skin breakdown or infection and will need to be changed.
8. Refasten straps at bottom of vest.	
9. Position patient on each side (or prone), and repeat steps 5 through 8.	Patient should be supported in side-lying position by another staff member so that nurse is free to provide necessary care.

Steps   *Additional Information*

Showering Patient with Halo Jacket with Velcro Sheepskin Liner

1. Position patient sitting in shower chair (or side lying on cart if unable to sit for shower).

   Do not transfer patient without liner in place.

2. Detach sheepskin liner, starting at shoulders and working downward.

   Liner is usually in two pieces, an anterior and a posterior piece.

3. Remove liner pieces.
4. Shower patient.
5. Dry patient's exposed skin.
6. Use dry washcloth to dry inside of halo jacket and patient's trunk.
7. Replace sheepskin liner, starting at shoulders and working downward.

   Patient may now be transferred.

8. If replacement sheepskin liner is available, shower patient with sheepskin liner in place.

   After showering, remove wet sheepskin liner, dry patient, and replace liner with dry sheepskin liner. Wet sheepskin liner may be dried in dryer with gentle heat.

PROCEDURES, THORACOLUMBAR SACRAL ORTHOSES: JEWETT ORTHOSIS

General Considerations for Jewett Orthosis

1. The Jewett orthosis restricts anterior flexion of the thoracolumbar sacral spine. Maximum orthotic support is provided by applying and maintaining the Jewett orthosis in the following positions:
   - sternal pad is ½ inch below the suprasternal notch;
   - suprapubic pad is ½ inch above the symphysis pubis;
   - lateral bars riding above the iliac crest; and
   - back pad centered at the small of the back.
2. Routine skin checks are to be performed. Special attention should be given to the pressure points, which include the symphysis pubis, the sternum, and the iliac crests. Notify the physician of reddened areas, and plan for pressure relief.
3. No substantial padding is permitted without a physician's prescription. Tee shirts should be worn under the Jewett brace and should be one to two sizes larger than usual.

4. When the brace is removed to take off a tee shirt before hygiene procedures, a prescription must be written. While the brace is off, the patient is on spinal precautions. The brace must be reapplied before showering. After showering, position the patient supine. Remove the brace, dry it, and reapply it.
5. The Jewett orthosis provides pressure to the abdomen. When the orthosis is removed, monitor for orthostatic hypotension, trunk instability, and changes in the patient's voiding pattern.
6. The Jewett orthosis limits flexion and hyperextension of the thoracolumbar sacral spine. Therefore, the patient may not be able to sit at 90°.

Steps   *Additional Information*

To Apply Jewett Orthosis

1. Logroll patient supine.

   Patient is on spinal precautions.

2. Center sternal (thinner) pad ½ inch below suprasternal notch.
3. Center suprapubic (wider) pad ½ inch above symphysis pubis.
4. Align lateral sections.

Steps	*Additional Information*

5. Feed thoracolumbar pad underneath small of patient's back.
6. Attach thoracolumbar pad to lateral frame.

To Remove Jewett Orthosis

Steps	*Additional Information*
1. Position patient supine.	Observe spinal precautions when brace is off.
2. Detach thoracolumbar pad from lateral frame.	
3. Remove thoracolumbar pad from underneath patient.	
4. Lift off anterior portion of orthosis.	
5. Change tee shirt, dry brace, and perform skin care, as appropriate.	A prescription must be written to remove shirt for hygiene. Clean brace pieces with alcohol. Dry thoroughly before reapplying.

PROCEDURES, THORACOLUMBAR SACRAL ORTHOSES: KNIGHT-TAYLOR ORTHOSIS

General Considerations for Knight-Taylor Orthosis

1. The Knight-Taylor orthosis restricts anterior flexion, posterior extension, and lateral movements of the thoracolumbosacral spine. The addition of a chin piece can result in limitations of the cervical spine.
2. Maximum orthotic support is provided by applying and maintaining the Knight-Taylor orthosis in the following positions:

   • vertebral spinal process should lie between the paraspinal bars or along the main bar;

   • lateral lower edge of the orthosis should lie above the head of the femur and below the iliac crest;

   • shoulders should be slightly retracted; and

   • if a chin piece is used, the head should be maintained in a neutral position.
3. Minor orthotic adjustments (e.g., tightening or loosening straps and changing the level of the chin cup) are to be anticipated and performed by a nurse whenever a patient's position is changed. Shifting of body mass requires adjustment to maintain desired position and support.
4. Patient weight gain or loss must be monitored weekly because it can affect the orthotic fit.
5. The Knight-Taylor orthosis provides support to the abdomen. When the orthosis is removed, monitor for orthostatic hypotension, trunk instability, and changes in the patient's voiding pattern.

Steps	*Additional Information*

To Apply Knight-Taylor Orthosis

Steps	*Additional Information*
1. Logroll patient to side-lying position. Two people should stabilize patient.	Observe spinal precautions. When orthosis is applied, the detachable pectoral horn should be bottom-most and removed. If paraspinal bars are present, be sure that the vertebral spinal processes lie between them.
2. Center posterior of orthosis on back.	
3. Align lower edge of orthosis so that lateral sides are centered between trochanter and iliac crest.	
4. Feed lateral side of orthosis and corset under patient.	

Steps	*Additional Information*
5. Tighten and fasten straps of anterior corset from bottom up.	Make sure it is snug so as to prevent sliding up when patient sits.
6. Feed pectoral horn under patient's axilla that is against bed (feed shoulder strap over shoulders if present).	
7. Screw pectoral horns into place as noted previously.	Screw tightly. Note if thread becomes stripped and screw slips.
8. Turn patient to supine position, holding posterior orthosis firmly against patient.	No need to logroll if corset and pectoral horns are in place.
9. Fasten chin piece if present.	
10. Adjust shoulder straps if present to position shoulders in retraction and external rotation.	
11. Assess fit.	Orthosis should restrict anterior flexion, posterior extension, and lateral movements of thoracolumbosacral spine. Chin piece limits cervical spine movement.

To Remove Knight-Taylor Orthosis

1. Position patient side lying.	Detachable pectoral horn should be bottom-most.
2. Unfasten shoulder strap, or unscrew and remove pectoral horn on which patient is lying.	At this time, patient begins on spinal precautions. Two people should stabilize patient. Note and mark holes from which screws were removed when removing pectoral horn.
3. Undo all straps on corset (and chin piece if applicable).	
4. Roll corset back under patient.	So that corset will not scrape patient's skin when removed, press brace against mattress to facilitate its removal and to prevent injury to patient.
5. Standing behind patient, gently pull off brace.	
6. Carefully raise patient's uppermost arm so that other pectoral horn does not catch or scratch arm.	
7. Logroll patient to desired position in correct alignment.	Transfers are not performed without orthosis applied.

Care of Patient Using Knight-Taylor Orthosis

1. Perform routine skin checks.	Special attention should be given to chin, scapulae, vertebrae, and anterior pectorals.
2. No substantial padding of orthosis is permitted without physician's prescription.	Tee shirts should be worn under Knight-Taylor brace and should be one to two sizes larger than regularly worn so as to avoid excessive movement when dressing or undressing.
3. Remove brace to take off tee shirt before hygiene procedures.	A prescription to remove brace for hygiene must be written if patient is to be on spinal precautions when brace is off. Do not transport patient with mechanical lifter when Knight-Taylor brace is off. These devices do not provide enough support. Transfer patient to cart first, then remove brace and tee shirt, shower, reapply brace, then transfer patient back to bed.
4. Reapply brace before showering if patient has extra corset to substitute.	An extra corset will allow for increased independence because patient will be able to shower when sitting up with brace on. Remove wet corset and apply dry corset after showering with patient supine or on spinal precautions. Allow wet corset to air dry. Use of a dryer may damage metal stays in corset.

PROCEDURES, THORACOLUMBAR SACRAL ORTHOSES: BODY JACKET

General Considerations for Body Jacket

1. Body jackets restrict anterior flexion, posterior extension, and lateral and rotating movements of the thoracolumbosacral and lumbosacral spine.
2. The body jacket may or may not indicate spinal instability. It may be used as a preventive measure for spinal deformities and respiratory compromise. It is important to ascertain the purpose of the body jacket.
3. When a body jacket is used as a preventive measure, spinal precautions are not necessary when the patient is not wearing the body jacket or when applying the body jacket. The patient may apply and remove the body jacket.
4. When the body jacket is used for spinal stability, the patient should be logrolled to one side for the nurse to position the posterior shell and then logrolled supine. The anterior shell should be positioned correctly and the straps secured.
5. Body jackets are individually created for each patient to fit his or her body. Weight gain and loss should be monitored at least weekly. A child's growth also needs to be monitored to ensure proper fit.
6. Notify the physician if the patient complains of pain after body jacket application or if weight gain or loss or growth occurs rapidly.

Steps	*Additional Information*
To Apply Body Jacket	
1. Position patient side lying.	If patient is on spinal precautions, logroll patient to side.
2. Place posterior shell behind patient, feeding lateral edge underneath side on which patient is lying.	
3. Position patient supine in posterior shell.	Logroll patient supine if on spinal precautions.
4. Apply anterior shell.	Body jacket should fit properly across chest and under arms to iliac crests.
5. Secure closures.	Patient is now off spinal precautions.
To Remove Body Jacket	
1. Position patient supine.	
2. Disengage side closures.	
3. Remove anterior shell of body jacket.	
4. Position patient on side.	Logroll patient to side if body jacket is used for spinal stability.
5. Remove posterior shell from patient.	If body jacket is used for spinal stability, logroll patient into desired position.

PROCEDURES, THORACOLUMBAR SACRAL ORTHOSES: CORSET

General Considerations for Corset

1. Corsets restrict anterior flexion, posterior extension, and lateral and rotating movements of the thoracolumbosacral and lumbosacral spine.
2. A corset may or may not indicate spinal instability. It may be used as a support to relieve back pain. It is important to ascertain the purpose of the corset.
3. When a corset is used as a support, spinal precautions are not necessary when the patient is not wearing the corset or when applying the corset. The patient may apply and remove it himself or herself.
4. When the corset is used for spinal stability, the patient should be logrolled to one side for the nurse to position the posterior portion of the corset correctly and then logrolled supine.
5. Notify the physician if weight gain or loss or periods of rapid growth occur because these will alter fit.

To Apply Corset

1. Position patient side lying.

Logroll to side if corset is used for spinal instability management.

2. Roll up far side of corset to facilitate easy pull through once patient is lying on corset.

Watch that clips do not scrape patient's skin.

3. Position corset under patient.

Center posterior portion of corset so that metal stays are symmetrically placed.

4. Position patient supine.

Logroll supine if corset is for spinal instability.

5. Gently pull out far side of corset.
6. Approximate edges of corset.

Anterior portion of corset should lie above anterior iliac crest.

7. Latch both edges of corset together.

If LSO corset, top anterior edge should lie below ribs. If TLSO corset, top anterior edge should lie over ribs.

To Remove Corset

1. Position patient supine.
2. Disengage corset latches.
3. Roll sides of corset distal to patient.
4. Tuck one side of corset under patient's far posterior side.
5. Turn patient side lying.

Logroll if corset is for spinal instability. Turn patient away from you.

6. Remove corset.
7. Reposition patient.

Logroll if corset is used for spinal instability.

DOCUMENTATION

1. Document the physician's prescriptions and related measures regarding the specific spinal orthosis.
2. Note any problems in the fit of the orthosis.
3. Note any problems that the patient is experiencing during adjustment to the orthosis.
4. Note the patient's tolerance and compliance.
5. Document any actions taken to remedy any problems.
6. Note the nursing measures that are currently in effect.

Straight-Plane Range of Motion (ROM)

PURPOSE

· To achieve safely the fullest range of functional motion possible within joints that have been affected by the consequences of disease, trauma, or immobility.

STAFF RESPONSIBLE

GENERAL CONSIDERATIONS

1. Decisions regarding the frequency and type of ROM to be used on selected joints are to be made by the nurse in conjunction with the physician's prescription and physical therapy advice. The specifics are to be recorded in the patient's nursing care plan.
2. ROM may be of the active, active assistive, or passive type as indicated.
3. Each joint being ranged is to be cupped in one hand to monitor it for resistance, pain, increased tone, or crepitus. Pain is the limiting factor. Resistance and tone can be overcome by proper movements. The joint is ranged no farther than its limits. Report changes in the limits to the physician and physical therapist.
4. Each joint is to be ranged singularly, slowly, and rhythmically, with each motion being repeated only as directed, usually three to five times.
5. Combine motions at wrist and hand and at ankle and foot.

6. Encourage the patient to deep breathe and to relax during ROM.
7. ROM can and should be combined with routine care and activities of daily living.
8. Periodically document the frequency of ROM, the patient's tolerance, and the effects of ROM.
9. Definitions of terms (see also Table 2-3):
   - Range of motion or range of joint motion (ROJM): the extent of movement within a given joint
   - Median: pertaining to or toward the middle or midline
   - Flexion: the bending of a joint in which the two adjacent parts approach each other
   - Extension: the straightening of a joint in which two adjacent parts are brought into straight alignment
   - Hyperextension: moving the joint in the direction of extension beyond a straight line
   - Abduction: movement away from the midline of the body
   - Adduction: movement toward the midline of the body
   - Internal rotation: turning toward the midline
   - Rotation: turning a joint on its own axis
   - External rotation: turning away from the midline
   - Pronation: turning the forearm so that the palmar surface of the hand is facing downward
   - Supination: turning the forearm so that the palmar surface of the hand is facing upward (also referred to as radial-ulna articulation)
   - Deviation: used to describe abduction or adduction of the wrist
   - Opposition: placing the palmar surface of the thumb so that it touches the base of the fingers

Table 2-3 Movements Possible at Each Joint with Patient Supine

Neck	Shoulder	Elbow	Wrist	Fingers and Thumb	Forearm	Hip	Knee	Ankle	Toes
Forward flexion	Flexion	Flexion	Flexion	Flexion	Supination	Extension	Flexion	Dorsiflexion (heel cord stretch)	Flexion
Extension	Extension	Extension	Extension	Extension	Pronation (radial-ulna articulation)	Flexion	Extension		Extension
Lateral flexion	Abduction		Abduction (ulna deviation)	Abduction		Abduction		Plantar flexion	Abduction
Rotation	Adduction		Adduction (radial deviation)	Adduction		Adduction		Inversion (in dorsiflexion)	Adduction
Hyper-extension	External rotation			Opposition (thumb)		Internal rotation		Eversion (in plantar flexion)	
	Internal rotation					External rotation			
	Protraction								
	Retraction								

- Dorsiflexion: ankle movement in which the upper surface of the foot approaches the anterior surface of the lower leg
- Plantar flexion: the movement of the ankle in which the foot is bent down in the direction of the sole
- Inversion: the turning of the foot so that the sole tends to face inward
- Eversion: the turning of the foot so that the sole tends to face outward
- Active ROM: those exercises in which the contraction of the person's muscle accomplishes the movement within the free range, entirely or in part, without the aid or opposition of some external force
- Active assistive ROM: those exercises in which the contraction of the person's muscles accomplishes the movement within the free range with the aid of some external force

- Passive ROM: Those movements within the free range of motion that are produced entirely by an external force without active contraction of the person's muscles
- Resistive ROM: those movements possible at the joint that are produced entirely by an external force producing muscle stretching or contraction

PATIENT AND FAMILY EDUCATION

1. Teach the patient and family to perform ROM as soon as possible, with special attention to the limiting factors of pain, following their own individualized program.
2. Teach the patient and family to report any pain, changes in joints and movements, concerns, and complications to the nurse or physician immediately.

PROCEDURES

Range of motion sequence includes movements to be done and verbal cues to patient, family, or staff.

Neck: To be done only by patient, sitting or supine without pillow, with cues from staff. Movements are contraindicated in patients with cervical orthoses.

Movement	*Patient Directions*
1. Flexion (Figure 2-11A)	"Chin on chest"
2. Extension (Figure 2-11B)	"Chin up"
3. Hyperextension (Figure 2-11C)	"Look at ceiling" (may be contraindicated in elderly patients; extreme ranges should be avoided)
4. Lateral flexion (Figure 2-11D)	"Ear to shoulder" (right and left)
5. Rotation (Figure 2-11E)	"Look over shoulder" (right and left; may be contraindicated in elderly patients; extreme ranges should be avoided)

A   B   C

Figure 2-11 Neck ROM. (**A**) Flexion, (**B**) Extension, (**C**) Hyperextension, (**D**), Lateral Flexion, (**E**) Rotation.

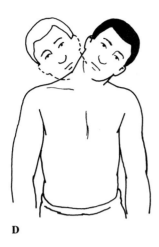

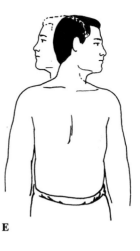

D

E

Shoulder: Start by protracting shoulder, arm pronated. Nurse places one hand over scapula to check movements as shoulder exercises are performed. Upward and outward movement of scapula accompanies shoulder movement.

Movement	*Patient Directions*
1. Flexion-extension (Figure 2-12A)	''Reach for headboard; down at side''
2. Abduction-adduction (Figure 2-12B)	''Move arm out and in''
3. External and internal rotation (Figure 2-12C)	First position arm out to side at shoulder level with elbow bent at right angle, ''Thumb a ride over same shoulder, move arm forward while turning thumb in at side ''

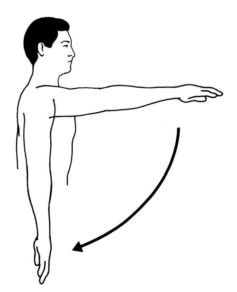

A

Figure 2-12 Shoulder ROM. (**A**) Flexion-Extension.

continues

Figure 2-12 continued

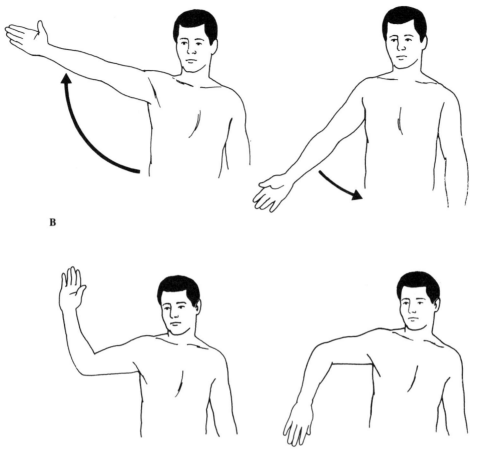

B

C

Figure 2-12 Shoulder ROM. (**B**) Abduction-Adduction, (**C**) External and Internal Rotation.

Elbow and forearm: Start with arm in supination.

Movement	Patient Directions
1. Flexion-extension (Figure 2-13A)	"Bend and straighten"
2. Supination-pronation (Figure 2-13B)	With elbow fixed, "Turn palm up, palm down"

Wrist and hand: Start by propping arm up on elbow, forearm pronated; one hand on wrist and thumb, other hand around fingers to facilitate natural tenodesis in hands.

Movement	Patient Directions
1. Wrist flexion and finger extension, abduction (Figure 2-14A)	"Down and out"
2. Wrist extension and finger flexion, thumb opposed (Figure 2-14B)	"Up and in"

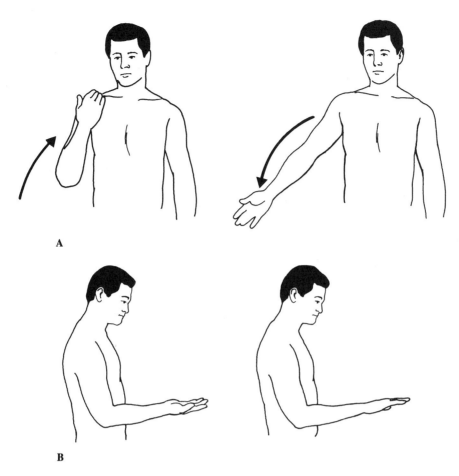

Figure 2-13 Elbow and Forearm ROM. (**A**) Flexion-Extension, (**B**) Supination-Pronation.

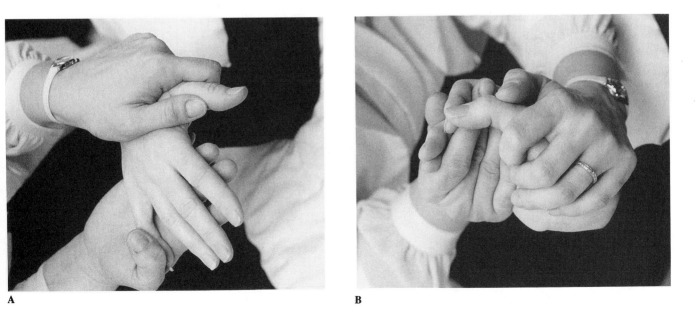

Figure 2-14 Wrist and Hand ROM. (**A**) Wrist Flexion and Finger Extension, Abduction; (**B**) Wrist Extension and Finger Flexion, Thumb Opposed.

Wrist: Start with arm straight and pronated.

Movement	Patient Directions
1. Ulnar and radial deviation (Figure 2-15)	"Turn wrist in and out in flat plane"

Hip: Start by protracting hip. Find trochanter with cupped hand, place other hand on back of calf.

Movement	Patient Directions
1. Flexion-extension (Figure 2-16A)	"Sole of foot to ceiling and down"
2. Abduction-adduction (Figure 2-16B)	"Move leg out and in"
3. External and internal rotation (Figure 2-16C)	"Use palms of hands only on thighs and shins, roll back and forth like a rolling pin"
4. Hyperextension (position patient prone or side lying) (Figure 2-16D)	Prone: "Lift straight leg toward ceiling (30° to 45° hyperextension)"
	Side lying: "Move top straight leg back toward side of bed"

Knee

Movement	Patient Directions
1. Flexion (Figure 2-17A)	"Bend your knee and raise toward your head"
2. Extension (Figure 2-17B)	"With leg in bent position, straighten your leg"

Ankle and foot: Start with one hand cupping heel, other around mid-section of foot. Besides dorsiflexion and inversion, a good stretch of the heel cords must be done by helper to decrease risk of tightening or fixation.

Movement	Patient Directions
1. Dorsiflexion and inversion (Figure 2-18)	Toes up, sole in: "Up and in"
2. Plantar flexion and eversion (Figure 2-19)	Toes down, sole out: "Down and out"

DOCUMENTATION

1. Specify frequency, type, position, and times of ROM.
2. Document any complications, patient complaints, and therapeutic effects noted.

3. Note effectiveness of patient and family teaching.

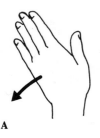

A

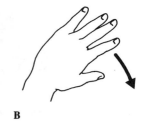

B

Figure 2-15 Wrist ROM. **(A)** Ulnar Deviation, **(B)** Radial Deviation.

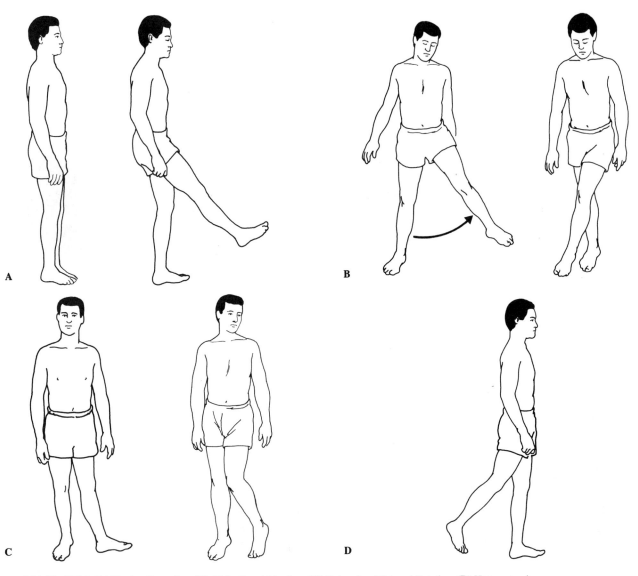

Figure 2-16 Hip ROM. (**A**) Flexion-Extension, (**B**) Abduction-Adduction, (**C**) External and Internal Rotation, (**D**) Hyperextension.

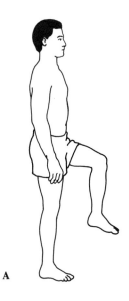 

Figure 2-17 Knee ROM. (**A**) Flexion, (**B**) Extension.

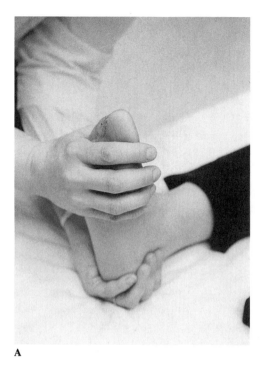

A

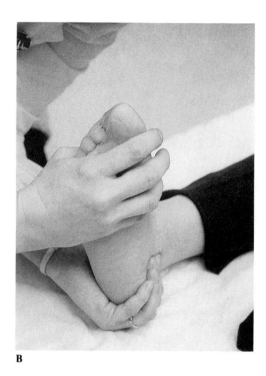

B

Figure 2-18 Dorsiflexion and Inversion. (**A**) View 1, (**B**) View 2.

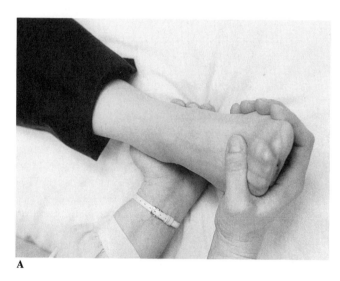

A

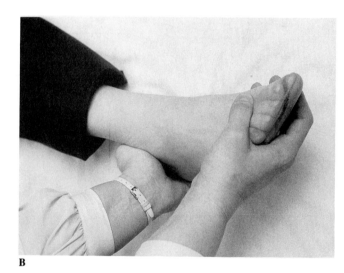

B

Figure 2-19 Plantar Flexion and Eversion. (**A**) View 1, (**B**) View 2.

Upper Extremity Self-Range of Motion for the Patient with Hemiplegia

PURPOSES

To maintain and/or increase the functional ROM of the affected extremity; to prevent deformities or contractures in the affected extremity; to promote awareness of the affected side of the body; to aid in decreasing edema in an affected hand; to provide some sensation to an affected extremity; to enhance strength and quality of movement when there is a return of voluntary motion.

STAFF RESPONSIBLE

GENERAL CONSIDERATIONS

1. ROM exercises are contraindicated in a "hot" joint, that is, a joint that is inflamed, red, warm, or swollen.
2. The following exercises should be carried out daily; each exercise is to be performed five to ten times.
3. Because the exercises may cause pain to the patient, movements should be carried out only to the point of pain.
4. Some patients may tend to over-range or inaccurately range themselves, thus producing pain or joint deformity (subluxation). Such patients should be guided to remain within the specific range and number of repetitions.
5. The patient should perform exercises while sitting down unless otherwise instructed.

PATIENT AND FAMILY EDUCATION

1. Teach the patient to self-range as soon as possible, to follow his or her own individualized ROM program, and to report pain or other complications to the nurse.
2. Patient should maintain good posture while performing exercises, breathe normally, move slowly, and allow joints to be stretched gradually.
3. Patient should hold the movements for several counts, moving only to the joint's limits and not pushing too hard to increase ROM.
4. Patient may enjoy listening to music while performing exercises.
5. Patient may substitute or change exercises from day to day. The first 11 exercises should consistently make up the core of daily exercises, or they can be used as a shortened exercise program.
6. Teach the patient to avoid pain by beginning with midrange movements and gradually increasing the range over time. The extremes of the range should be avoided.
7. Teach the patient to avoid shoulder pain by doing shoulder exercises while lying supine, which will support the shoulder blade.
8. Patient should avoid excessive overhead stretches.
9. Hand or finger edema can make movement of joints difficult. Teach the patient to minimize edema during rest periods by keeping the affected arm elevated when possible and massaging the affected arm in long, one-way strokes from finger tips to elbow.

PROCEDURES

1. *Side stretch* (Figure 2-20): "Shift weight over to right side as you look to ceiling on right side. Then reverse, shift weight over to left side looking to ceiling on left side. As you do this you should feel your trunk stretching out."
2. *Drop it* (Figure 2-21): Clasp hands together, hunch shoulders forward, and hang arms down between legs as close to ankles as possible. Then bring arms up into lap and sit up as straight as possible.
3. *Head diagonals* (Figure 2-22): Look up and over right shoulder, then down to left hip. Then reverse. Look up over left shoulder, then down to right hip. Remember to twist waist as you move.
4. *Shoulder shrugs* (Figure 2-23): Rest affected arm on top of strong arm. Push up to shrug right shoulder, then left. Now try to shrug both shoulders at the same time.
5. *Open the door* (Figure 2-24): Keeping weaker elbow in at side (inside of armrest of wheelchair), hold weaker forearm at wrist. Push forearm away from body, then back in.
6. *Reach for the sky* (Figure 2-25): Clasp hands together and raise arms up, then down to lap. Keep arms even. Avoid raising arms over head if painful or difficult to do.
7. *Stir the pudding* (Figure 2-26): Clasp hands together, reach arms out to right, in front, then out to left. Repeat in opposite direction.
8. *Chopping wood* (Figure 2-27): Clasp hands together and bend and straighten elbows by touching right shoulder and left knee. Repeat in opposite direction, bend and straighten elbows touching left shoulder and right knee.
9. *Push-pull* (Figure 2-28): Clasp hands together with thumbs facing up. Push affected wrist away (bend it out), then pull it back (bend it in). Thumbs should remain facing up.
10. *Finger bends* (Figure 2-29): Rest affected hand in other hand. Bend all three joints of all affected fingers into a fist. Straighten fingers out.
11. *Arm flip* (Figure 2-30): Clasp hands together, then touch back of right hand to right knee. Then reverse by touching back of left hand to left knee.

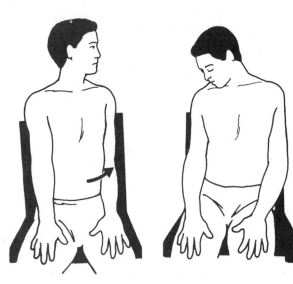

Figure 2-20 Side Stretch.

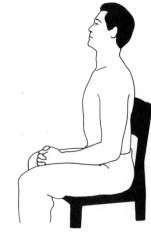

Figure 2-21 Drop It.

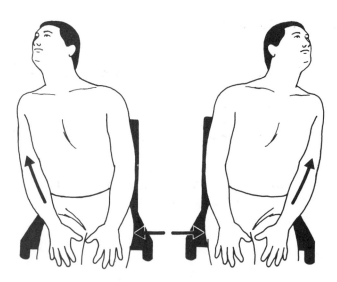

Figure 2-22 Head Diagonals.

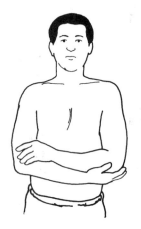

Figure 2-23 Shoulder Shrugs.

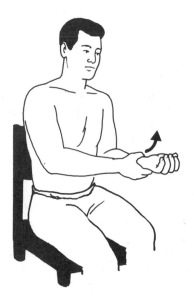

Figure 2-24 Open the Door.

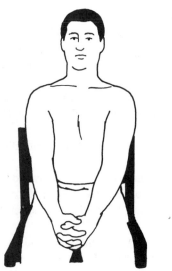

Figure 2-25 Reach for the Sky.

Figure 2-26 Stir the Pudding.

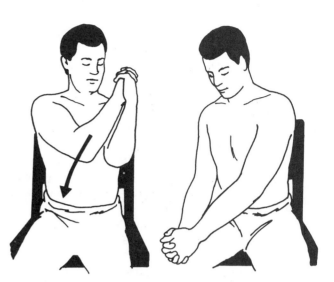

Figure 2-27 Chopping Wood.

Figure 2-28 Push-Pull.

Figure 2-29 Finger Bends.

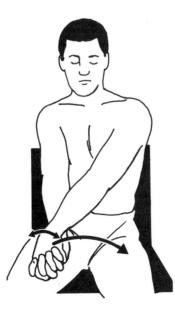

Figure 2-30 Arm Flip.

OPTIONAL OR ADDITIONAL EXERCISES

1. *Body slump* (Figure 2-31): Slump back in chair, then sit forward with back straight and head up.
2. *Side-to-side* (Figure 2-32): Look down toward floor on right side as you shift weight onto right side (buttock). Then reverse. Look down to floor on left side as you shift weight to left side.
3. *Head up* (Figure 2-33): Look up toward ceiling, then down to floor. Attempt to arch your back as you look up.
4. *Head turn* (Figure 2-34): Turn head to right, twisting waist as you look behind right shoulder. Then reverse, turn head to left, twisting waist as you look behind your left shoulder.
5. *Ear touch* (Figure 2-35): Looking straight ahead, touch right ear to right shoulder and attempt to shrug shoulder to meet ear. Reverse.
6. *Chin tuck* (Figure 2-36): Rest affected arm on top of other arm. Raise arms up to chin level. Then lower them. Keep elbows and arms even.
7. *Rock the baby* (Figure 2-37): Rest affected arm on top of strong arm. Rock arms to right and left. Attempt to lift right buttock off chair while shifting weight from side to side.

8. *Thumb circles and hitch a ride* (Figures 2-38 and 2-39): Hold tip of affected thumb with fingers of other hand. Turn in slow, large circles. Bend affected thumb across palm to touch little finger, then straighten thumb out.
9. *Weight-bearing* (Figure 2-40): Position affected arm on table straight in front with palm down. Do a reaching task over affected arm, moving items from side to side with other arm so that affected arm accepts light weight shifts.
10. *Two-arm grasp* (Figure 2-41): Clasp hands together. Reach for an object on one side, and move it over to other side. May also work high to low: reach for high object placed on unaffected side, and place it across and low on affected side.
11. *Two-arm towel stretch* (Figure 2-42): Clasp hands together and place arms on a towel, which is laid out on table. Move arms in figure-of-eight pattern and diagonals, and circle right and left.

DOCUMENTATION

1. Specify frequency, type, position, and times of ROM.
2. Note any complications, patient complaints, and therapeutic effects noted.
3. Note effectiveness of patient and family teaching.

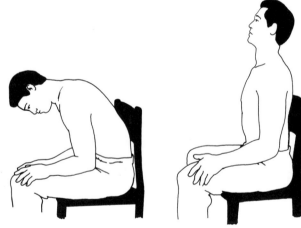

Figure 2-31 Body Slump.

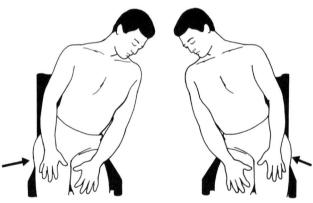

Figure 2-32 Side-to-Side.

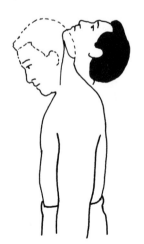

Figure 2-33 Head Up.

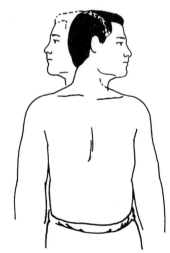

Figure 2-34 Head Turn.

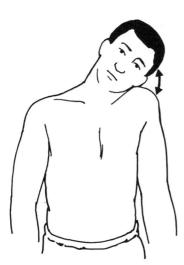

Figure 2-35 Ear Touch.

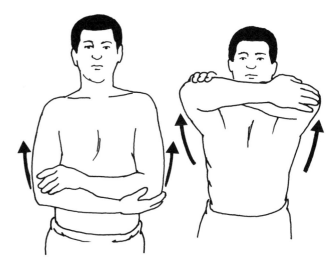

Figure 2-36 Chin Tuck.

Figure 2-37 Rock the Baby.

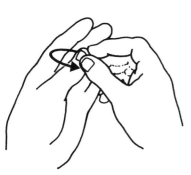

Figure 2-38 Thumb Circles.

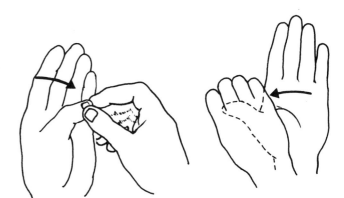

Figure 2-39 Hitch a Ride.

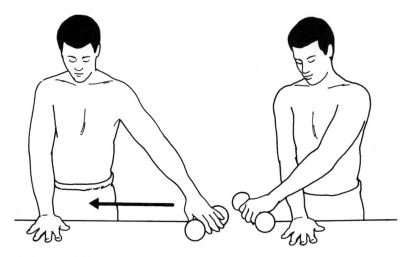

Figure 2-40 Weight-Bearing.

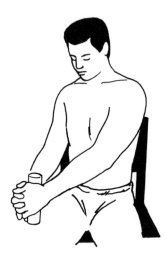

Figure 2-41 Two-Arm Grasp.

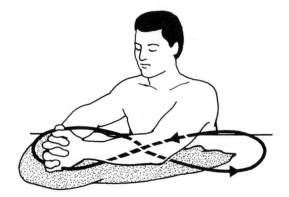

Figure 2-42 Two-Arm Towel Stretch.

Continuous Passive Range of Motion

PURPOSE

To promote maximal ROM of the knee through slow, progressive motion using a mechanical device.

STAFF RESPONSIBLE

EQUIPMENT

1. Continuous passive range of motion (CPM) machine (Figure 2-43). (See local/national manufacturer product information.)

2. Padding for femur and lower leg and foot supports (dispose after each patient's use).

GENERAL CONSIDERATIONS

1. A physician's prescription is required for the use of the CPM machine. The prescription should include the flexion-extension setting, frequency, and speed. The machine may be set to run on automatic or manual mode (depending on the unit).
2. CPM is indicated to increase and maintain knee ROM to prevent joint stiffness, especially during the postoperative period, and to reduce pain, throbbing sensation, and edema.
3. The hip and knee should be in the extended position when the device is turned on and off.
4. The flexion-extension setting should be checked before starting the device.

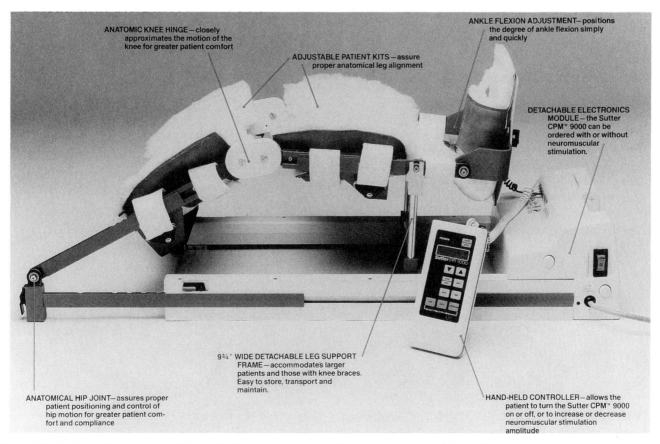

Figure 2-43 Continuous Passive Range of Motion Machine. *Source:* Courtesy of Sutter Corporation, San Diego, CA.

5. Discontinue use of the machine if the patient complains of increased pain or impaired skin integrity that prevents back lying.
6. Do not raise the head of the bed above 30° from the horizontal.
7. When installing or removing the device, always set the device on its lowest setting.

PATIENT AND FAMILY EDUCATION

1. Teach the patient and family the purpose of the machine, its benefits, and how to use it.
2. Assess issues of noncompliance in using the device and notify physician if appropriate.

PROCEDURES

Steps	Additional Information

Measurements

1. Measure patient's leg (in inches) from greater trochanter to knee axis.	
2. Adjust thigh bar (if present) to equal this measurement.	Number on thigh bar should line up with proximal end of latch.
3. Measure patient's leg (in inches) from knee axis to lateral malleolus.	
4. Adjust calf bar (if present) to equal this measurement.	Number on calf bar should line up with distal end of each latch.
5. Add thigh and calf measurements together.	
6. Set hip extension bar to this number, to nearest whole inch.	Measurements of total leg length should line up with end of device.
7. Use up and down arrows to increase or decrease parameters.	Whatever is flashing on screen can be changed with arrows.

Programming the Device

1. *Limit button:* Press the limit button. Use up and down arrows to adjust desired degree of extension.	"Extension" will flash on screen.
Press limit button again. Use up and down arrows to adjust desired degree of flexion.	"Flexion" will flash on screen.
2. *Rate button:* Press rate button. Use up and down arrows to adjust desired rate.	"Rate" will flash on screen.
3. *Time button:* Press time button.	Panel should read "Continuous Time." If it does not, press up arrow until it does.

Starting CPM

1. Place padding on calf and foot.	New padding is used for each patient.
2. Place machine on bed.	Attach to footboard.
3. Angle machine slightly toward outside corner of bed.	This slight abduction will maintain proper anatomical alignment.
4. Place leg in device so that knee is centered with white knee hinge.	Leg should be extended.
5. Press start-stop button.	Make sure device is plugged in and that green power switch is turned on.

Discontinuing CPM

1. Press start-stop button.
2. Remove leg from device.
3. Turn off green power switch.
4. Unplug machine.

Stop device when leg is extended straight.

DOCUMENTATION

1. Record flexion-extension settings.
2. Note patient compliance, tolerance, and effects of treatment.
3. Note effectiveness of patient and family teaching.
4. Note length of time of the treatment.

Positioning the Patient Three-Quarters Prone

PURPOSE

. To relieve pressure on bony prominences in patients with normal or decreased tone.

STAFF RESPONSIBLE

EQUIPMENT

1. Four to five pillows.
2. Eggcrate mattress.
3. Two to four foam blocks (3 × 6 × 18 inches).
4. Full-length sheepskin.

GENERAL CONSIDERATIONS

1. Advantages of the three-quarters prone position are:
   - it relieves most pressure on bony prominences because the iliac crest and trochanter are bridged (Figure 2-44);
   - it is easier to do than full prone (requires one staff member);
   - it is easier for the patient to breathe, and it provides more comfort than the full prone position; and
   - it can reduce the number of turns at night.
2. Position the eggcrate mattress with the eggcrate surface away from the patient (smooth surface toward the patient's skin). This will offer less resistance when bridging with foam blocks.
3. The full-length sheepskin is used for comfort and for ease in bridging the trochanter.

4. In the three-quarters prone position, the patient should be able to change to side lying by pushing up and over with the side rail. Then, when side lying, the patient can roll himself or herself three-quarters prone by rolling forward.

PATIENT AND FAMILY EDUCATION

Teach the patient and family this procedure to maximize turning tolerance time during the night.

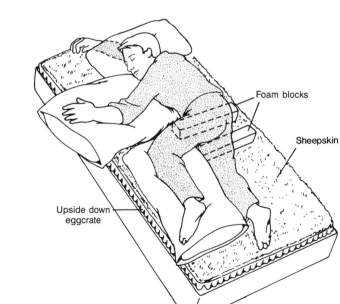

Figure 2-44 Three-Quarters Prone Position.

PROCEDURE

Steps	Additional Information
1. Place full-length sheepskin lengthwise under patient.	
2. Position patient on his or her side on top of sheepskin, close to edge of bed. Extend patient's down-side arm, and tuck it slightly under body.	Head may rest on pillow, depending on patient's comfort.
3. Place pillows to bridge chest, and position top leg in front of bottom leg on top of two to four pillows positioned horizontally.	More than two pillows under legs may be needed to keep ankle, knee, and hip in same horizontal plane.
4. Place your arm closest to patient's head under small of patient's back, and hold his or her down-side forearm with your arm palm down.	
5. Turn patient over onto chest, facing away from you, by pushing at hip and pulling bottom-most arm toward you.	Placing top arm temporarily over side rail will assist in keeping patient positioned while adjusting pillow under chest.
6. Lift up on sheepskin, and slide foam blocks lengthwise underneath sheepskin, above and below iliac crest (Figure 2-44).	
7. Assess for adequate bridging by sliding your hand under trochanter between foam blocks.	Additional foam blocks may be used to provide adequate bridging.
8. Ensure that patient is comfortable.	

DOCUMENTATION

1. Note turning tolerance.

2. Note any untoward reactions during the procedure.

Care of the Patient in a Solid or Bivalve Cast

PURPOSES

To immobilize a bony structure to promote healing of a fracture, dislocation, or surgical site; to maintain or increase ROM through serial application or use of dropout casting; to facilitate positioning through use of bivalve casts; to preserve circulation and skin integrity under the casted area.

STAFF RESPONSIBLE

EQUIPMENT

1. Flashlight.
2. Waterproof cast tape.

GENERAL CONSIDERATIONS

1. Keep the cast clean and dry at all times. When a cast gets wet, it may soften and crack.
2. Nursing assessments of a casted extremity include:
   - neurological and vascular status;
   - presence, amount, color, and change in drainage; and
   - skin characteristics.
   Any impairment should be reported to the physician immediately.
3. Impaired circulation can be identified by:
   - patient complaints of localized pain;
   - absence of pulse under the cast;
   - symptoms of coldness, pallor, duskiness, or cyanosis;
   - edema;
   - loss of movement;
   - numbness; and
   - slow capillary refill with blanching.

In unresponsive or cognitively impaired patients, increased agitation or restlessness after cast application should be investigated.

4. Any drainage noted should be circled with a ball-point pen and labeled with the date and time.
5. Any unexplained, offensive odors from beneath the cast should be reported immediately because these may be evidence of skin breakdown.
6. A window may be cut in the cast by the physician to allow for:
   - removal of pressure from a bony prominence,
   - checking of circulation and pulse,
   - changing of dressing, or
   - checking of surgical site.
7. The cast may be bivalved in such a manner as to make it removable when it is no longer necessary for constant wear. The bivalved cast is held together by Velcro straps or Ace bandages and is used for positioning as prescribed. Increased circulation and decreased tone can result from the use of a bivalved cast.
8. No showers or tub baths are given unless you have a cast guard or are able to cover the cast tightly with plastic bags and tape. Give sponge baths. Bivalved casts can be removed for hygiene purposes if specifically prescribed by a physician.
9. Do not allow weight-bearing on a casted extremity unless prescribed by the physician.
10. Any writing on the cast must be done with materials that will not seal the cast and prevent it from "breathing." Color crayons, Magic Markers, and pens are acceptable; paint and other oil-based materials are not to be used.
11. A cast cutter for emergency removal of a cast should be available at all times.
12. Stains (food, dirt, grime, or excrement) can be removed with the use of a damp (not wet) cloth, kitchen cleanser, and gentle rubbing.
13. To protect the cast from incontinence:
    - cover perineal area of cast with plastic sterile drape or plastic wrap, and check skin frequently for moisture build up or irritation;
    - use Pampers or small diapers tucked into the groin area, and change them frequently; or
    - place the patient in a prone position with the head higher than the feet to facilitate drainage when in a hip spica cast.

PATIENT AND FAMILY EDUCATION

Teach the patient and family the purpose and benefits of the cast, how to care for the cast (if it will be used at home), and how to assess circulation and signs and symptoms of cast problems or emergency situations.

PROCEDURES

Steps	*Additional Information*
Care of Wet or Damp Cast	
1. Leave cast exposed to air until dry.	Fiberglass cast dries immediately. Plaster cast dries in 24 to 48 hours, depending on size. Plaster hip spica or body cast dries in 48 to 72 hours.
2. Place pillows to support cast (lengthwise), especially under hips and knees.	Cast will flatten over bony prominence, causing tissue damage if wet or damp and unsupported on hard surfaces. Use foam pillows, not feather pillows.
3. Position properly to prevent depression in cast.	Depressed areas can cause tissue breakdown, dependent edema, and impaired circulation.
4. Lift cast with palms of hands, not fingers.	Do not use abduction bar as a handle when lifting or turning patients.
5. If necessary, turn patient with two staff members.	This ensures patient comfort and prevents cast destruction. Turn to uncasted side as much as possible.
6. Elevate casted extremity.	This decreases or prevents edema in extremity.
7. Assess neurological and vascular status, drainage patterns, skin, and odor every 4 hours and as needed.	

Skin Care of Casted Extremity

1. Check skin around all edges of cast with flashlight.

2. Wash exposed part of extremity with soap and water, rinse well, and dry.

3. Apply lotion sparingly around cast edges if skin is dry and cracking. Do not put inside cast.

4. Check for any signs of complications.

Observe for redness, any change in color, broken skin areas, or offensive odor.
Do not get cast wet.

Lotions and moisture may cause skin breakdown in an enclosed area.
Check for discomfort, pulses, edema, skin temperatures, and color below casted area.

DOCUMENTATION

1. Note any changes in neurovascular status, presence and amount of drainage, presence of odor, and any complications of immobility.

2. Note the use of bivalve casts, wearing times, positioning recommendations, and routine cast care.

Kinetic Therapy Bed

PURPOSES

To facilitate the selection of patients whose care would be enhanced by kinetic therapy; to use properly a kinetic therapy bed.

STAFF RESPONSIBLE

EQUIPMENT

1. Kinetic therapy bed (see local/national manufacturer product information).

GENERAL CONSIDERATIONS

1. The bed is used to prevent the effects of immobility.

2. Severe, uncontrollable claustrophobia is the only contraindication.

3. Precautions need to be taken with:
   - pathologic or traumatic rib fractures—adjust rotation to avoid weight-bearing on affected side;
   - large cranial defect—adjust head pack accordingly;
   - comatose patients in an extremely agitated state, who may become more agitated; and
   - severe uncontrollable diarrhea because the bed stimulates peristalsis.

4. The bed is adjusted to fit each individual patient's need and size. See the instruction manual or kinetic therapist.

5. The kinetic therapy bed should be kept in rotation at all times except for specific treatment.

6. In case of a power failure or motor malfunction, the bed can be turned manually or locked in a central position. Turning and pressure relief should be provided according to the patient's tolerance. If an empty bed is available, move the patient to a regular hospital bed.

7. Safety straps must always be used.

8. Never attempt to rotate a patient in a sitting position.

9. Generally the company will provide demonstrations before implementation.

10. A booklet outlining all the procedures discussed is kept with the bed at all times.

PROCEDURES

Procedure is written for the RotoRest® bed.

Steps	Additional Information

To Transfer Patient from Kinetic Therapy Bed*

1. Have wheelchair nearby.
2. Disengage bed rotation:
   - hold lowest end of footboard;
   - put green handle down;
   - turn patient slowly to back-lying position; and
   - push black knob into stop position.
3. Gather patient's clothes if necessary.
4. Remove straps.
5. Remove both knee pieces.
6. Remove both interior leg pieces.
7. Dress lower extremities as appropriate.
8. Lift shoulder pieces away.
9. Remove arm piece, exterior long leg piece, arm cradle, pillow, and pad from same side.
10. Position wheelchair next to bed.
11. Put bed in low position by pressing "raise bed" switch.
12. Sit patient up in bed by pressing "sit up" switch.
13. Transfer patient to wheelchair, lifting arm from remaining arm piece to facilitate transfer.
14. Turn fan off at end of bed.
15. Turn vibrator off.
16. Place all bed parts in box appropriately marked.
17. Dispose of soiled linens.
18. Check all foam pieces for wetness or soiling.

Additional Information (aligned to steps above):

Safety feature: Connecting arm (green handle) is designed to release only if weight is relieved from mechanism by grasping footboard and pushing down on its lower side. *(step 2)*

This switch is found at foot of table on control panel. *(step 11)*
This switch is located on center post at foot end of table. *(step 12)*

See switch on cord. *(step 15)*

All pieces are covered with Gore-Tex, which provides low-shear and low-friction breathable surfaces that are easy to clean. *(step 18)*

To Position Patient in Kinetic Therapy Bed

1. Check to see if bed is ready for patient:
   - ensure that all pieces and linen are dry and clean;
   - place long leg side piece, short arm piece, arm cradle, and pillow on same side of bed; and
   - ensure that all necessary wedges and foam pieces for bridging are in place.

     A wedge is available to increase angle of head of bed. Coccyx bridging may be necessary in agitated patients who move their trunk and buttocks. A bridge is needed at space between back and buttock dropout pieces.

2. Position wheelchair next to bed.
3. Remove patient's shirt.
4. Transfer patient to bed.

*Note: Refer to booklet for additional information.

Steps	*Additional Information*

5. Put silver post in place between knees.
6. Put interior left leg piece in place (distal portion of this piece goes on outside of post at foot of bed).
7. Put interior right leg piece in place.

Distal portion is placed on outside of post at foot of bed.

8. Take patient's pants off if appropriate.
9. Attach knee pieces.

Move each piece down as many notches as possible to promote extension. If patient moves leg, pad knee pieces with thin blue pad in pillow case.

10. Make sure leg pads (blue foam wedges) are under legs with thin section of pad at top of thighs, and tuck part of wedge under heel.

It may be necessary to put additional pad under each ankle to prevent heel pressure.

11. Place right side long leg piece and short arm piece in appropriate holes.

Padding goes next to patient. Point of arm piece points toward axilla. Patient's arm must be at 90° for proper measurement of arm piece.

12. Place foot support in foot assembly.

In no instance should feet be prevented from moving freely. Foot support should be left in place no longer than 2 hours each shift.

13. Put straps across patient from left to right.

Criss-cross top two straps. There are three straps. They do not have to be pulled tight.

14. Put right arm cradle in place.
15. Place pillow in cradle, and put foam pad next to arm piece.
16. Position right arm between foam pad and pillow.
17. Repeat steps 14 through 16 for left arm.
18. Move shoulder pieces down.

There should be 1 inch between shoulder and shoulder piece to prevent pressure areas on shoulder.

19. Place flat pillow or blanket under patient's head. Pull blanket up at each end.

This protects patient's head from blue padded head pieces.

20. Plug in vibrator, and turn it on.
21. Check to see that accessory switch is on.
22. Check to see that fan switch is on.

Vibrator is found under bed on back dropout piece if used.
The ''set up'' button must be completely down.
Never run fan with air intake completely closed because this will cause serious overheating.

23. Place sheet over patient in tentlike fashion over lower extremities and stomach.
24. Check patient's bed placement:
   - there should be space for two or three fingers between axilla and arm piece;
   - no pressure should be on patient's upper arms;
   - bridging should be checked;
   - all pieces should be checked for proper fit;
   - all padding on pieces should face downward; and
   - safety straps should be checked.
25. Press ''raise bed'' button to raise bed to highest position.
26. Lift green handle at foot of bed.

Never unlock bed without holding onto footboard handle to prevent rapid table turning.

27. Pull black knob to engage bed, and turn slowly until bed is engaged.

To Use Rectal Hatch Door for Elimination

1. Turn bed to extreme lateral position.
2. Open rectal hatch door, and remove cushion.

Steps	*Additional Information*
3. Put bedpan in place; give bowel program if appropriate.	A full-size bedpan should be used because fracture pan could spill when removed.
4. Close hatch door to hold bedpan in place.	
5. Place table in horizontal position during evacuation.	To take rectal temperature or place suppository, remove knee pack, lift patient's leg, and insert thermometer or suppository. This may also be done through rectal hatch, but this is generally more difficult.
6. To remove, place bed in 40° position. Remove bedpan carefully. Replace pack, and close hatch. Engage rotation.	

To Use Back Hatch Door

1. Turn bed to extreme lateral position.
2. Open back hatch door, and remove cushion.
3. Perform back care.
4. Replace pack, and close hatch.
5. Engage rotation.

DOCUMENTATION

1. Document the type of bed used and any special instructions.

2. Note the patient's response to the bed and any untoward effects.

Bed Positioning in the Presence of Increased Tone (Spasticity)

PURPOSES

To normalize muscle tone, while in bed, for patients with increased tone or spasticity; to prevent contractures or deformities in patients prone to increased tone or spasticity; to maintain functional ROM with bed positioning; to improve gastrointestinal and respiratory function (secondary effect of trunk extension).

STAFF RESPONSIBLE

EQUIPMENT

1. Foam blocks.
2. Pillows.
3. Pillow cases.

GENERAL CONSIDERATIONS

1. Normal muscle tone is defined as enough muscle contraction to allow for movement against gravity and full ROM of the joints. Increased tone results in positions against gravity, which occur in patterns (synergies), leading to nonfunctional and fixed postures in the trunk and extremities and possibly decreased ROM.
2. Patients exhibiting mild to severe increases in tone with synergy should have their trunk, head, and affected limbs positioned in opposite patterns to normalize tone. Always begin by assessing and positioning the trunk, then the head, and then the extremities (proximal to distal). Consult the physical therapist and occupational therapist for assistance.
3. Increased tone patterns may be unilateral (as in the hemiplegic patient) or bilateral (as in the head trauma patient). With unilateral tone patterns, the affected side is to be considered the weaker or shortened side in the rest of these procedures. These procedures are to be used with patients whose increased tone patterns are primarily flexion, extension, or mixed.
4. Identify shortening of the trunk with the patient supine or sitting. Consider the shortened side the weaker or affected side. Instead of positioning the patient side lying, position him or her three-quarters prone with the affected side up and three-quarters supine with the affected side up or down. Position the patient supine and prone. Difficulties in the prone position (discomfort, increased tone, or res-

piratory distress) need to be closely monitored and the position discontinued if necessary. The most common contraindication to prone positioning is obstruction of the airway (i.e., if the patient has a tracheostomy or buries his or her face in the pillow).

5. Some patients with abnormal tone may exhibit the asymmetric tonic neck reflex (fencing reflex), in which the head turns away from the flexed side of the body. Carefully position such a patient's head in neutral and midline with foam blocks or a pillow to prevent activation of this reflex. Some patients have increased flexion of the neck. These patients respond well to a flat pillow or no pillow under their head, which actually encourages hyperextension but results in neutral and midline positioning.

6. Patients with increased tone tend to adduct their shoulders and hips, resulting in contractures. Position their extremities with the shoulder and hip abducted. Protract and flatten the scapula before abducting and externally rotating the shoulder. Externally rotate and abduct the hip in slight flexion.

7. Weight-bearing or placement in a weight-bearing position decreases spasticity.

8. When handling patients, use firm, palmar pressure. Avoid finger-tip and light touch. Use two hands. Movements are to be slow and smooth. Use your whole body (i.e., your voice, body, and movement).

9. Try to combine or maximize relaxation techniques: showering, warm towels, partial bathing, room temperature, fluids, soothing music, fan for cooling, and removal or reduction of noxious stimuli (full bladder, infection, fever, skin problems, bowel problems, orthopedic problems, or deep vein thrombus).

10. Position the patient on a firm surface (exception: patients with predominant extensor tone need to sag), and select an appropriate mattress topper. Use small, firm positioning aids such as foam blocks, pillows, rolls, bolsters, and wedges. Blankets and towels have smooth, soft surfaces and thus will decrease tone. Many patients have an increase in autonomic response with resulting diaphoresis, so that absorbent material will aid in patient comfort. If the patient has low tone (flaccid), use rough surfaces to increase tone. Close monitoring is necessary to validate the response and objective of increasing or decreasing tone. Coordinate use of splints, bivalved casts, and the like with the therapists, and devise a positioning schedule.

11. Facilitate follow-through with optimal positioning by drawing or taking pictures of the patient in these positions. Post the picture or drawing over the patient's bed or in the room. Practice placing the patient in these positions with staff members.

12. Monitor the patient after positioning for discomfort, restlessness, and increased diaphoresis which would indicate the patient's tolerance or response.

13. If you have a patient with a combination of flexion and extension patterns (which is often the case), remember to position the patient out of those patterns to increase normal tone and movement.

PROCEDURES

Steps	*Additional Information*

Supine Position To Minimize Flexion Spasticity on Affected Side

1. Position patient supine in middle of bed.	Start with bed flat and no pillows or blocks under patient.
2. Turn patient on unaffected side to place positioning props.	Make sure that side rail is up. Some patients may not have to be turned to place towels.
3. Place folded towel under affected scapula and hip.	This will facilitate shoulder and hip protraction. For severe spasticity, a foam block placed lengthwise under affected scapula down to hip may be necessary.
4. Roll patient back to supine position.	
5. Place small, firm pillow under or next to patient's head to keep it in midline.	This is to facilitate positioning of head in neutral and midline; no pillow may be needed.
6. Position upper and lower extremities in abduction and extension as much as possible with towels, small pillows, or foam blocks.	Start with shoulder, and work down arm to hand. Then start at hip and work down to foot.

Supine Position To Minimize Extension Spasticity on Affected Side

1. Position patient supine in middle of bed.	Start with bed flat and no pillows or blocks under patient. Patients who have severe rigidity may require elevation of head of bed to 30°. This facilitates trunk flexion.

Steps	*Additional Information*
2. Place small pillow under occiput.	To flex head forward to neutral, midline.
3. Place small, folded towel under scapula, and put upper extremity in slight flexion.	This protracts shoulder, producing relaxation of arm. Slight flexion of elbow will break up extension synergy. Pillow under affected arm may be used to prevent edema.
4. Place small, folded towel or foam block under hip.	This protracts hip, which relaxes extremity. Patients with severe rigidity may require elevation of knee gatch to 15° to 20°. This is to facilitate slight flexion of hips and knees.
5. Place small roll under leg slightly above knee.	This facilitates flexion of knee and at same time prevents occlusion of popliteal artery.
6. Place pillow between feet and foot of bed.	Firm-surfaced footboard should be avoided because it may increase extension. Do not place anything under ball of foot because this will increase tone.

Three-Quarters Supine Position To Minimize Flexion Spasticity on Affected Side

1. Position patient supine in center of bed.	Start with bed flat and no pillows or blocks under patient.
2. Roll patient onto either side.	
3. Place pillows or foam blocks across back at subscapular level, or at small of back (or both) or one foam block above small of back.	Number and position of pillows or foam blocks is dependent on amount of tone and size of patient.
4. Roll patient back over these blocks to three-quarters supine position, and pull blocks through.	This will encourage extension of head, shoulder protraction, and scapular flattening on affected side.
5. Position head in neutral, midline position.	Place small, rolled towel or pillow under head to block rotation in patients with severely increased tone.
6. Gently abduct both arms:	Use pillows or foam blocks to facilitate abduction and support arms.
• Affected arm in bottom position: position this arm in extension and forearm in supination (or neutral).	Place small pillow under forearm or hand to minimize edema.
• Affected arm in top position: position this arm in extension with pillow supporting arm in horizontal plane. Forearm is slightly supinated or neutral.	
7. Gently abduct both legs:	
• Affected leg in bottom position: position leg forward and in slight flexion. Hip is protracted.	
• Affected leg in top position: position leg in slight flexion behind bottom leg. Support leg in a horizontal plane with pillows.	
8. Use foam blocks to bridge any bony areas as needed.	

Three-Quarters Prone Position To Minimize Flexion Spasticity on Affected Side

1. Position patient supine in center of bed.	Start with bed flat and no pillows or blocks under patient.
2. Move patient to side of bed closest to unaffected side.	
3. Place trunk roll, foam blocks, or firm pillow next to affected side of trunk below axilla level.	
4. Roll patient forward over roll, foam blocks, or firm pillow.	This will stretch both sides of the trunk. Pad side rail closest to affected side.
5. Position affected upper extremity behind trunk.	This encourages shoulder abduction and protraction.

Steps	*Additional Information*
6. Turn head toward unaffected side.	Place small pillow under head to facilitate neutral positioning if needed.
7. Position topmost upper extremity to front, rolling shoulder forward.	
8. Position affected lower extremity in back of lower extremity on bottom, extending hip and bending knee slightly.	This will promote hip extension, abduction, and protraction.

DOCUMENTATION

1. Record the response to positioning (i.e., increased or decreased tone).

2. Document patient and family teaching.

Nursing Care for the Patient with the Functional Electrical Stimulation or Transcutaneous Electrical Nerve Stimulation Unit

PURPOSES

Functional electrical stimulation (FES): To stimulate contraction of a specific muscle to enhance movement; to increase strength in weak muscles; to decrease spasticity of specific muscles by stimulating the antagonistic muscles; to help resolve shoulder subluxations; to promote sensory motor integration; to increase venous return.

Transcutaneous electrical nerve stimulation (TENS): To block specific localized pain or nerve irritation.

STAFF RESPONSIBLE

EQUIPMENT

See local/national manufacturer product information.

1. Electrodes (patches).
2. Lead wires.
3. FES or TENS unit.
4. Instructions for prescribed use.

GENERAL CONSIDERATIONS

1. The nurse's support and belief in a treatment modality such as FES or TENS may have an effect on the patient's compliance and satisfaction with the treatment. When a device such as TENS is used, the nurse's belief that the patient is in pain, that the pain is real, and that TENS can help alleviate it influences the patient in a positive manner. Other pain relief methods such as massage, imagery, progressive relaxation exercises, cold packs or icing, warm moist packs, and medications should be incorporated in the pain relief program as appropriate and effective.
2. The physical therapist or physician is responsible for placement of electrodes and setting of dials on the FES or TENS unit. Electrodes may be left in place for 1 week, provided that they remain secure.
3. The physical therapist or physician will supply nursing with specific instructions for dial settings, frequency and duration of the treatment, positioning of the patient during treatment, and the patient's level of independence in the treatment.
4. The physical therapist initiates the use of the FES or TENS unit and notifies nursing of the treatment.
5. Nursing requires a physician's prescription to use FES and TENS on the patient unit.
6. Showering is not contraindicated with this treatment. The electrodes can become wet and do not need to be covered, but they should be disconnected from the unit before showering the patient.
7. The TENS or FES unit is kept with the patient or is locked up when not in use.

PROCEDURE

Steps	*Additional Information*
1. Review with physical therapist the individualized patient instructions before initial use of FES or TENS unit on patient unit.	FES is contraindicated in patients with cardiac pacemakers or orthopedically unstable areas unless they are immobilized.
2. Position patient in specified position as instructed by physical therapist or physician.	
3. Check placement of electrodes.	Check for electrode adherence to skin and proper placement over desired muscle. If electrode has become loose along edges, it can be reinforced with paper tape. If electrode has fallen off completely, ask physical therapist to replace in proper position. Do not continue with treatment.
4. Check lead wires for any fraying that could indicate an electrical hazard.	If this is found, do not continue with treatment. Notify physical therapist as soon as possible.
5. Check that FES or TENS unit is off.	
6. Plug appropriate lead wires into electrodes and into FES or TENS unit per physical therapist's or physican's instructions.	
7. Check dials on FES or TENS unit for proper settings.	Verify with physical therapist's instruction sheet.
8. Check patient's pulse and blood pressure before, during, and after FES.	
9. Turn unit on.	Units vary in that some require that nurse set voltage dial.
10. Check patient comfort.	If patient complains of burning sensation, check for loosening of electrodes or inadequate gel.
11. After designated treatment time has elapsed, switch unit off.	Unit is set to shut off automatically after designated treatment time has elapsed (usually 15 to 20 minutes). Switch is still on, however, and wears out FES or TENS unit batteries.
12. Disconnect all lead wires from electrodes.	

DOCUMENTATION

1. Note the time of treatment and the patient's response.

2. Note any problems or concerns.

Applying Elastic Bandages to Amputated Extremities

PURPOSE

To decrease edema and shape residual limb before prosthetic fitting.

STAFF RESPONSIBLE

EQUIPMENT

1. Tape.
2. Elastic bandages.

GENERAL CONSIDERATIONS

1. Stump shrinkage is desirable, even for patients who are not candidates for prostheses, to decrease pain and to enhance healing of the residual limb.
2. Wash bandages at least every 48 hours in mild soap and lukewarm water. Rinse them thoroughly, and dry them flat.

Do not hand wring or place them in a dryer. Avoid direct heat and sunlight.
3. Elastic bandages should be removed and the stump inspected in the morning and evening for skin problems. Notify the physician of any problems.
4. Elastic bandages should be worn at all times except during hygiene procedures, massage, and exercise.
5. The stump should be rewrapped during morning and evening care as well as whenever the bandage becomes too tight or loose. Bandages should be wrapped in an overlapping manner, smoothly, and without wrinkles.
6. A patient with open skin areas on the stump should follow the prescribed treatment plan.
7. Tape should be used in place of safety pins or metal hooks to anchor the wrap, especially in patients with sensory loss.

PATIENT AND FAMILY EDUCATION

1. Careful patient and family instruction is necessary to prevent complications from poor wrapping technique.
2. Always wrap or assist in wrapping the residual limb with the patient positioned as if he or she was wrapping it. This position facilitates patient teaching and minimizes confusion.

PROCEDURES

Steps   *Additional Information*

Above-Knee Amputation

1. Use double-length, 6-inch elastic bandage.

2. Begin with an oblique turn on anterior aspect of residual limb at a point below trochanter (Figure 2-45).
3. Pass bandage over anterior medial aspect of distal end. Run bandage posteriorly to lateral side (Figure 2-45).
4. Bring bandage up and around medial side and down posteriorly to lateral distal end of residual limb (Figure 2-46). Continue making oblique and figure-of-eight turns (Figure 2-47) until firm pressure is obtained distally. Overlap half the bandage width on each turn.
5. Proceed up residual limb combining figure-of-eight and oblique turns, bringing bandage high into groin area to prevent possibility of adductor roll (Figure 2-48).

Patient may be supine with residual limb extended or may sit on edge of bed or chair.
Keep bandage free of wrinkles to avoid skin irritations.

Pressure should be greatest at distal end and decrease as bandage is wrapped toward hip.
Pressure must always be up and out at distal end of residual limb to prevent formation of skin creases. Do not include both medial and lateral aspects of end portion of residual limb in same turn because this tends to cause skin creases. Do not use circular turns because this can constrict circulation.

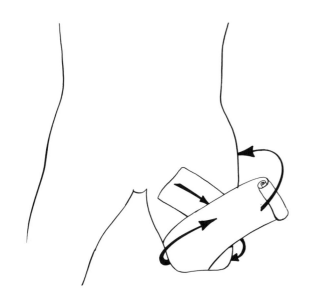

Figure 2-45 Above-Knee Stump Wrapping. *Source:* From *Pre-Prosthetic Care for Above-Knee Amputees* (p. 6), 1978, Chicago, IL: Physical Therapy Department, Rehabilitation Institute of Chicago. Copyright 1978 by Rehabilitation Institute of Chicago. Reprinted by permission.

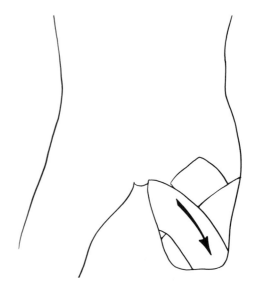

Figure 2-46 Above-Knee Stump Wrapping (continued). *Source:* From *Pre-Prosthetic Care for Above-Knee Amputees* (p. 6), 1978, Chicago, IL: Physical Therapy Department, Rehabilitation Institute of Chicago. Copyright 1978 by Rehabilitation Institute of Chicago. Reprinted by permission.

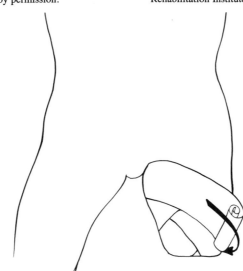

Figure 2-47 Above-Knee Stump Wrapping (continued). *Source:* From *Pre-Prosthetic Care for Above-Knee Amputees* (p. 6), 1978, Chicago, IL: Physical Therapy Department, Rehabilitation Institute of Chicago. Copyright 1978 by Rehabilitation Institute of Chicago. Reprinted by permission.

Steps

6. Start hip spica from anterior lateral aspect of residual limb, and run it medially across anterior surface of residual limb (Figure 2-48).
7. Cross over uninvolved hip at level of iliac crest. Carry bandage around body (Figure 2-49).
8. Cross greater trochanter of involved side (Figure 2-49).
9. Run bandage obliquely to medial distal end of residual limb (Figure 2-50).
10. Finish bandage by making oblique turns on end of residual limb (Figure 2-50).
11. Anchor bandage over lateral or anterior surface with tape (Figure 2-50).

Additional Information

Hip spica is used if above-knee residual limb is too short for elastic bandage to stay on. Hip spica further secures bandage to extend time between wrappings.

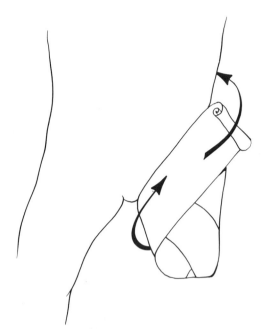

Figure 2-48 Above-Knee Stump Wrapping (continued). *Source:* From *Pre-Prosthetic Care for Above-Knee Amputees* (p. 6), 1978, Chicago, IL: Physical Therapy Department, Rehabilitation Institute of Chicago. Copyright 1978 by Rehabilitation Institute of Chicago. Reprinted by permission.

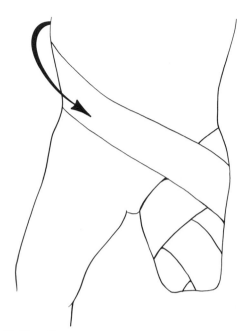

Figure 2-49 Above-Knee Stump Wrapping (continued). *Source:* From *Pre-Prosthetic Care for Above-Knee Amputees* (p. 6), 1978, Chicago, IL: Physical Therapy Department, Rehabilitation Institute of Chicago. Copyright 1978 by Rehabilitation Institute of Chicago. Reprinted by permission.

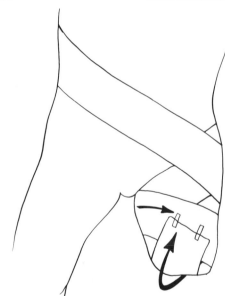

Figure 2-50 Above-Knee Stump Wrapping (completed). *Source:* From *Pre-Prosthetic Care for Above-Knee Amputees* (p. 6), 1978, Chicago, IL: Physical Therapy Department, Rehabilitation Institute of Chicago. Copyright 1978 by Rehabilitation Institute of Chicago. Reprinted by permission.

Steps	*Additional Information*

Below-Knee Amputation

1. Use double-length, 4-inch elastic bandage.	Patient may be supine or sitting with knees extended.
2. Begin with an oblique turn on anterior aspect of residual limb inferior to knee joint (Figure 2-51).	
3. Pass bandage over anterior medial aspect of distal end. Run bandage posteriorly to lateral side (Figure 2-51).	Keep bandage free of wrinkles to avoid skin irritations.

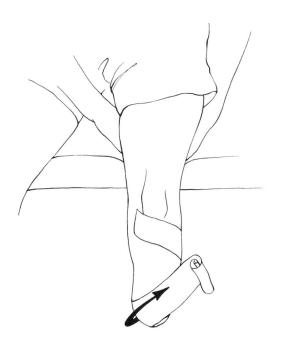

Figure 2-51 Below-Knee Stump Wrapping. *Source:* From *Pre-Prosthetic Care for Below-Knee Amputees* (p. 6), 1978, Chicago, IL: Physical Therapy Department, Rehabilitation Institute of Chicago. Copyright 1978 by Rehabilitation Institute of Chicago. Reprinted by permission.

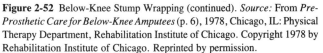

Figure 2-52 Below-Knee Stump Wrapping (continued). *Source:* From *Pre-Prosthetic Care for Below-Knee Amputees* (p. 6), 1978, Chicago, IL: Physical Therapy Department, Rehabilitation Institute of Chicago. Copyright 1978 by Rehabilitation Institute of Chicago. Reprinted by permission.

Figure 2-53 Below-Knee Stump Wrapping (continued). *Source:* From *Pre-Prosthetic Care for Below-Knee Amputees* (p. 6), 1978, Chicago, IL: Physical Therapy Department, Rehabilitation Institute of Chicago. Copyright 1978 by Rehabilitation Institute of Chicago. Reprinted by permission.

Steps	*Additional Information*
4. Bring bandage up and around medial side and down to posterior, lateral, distal aspect of residual limb (Figures 2-52 and 2-53).	
5. Continue making oblique and figure-of-eight turns until firm pressure is obtained distally (Figure 2-54).	Pressure must always be up and out at distal end of residual limb to eliminate formation of skin creases.
6. Reduce pressure from distal to proximal, and proceed with figure-of-eight turns at least 2 inches above superior border	

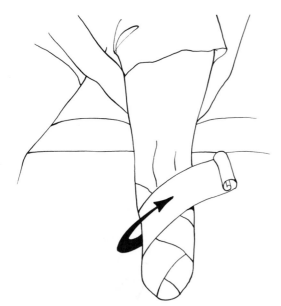

Figure 2-54 Below-Knee Stump Wrapping (continued). *Source:* From *Pre-Prosthetic Care for Below-Knee Amputees* (p. 6), 1978, Chicago, IL: Physical Therapy Department, Rehabilitation Institute of Chicago. Copyright 1978 by Rehabilitation Institute of Chicago. Reprinted by permission.

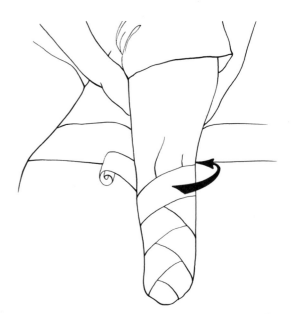

Figure 2-55 Below-Knee Stump Wrapping (continued). *Source:* From *Pre-Prosthetic Care for Below-Knee Amputees* (p. 7), 1978, Chicago, IL: Physical Therapy Department, Rehabilitation Institute of Chicago. Copyright 1978 by Rehabilitation Institute of Chicago. Reprinted by permission.

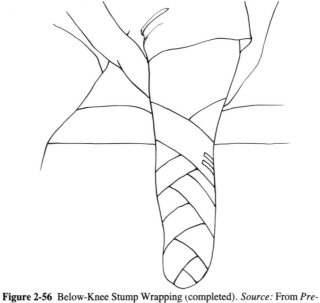

Figure 2-56 Below-Knee Stump Wrapping (completed). *Source:* From *Pre-Prosthetic Care for Below-Knee Amputees* (p. 7), 1978, Chicago, IL: Physical Therapy Department, Rehabilitation Institute of Chicago. Copyright 1978 by Rehabilitation Institute of Chicago. Reprinted by permission.

Steps	*Additional Information*

of patella (Figure 2-55). Overlap half the bandage width on each turn.

7. Return to below knee and finish bandage with oblique or figure-of-eight turns. Secure with tape (Figure 2-56).

DOCUMENTATION

1. Note the schedule for use of elastic bandages.
2. Note the skin status, shrinkage and shape of the stump, and the patient's tolerance for the bandage.

3. Note the patient's self-bandaging ability and consistent follow-through with the bandaging schedule.

Applying the Removable Rigid Dressing in Below-Knee Amputation

PURPOSES

To decrease the swelling and to shape the residual limb.

STAFF RESPONSIBLE

EQUIPMENT

1. Stump socks.
2. Rigid dressing (includes molded cast, cover sock, and cuff).
3. Nonadhesive dressing (i.e., Telfa pads) if needed.

GENERAL CONSIDERATIONS

1. Stump shrinkage is desirable, even for patients who are not candidates for prostheses, to decrease pain and to enhance healing of the residual limb.

2. A patient with open skin areas on the stump should follow the prescribed treatment plan.
3. The rigid dressing should be removed every morning and evening and the skin checked for red areas, blisters, or open areas. Notify the physician of any problematic skin areas.
4. The rigid dressing is to be worn at all times except when bathing or exercising.
5. The knee should be kept in an extended position as much as possible.
6. Assess patient complaints of pain, burning, and so forth, and promptly inspect the residual limb for alterations in vascular status, color, temperature, edema, or pulse.

PATIENT AND FAMILY EDUCATION

Teach the patient and family to apply and remove the removable rigid dressing for skin checks and hygiene procedures.

PROCEDURE

Steps	*Additional Information*
1. Explain procedure to patient.	
2. Inspect skin for red areas, blisters, or open areas. Notify physician if any new areas have developed.	Open areas may be covered with nonadhering dressing as prescribed by physician.
3. Skin care should be performed every morning and evening.	
4. Perform any stump treatments as prescribed by physician.	
5. Apply socks (Figure 2-57A).	Socks have various thicknesses. To obtain proper fit, only socks provided by physical therapist should be used.
6. Apply molded cast (Figure 2-57B). Cast is marked to indicate center front. Top rim of cast should come to middle of patella. If rim is lower than middle of patella, remove some socks. If the cast is higher than middle of knee cap, apply more socks.	Cast must be applied properly to achieve proper pressure for shrinkage and to avoid pressure areas and skin problems.
7. Apply cover sock (long sock tied in a knot at end) over cast (Figure 2-57C).	
8. Apply cuff snugly (Figure 2-58A). Cuff is placed slightly higher than knee. Center front of cuff is marked. Top outside of cuff is lined with Velcro.	Cuff needs to be snug to hold cover sock and cast in place.
9. Pull both inner sock(s) and cover sock up to eliminate any wrinkles (Figure 2-58B). Then pull socks down over top of cuff across Velcro strip (Figure 2-58C). Tuck excess socks under bottom edge of cuff to help secure cast and socks.	

DOCUMENTATION

1. Document the use of the removable rigid dressing.
2. Note the skin status and the patient's tolerance.

3. Note the patient's and family's education and mastery of application.

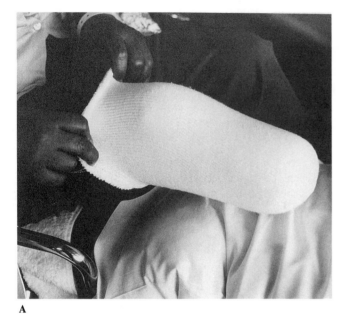

A

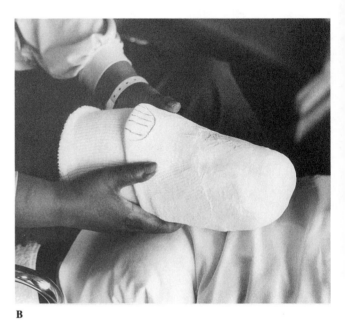

B

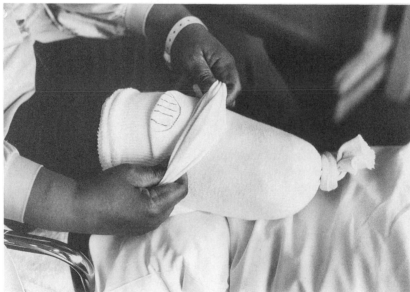

C

Figure 2-57 Applying Removable Rigid Dressing in Below-Knee Amputation. (**A**) Applying Socks, (**B**) Applying Molded Cast, (**C**) Applying Cover Sock.

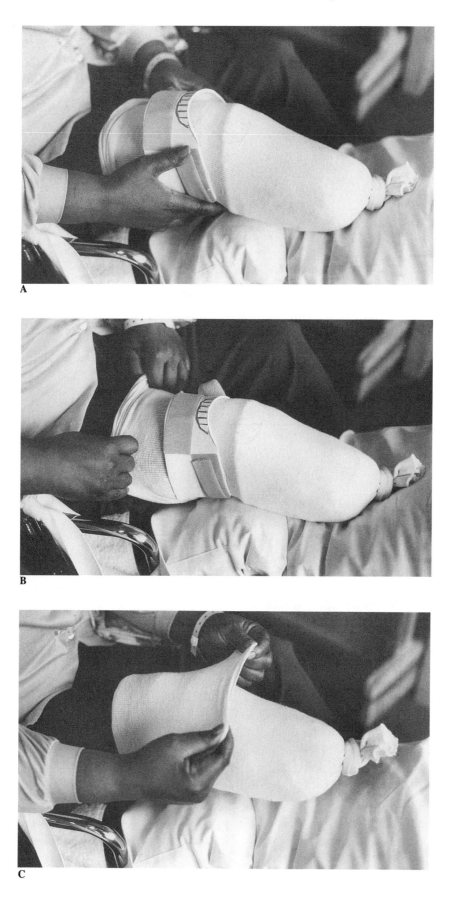

Figure 2-58 Applying Removable Rigid Dressing in Below-Knee Amputation. (**A**) Applying Cuff, (**B**) Pulling up Socks, (**C**) Folding over Sock Edges.

Positioning the Patient with Lower Extremity Amputation

PURPOSE

To prevent shortening of soft tissue, joint contracture, and edema in the residual limb.

STAFF RESPONSIBLE

EQUIPMENT

1. Lying: no equipment necessary.
2. Sitting: second chair or small (sliding) board.

GENERAL CONSIDERATIONS

1. Common contractures with lower extremity amputation are:
   - hip flexion,
   - hip abduction,
   - hip external rotation, and
   - knee flexion.
2. Avoid the use of pillows under the residual limb in bed because this may contribute to joint contractures, especially in below-knee amputation (Figures 2-59 and 2-60).
3. Ambulation should be encouraged when ordered by the physician.

PATIENT AND FAMILY EDUCATION

Teach the patient and family to assume these positions several times daily to prevent contractures that could complicate prosthetic fitting, ambulation, or cosmesis.

PROCEDURE

Steps	*Additional Information*
1. Assist patient as necessary to lie prone several times during the day.	Check with physician before positioning patient prone, especially spinal cord–injured or geriatric patients or those with respiratory or cardiac problems. Sleeping in prone position, if tolerated, is highly recommended.
2. When supine, patient with above-knee amputation should lie with pelvis neutral and hip joint in extension. Hip should be in neutral rotation and neutral abduction-adduction. Patient with below-knee amputation should lie as above and knee extended.	
3. When sitting, patient with below-knee amputation should be assisted as necessary to keep residual limb extended. Use second chair to support residual limb (Figure 2-61), or use board placed under wheelchair cushion to support residual limb.	Extension of residual limb is necessary to prevent contracture and edema even if shrinkage device is being used.

DOCUMENTATION

1. Note the patient's positioning methods and schedule.
2. Note the patient's tolerance to positioning, presence of joint contracture, or presence of edema in the residual limb.
3. Note the effectiveness of patient and family education.

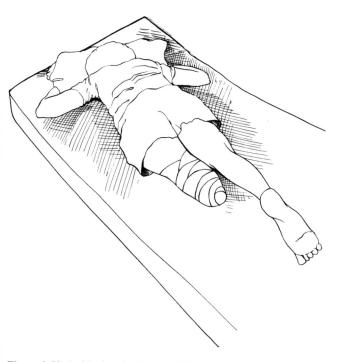

Figure 2-59 Positioning the Patient with Lower Extremity Amputation: Prone Lying. *Source:* From *Lower Extremity Amputation: A Guide to Functional Outcomes in Physical Therapy Management* (p. 10) by L.A. Karacoloff, 1986, Rockville, MD: Aspen Publishers, Inc. Copyright 1986 by Aspen Publishers, Inc.

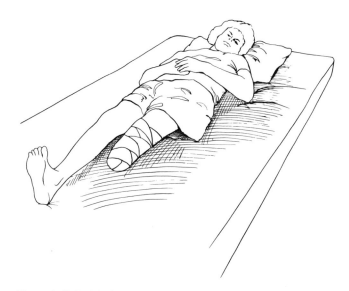

Figure 2-60 Positioning the Patient with Lower Extremity Amputation: Supine Lying. *Source:* From *Lower Extremity Amputation: A Guide to Functional Outcomes in Physical Therapy Management* (p. 10) by L.A. Karacoloff, 1986, Rockville, MD: Aspen Publishers, Inc. Copyright 1986 by Aspen Publishers, Inc.

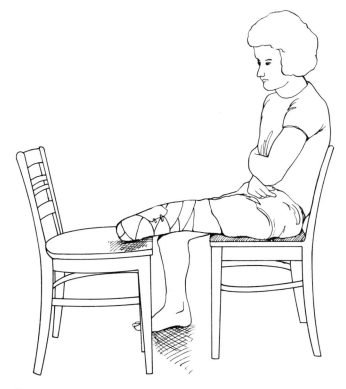

Figure 2-61 Positioning the Patient with Lower Extremity Amputation: Sitting. *Source:* From *Lower Extremity Amputation: A Guide to Functional Outcomes in Physical Therapy Management* (p. 11) by L.A. Karacoloff, 1986, Rockville, MD: Aspen Publishers, Inc. Copyright 1986 by Aspen Publishers, Inc.

Moving Forward and Backward in Wheelchair

PURPOSE

To position patient properly in a wheelchair before or after transfers or to improve posture.

STAFF RESPONSIBLE

GENERAL CONSIDERATIONS

1. To facilitate normal movement and tone, the patient should be encouraged to participate as much as possible (for example, a patient with hemiplegia may be able to slide the unaffected side of his or her body forward in the chair in preparing to transfer).
2. Technique 1 should be used with patients who can also do the dependent pivot transfer. Contraindications are:

- patients with leg casts or body casts;
- patients with CTO, TLSO, CTLSO, or LSO devices;
- patients with trunk extension contractures;
- patients with labile orthostatic hypotension or chronic obstructive pulmonary disease; and
- patients with arthritis or other diseases that prohibit flexion of hip and knee joints while weight-bearing.

3. Technique 2 should be used when contraindications exist for the use of technique 1.
4. When sitting, the patient will be more functional if he or she assumes and maintains an anterior pelvic tilt, symmetrical trunk, and head in midline alignment. Recognizing deviations from this position allows for prompt correction, increased function of the patient, and safety for all.

PATIENT AND FAMILY EDUCATION

Teach this technique to the family to facilitate the transfer process. As the procedure is repeated, the patient may be able to assist more.

PROCEDURES, TECHNIQUE 1

Steps | *Additional Information*

Moving Forward

1. Position wheelchair for transfer (90° to other surface).
2. Remove footrests.
3. Lock brakes.
4. Remove armrests.
5. Remove safety strap.
6. Have patient assist as much as possible. Face patient with wide base of support. Bend knees.

Patient's feet should be securely on floor with wide base of support and toes a little behind knees. If patient's legs do not touch floor, be prepared to brace patient more forcefully; this procedure should move patient forward so that feet will touch floor.

7. Place your right shoulder against patient's right shoulder (Figure 2-62A).
8. Encircle patient's trunk with your arms, and cup patient's left scapula with your right hand (Figure 2-62B).
9. Place your left hand on patient's right buttock.
10. Lean patient forward and to left side while supporting the left side with your right arm, and pull patient's right buttock toward front of wheelchair (Figure 2-62C).

Buttock may come forward only a small amount. This usually indicates a need to lean patient forward and to the side more.

11. Move your left hand from patient's right buttock to right scapula.

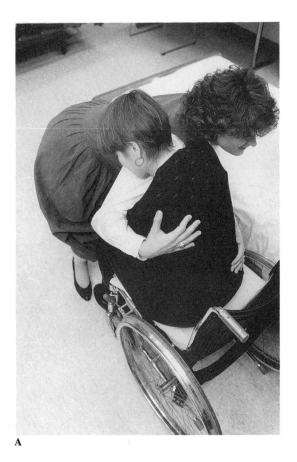

A

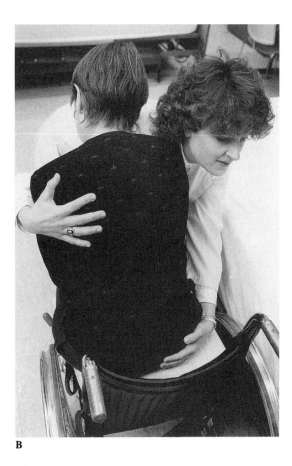

B

C

Figure 2-62 Moving the Patient Forward in a Wheelchair (Technique 1).

Steps   *Additional Information*

12. Move your right hand from patient's left scapula to left buttock.
13. Lean patient forward and to right side while supporting right side with your left arm, and pull patient's left buttock toward front of wheelchair.
14. Continue steps 9 through 13 until patient is sitting on front half to two-thirds of wheelchair cushion.

Moving Backward

1. Remove footrests.
2. Lock brakes.
3. Remove safety strap.
4. Have patient assist as much as possible.
5. Lean patient forward over either of your hips (Figure 2-63B).   Patient's feet should be securely on floor with wide base of support and toes quite a bit behind knees. If patient's feet do not touch floor, use technique 2.
6. Encircle patient's trunk with your arms, grasping your wrists under patient's breasts (Figure 2-63B).
7. Rock patient forward.
8. When patient's weight is over his or her legs, push against patient's shins or knees to move patient backward in chair (Figures 2-63A and 2-63C).
9. Allow patient to come in contact with seat of wheelchair.
10. Continue steps 7 through 9 until patient is in appropriate sitting position.

PROCEDURE, TECHNIQUE 2

Moving Forward or Backward

1. Get another person to assist you.
2. Stand behind patient, facing same way as patient.
3. Second person stands in front of patient, facing patient.
4. Second person places right shoulder to patient's right shoulder.
5. Second person leans patient forward and holds him or her there by cupping his or her scapulae.
6. First person encircles patient's chest under axillae, and with left hand grasps patient's right wrist and with right hand grasps patient's left wrist (Figure 2-64A).
7. Second person lets patient rest back against you, moves to face patient, and places a hand under each thigh above knee (Figure 2-64B).   Second person should hold patient's thighs close to his or her own chest, bend knees, and have wide base of support.
8. On count of three, lift up patient's trunk by lifting patient with your forearms against patient's ribs. Second person lifts patient's thighs and buttocks back or forward in wheelchair (Figure 2-64C).
9. Continue with transfer techniques, or complete appropriate patient positioning in wheelchair.

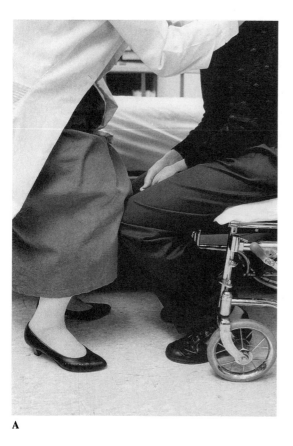

A

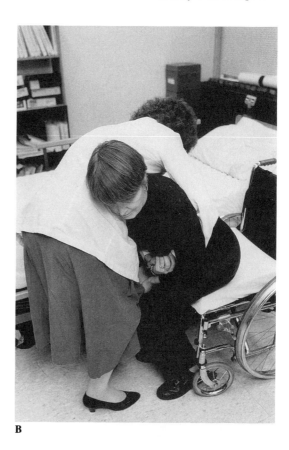

B

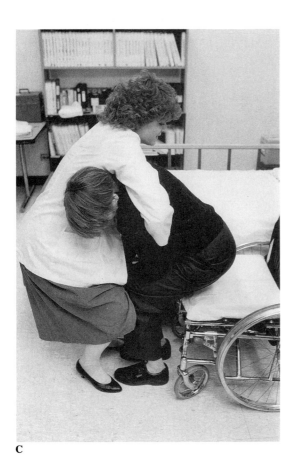

C

Figure 2-63 Moving the Patient Backward in a Wheelchair (Technique 1).

A

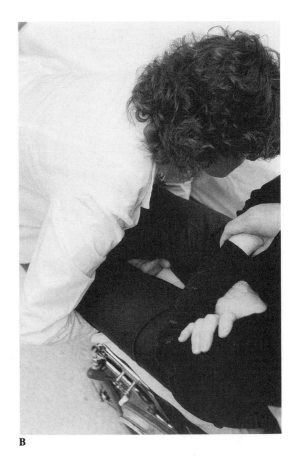

B

Figure 2-64 Moving the Patient Forward or Backward in a Wheelchair (Technique 2).

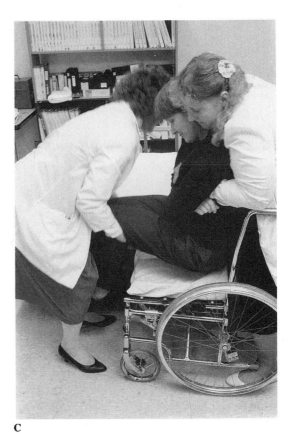

C

DOCUMENTATION

1. Note the effectiveness of patient and family teaching.
2. Document any unusual occurrences.
3. Note any change in the amount of assistance needed.
4. Note the amount and kind of assistance needed.
5. Note any special precautions, needs, or equipment.

Dependent or Sitting Pivot Transfer

PURPOSE

To transfer a patient safely from one surface to another.

STAFF RESPONSIBLE

EQUIPMENT

1. Wheelchair.
2. Bed or mat.
3. Shower chair.

GENERAL CONSIDERATIONS

1. This type of transfer is ideal for patients who have quadriplegia with increased tone, but it can be used with any patient who can bear weight on his or her legs (involuntarily or voluntarily). The patient need only be able to cooperate minimally but at least should not resist the procedure.
2. The use of a sliding board may facilitate the procedure, particularly with heavy or tall patients.
3. The transferer must use good body mechanics to perform this procedure safely (i.e., keep the back straight and knees bent, have a wide base of support, pivot rather than twist, and carry weight at the center of the body).
4. Contraindications to using this transfer include:
   - patients with leg or body casts;
   - patients with CTO, CTLSO, TLSO, or LSO devices;
   - patients with trunk extension contractures;
   - patients with labile orthostatic hypotension or chronic obstructive pulmonary disease; and
   - patients with arthritis or other diseases that prohibit flexion of hip and knee joints while weight-bearing.

PATIENT AND FAMILY EDUCATION

Teach this technique to the family. This method is recommended particularly for car transfers.

PROCEDURE

Steps	*Additional Information*
1. Explain procedure to patient.	
2. Position wheelchair 90° to bed. Remove footrests, and lock brakes. Remove armrest closest to bed or chair.	Face patient, use wide base of support, and bend your knees, not your back.
3. Move patient forward in wheelchair or to side of bed so that feet are flat on floor and toes are behind knees with wide base of support (Figure 2-65A).	See procedures for moving patient forward or backward in wheelchair. Ensure that patient is in anterior pelvic tilt, that trunk is symmetrical, and that head is in midline.
4. Lean patient forward so that patient's shoulder rests against your hip opposite to surface to which patient is being transferred (Figure 2-65B).	Place patient's arms in patient's lap.
5. Reach under patient's breasts and clasp your wrists while leaning patient forward and placing your chest against patient's upper posterior trunk (Figure 2-65C).	Bend your legs and lean slightly backward. If patient feels heavy, try bending your knees more and leaning patient forward. Patient will be unable to resist transfer procedure.
6. Rock patient's body forward a little and toward bed or chair, set patient down for a moment, then rock patient forward and over again until he or she is firmly on bed or chair (Figure 2-65C).	If patient is heavy or too tall for transfer, a sliding board may be used to assist. A spotter may assist by positioning himself or herself behind patient's back and chair and helping lean and rock patient forward as needed.
7. Position patient appropriately in wheelchair or bed.	

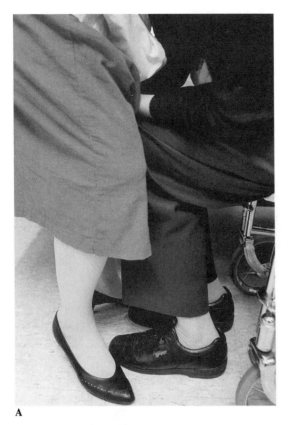

A

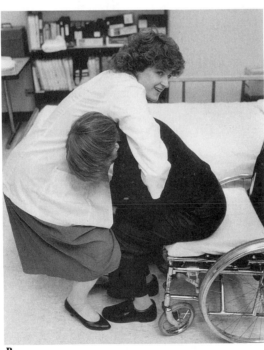

B

Figure 2-65 Dependent or Sitting Pivot Transfer.

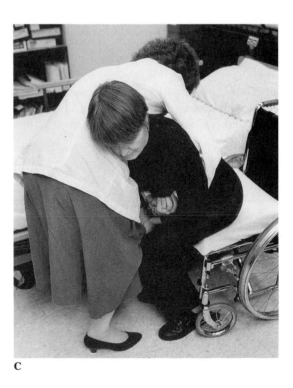

C

DOCUMENTATION

1. Note the effectiveness of patient and family teaching.
2. Note the type of transfer.
3. Document the amount and kind of assistance required.
4. Note any special precautions, needs, or equipment.
5. Note any difficulty in completing the transfer.
6. Document any unusual occurrences.
7. Note any change in the amount of assistance needed.

Standing Pivot Transfer

PURPOSE

To perform a safe standing pivot transfer to any surface.

STAFF RESPONSIBLE

EQUIPMENT

1. Wheelchair.
2. Shower chair.
3. Toilet.
4. Bed.

GENERAL CONSIDERATIONS

1. In most cases, if the patient can voluntarily bear weight on one or both legs, a standing pivot transfer can be performed.
2. The patient with hemiplegia or brain damage may have any or all of the following problems:
   - partial or complete loss of function on one side of the body;
   - partial or total lack of sensation;
   - increased or decreased tone in the involved side;
   - aphasia;
   - perceptual problems;
   - neglect of one side of the body;
   - confusion;
   - emotional liability;
   - intellectual impairment; or
   - impaired vision.
3. The person with hemiplegia has a sound arm and leg that should be utilized to their fullest extent when performing a transfer.
4. The less variance there is in the physical environment, the easier it is for the patient to transfer. Repetition in the same situation is valuable.
5. The armrest may or may not be removed, depending on the patient's level of ability. Removable legrests are desirable.
6. Familiarize yourself with body mechanics and transfer techniques so that you can perform the transfer properly.
7. Complete the following activities before doing the transfer:
   - assess the patient's strengths and weaknesses;
   - observe the patient's activity, and determine his or her ability to assist;
   - observe the patient's posture and balance; and
   - evaluate the patient's comprehension and ability to follow instructions.

PATIENT AND FAMILY EDUCATION

Teach this technique to the patient and family. After repetition of the technique, the patient may be able to perform the transfer with less assistance or fewer cues.

PROCEDURES

Steps	*Additional Information*
Preparation for Transfer	
1. Review procedure with patient.	Keep instructions to one- or two-step commands if patient has comprehension problems.
2. Position wheelchair at 90° angle to surface from which you are transferring patient.	If hemiplegia exists, initially position wheelchair so that patient is able to lead with strongest side until transfers are perfected. Ideally, a patient with hemiplegia should be able to transfer from both sides for optimal community reentry.
3. Lock brakes on wheelchair.	
4. Remove armrest closest to patient (if not needed), and move legrests out of way.	Patients needing minimal assistance may use armrest to push to standing.
5. Adjust height of bed.	Adjust bed so that patient's legs will be flat on floor when sitting on edge of bed.

Steps   *Additional Information*

6. Place proper, nonslip shoes on patient.
7. Lower side rail closest to wheelchair, and remove safety strap.

Bed to Wheelchair or Shower Chair: Maximal Assistance

1. Assist patient to sitting position.

Do this by cradling trunk below shoulders while grasping lower extremities under knees. Simultaneously raise patient's head and slide legs off side of bed, pivoting trunk.

2. Stand in front of patient.
3. Place patient's feet on floor with wide base of support and heels behind knees.
4. Place your legs on either side of patient's weak leg, and bend your knees (Figure 2-66A).
5. Put your hands on both sides of patient's chest, and place your right shoulder to patient's right shoulder (or your left shoulder to patient's left shoulder) (Figure 2-66B).

It is sometimes helpful to place safety belt or transfer belt around patient's waist to give you something firm to grasp. Depending on your size and patient's size, it is sometimes helpful also to place your hands under patient's buttocks. Do not allow patient to put arms around your neck. Instead, instruct patient to use arms to push off bed or to clasp hands and extend arms in front of himself or herself to weaker side. A rocking motion helps.

6. Have patient lean as far forward as possible and, on count of three, come to standing position (Figure 2-66C).

Rock patient forward rhythmically three times, and, on third time, stand. If patient is able, have him or her extend both arms straight out in front; otherwise keep patient's arms in his or her lap. Leaning forward will prevent patient from falling backward into wheelchair.

7. Pivot patient toward wheelchair, stop when patient is in front of it.
8. Bend at knees to lower patient to chair.

Bed to Wheelchair or Shower Chair: Minimal Assistance

1. Have patient come to sitting position with feet flat on floor (toes under knees).

Assistance may be needed to maintain balance (put your hands on either side of patient's chest, or give step-by-step directions).

2. Have patient place his or her strong hand on armrest of chair or side of bed.
3. Have patient lean forward, push against chair, and come to standing position.

Have patient look up when standing and look toward direction in which he or she is moving. Allow patient to get balance before pivoting.

4. Have patient pivot toward chair.
5. Have patient bend at waist and lean forward.
6. Have patient sit down.

You may want to have patient reach back to touch surface before sitting down.

7. Adjust safety belt around patient's waist.

This is optional.

8. Replace armrests or legrests.

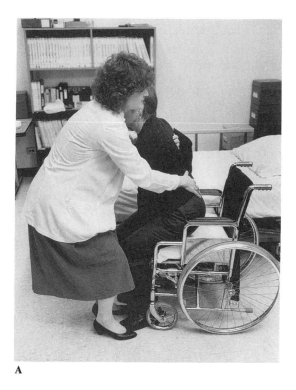

A

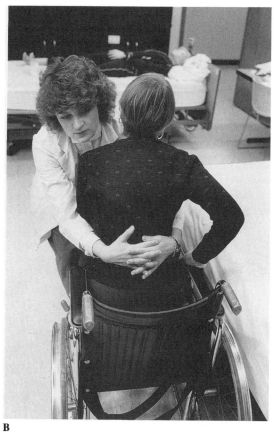

B

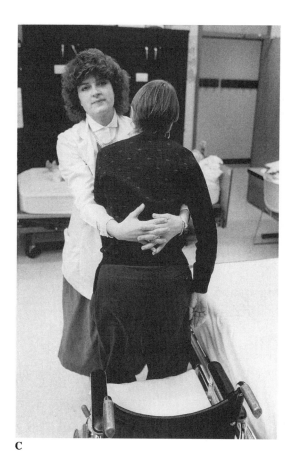

C

Figure 2-66 Standing Pivot Transfer, Maximal Assistance.

Wheelchair to Bed or Shower Chair: Maximal Assistance

1. Prepare for transfer.
2. Move patient forward in chair by means of the following steps:
   - Tell patient to slide or scoot forward, if possible.
   - Stand in front of patient.
   - Place patient's feet well behind his or her knees on floor.
   - Place patient's shoulder against yours (right to right or left to left).
   - Place one of your hands on patient's scapula and other on patient's opposite buttock.
   - Lean patient forward.
3. With patient in posterior pelvic tilt and maximum assistance needed, pull legs forward gently.
   - Assist patient to edge of wheelchair by pulling patient forward while tilting trunk to opposite side.
   - Change hands and repeat.
4. Place feet on floor with wide base of support and feet slightly behind knees.
5. Follow maximal assistance (bed to wheelchair) steps.

Follow steps given above.

Wheelchair to Bed or Shower Chair: Minimal Assistance

1. Prepare for transfer.
2. Follow minimal assistance (bed to wheelchair) steps.
3. Position patient in bed, and raise side rails.
4. Replace armrests and legrests.

DOCUMENTATION

1. Document the type of transfer.
2. Note the amount and kind of assistance needed.
3. Note any special precautions, needs, or equipment.
4. Note any difficulty in completing the transfer.
5. Document any unusual occurrences.
6. Note any change in the amount of assistance needed.
7. Note the effectiveness of patient and family teaching.

Sliding Board Transfer

PURPOSE

To transfer a patient safely from one surface to another.

STAFF RESPONSIBLE

EQUIPMENT

1. Wheelchair.
2. Shower chair.
3. Transfer board.

GENERAL CONSIDERATIONS

1. This type of transfer may be used with a wide range of patients, from those requiring no assistance to those who

are totally dependent. The patient need only be able to cooperate minimally but at least should not resist the procedure. This transfer technique is especially helpful with car transfers.

2. The transferer must use good body mechanics to perform this procedure safely (i.e., keep the back straight and knees bent, have a wide base of support, pivot rather than twist, and carry weight at the center of the body).
3. Contraindications to using this transfer include:
   - patients with trunk extension contractions, and
   - patients who are resistive to the technique or who are uncooperative.

4. This type of transfer is often the first step in developing an independent lateral transfer for patients with paraplegia or paresis. The amount of energy and upper extremity strength required is substantially less when the sliding board is used.

PATIENT AND FAMILY EDUCATION

Teach this technique to the patient and family. It is especially helpful in performing transfers across uneven surfaces, including car transfers.

PROCEDURE

Steps	*Additional Information*
1. Explain procedure to patient.	
2. Position wheelchair 90° to bed.	
3. Remove footrests.	
4. Lock brakes.	
5. Remove armrest closest to bed or chair.	
6. Remove safety strap.	
7. Move patient forward in wheelchair or to side of bed so that feet are flat on floor and toes are behind knees with wide base of support.	Patients with casts or who cannot bear weight may have legs on bed but must compensate by leaning forward.
8. Lean patient to side away from chair or bed.	Optimally, patient should be moving from higher surface to lower one.
9. Holding board at 45° to bed or chair, slide it under patient's upper thighs (not buttocks) (Figure 2-67A).	
10. Reposition patient upright.	
11. Aim free end of board to distant rear corner of chair or middle of bed (Figure 2-67B).	
12. If patient is dependent:	
• lean patient forward over your hip opposite to surface to which patient is being transferred;	Place patient's arms in his or her lap.
• circle patient's chest under breasts with your arms, and clasp your wrists; and	Alternatively, lean patient over your shoulder, and grasp waistband of patient's pants (not belt loops).
• slide patient along board (Figure 2-67C).	
13. If patient is able to assist, have patient lean forward and slide himself or herself by shifting weight.	Guard patient by placing your arms around patient's chest or waist and your legs between patient's legs. If patient's legs give out, lean patient forward more and brace his or her shin with yours.
14. If patient is independent, have him or her perform as many steps as possible.	Eventually, as upper extremity strength and endurance increase, the sliding board becomes unnecessary.
15. Position patient in wheelchair or bed as appropriate.	

DOCUMENTATION

1. Note the type of transfer.
2. Document the amount and kind of assistance needed.
3. Document any special precautions, needs, or equipment.
4. Note any difficulties in completing the transfer.

5. Note any unusual occurrences.
6. Note any change in amount of assistance needed.
7. Document the effectiveness of patient and family teaching.

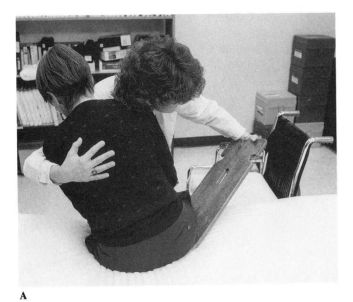

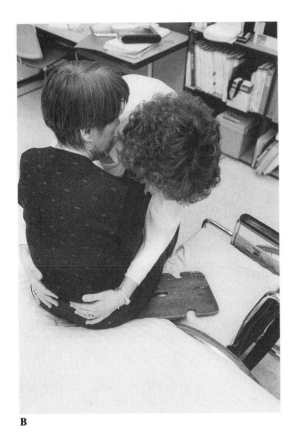

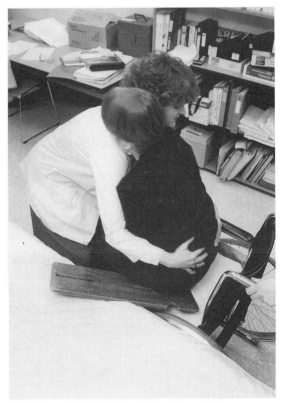

Figure 2-67 Sliding Board Transfer for Dependent Patient.

A

B

C

Two-Person Lift

PURPOSE

To lift a patient safely from one surface to another.

STAFF RESPONSIBLE

EQUIPMENT

1. Wheelchair with removable armrests and legrests.
2. Shower chair.
3. Toilet.
4. Bed or mat.

GENERAL CONSIDERATIONS

1. In most cases, any patient who sits at 60° or higher can be transferred by the two-person lift technique.
2. Patients who consistently require a two-person lift should consider using a mechanical lifting device (Trans-aid or Hoyer lift) or transfer assistance device (sliding board, slings, or loops). Such a patient may also be a candidate for a dependent pivot transfer. The physical therapist should be consulted regarding this decision.

3. Patients requiring a two-person lift may have any or all of the following problems:
   - paralyzed upper or lower extremities (or both);
   - loss of sensation;
   - loss of position sense;
   - spasticity;
   - loss of trunk stability or balance in sitting; or
   - contraindicated weight-bearing in trunk or legs (i.e., fractures, contractures, or arthritis).
4. Familiarize yourself with body mechanics and transfer techniques so that you can perform the transfer properly.
5. Complete the following activities before performing the transfer:
   - assess the patient's strengths and weaknesses;
   - observe the patient's activities, and determine his or her ability to assist;
   - observe the patient's posture and balance;
   - evaluate the patient's comprehension and ability to follow instructions; and
   - consider the patient's height and weight (patients weighing more than 150 lbs should not be lifted).

PATIENT AND FAMILY EDUCATION

1. The patient is not able to assist with this procedure.
2. The procedure requires two persons (not always available in the community setting), good body mechanics, and strength.

PROCEDURES

Steps	Additional Information

Bed to Wheelchair or Shower Chair

Steps	Additional Information
1. Review procedure with patient.	
2. Move patient to side of bed where transfer will take place, securing catheter, IV, tubing, and so forth from harm.	Depending on environmental setup, this may be either right or left side.
3. Move wheelchair parallel to side of bed at hip level and facing foot of bed.	
4. Lock wheels. Remove armrest closest to bed and both legrests if possible.	Legrests can be moved out of the way; if not removable, raise them.
5. Raise bed so that it is at same level or slightly higher than seat cushion of wheelchair.	

Steps	*Additional Information*
6. Bring patient to sitting position.	For those patients who experience orthostatic hypotension, head of bed should be raised 5 to 10 minutes before transfer. This may also help if patient has poor trunk balance or is obese.
7. Have patient cross arms on chest, or cross them for him or her.	
8. Stand behind patient with one knee on bed, slide arms under patient's axillae, and firmly grasp patient's forearms (Figure 2-68A).	Put firm pressure with your forearms against patient's ribs rather than axillae. The humeral head can be forced into subacromial arch, causing pain on lifting.
9. The second person stands facing bed in front of wheelchair and places one arm under patient's thighs and one arm under knees (Figure 2-68B).	This person should have wide base of support, bend at knees, and keep back as straight as possible.
10. On the count of three, patient is lifted into chair. Shift weight from knee on bed to leg behind chair; other person should step back (Figure 2-68C).	Lift completely and slowly so as not to cause trauma to patient's skin or extremities. Be sure that patient is held close to your body (center of gravity), and do not bend your back.
11. Adjust patient's position as necessary.	
12. Attach safety belt, replace armrests, and adjust legrests.	For patients with poor trunk stability, person at feet should stabilize patient until safety strap is attached.

Wheelchair or Shower Chair to Bed or Mat Table (Mat)

1. Review procedure with patient.	
2. Move wheelchair or shower chair parallel to bed or mat at hip level and facing foot of bed.	Estimate position that patient will assume in bed to eliminate need to move patient up or down after transfer.
3. Lower bed to lowest level.	
4. Lock wheelchair or shower chair brakes.	
5. Remove armrest closest to bed or mat.	
6. Remove both footrests.	
7. Move patient forward in chair.	Approximately one-third of wheelchair cushion should be exposed behind patient.
8. Position one person behind wheelchair (person 1) and one person in front of wheelchair (person 2).	
9. Person 1 should place arms around patient's chest and hold patient's forearms so that patient cannot pull away (Figure 2-68A).	Person 1 should place knee closest to bed or mat on bed or mat.
10. Person 2 places patient's legs on bed or mat unless contraindicated.	
11. Person 2 turns to face bed or mat, crouches down with wide base of support, and places one arm under patient's thighs as high up as possible and other arm under patient's lower thighs (Figure 2-68B).	Person 1 may lean patient backward so that person 2 can get arms high up under patient's thighs.
12. On count of three, patient should be lifted into bed or onto mat (Figure 2-68C).	Person 1 should shift weight from straight leg to knee on bed or mat. Person 2 should take a step forward to come to standing position with back straight.
13. Adjust patient's position.	If patient has landed on edge of bed, either position side lying or move to center of bed from other side.

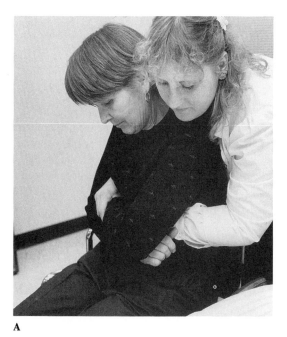

A

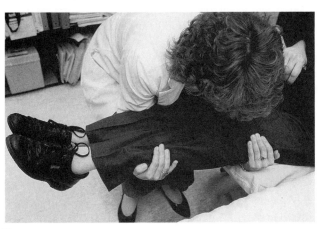

B

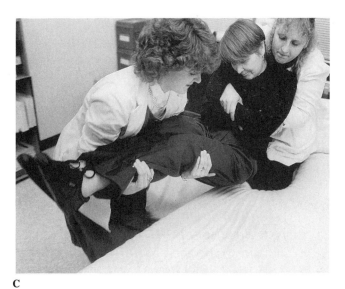

C

Figure 2-68 Two-Person Lift.

DOCUMENTATION

1. Note the type of transfer.
2. Document the amount and kind of assistance needed.
3. Note any special precautions (e.g., painful shoulders).
4. Note any difficulties in completing the transfer.
5. Note any unusual occurrences.
6. Document the effectiveness of patient and family teaching.

Three-Person Lift

PURPOSE

To perform a safe three-person lift transfer to all flat surfaces.

STAFF RESPONSIBLE

EQUIPMENT

1. Bed.
2. Cart.
3. Reclining wheelchair.

GENERAL CONSIDERATIONS

1. The criterion for selecting a three-person lift is spinal precautions. Generally, any patient who cannot sit above 30° can be transferred by Trans-aid or other devices.
2. The Surgilift mechanical lifting device should be considered for use on anyone who would require a three-person lift but is not on spinal precautions.

PATIENT AND FAMILY EDUCATION

Explain the procedure to the patient and family.

PROCEDURE

Steps	Additional Information
1. Position cart or wheelchair perpendicular to bed or surface from which patient will be transferred.	Position equipment to which patient will be transferred so that end where patient's head will be is currently at patient's foot (Figure 2-69A).
2. Lock all wheels (bed and cart or wheelchair).	If unable to lock cart or bed, a fourth person should stabilize it. Have pillows or positioning equipment ready and available for final positioning.
3. Position patient on back, and raise bed to comfortable level for tallest person.	
4. Tallest person stands at head of patient, second tallest person stands at waist, and third person (shortest) stands at knees (Figure 2-69B).	Remove any articles such as watches or bracelets that may scratch patient.
5. Arms are placed under patient, one at a time:	
• Tallest person places arms under neck to hold far shoulder and under lumbar area, reaching up to lower chest to hold patient's opposite forearm (Figure 2-69C).	Place palms up, and press down on mattress. Arms may be crossed to provide more stability. You may need an additional person to support patient's neck if patient has poor head control or is on spinal precautions.
• Second tallest person places arms under lumbar area, reaching up next to tallest person's lower arm to hold patient's opposite forearm, and under upper thighs.	An additional person may assist if patient is tall or heavy at second person's position.
• Shortest person places arms under upper thighs next to second tallest person's lower arm and above knees.	
6. Move patient to side of bed on count of three (Figure 2-69D).	This is the only lifting that should occur in transfer. Tallest person gives directions and counts.
7. All persons should ensure wide base of support. Their chests should be against patient's closest side, and they should have solid grip before proceeding.	
8. Roll patient onto your chests (sternums) on count of three (Figure 2-69E).	When rolling patient onto chests, all lifters must be at bed level to eliminate need to lift. Once patient is rolled, lifters must arch their backs to keep patient on their sternums and not allow patient to roll down onto their arms.
9. Pause momentarily to make sure that weight can be managed.	If not, place patient on bed and seek additional assistance.

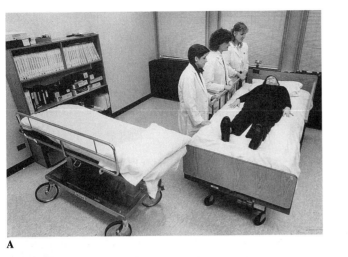
A

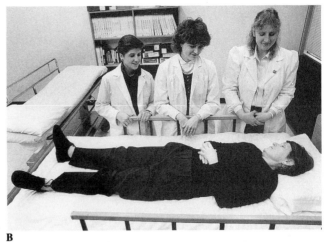
B

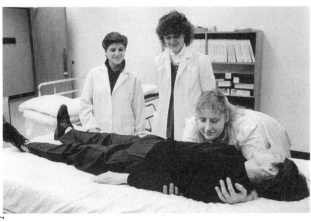
C

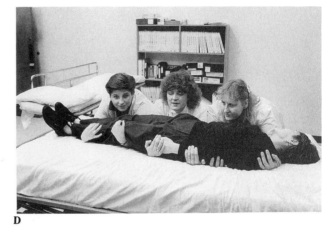
D

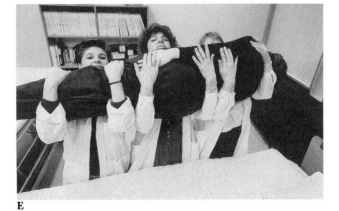
E

Figure 2-69 Three-Person Lift.

Steps	*Additional Information*
10. Shortest person directs transfer to new surface (bed, cart, or mat)	This person should be only one who can see over patient.
11. Shortest person directs lowering of patient to new surface.	Patient should not be dropped to new surface. All lifters should bend their knees to lower patient.
12. Position patient comfortably.	
13. Put side rails up.	

DOCUMENTATION

1. Document any unusual circumstances or any patient problems.

2. Note the type of transfer.
3. Note any special precautions.

Hoyer Lift Transfer

PURPOSE

To move patient safely with a mechanical lifter.

STAFF RESPONSIBLE

EQUIPMENT

1. Hoyer lift and sling.
2. Wheelchair.

GENERAL CONSIDERATIONS

1. It is recommended for use with patients who are too heavy to lift or who cannot bear weight, who do not have excessive tone, or who are oriented and able to cooperate or follow instructions.
2. Arrange all items necessary for a smooth procedure—lifter, slings, wheelchair.
   - Place the wheelchair at either the head or the foot of the bed so that it is both parallel to it and about 3 feet away. The pivot wheels of the wheelchair should be in line with either the headboard or the footboard, leaving a radius in which to swing the horseshoe base of the lifter. Be sure that the wheelchair brakes are locked.
   - Move the lifter through the path over which the transfer will be made to ensure that no obstructions are present. Check to be sure that the horseshoe base is wide enough to straddle the wheelchair.

3. The patient should be slightly off center in the bed.
4. A second person should be available to assist initially.
5. In transferring the patient to a wheelchair or commode, always check to be sure that the brakes are locked before initiating the transfer.
6. Commode transfer: adjust the patient's clothing before moving the lifter to straddle the commode. Keep the chains taut to hold the patient in a comfortable sitting position.
7. Car transfer: use the straight bar instead of the V-swivel bar. Hook the chains short. The boom should be approximately at the level of the patient's chin when he or she is sitting on sling. Three- and 4-inch casters are available for low cars.
8. Slings are available in a one-piece seat and back or in two pieces. A commode seat can be obtained with either model. A head support extension is available with the one-piece model. The one-piece seat and back sling is safer to use for patients who lack shoulder girdle stability and the ability to hold onto the chains. It has the disadvantage of being bulky while the patient is sitting, whereas the back portion of the two-piece model may be removed.
9. Slings are available in three fabrics: canvas, nylon, and mesh. For transferring and sitting when the patient is fully clothed, the nylon material is slippery and hot to sit on. For showering and toileting, the nylon or mesh material is preferred because it dries quickly and is easiest to clean. The user may wish to obtain two sets of slings for maximum utility.

PATIENT AND FAMILY EDUCATION

1. Teach this procedure to the family for use at home.
2. Evaluate and reinforce the family's or caregiver's liability to use the lift safely.

PROCEDURE

Steps	*Additional Information*
1. Roll patient on side away from you.	
2. Place sling, folded halfway, under patient so that lower edge of seat is slightly below knees (like placing a draw sheet).	

Steps	*Additional Information*
3. Roll patient back to other side. Pull sling through.	Patient should be centered on canvas with lower edge right behind his or her knees.
4. If patient is in a hospital bed, it will help to roll up head of bed at this time.	
5. Attach open S-hooks of *shorter* portion of chains into holes on back; attach open S-hooks of *longer* part of chains into holes in seat.	S-hooks should be hooked all the way into holes, away from patient and toward outside of sling.
6. Move lifter so that open end of horseshoe base is under side of bed pointing toward center of patient.	
7. Hook closed S-hooks of chains into end of swivel bar.	They should be placed an equal distance from both sides. They must be hooked all the way into swivel bar.
8. Close release valve by turning knob gently to right.	It is advisable to have patient's arms outside chains if he or she is capable of hanging on.
9. Begin pumping hydraulic handle.	It is necessary to support patient's head until he or she has reached 45° sitting unless he or she has full neck control or neck support extension on sling.
10. Make any needed adjustment for patient's comfort and safety before raising patient clear of surface area.	Check that chains and S-hooks are properly positioned.
11. When patient's trunk has been lifted clear of bed, swing feet off bed.	Position patient's legs on either side of steering bar.
12. Grasp steering handles, and move patient away from bed.	
13. Move patient over wheelchair so that horseshoe base straddles wheelchair and patient's buttocks are touching back panel.	
14. Turn release valve slowly and gently to left to lower patient.	Guide patient's descent by pushing firmly on knees as he or she is being lowered so that correct sitting posture can be attained. Positioning is improved if knee pressure is sufficient to tip wheelchair backward slightly as patient's buttocks slide down back panel. Be cautious that boom of lifter does not descend and strike patient's head.
15. Before removing chains, check that correct sitting posture has been achieved.	Raise patient and reposition if necessary.
16. Detach S-hooks, remove chains, and move lifter away.	
17. Patient remains seated on sling. Make certain that sling is not wrinkled under patient.	
18. To return patient to bed, reverse this procedure.	Check carefully that S-hooks are not caught on wheelchair arms when patient is raised. Patient should be centered over bed after legs have been positioned on bed.

DOCUMENTATION

1. Document the type of transfer.
2. Note any special precautions, needs, or equipment.
3. Note any difficulty in completing the transfer.

4. Note any unusual occurrences.
5. Document the effectiveness of patient and family teaching.

Trans-aid Lift

PURPOSE

To provide safe and comfortable transfer of patients to and from a bed, cart, or wheelchair by means of a mechanical lifter.

STAFF RESPONSIBLE

EQUIPMENT

1. Slings (regular, with commode cut-out, or extra wide).
2. Trans-aid lifter (Figure 2-70).
3. Bed, cart, wheelchair, or commode.

GENERAL CONSIDERATIONS

1. Two persons (excluding the person being lifted) should be in attendance when doing a Trans-aid lift.
2. During a commode transfer, adjust the patient's clothing before moving the lifter to straddle the commode. Once the patient is in place on the commode, disconnect the wraparound leg flaps, and replace them when the patient is ready to transfer.
3. There are three different sizes of slings (regular, with commode cut-out, and extra wide). The sling for commode use (cut-out seat and wraparound leg flaps) is recommended for transferring patients with increased tone at any time.
4. Different types of Trans-aid lifters are available. One heavy-duty lifter will lift up to 600 pounds. The standard Trans-aid lifter will lift up to 400 pounds. A special lifter arm is available from the manufacturer that increases the height to which the patient can be lifted for cart to wheelchair transfers. All lifters can lift the patient from the floor.
5. A headrest attachment may be obtained and placed behind the patient's neck; each side is then hooked to the top links of the boom.
6. Malfunctions should be reported to the appropriate person (or manufacturer's representative). Do not use the lifter until repair has been made.
7. The base of the lifter is U shaped and designed to fit under low structures with only 4 ¾ inches clearance. For it to fit under most hospital beds, the bed should have casters.

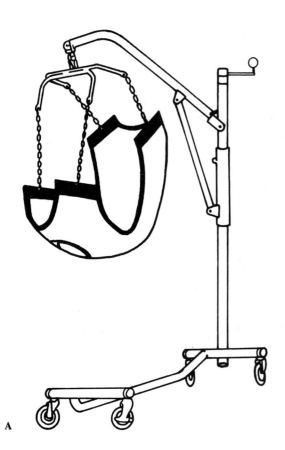

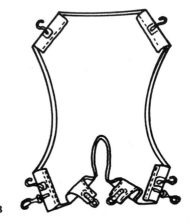

Figure 2-70 Trans-aid Lifter. (**A**) Lifter, (**B**) Slings. *Source:* Drawing prepared by Rehabilitation Institute of Chicago from literature distributed by Guardian, a division of Sunrise Medical, Arleta, CA. Used with permission.

8. Slings for the Trans-aid should be kept with the lifter when not in use. Additional slings for the Trans-aid may be ordered.
9. Trans-aid slings are to be washed daily with warm water and disinfectant, rinsed well, and air dried.
10. The Trans-aid sling is washed in the washer with hot water (140°F or hotter) and bleach after *each use* by patients who contaminate the sling with body secretions of any type (i.e., drainage that has soaked through a dressing, incontinency of urine, and the like).
11. By altering the number of chain links into which the canvas is hooked, the patient can be transferred in a 30° to 90° sitting position, which is ideal for someone using a recliner wheelchair.

PATIENT AND FAMILY EDUCATION

1. The physical therapist should complete the patient and family teaching before the patient and family perform car transfers with this lifter.
2. Teach the patient and family how to operate the lifter as soon as possible.

PROCEDURE

Steps	*Additional Information*
1. Place wheelchair at foot of bed, parallel to it and approximately 3 feet away.	Elevate footrests, or swing them to side.
2. Lock wheelchair.	An electric wheelchair should be turned off.
3. Move lifter through transfer path to ensure that no obstructions are present.	
4. Check that base is wide enough to straddle wheelchair.	
5. Obtain proper size sling.	
6. Roll patient onto his or her side and to side of bed.	
7. Identify top and bottom of canvas.	In the commode sling option, the top part is solid closed end, and bottom part is end with wraparound leg straps.
8. Place sling fan-folded lengthwise under patient as far as possible.	Top of sling should be at shoulder, hole at buttocks, and leg flaps slightly above knee.
9. Roll patient to his or her back, and pull sling through to opposite side.	Take care not to scratch or injure patient with metal hooks.
10. Center patient on sling.	
11. Wrap leg straps around patient's leg above knee and attach to snap hooks	This may be used for patient in whom spasticity or uncontrollable movements are *not* a problem.
or	
Connect leg straps going under adjacent leg and over opposite leg into snap hook.	This is preferred method for securing patient's leg when increased tone or uncontrollable movement is a problem.
12. Move lifter perpendicular to and under bed.	Be careful that boom does not hit patient. Shallow curve of boom should be toward patient's head and deep curve toward feet.
13. Connect each hook on sling to appropriate chain on boom.	Chain lengths may vary, but generally top hooks into fifth link of boom chain and bottom hooks into seventh link of boom chain. This will result in patient sitting at 90° during transfer.
14. Ensure that all hooks are satisfactorily in place and not pinching patient.	
15. Cross patient's arms inside sling apparatus.	Do this to avoid pinching patient's fingers or hands and to steady patient's body during transfer.
16. Support patient's head until he or she has reached 45° sitting angle if he or she has poor neck control.	
17. Raise patient by turning ball crank clockwise.	Put bed in its lowest position so that lift will clear bed.
18. Make any needed adjustments for patient's comfort and safety before moving patient clear of surface area.	

Steps	*Additional Information*
19. Swing patient's feet off the bed, and let them dangle freely. Position patient's feet and legs so that steering column is between patient's legs and patient's feet rest on baseboard.	This further increases patient's stability while in lifter.
20. Grasp steering handles, and move patient toward wheelchair. Stop when patient's buttocks touch back panel of wheelchair.	Base of lifter should straddle wheelchair.
21. One person behind wheelchair should grasp sling and hold patient's buttocks against back of wheelchair.	
22. A second person turns crank counterclockwise while simultaneously guiding the patient's descent.	Do this by pushing firmly on patient's knees as he or she is being lowered so that correct sitting position is attained. Use caution so that boom does not strike patient's head.
23. Check that correct sitting posture has been achieved.	Raise and reposition patient if necessary.
24. Detach hooks from chain on top and bottom, and carefully move lifter away.	
25. Unsnap rings of leg straps from snap hooks on both sides.	If patient is to remain on sling, disconnect leg fasteners to avoid thigh constriction.
26. Remove leg straps from under patient's legs. Push leg straps to side and back toward patient's buttocks.	
27. Lean patient forward, supporting his or her torso, and carefully remove sling.	
28. Reverse procedure to return patient to bed.	
29. Check that hooks are not caught on wheelchair when patient is raised by lifter and that safety strap is removed.	
30. Center patient over bed after his or her legs have been positioned on bed.	

DOCUMENTATION

1. Note the type of lifter.
2. Note any special sling sizes, precautions, needs, or equipment.
3. Document any unusual circumstances.
4. Document any difficulty completing the transfer.
5. Note the effectiveness of patient and family teaching.

Surgilift Transfer

PURPOSE

To transfer a patient safely by means of the Surgilift for bed or cart transfers or showers.

STAFF RESPONSIBLE

EQUIPMENT

1. Surgilift.
2. Surgilift netting.
3. Restraint straps (optional, as needed).

GENERAL CONSIDERATIONS

1. Use of the Surgilift permits safe transfer of a patient by one staff member and minimizes strain on personnel and the patient.
2. The Surgilift should not be used on patients with unstable spines while braces are off unless specific prescriptions are written by the physician.

3. Beds with casters removed do not permit Surgilift use because of low ground clearance.
4. The Surgilift safely carries 400 pounds. Surgilift netting should be monitored for wear on the straps and replaced when this becomes evident.
5. The spring locks on the Surgilift frame are designed to lock tighter the more weight that is placed on the netting.
6. Surgilift netting is washed daily. Wash with warm water and disinfectant, rinse well, and air dry.

7. Surgilift netting is washed in the washer with hot water (140°F) and bleach after each use by patients who contaminate the netting with body secretions of any type during use (i.e., drainage that has soaked through dressing, incontinence of urine, and the like).
8. Patients can be showered while on the Surgilift. Netting allows for washing, rinsing, and drying of back and legs.

PROCEDURE

Steps	Additional Information
1. Place patient's bed in flat position.	
2. Position patient to side of bed with head in position in which it will be on netting.	Try placing lifter over bed so that you can position patient such that lifter will fit around bed wheels and patient's head will be supported.
3. Fan-fold Surgilift netting, and place it under patient.	This can be done by rolling patient from side to side. Top of patient's head should be even with top end of netting.
4. Raise Surgilift frame to bed level by turning crank on side clockwise.	
5. Lift frame to vertical position.	
6. Slide wheels of Surgilift under bed while holding frame in vertical position.	
7. Gently lower frame over patient, encircling him or her.	Patients taller than 7 feet will be too long for frame. Their legs can be positioned so that they are supported with a pillow over top of frame, or they can be suspended in netting so that legs clear below frame.
8. Lift up latches of spring locks, and thread netting straps through them.	Secure locks by pressing down on latches when straps are all in place.
9. Place restraining straps if needed over patient (e.g., if patient is agitated, impulsive, spastic, or mobile).	*Do not* leave patient unattended on Surgilift.
10. Raise Surgilift by turning knob so that patient's trunk is high enough to clear bed.	Lower bed to lowest position to facilitate clearance.
11. Take patient to desired location.	
12. Reverse procedure to take patient off Surgilift.	

DOCUMENTATION

1. Document the type of transfer.
2. Note any unusual occurrences during the Surgilift procedure.
3. Note any special precautions, needs, or equipment.
4. Note any difficulties in completing the transfer.

BIBLIOGRAPHY

Agee, B.L., & Herman, C. (1984). Cervical logrolling on a standard hospital bed. *American Journal of Nursing, 84*, 314–318.

American Academy of Orthopaedic Surgeons. (1981). *Atlas of limb prosthetics: Surgical and prosthetic principles*. St. Louis, MO: Mosby.

Banerjee, S.N. (1982). *Rehabilitation management of amputees*. Baltimore, MD: Williams & Wilkins.

Bobath, B. (1978). *Adult hemiplegia: Evaluation and treatment* (2nd ed.). London: Heinemann Medical Books.

Browse, N.L. (1965). *The physiology and pathology of bedrest*. Springfield, IL: Thomas.

Carnevali, D., & Brueckner, S. (1970). Immobilization: Reassessment of a concept. *American Journal of Nursing, 70*, 1502–1507.

Carr, J., & Shepherd, R. (1983). *A motor relearning programme for stroke*. Rockville, MD: Aspen.

Engstrom, B., & Van De Ven, C. (1985). *Physiotherapy for amputees*. New York: Churchill Livingstone.

Gee, Z.L., & Passarella, P.M. (1978). Starting right. *American Journal of Nursing, 87*, 802–808.

Gee, Z.L., & Passarella, P.M. (1985). *Nursing care of the stroke patient*. Pittsburgh, PA: AREN.

Hanak, M., & Scott, A. (1983). *Spinal cord injury: An illustrated guide for health care professionals*. New York: Springer.

Hart, L.K., Reese, J.L., & Fearing, M.O. (1981). *Concepts common to acute illness*. St. Louis, MO: Mosby.

Jacobs, M.M., & Geels, W. (1984). *Signs and symptoms in nursing*. Philadelphia, PA: Lippincott.

Johnstone, M. (1976). *The stroke patient: Principles of rehabilitation*. Edinburgh: Churchill-Livingstone.

Johnstone, M. (1978). *Restoration of motor function of the stroke patient*. Edinburgh: Churchill-Livingstone.

Karacoloff, L.A. (1986). *Lower extremity amputation: A guide to functional outcomes in physical therapy management*. Rockville, MD: Aspen.

Kostiuk, J.P. (1981). *Amputation surgery and rehabilitation: The Toronto experience*. New York: Churchill-Livingstone.

Kovich, K.M., & Bermann, D.E. (1988). *Head injury: A guide to functional outcomes in occupational therapy*. Rockville, MD: Aspen.

Matthews, P.J., & Carlson, C.E. (1987). *Spinal cord injury: A guide to rehabilitation nursing*. Rockville, MD: Aspen.

Mueller, D.G. (1987). Clinical applications in spinal orthotics. *Topics in Acute Care and Trauma Rehabilitation, 1*, 48–61.

O'Brien, M.T., & Pallett, P.J. (1978). *Total care of the stroke patient*. Boston: Little, Brown & Company.

Olson, E.V. (1967). The hazards of immobility. *American Journal of Nursing, 67*, 780.

Pallett, P.J., & O'Brien, M.T. (1985). *Textbook of neurological nursing*. Boston: Little, Brown & Company.

Rehabilitation Institute of Chicago. (1978). *Pre-prosthetic care for above-knee amputees*. Chicago: Rehabilitation Institute of Chicago.

Rehabilitation Institute of Chicago. (1978). *Pre-prosthetic care for below-knee amputees*. Chicago: Rehabilitation Institute of Chicago.

Wu, Y., & Krick, H. (1987). Removable rigid dressing for below-knee amputees. *Clinical Prosthetics and Orthotics, 11*, 33–44.

Zejdlik, C.M. (1983). *Management of spinal cord injury*. Belmont, CA: Wadsworth.

chapter 3

Procedures To Establish and Maintain Elimination

INTRODUCTION

Patients with physical disability, bowel and bladder incontinence, or complicated bladder management routines can experience major impediments in their ability to work and socialize or to reenter the community life.

Management of the urinary tract may be one of the most significant factors in the patient's ability to function in his or her daily life and may profoundly affect his or her longevity. Urinary tract complications may lead to life-threatening situations in the patient with disability. An unmanaged bowel may cause the complications of constipation leading to impaction or incontinent bowel movements. With the help of skillful rehabilitation nurses, many of these problems can be prevented. The information in this chapter provides the nurse with current knowledge and techniques to avoid such problems. The following procedures should help establish simple, effective bladder programs and regular bowel habits.

The chapter is divided into two main sections: bowel elimination procedures and urinary elimination procedures. The bowel elimination procedures include establishing bowel programs, preventing complications, rectal digital stimulation techniques, and administration of suppositories. The urinary elimination procedures include establishing bladder programs, indwelling catheters, catheterizations, and home care procedures on preparation of solutions and disinfecting urinary equipment.

Aseptic technique is vital in the care of patients requiring bladder management. Effective hand-washing techniques before and after implementing each procedure are essential in prevention of iatrogenic complications. The goals of the elimination procedures are to:

1. prevent complications of the bowel and urinary tracts by
   - establishing programs for each patient that will minimize complications, and
   - carefully adhering to established guidelines for avoidance of complications (e.g., principles of asepsis) when carrying out these procedures.
2. establish bowel and bladder programs that will maximize the patient's ability to function in his or her chosen lifestyle.
3. promote the patient and primary caregiver's ability to facilitate the maintenance of a healthy bowel and urinary tract.

Establishing and Revising a Bowel Program

PURPOSE

To establish a reliable, safe, inexpensive, and convenient method of managing bowel evacuation or fecal incontinence. The goals of any bowel program include:

1. development of a method to establish regular bowel elimination and habit time;
2. management of fecal incontinence through establishment of fecal continence; and
3. assistance in development of positive patient self-esteem.

STAFF RESPONSIBLE

GENERAL CONSIDERATIONS

1. A bowel program utilizes a method of rectal stimulation: chemical stimulation (suppository administration) or mechanical stimulation (digital stimulation). Other methods utilized include diet, fluid, medications, activity level, and establishing a habit time.
2. Review the patient's past bowel habits:
   - frequency and pattern before disability,
   - use of laxatives and enemas,
   - fluid intake,
   - eating patterns and food preferences,
   - age and level of activity, and
   - gastrointestinal history (diarrhea, constipation, hemorrhoids, or diverticulitis).
3. Further, consider any present factors that affect regular bowel evacuation:
   - immobility or inactivity,
   - spinal precautions,
   - postural or tone abnormalities,
   - use of medications (stool softeners; laxatives; and medications causing sensitivity, diarrhea, or constipation; Table 3-1),
   - tube feeding schedule,
   - diet (ability to chew and swallow and volume of fluid taken in), and
   - present program or use of suppositories.

4. Assess the patient's ability to communicate the need to defecate. Level of sensory awareness and state of arousal must also be evaluated before a successful bowel program can be established.
5. The patient populations that can benefit from a regular bowel program include those with spinal cord injury, neuromuscular disease, traumatic brain injury, or cerebrovascular problems.
6. Precautions to be considered include the following:
   - Maintain spinal stability as appropriate for each individual patient, or work around postural tone abnormalities that prevent the patient from sitting upright at 90° angles.
   - Observe for signs and symptoms of autonomic dysreflexia in persons with spinal cord injury above T-6 and in some with traumatic brain injuries.
7. Bowel programs are developed in collaboration with the patient's attending physician as well as with the patient.
8. When initiating a program, start with a thorough assessment and the simplest yet most effective program for that patient. Patients with lower motor neuron lesions seem to respond best to a program with carbon dioxide suppository use or manual removal. Patients with upper motor neuron lesions may start with a daily bisacodyl suppository, advance to every other day use, and eventually substitute digital stimulation every other day. A glycerine suppository to provide local rectal irritation on a daily basis may be what is necessary for a patient with head injury or stroke.
9. Consider all aspects of the bowel program, including:
   - medications
     - —softeners
     - —laxatives
     - —suppositories
   - mechanical stimulation
     - —digital stimulation to relax rectal sphincter
     - —suppositories (most effective after meals when peristalsis is increased)
     - —diet and bulk intake
     - —fluid intake
     - —level of activity
     - —timing (establish a consistent time)
10. Review or familiarize yourself with suppositories and medications available at your institution or facility.
11. Consider the patient's stage of growth and development.
12. Enlist the support of the patient, family, and staff through education.
13. When making changes, change only one aspect of a program at a time and evaluate the change through three

Table 3-1 Suppositories and Medications Used for Bowel Programs in Patients with Spinal Cord Injury

Product	Action	Considerations
Laxatives		
Stimulant (contact laxative) Glycerine Bisacodyl	Acts on colonic mucosa to produce normal peristalsis through parasympathetic reflexes.	Very effective for initial bowel regulation for upper motor neuron lesion (reflex bowel); can be irritating to persons with rectal sensation.
Carbon dioxide evacuant	Acts by releasing carbon dioxide into rectum, stimulating peristalsis.	Expensive; may cause autonomic dysreflexia.
Medications		
Stool softeners Colace Surfax	Wetting agents that promote absorption of water and emulsifying fats.	Works well initially with Dulcolax suppository for patients with upper motor neuron lesion (reflex bowel).
Peristaltic stimulators Pericolace Doxidan Senecot (stimulator only)	Most are stool softeners and mild irritants that stimulate peristalsis.	Indicated initially for those with delayed response to bowel program.
Bulk formers Metamucil Fibermed	Dietary fibers that aid in absorbing water from intestinal contents and provide bulk.	Ensure adequate fluid intake. Effective with patients who have recurring problem of loose or semiformed stools and who are unable to get bulk from foods (i.e., on tube feedings).
Lactinex	Assist in reinstating normal gastrointestinal flora.	Indicated for persons with prolonged loose stools associated with antibiotic therapy.
Yogurt		

Source: From *Spinal Cord Injury: A Guide to Rehabilitation Nursing* (p. 113) by P.J. Matthews, C.E. Carlson, and N.B. Holt, 1987, Rockville, MD: Aspen Publishers, Inc. Copyright 1987 by Aspen Publishers, Inc.

or four administrations before making further changes. This approach allows for objective evaluation of the one component and of demonstrated consistency relating to the change.

14. Being consistent with time of suppository administration each day assists in establishing the pattern. Repeating the suppository if there are no results is important.

15. Always provide privacy for bowel procedures.

PATIENT AND FAMILY EDUCATION

Teach the patient and family:

1. basic gastrointestinal tract anatomy;
2. basic bowel physiology and pathophysiology as they relate to etiology or patient needs;
3. five basic aspects of good bowel function:
   - diet,
   - fluids,
   - activity,
   - medication (see Table 3-1), and
   - habit time.

Discuss the rationale for and choice of bowel program and explain the specifics. Discuss problem solving, and provide practice in problem solving.

PROCEDURE: ESTABLISHING A BOWEL PROGRAM

Steps	*Additional Information*
1. Complete nursing assessment.	Include rectal check to rule out impaction, and check consistency of stool. For patients with sensation or autonomic dysreflexic problems, consider use of anesthetic ointment to minimize discomfort.
2. Review factors influencing bowel program: diet, fluid, medications, and level of activity.	Identify problems, and implement appropriate action to correct as needed.
3. For patients with spinal cord injury, neuromuscular disease, or history of severe constipation or poor bowel	

Steps	Additional Information
results, begin with daily bisacodyl suppository, repeating application if there are no results in 30 to 60 minutes.	
4. Record results and evaluate patient response for three to four administrations.	When evaluating results, look for any emerging patterns (i.e., inconsistencies or lack of results). Program can be reviewed or revised when a consistent pattern is identified.

DOCUMENTATION

1. Document the results of the assessment.
2. Note all elements and the time of administration of the bowel program.
3. Note the patient and family education.
4. Document the results of the bowel program.
5. Note the patient's response to the program.

PROCEDURE: REVISING A BOWEL PROGRAM

Steps	Additional Information
1. Review bowel record, and identify patterns and results.	
2. Change only one aspect of bowel program at a time:	Allow 7 days or three to four administrations before making further changes.
• suppository frequency, *or*	
• number of suppositories, *or*	
• suppository type, *or*	
• diet (change to tube feeding, increase bulk, add prune juice or prunes as able), *or*	
• fluid volume, *or*	
• activity, *or*	
• medication.	
3. Upgrade program until:	
• fecal continence is achieved,	
• management of fecal incontinence is achieved, or	
• regular routine bowel elimination or habit time is established.	

DOCUMENTATION

1. Note any changes or adaptations in the nursing care plan as indicated.
2. Document the results and patient response.

Prevention and Control of Complications Related to Bowel Management

PURPOSE

To assist in the prevention of complications related to bowel management, or to reduce or eliminate complications related to bowel management. The complications to be addressed are constipation and impaction, diarrhea, hemorrhoids, delayed bowel program results, and autonomic dysreflexia.

STAFF RESPONSIBLE

EQUIPMENT

1. Bowel record or nursing admission or health history form.

GENERAL CONSIDERATIONS

1. Constipation is defined as the infrequent passage of hard stool. It is usually associated with straining or a feeling of fullness, distention, cramping, anorexia, and malaise. Occasional complaints of lower left quadrant tenderness may be present. If constipation is left untreated, it may result in impaction. Frequent problems with constipation may contribute to the development of hemorrhoids.
2. A decrease in activity level may help promote constipation. Keeping the person as active as possible (i.e., allowing regular participation in all activities of daily living and allowing for a regular exercise program) helps alleviate problems with constipation.
3. Some foods may cause constipation. Patients should be encouraged to experiment with their diet and to avoid foods that cause problems. Adhering to a regular bowel program will also assist in the prevention of constipation and other bowel complications.
4. Diarrhea is the frequent passage of watery stool. It may be accompanied by abdominal cramping. Infection, drug side effects, and dietary intake are a few of the causes of diarrhea.
5. Adhering to a regular bowel program will assist in the prevention of these complications.
6. Prevention of bowel complications includes patient education regarding choice of diet and fluid intake. Assisting patients with education relative to medication side effects is also helpful.
7. Adjust diet, fluid, medication, level of activity, and frequency of suppositories as needed for the individual patient.
8. Patient populations who may experience problems with bowel complications include elderly patients and those with spinal cord injuries, neuromuscular disease, and traumatic brain injury.

PATIENT AND FAMILY EDUCATION

Teach the patient and family:

1. the signs and causes of constipation and corrective action;
2. the signs and causes of impaction and corrective action;
3. the signs and causes of diarrhea and corrective action;
4. the signs and causes of hemorrhoids and corrective action;
5. methods to correct delayed results; and
6. the signs and causes of autonomic dysreflexia and corrective action.

PROCEDURES

Steps	Additional Information

Preventing Constipation

Steps	Additional Information
1. Complete nursing assessment to ascertain cause or causes of constipation. Investigate: • diet, • fluid intake, • decreased activity, • medication, • problems adhering to bowel program, • availability of primary caregiver, and • accessibility of bathroom.	
2. Adjust present program.	If there are no results from suppository program, repeat suppository in 30 to 60 minutes. If no results at that time or if results are small, repeat on next day. If stool is hard or if results take too long, add 4 to 6 oz of prune juice or four to six prunes to diet. Bran also may be needed as an addition to diet.
3. Consult physician about need to increase or start stool softener or laxative.	

Eliminating Fecal Impaction

1. Ascertain that problem being dealt with is indeed fecal impaction.

   Remember that leakage of watery stool around impaction may be interpreted as diarrhea rather than impaction. A kidney-ureter-bladder (KUB) x-ray is the best way to differentiate between these two complications when impaction is high in bowel. A KUB is not needed for low impaction.

2. Attempt to remove impaction with gloved and lubricated finger.

   Anesthetic ointment may be needed for decreasing noxious stimuli. Cardiac precautions may contraindicate this procedure.

3. If impaction is high up in bowel, consult physician for oral medications (e.g., bisacodyl tabs or magnesium citrate).

4. Use oil retention enema in combination with above to loosen stool.

5. Use tap water enema if there are no results from oil retention. Repeat until clear.

6. When problem is alleviated, adjust program to remove cause.

Controlling Diarrhea

1. Assess patient to ascertain cause or causes.

   Evaluate for factors that cause diarrhea, such as increased alcohol consumption, diet, or stool softeners. Perform rectal check to rule out impaction. Note fever because diarrhea may be caused by medical illness. Presence of diarrhea requires meticulous hygiene to prevent skin breakdown.

2. If diet is cause, remove offending foods or fluids.

3. If stool softeners are possible cause, request medication hold order from physician.

   Consult physician regarding adjusting medications or stool softener to achieve desired stool firmness or to treat medical illness.

4. Resume program after diarrhea is no longer an issue.

Management of Hemorrhoids

1. Assess patient for red, bulging areas inside and outside rectum, pain (if sensation is present), bleeding, and history or presence of constipation.

2. Consult with physician regarding treatment plan (may order such treatments as stool softeners, oil retention enema, sitz bath, ice, creams, and the like).

3. Correct and manage constipation if present.

4. Consult with physician regarding administration of mild laxative for short period of time.

5. Discourage straining and use of digital stimulation.

6. Return to previous program when flare-up is decreased. Include methods in program to manage or eliminate hard stool or constipation.

Methods To Correct Delayed Bowel Program Results

1. Any one or a combination of the following methods may correct delayed results:
   - Give suppository close to mealtime or in conjunction with hot or cold drink (mealtimes produce increased peristalsis; hot or cold drinks stimulate gastrocolic reflex to aid in evacuation).
   - Repeat digital stimulation frequently to relax rectal sphincter.
   - Repeat suppository to increase chemical stimulation of bowel.
   - Assist patient with abdominal massage (right to left) to increase peristalsis.
   - Assist patient to assume upright or squatting position (position patient on commode or in shower chair, or place patient's feet on stool and lean trunk forward).
   - Try using two suppositories as part of program.

Managing Autonomic Dysreflexia

1. See Chapter 6, protocol for prevention, identification, and treatment of autonomic dysreflexia.

DOCUMENTATION

1. Note the assessment, describe the complication (type and frequency), and document the patient's response.

2. Document notification of the physician.
3. Note any interventions and changes in the program.

Rectal Digital Stimulation

PURPOSE

To produce bowel evacuation through relaxation of the anal sphincter to produce reflex defecation.

STAFF RESPONSIBLE

EQUIPMENT

1. Water-soluble lubricant.
2. Incontinence pads.
3. Gloves, soap, water, and washcloth.
4. Medicinal lubricant as prescribed by physician.

GENERAL CONSIDERATIONS

1. Digital stimulation of the anal sphincter produces mechanical relaxation of the sphincter, which may produce a bowel evacuation, speed up the effect of a suppository, or

assist in complete bowel emptying. Digital stimulation also may precede suppository insertion to relax the anal sphincter and to aid in suppository administration.

2. If digital stimulation is used to facilitate the effect of a suppository, experience has shown that it is more effective to wait at least 15 minutes after suppository insertion to perform it. Digital stimulation may follow bowel evacuation to ensure complete emptying.

3. Digital stimulation is contraindicated in patients with a cardiac history and in whom there is indication of nausea and vomiting, abdominal pain, rectal bleeding, or increased sphincter spasticity.

4. Patients with sensation may find the procedure painful.

5. As with all bowel-related procedures, adhere to infection control practices and indications.

6. Further complications are present with spinal cord injury above T-6. If the patient is prone to autonomic dysreflexia, he or she should be observed for symptoms (e.g., sudden pounding headache, unexplained sweating, flushing, chills, or sudden increased blood pressure).

7. An anesthetic ointment can be used with patients who experience autonomic dysreflexia during digital stimula-

tion or if hemorrhoids or pain are a problem. Deep breathing may also help relieve discomfort.

8. Digital stimulation is also contraindicated in patients with a flaccid sphincter secondary to a lower motor neuron lesion because it is usually not effective in producing bowel results.

9. Digital stimulation can be performed with the patient side lying in bed or positioned on a commode chair or toilet. It is most effective, however, when the patient is in a sitting position to defecate because the stool evacuation is then aided by gravity.

PATIENT AND FAMILY EDUCATION

1. Teach the patient and family the basic general considerations.

2. Demonstrate the procedure, and then encourage a return demonstration.

3. Discuss the role of digital stimulation in the present bowel program.

4. Discuss the need to evaluate and problem solve. Provide practice situations.

PROCEDURE

Steps	*Additional Information*
1. Wash hands.	
2. Assist patient with transfer to toilet or commode chair, or place incontinence pads under side-lying patient in bed.	
3. Glove dominant hand, and lubricate index or middle finger.	
4. Locate anal opening, and insert index or middle finger to check for stool.	
5. If stool is present, gently remove it.	
6. Reapply lubricant if needed, and reinsert finger approximately ½ to 1 inch into anal opening.	
7. Gently rotate finger in circular motion against wall of anal sphincter for 30 seconds. May need to continue for 30 to 60 seconds and up to 2 minutes until sphincter relaxes.	Digital stimulation need not be continuous depending on amount of relaxation or defecation achieved.
8. Wait about 15 to 20 minutes for reflex peristalsis to produce bowel movement.	
9. If no bowel movement occurs, repeat digital stimulation or use suppository if these are the only elements in bowel program.	

DOCUMENTATION

1. Note the date, time, and method utilized, the time of evacuation, and the characteristics of the results.

2. Note the effectiveness and frequency of digital stimulation.

3. Note any complications or difficulties encountered during the procedure.

4. Document patient and caregiver education.

Rectal Suppository Administration

PURPOSE

To achieve proper insertion and placement of rectal suppository.

STAFF RESPONSIBLE

EQUIPMENT

1. Incontinence pads.
2. Commode chair or shower chair.
3. Gloves.
4. Water-soluble lubricant.
5. Glycerine suppository.
6. Bisacodyl suppository.
7. Other suppository.
8. Anesthetic ointment.

GENERAL CONSIDERATIONS

1. Administering the suppository with the patient positioned on the left side is ideal because anatomically it eases suppository insertion and maintains the suppository position in the bowel.
2. A lubricant may be necessary, especially if the patient experiences autonomic dysreflexia during administration. An anesthetic ointment may be prescribed in these cases or when the patient finds suppository insertion painful.

3. Generally, glycerine suppositories act mechanically to stimulate rectal mucosa, and bisacodyl suppositories act chemically to stimulate bowel movements. Familiarize yourself with the actions and uses of suppositories available in your facility. Obtain a medical order for suppository use.
4. Before administering any suppository, the nurse should assess the patient as outlined in the procedure for establishing a bowel program.
5. Use proper infection control guidelines: wash hands before and after the procedure, and dispose of all wastes according to infection control policy.
6. Observe patients who are prone to autonomic dysreflexia for symptoms of sudden onset of headache, flushing, chills, unexplained diaphoresis, or increase of blood pressure.
7. If patient complains of nausea, vomiting, severe abdominal pain, or other symptoms of bowel impactions or obstruction, or if rectal bleeding is noted, report to the physician or make appropriate changes in the bowel program as needed.

PATIENT AND FAMILY EDUCATION

Teach the patient and family:

1. the general considerations;
2. the role of the suppository in the bowel program and any side effects if the suppository is medicated; and
3. the basic procedure.

Obtain a return demonstration, and evaluate effectiveness and problem solving.

PROCEDURE

Steps	*Additional Information*
1. Wash hands.	
2. Prepare bed with incontinence pads. Place patient on *left* side with *right* top knee flexed.	This is to aid access to intestine.
3. Apply gloves. Unwrap suppository if necessary.	
4. Lubricate index or middle finger of dominant hand.	
5. Locate anal opening, and gently insert finger.	
6. If stool is present, remove only stool blocking anal opening.	
7. Assess need for additional lubrication or use of anesthetic ointment.	The carbon dioxide suppository should be activated by inserting the suppository in a cup of water until it starts to fizz. Do not lubricate suppository itself because this decreases its effectiveness.

Steps	*Additional Information*
8. Insert narrowest end of suppository into rectum. Turn suppository and place it along rectal wall as far up as possible, making certain that it is placed against wall of colon above sphincter and not embedded in stool.	The carbon dioxide suppository does not need to be placed against intestinal wall.
9. Allow 15 to 20 minutes to pass before performing digital stimulation or transferring patient to toilet (most suppositories work within 15 to 60 minutes of insertion; see product information).	
10. Cleanse patient.	
11. Dispose of all materials.	Use infection control procedures.

DOCUMENTATION

1. Note the time and date of suppository insertion, the time at which evacuation occurred, and the characteristics of the results (amount and consistency).

2. Note the effectiveness, time, and frequency of digital stimulation if used.

3. Document any complications or difficulties encountered during the procedure.

Enema Administration

PURPOSE

To introduce a solution into the colon to aid in stimulating peristalsis to promote bowel evacuation.

STAFF RESPONSIBLE

EQUIPMENT

1. Enema or enema kit.
2. Bedpan or commode.
3. Incontinence pads.
4. Toilet tissue.
5. Linen.
6. Lubricant.

GENERAL CONSIDERATIONS

1. A physician's order is generally needed to administer an enema and should include the type and amount of solution to instill.

2. Caution should be exercised if the patient has complained of nausea, vomiting, or abdominal pain or if the temperature or white blood cell count is elevated. The patient should be evaluated for signs and symptoms of impaction.

3. Before enema administration, thorough assessment of the patient's physical status, cardiac concerns, and bowel history is essential. Approximate recommended volume amounts that may be instilled are as follows:
   - adult, 500 to 1,000 mL;
   - child, 250 to 400 mL;
   - infant, 15 to 60 mL.

4. Large quantities of hypotonic solutions such as tap water can be absorbed through the bowel and cause water intoxication. Observe the patient for symptoms of weakness, pallor, vomiting, coughing, or dizziness.

5. Autonomic dysreflexia can be triggered by distention created by the enema solution.

6. Some patients with spinal cord injury may be unable to expel the enema solution.

PATIENT AND FAMILY EDUCATION

1. Teach the patient and family the general considerations and precautions.

2. Demonstrate the procedure, and obtain a return demonstration.

3. Discuss the role of the enema to treat constipation or impaction.

4. Evaluate effectiveness and problem solving.

PROCEDURE

Steps	*Additional Information*
1. Evaluate and assess patient and need for enema.	
2. Check or obtain physician order.	
3. Wash hands.	
4. Gather equipment. Prepare solutions as prescribed.	
5. Explain procedure and reason for enema administration to patient. Provide privacy.	
6. Position patient on left side with knees flexed, and prepare bed with incontinence pads and linens.	This is to aid access to intestine.
7. Locate rectal opening (anus), and gently insert lubricated tip.	
8. Encourage patient to take slow, deep breaths while liquid is being instilled.	
9. Remove tip from rectum when all liquid is instilled, and encourage patient to hold solution as long as possible (at least 10 to 15 minutes).	
10. Assist patient into safe and comfortable position to expel enema (toilet, commode, or bedpan).	
11. Observe amount, consistency, color, or unusual odor of returned enema.	
12. Clean patient, and reposition him or her in clean, safe, and comfortable environment.	
13. Dispose of all materials according to infection control guidelines.	

DOCUMENTATION

1. Note the date and time of enema administration, the time of evacuation, and the characteristics of the results.
2. Note the volume of contents expelled.
3. Document any complications or difficulties encountered during the procedure.

Removal of Fecal Impaction

PURPOSE

To remove stool manually from the bowel to promote evacuation, to treat or relieve impaction, or to clear the rectum before suppository insertion.

STAFF RESPONSIBLE

EQUIPMENT

1. Gloves.
2. Lubricant.
3. Incontinence pads.
4. Soap, water, washcloth, and towel.

GENERAL CONSIDERATIONS

1. The procedure must be performed gently to avoid injury to the bowel wall or to hemorrhoids, if present.
2. If the stool is high up in the intestine, a small oil retention enema may be used to help soften hard stool.
3. Prevention of constipation and impaction is the key to management.

PATIENT AND FAMILY EDUCATION

1. Teach the patient and family the general considerations as they apply.

2. Demonstrate, and obtain a return demonstration.
3. Discuss problem solving and follow up.
4. Discuss changes in the program to alleviate constipation or impaction.

PROCEDURE

Steps	Additional Information
1. Explain procedure.	
2. Place incontinence pads beneath patient.	
3. Position patient on left side.	This is to aid access to intestine.
4. Apply gloves.	
5. Lubricate index or middle finger.	
6. Insert gloved finger into patient's rectum.	
7. Remove any hardened stool gently and dispose of properly.	Dispose of all materials according to infection control guidelines.
8. Cleanse patient, and dry his or her skin.	

DOCUMENTATION

1. Note the date and time of the procedure, the amount of stool removed, and the characteristics of the results.

2. Document any complications or difficulties encountered during the procedure.

Intermittent Catheterization

PURPOSES

To provide complete and regular bladder drainage, either permanently or until reflex voiding is well established; to decrease trauma to the bladder and urethra associated with the use of an indwelling catheter; to prevent incontinence by combining intermittent catheterization with regulated fluid intake; to minimize the occurrence of urinary infections.

STAFF RESPONSIBLE

EQUIPMENT

1. Catheterization pack.
2. External catheter (optional).
3. Incontinence pads or panties (optional).
4. Measurement device to measure urine volume (if not in pack).
5. Disposable sterile gloves (nonsterile gloves for clean technique).
6. Syringe to deflate balloon of indwelling catheter (when appropriate).

GENERAL CONSIDERATIONS

1. The return of adequate reflex bladder activity is favorably influenced by the avoidance of overdistention and chronic infection, which can damage the neural and muscular elements of the bladder wall. Maintenance of a good blood supply to the bladder by avoiding increased pressures caused by bladder overdistention is thought to be a key factor in the prevention of urinary tract infection.
2. It is possible to decrease significantly the incidence of urinary infection by using sterile intermittent catheterization rather than an indwelling catheter. An indwelling catheter can provoke sepsis if it becomes obstructed and allows the bladder to overdistend markedly. Bladder overdistention is also thought to contribute to the development of vesicoureteral reflux. Infection also occurs if bacteria enter the bladder during catheterization and multiply because of prolonged intervals between catheterizations.

3. In the hospital, sterile intermittent catheterization is recommended to avoid introduction of bacteria into the bladder and cross-contamination of bacteria, especially resistant strains.
4. High residual urine volumes are thought to interfere with the antibacterial action of the bladder wall. Incomplete emptying of the bladder allows bacteria present to increase rapidly, whereas complete emptying of the bladder can help to eliminate bacteria and result in a sterile urine.
5. A physician's prescription is required when initiating or changing any individual's intermittent catheterization program.
6. Complications and related problems include the following:

- Bladder-sphincter dyssynergia (intravesical pressure not adequate to overcome resistance at bladder neck)—signs of bladder overdistention secondary to bladder-sphincter dyssynergia may indicate a need for immediate catheterization. Medication may be ordered to relax the bladder neck. The patient may need to continue on lifelong intermittent catheterizations, undergo surgical intervention, or have a Foley catheter inserted.

- Perineal or genital dermatitis—excoriation and rash experienced by some patients are primarily a result of the procedure used to apply and maintain the external catheter, the need for more frequent changing of incontinence devices, or poor hygiene. Prevention of incontinence in patients on long-term or permanent intermittent catheterization may require drug therapy to decrease incontinence.

- Hydronephrosis—hydronephrosis, which may develop with sterile urine and no overt symptoms, has been seen in patients who are catheter free. Obstruction, infection, reflux, and neurogenic factors can contribute to hydronephrosis (Shields, 1981). The threat of this complication is reduced when patients thoroughly understand and follow the bladder program. Close postdischarge follow up is indicated to prevent this condition. If hydronephrosis is detected, an alternate method of bladder drainage may be initiated (i.e., indwelling catheter or surgical intervention).

- Autonomic dysreflexia (hyperreflexia)—the symptoms may be caused by bladder distention or infection and may be seen for the first time when intermittent catheterization is started. This is a medical emergency and demands prompt evaluation and treatment (see Chapter 6, protocol for prevention, identification, and treatment of autonomic dysreflexia). Frequent episodes of dysreflexia may be severe enough to warrant discontinuing an intermittent catheterization program.

- Other reasons for unsuccessful intermittent catheterization programs include previously acquired urinary tract complications (periurethral abscess, penoscrotal fistula, strictures, and the like). Meticulous attention to indwelling catheter care from the start of the disability and early placement on intermittent catheterization programs may be keys to preventing these problems. A failure to develop spontaneous voiding, high residual urine volumes, lack of patient problem-solving abilities, and poor cooperation may also interfere with attempts to become catheter free.

- Decreasing manual dexterity in people with progressive disabilities and the inability to adjust to procedural routines may be contraindications to home catheterization programs. For patients who are dependent in self-catheterizations, postdischarge intermittent catheterization may be impractical if the caregiver's assistance is inadequate.

7. If incontinence between catheterizations interferes with activities, an external condom collecting device should be applied. An external device is not necessary for the individual who has not started to void. External condom collecting devices applied with fixatives on the penis itself (Crixiline strips, Freedom, Skin Bond, Urosan, and so forth) are considered only when postvoiding residual is done no more frequently than daily. When obtaining a postvoiding residual, a padded urinal can be propped for male patients to void into before catheterization. For female patients, sanitary pads, external catheters, or incontinence pants with liners may be used. When the goal is dryness, incontinence must be recorded and reported to the attending physician to maintain effective management of the pharmacologic regimen.

8. The program is started as early as possible to avoid complications associated with an indwelling catheter. The physician writes specific orders regarding fluids and catheterization schedule.

9. When voiding is completely absent, catheterizations are initially performed every 4 hours, day and night, and more often if bladder overdistention is observed. Ideally, catheterized urine volumes should not exceed bladder capacity (which may be as little as 100 to 200 mL). In the absence of data on bladder capacity, it is generally recommended that volumes not exceed 400 mL.

10. Some individuals may experience bladder overdistention at night and in the early morning. Individuals with lower-extremity paralysis may develop dependent edema during the day and then diurese when supine. If they do not void, bladder overdistention could occur. This may be minimized by doing one or more of the following:

- elevating the lower extremities periodically during the day;
- wearing support stockings;
- increasing the frequency of catheterizations during the night; or
- limiting or eliminating fluids early in the evening and throughout the night.

11. Medical assessments (Table 3-2) are recommended for patients with neurogenic bladders. Intravenous pyelography (IVP) and measurements of serum creatinine and blood urea nitrogen are used to evaluate kidney function. IVP should be done during the first admission and every 6 to 12 months after discharge. After baseline IVP, renal ultrasonography may be used for follow up. Voiding cystourethrography (VCG) is used to assess bladder capacity, reflux, reflex voiding, and sensation for distention. Urodynamics procedures assess the bladder-urethral pressure profile; findings are used to diagnose detrusor-sphincter dyssynergy. The physician determines the appropriateness of diagnostic tests. There is some controversy surrounding the criteria and timing of performing VCG and measuring urodynamics.

12. When monitoring the patient for spontaneous voiding, it is sometimes found that patients with normally flaccid bladders may urinate a small amount. If the patient is catheterized after a small void and if the volume of the catheterization is high, it is likely that the patient did not have a true void. This is considered an overflow incontinence.

13. Initially it may be helpful to structure the program by instructing the patient to drink a specific amount every hour or two. At the start of the program, fluids may be restricted after 8 or 9 p.m. (except small amounts) to avoid bladder overdistention. After a patient begins to void spontaneously, fluid restrictions can be liberalized or eliminated if bladder distention does not occur. If the patient does not have spontaneous voids and is to be on long-term intermittent catheterization, experimentation with fluid intake and catheterization schedule to provide flexibility is advised.

14. The parasympathetic nervous system is primarily responsible for bladder emptying, and drugs that stimulate or inhibit this system can be used either to aid weak bladder contractions or to decrease overactivity of bladder contractions. Urecholine (bethanechol chloride) has probably been the most widely used cholinergic drug to increase bladder contraction. *Caution is necessary because reflux of urine can occur if dyssynergia is present.* Anticholinergic drugs, such as pro-Banthine and Ditropan, have been used for patients with uncontrolled bladder contractions and incontinence. They are particularly important in female patients who are incontinent. The sympathetic nervous system influences the bladder neck (internal sphincter region), and drugs that modify internal sphincter resistance can be used to decrease resistance to

Table 3-2 Common Tests for Assessing Urinary Tract Function

Test	Purpose	Procedure
Intravenous Pyelogram (IVP)	To demonstrate kidney function and rule out stones, obstructions, stenosis. Recommended every year (every 6 mos. for high risk).	Contrast dye administered IV followed by serial x-rays as dye is excreted. Requires bowel prep prior to procedure.
Renal Ultrasound	As above. May be used in place of follow-up IVP. Ideally, patient should have a baseline IVP initially.	Noninvasive. Requires bowel prep prior to procedure.
Cystourethrogram	To assess bladder capacity, reflux, reflex voiding, and sensation for distention.	Indwelling catheter is placed. Dye is instilled into bladder. X-ray is taken and catheter is removed and patient tries to void.
Urodynamics	To assess bladder-urethral pressure profile and diagnose detrusor-sphincter dyssynergy.	Indwelling catheter is placed. Fluid is instilled into bladder and sensor placed to detect detrusor pressure and sphincter contraction.
Serum Creatinine	Normal value: .5–1.0.	Blood drawn.
Blood Urea Nitrogen	Normal value: 10–20.	Blood drawn.
Urinalysis	To determine presence and amount of bacteria, glucose, blood, protein in urine.	Random sample of urine. Does not have to be sterile.
Culture and Sensitivity	To determine type of bacteria and its sensitivity to antibiotics.	Requires sterile specimen either through aspiration from indwelling catheter, sterile catheterization, or midstream void.

Source: From *Spinal Cord Injury: A Guide to Rehabilitation Nursing* (p. 103) by P.J. Matthews, C.E. Carlson, and N.B. Holt, 1987, Rockville, MD: Aspen Publishers, Inc. Copyright 1987 by Aspen Publishers, Inc.

urine outflow, which can help combat urine retention. Therefore, sympatholytic drugs such as Dibenzyline may decrease resistance at the bladder neck and contribute to more complete emptying. Drugs affecting the autonomic nervous system can have serious side effects. Patient and family education and close monitoring of patient response are of primary import.

15. A clean intermittent catheterization procedure is frequently recommended for use after discharge. Use of clean technique in the hospital remains controversial.

PATIENT AND FAMILY EDUCATION

1. For successful outcomes, the patient must participate fully in the program. Initiation of the program, fluid restrictions, action and side effects of medications, frequency of catheterization, progress, and termination of the program must be thoroughly explained to the patient and family. The attending physician and nurse are responsible for the initial explanation of the program and goal identification.
2. If injury to the spinal cord is above T-6, the patient or caregiver is taught about the possibility of autonomic dysreflexia before beginning on an intermittent catheterization program.
3. Before discharge, the patient or caregiver must understand the importance of routine reevaluation.
4. A home health referral is usually indicated to assist with community adjustment to the program and to provide reinforcement.
5. Clean intermittent catheterization is generally recommended for home use. This can be taught for use on weekend passes, or it could be taught and practiced shortly before discharge.

PROCEDURE

Steps

Additional Information

1. Nursing assessment includes the following:
   - type of neurogenic bladder (reflexic or areflexic);

A reflexic bladder results with lesions above the sacral spinal cord segments. Reflex voiding with varying degrees of residual urine occurs.

Steps	*Additional Information*
	An areflexic bladder results from lesions in the sacral reflex center or in the spinal roots. This type of bladder is characterized by retention of urine with bladder overdistention. Areflexic bladders can occur during spinal shock.
• sensation for distention; • sensation for voiding; • history of dysreflexia;	If patient has frequent episodes of dysreflexia from bladder-related causes and if small volumes trigger episodes, he or she may not be a good candidate for intermittent catheterization.
• condition of urinary meatus and external genitalia (discharge, skin irritation, potential problems with fitting of external catheter); • pattern and adequacy of fluid intake and pattern of output, with particular attention to patterns of sudden diuresis (see general considerations 9); • medication (urologic, other); • concurrent medical conditions (e.g., infection, renal disease, hydration status, electrolyte imbalance); and • patient and caregiver problem-solving ability, motivation, cognitive status, and knowledge of urinary system and intermittent catheterization program.	Some patients are unable to restrict their fluids because of concurrent medical problems or excessive thirst. These patients may not be good candidates at this time. Patients and caregivers who are poorly motivated, unreliable, or poor problem solvers may not be good candidates for this program.
2. Physician writes an order to begin program, including frequency of catheterizations and fluid restrictions.	Physician's order is required to alter frequency of catheterizations and fluid restriction.
3. Instruct patient in purpose of program, frequency of catheterizations, and fluid restrictions. Also instruct patient in monitoring for voids. Patient is to notify nurse if he or she voids or feels distended.	Some patients may have normal sensation for distention and voids. Other patients may notice subtle sensations (i.e., flushing, tingling, goosebumps). Still others will not have any sensation.
4. Catheterize patient at prescribed frequency. If patient has spontaneous void, catheterize immediately to obtain postvoid residual.	
5. Document all spontaneous voids and catheterization volumes. Note time of each event.	
6. Reinforce that patient must request fluids at appropriate intervals.	It is important that patient and caregiver begin to take responsibility for program well before discharge.
7. Monitor catheterization volumes and notify physician if: • volumes are too high,	Patient may need to decrease fluids or to increase frequency of catheterizations. Overdistention is thought to contribute to infections and vesicoureteral reflux and interferes with reflex activity.
• volumes are too low, or	Patient may need to increase fluids or to decrease frequency of catheterizations. Patient will need adequate volume to trigger void if reflex activity is present.
• patient is having spontaneous voids with low postvoid residuals.	If patient is voiding and if catheterization volumes never exceed 300 to 400 mL, he or she no longer needs fluid restriction. If postvoid residuals are consistently low, program may be discontinued with occasional checking of postvoid residuals.
8. If patient is having spontaneous voids: • obtain and apply external catheter, or • attempt to stimulate voids at regular intervals and before catheterizations.	See procedure on external catheters. See procedure on methods to stimulate voids.

Steps	*Additional Information*
9. Well before discharge, assess appropriateness of program for home.	Adequate resources must exist for patients to be considered safe with an intermittent catheterization program at home (i.e., independent with procedure; adequate caregivers, supplies, problem-solving abilities).
10. If patient will be catheterized at least every 6 hours, teach patient and caregiver clean catheterization technique for home use. Obtain physician order to begin this program.	Sterile self-catheterization for home use is expensive. Clean intermittent catheterization is easier to perform and maintain in routines of daily living at home. Clean intermittent catheterization has been found to be safe in home environment.

DOCUMENTATION

1. Record all urine measurements. It may be helpful to keep a flow sheet at the bedside for this purpose.
2. It is important that voiding between catheterizations be recorded. Note the time and amount.
3. Document all patient and caregiver education regarding the program.
4. Document when the program starts and when changes occur. Inability to comply with the program is significant and should be documented.

Establishing Bladder Programs for Patients with Brain Damage

PURPOSES

To eliminate the use of indwelling catheters; to avoid catheter-related complications; to achieve urinary continence through scheduled voidings and fluid restrictions if needed; to promote the individual's self-esteem.

STAFF RESPONSIBLE

EQUIPMENT

1. Commode chair, bedpan, toilet, or raised toilet seat.
2. Incontinence pads or briefs or external catheters.
3. Adaptive clothing and equipment.

GENERAL CONSIDERATIONS

1. Voluntary inhibition of the micturition (voiding) reflex is mediated through the influence of the midbrain and other centers of the brain. These centers inhibit bladder contractions and facilitate relaxation of the external urinary sphincter and pelvic floor to allow bladder emptying. Since bladder function in the cerebral cortex is bilateral, patients with unilateral injury generally have successful bladder retraining (O'Brien & Pallett, 1978).

2. A brain lesion that disrupts the inhibitory centers can result in frequent, uninhibited bladder contractions (uninhibited bladder). Urinary frequency, urgency, and incontinence are symptoms of this condition. Bilateral brain damage may result in loss of voluntary micturition.
3. Most patients with brain damage from a stroke can be continent of urine because bladder emptying is possible: the sacral reflex arc remains intact, and there is at least partial sensation of bladder filling along with partial voluntary control of bladder emptying.
4. Other factors contributing to incontinence after brain damage include:
   - impaired sensory feedback,
   - impaired motor ability,
   - impaired cognition, and
   - impaired communication or organic problems such as urinary tract infection, changes due to aging, disease, or trauma.
5. Before implementing bladder programs, the nurse assesses the patient to determine the etiology of the bladder incontinence. Assessments of present voiding patterns, factors contributing to incontinence, appropriateness of toileting schedule, and appropriateness of present bladder program are important in identifying any limiting factors. Bladder toileting programs are based on the etiology of incontinence, the data base obtained through assessment, and the goals of patient care.
6. Once the program is established, communication to the nursing staff (by means of the nursing care plan and

incontinence flow sheet), physician, patient, family, and interdisciplinary team is essential for its success.

7. The incontinence flow sheet is a worksheet for assessing the pattern of incontinence and fluid intake and factors contributing to incontinence and for monitoring the effectiveness of a toileting program.

8. Initial goals of bladder programs are usually very modest (i.e., daytime continence). External catheters or incontinence briefs or pads may be utilized through the night.

9. It is important to provide privacy for urinary elimination. Consideration of the patient's self-esteem and dignity is essential to a successful program, along with consideration of the toileting facility to be utilized and the position of the patient for voiding.

10. Consultation with the occupational therapy department may be needed to assist with the fabrication of adaptive clothing. Velcro closures, zipper pulls, or hooks may be useful.

11. Generally speaking, if an indwelling catheter has been in place for several months, a urinary system evaluation may be ordered by the physician.

12. If pharmacologic management is necessary to improve bladder tone, the patient should be observed for medication effect on the program and for side effects.

13. Meticulous skin care is needed to prevent perineal skin irritation related to incontinence.

14. Constipation can contribute to urinary incontinence. Assess and treat constipation.

PATIENT AND FAMILY EDUCATION

1. Teach the patient and family the general considerations as they apply to the patient, inclusive of basic anatomy and physiology.

2. Teach the goals of the bladder program.

3. Explain the present program, responsibilities for the program, and the use of the incontinence flow sheet.

4. Evaluate the program's effectiveness and the patient's problem-solving skills.

5. Note the care of equipment if used.

PROCEDURE

Steps	*Additional Information*
1. Obtain history of incontinence from patient or family members. Assess: • ability to communicate bladder fullness, • awareness of sensation of fullness, • frequency of incontinence, and • sensation of urgency.	Initial assessment of present bladder function is important to any retraining program. A 24-hour record of fluid intake and output provides baseline data.
2. Initiate recording of intake and output.	
3. Place call light within reach, and instruct patient in use.	If patient is aphasic, develop system to communicate need to toilet. Place commode near bed if urgency is severe.
4. Initiate incontinence flow sheet (Exhibit 3-1), and indicate bladder program, goals, and fluid and toileting directions.	Flow sheet can be used to assess pattern of incontinence if patient is not on a bladder program or effectiveness of current bladder program. Notify patient, family, and appropriate interdisciplinary staff.
5. To use flow sheet: • Chart fluid and toileting amounts in measured volumes in proper cells and columns. Estimate volume of incontinence on basis of following amounts: small, 50 to 100 mL; medium, 100 to 175 mL; large, more than 200 mL.	Knowledge of relationship between amount of fluid taken in and voiding intervals will assist when developing bladder program. If there is no void when patient is toileted, toilet patient 1 hour later. Toilet time or prompt is specified time from the last void. For example, patient may drink small amount of fluids and be incontinent in 30 to 40 minutes, or patient may drink 400 mL with incontinence 2 hours later. Toileting needs will vary in these situations.
• Use comments section or mentation column to indicate patient's mental status, location of patient, or other circumstances under which incontinence occurred.	Knowledge of patient's mental status or level of awareness and location at time of incontinence will assist in progressing or developing plan.
• Indicate in comments section if incontinence occurred off nursing unit, in bed, on the way to toilet, and so on.	Knowledge of patient position may be helpful; for example, in supine position it is difficult to relax perineal muscles com-

Exhibit 3-1 Incontinence Flow Sheet

	DATE: 12/13/85				DATE:				DATE:				DATE:				DATE:				
	FLUID INTAKE	TOILETED AMOUNT	INCONTINENT AMOUNT	MENTATION	FLUID INTAKE	TOILETED AMOUNT	INCONTINENT AMOUNT	MENTATION	FLUID INTAKE	TOILETED AMOUNT	INCONTINENT AMOUNT	MENTATION	FLUID INTAKE	TOILETED AMOUNT	INCONTINENT AMOUNT	MENTATION	FLUID INTAKE	TOILETED AMOUNT	INCONTINENT AMOUNT	MENTATION	
8-9a	250																					
9-10a		100																				
10-11a	100																					
11-12a		0																				
12-1p	300																					
1-2p		300																				
2-3p	150																					
3-4p		0																				
4-5p	250																					
5-6p		100																				
6-7p	100																					
7-8p		300																				
8-9p	150																					
9-10p		0																				
10-11p																						
12-1a																						
1-2a	50	200		0																		
2-3a																						
3-4a																						
4-5a			approx 100	S/A																		
5-6a																						
6-7a																						
7-8a	50	0																				

COMMENTS:
Include cath time and amts.
coffee in a.m. & at dinner
does not drink a lot of fluids
requested toileting at 1 a.m.
incontinent at 4:30 a.m.

COMMENTS:
Include cath time and amts.

COMMENTS:
Include cath time and amts.

COMMENTS:
Include cath time and amts.

COMMENTS:
Include cath time and amts.

JOHN DOE
DR. P. BROWN
Rehabilitation Institute of Chicago
Division of Nursing

INCONTINENCE FLOW SHEET

PRESENT PROGRAM (include MD's order for caths if no void in a specific time):

Toilet every 2 hours during day
Toilet every 4 hours during night
No fluid restrictions
Push Fluids!!

KEY

Fluid Intake = amount in cc's
Toileted Amount = amount in cc's, indicate 0 if no void

Mentation = C - Confused
S - Sleeping
O - Oriented
A - Aware Wet

Source: Courtesy of Division of Nursing, Rehabilitation Institute of Chicago.

Steps	*Additional Information*
	pletely. This may result in incomplete emptying. Privacy is important for many patients for complete bladder emptying. Patients may be incontinent when in unfamiliar environments.
• Indicate in comments section any unusual occurrences (i.e., frequency, urgency, burning).	Urinary infection contributes to urgency and frequency.
6. Assess baseline data on incontinence flow sheet for patterns.	Pattern is usually noted in 2 to 3 days but may take longer. Toileting schedule *must* be consistent. If pattern is obscure, offer toileting every 2 hours (or prompt patient).
7. Revise toileting frequency on basis of patterns of incontinence observed.	If patient has frequent periods of dryness, increase intervals between toileting and evaluate. Decrease intervals to 1 hour if incontinence has not improved. Advance to establishing voiding pattern by offering toileting at key times: in early morning, before and after meals, before scheduled therapies, before rest periods, or at bed time. Nighttime toileting with restricted fluids may be scheduled for every 3 to 4 hours.
8. Review findings with physician.	If medications are ordered to treat urinary tract infection, urgency, or frequency, evaluate effectiveness and for side effects. Continue use of flow sheet for evaluation.
9. Review total fluid intake for adequacy, and evaluate need for restriction of fluids.	Establish fluid schedule every 2 hours if there is no clear incontinence pattern or if patient intake is poor. If incontinence occurs through night and if medical condition allows, restrict amount of fluids after 8 p.m. Limiting fluids at night is not indicated if patient is dehydrated or if other medical condition contraindicates. Eventually, most patients do not need strict fluid schedule.
10. Consider use of behavioral intervention program if timed fluids, toileting, and medication are ineffective.	Behavioral programs are individualized and somewhat complex. Refer to McCormick, Scheve, and Leahy (1988) for extensive references.

DOCUMENTATION

1. Document the amount, frequency, and circumstances related to incontinence, intake, and output.
2. Document your evaluation of emerging patterns of incontinence and of progress toward goals.
3. Document the patient and family response to the program.

4. Document the elements of the plan to control incontinence and to achieve continence: goals, fluids (type, amount, and frequency), toileting frequency, prompts (cueing, if used), and protective devices or clothing used.

Methods To Stimulate Voiding and To Empty the Bladder in Patients with Spinal Cord Injuries

PURPOSE

To initiate voiding or to empty the bladder in the patient with spinal cord injury.

STAFF RESPONSIBLE

EQUIPMENT

1. Nonsterile gloves.
2. Water-soluble lubricant (for anal stretch).

GENERAL CONSIDERATIONS

1. Methods of stimulation should *not* be used if the patient has detrusor-sphincter dyssynergia because it could cause reflux of urine into the ureters and kidney.

2. Urodynamic studies should be performed to evaluate the effects of Credé and Valsalva maneuvers, abdominal tapping, and anal stretch techniques.
3. Anal stretch is used with patients with complete spinal cord lesions above the sacral segments or with a reflex neurogenic bladder.
4. Anal stretch requires a physician's orders.
5. When using anal stretch, the patient may also need to do Credé or Valsalva maneuvers to empty the bladder because anal stretch inhibits detrusor and urethral sphincter contractions (Matthews, 1987).
6. Credé and Valsalva maneuvers may be effective for patients with lower motor neuron lesions that have resulted in an areflexic bladder. To avoid vesicoureteral reflux, detrusor-sphincter dyssynergia should be ruled out or voiding should be initiated before using Credé maneuver.
7. Credé maneuver requires a physician's order.
8. For more information about types of bladder dysfunction, see Matthews (1987).

PATIENT AND FAMILY EDUCATION

1. Education should include the purpose of the procedure, the proper technique to stimulate voiding, measuring the effectiveness of the technique, and any possible complications.
2. Whenever possible, involve the patient and family in the procedure.

PROCEDURES

Steps	*Additional Information*

Anal Stretch

1. Obtain physician's order.

This procedure may cause vesicoureteral reflux in patients with detrusor-sphincter dyssynergia.

2. Explain purpose and procedure to patient. Provide privacy.
3. Position patient comfortably on side or on toilet.
4. Don glove, and lubricate index and middle fingers.
5. Insert first one then two fingers gently into rectum (Figure 3-1A).

Go only as far as necessary to stretch anal sphincter (usually about 3 cm).

6. Spread fingers apart (Figure 3-1B).

If patient begins to void, have him or her perform Valsalva or Credé maneuver to increase intra-abdominal pressure to facilitate emptying.

7. Withdraw fingers gently once voiding is complete.
8. Clean patient, and make him or her comfortable.
9. Catheterize for residual urine as ordered by physician.

Observe for signs and symptoms of autonomic dysreflexia.
Assess for bowel movement.
Dispose of soiled materials according to infection control procedures.

10. Document according to guidelines.

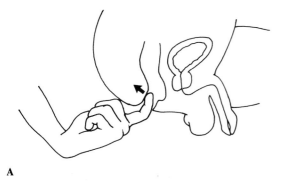

A

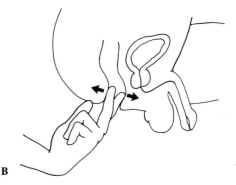

B

Figure 3-1 Procedure for Anal Stretch. *Source:* From "Sphincter Stretch: New Technique Resulting in Continence and Complete Voiding in Paraplegics" by Kiviat, Zimmermann, and Donovan, 1975, *Journal of Urology, 114*, pp. 895–897. Copyright 1975 by Williams & Wilkins Company. Reprinted by permission.

Steps	*Additional Information*

Credé Maneuver

1. Obtain physician's order.	This procedure may cause vesicoureteral reflux in patients with detrusor-sphincter dyssynergia.
2. Explain purpose and procedure to patient. Provide privacy.	Patient may be positioned in Fowler's position in bed or seated on toilet or commode.
3. Place hands flat against patient's abdomen lateral to and below umbilicus.	
4. With hands, use firm downward and medial stroke toward bladder, then press with both hands directly over bladder.	This will manually express urine from bladder.
5. Repeat several times.	
6. Catheterize for residual urine if ordered by physician.	
7. Return patient to comfortable position and appropriate dress.	
8. Document according to guidelines.	

Valsalva Maneuver

1. Explain purpose and procedure to patient. Provide privacy.	Patient may be positioned in Fowler's position in bed or seated on toilet or commode.
2. Instruct patient to hold breath while straining to urinate and move bowels.	
3. Repeat several times.	
4. Catheterize for residual urine if ordered by physician.	
5. Document according to guidelines.	

Other Techniques for Patients with Automatic Reflex Bladders

1. Explain purpose and procedure to patient. Provide privacy.	See Shields (1981) for further information about other techniques.
2. Tap with fingers over patient's suprapubic region for 2 to 3 minutes (about 50 taps). If ineffective, stop and wait 1 minute.	
3. Try stroking medial thigh in area along adductor magnus for 2 to 3 minutes. If ineffective, stop and wait 1 minute.	
4. Try pinching abdomen above inguinal ligaments for 2 to 3 minutes. If ineffective, stop and wait 1 minute.	
5. Try pulling patient's pubic hair for 2 to 3 minutes. If ineffective, stop and wait 1 minute.	
6. Try massaging the male patient's penoscrotal area. If ineffective, stop and wait 1 minute.	
7. Try pinching posterior aspect of male patient's glans penis for 2 to 3 minutes. If ineffective, stop.	
8. Catheterize for residual urine if ordered by physician.	
9. Document according to guidelines.	

DOCUMENTATION

1. Document the procedure, the effectiveness of the techniques, the most successful methods to stimulate voiding or to empty the bladder, the amount voided, and the type of catheterization.

2. Document any complications or unusual observations.

3. Document patient and primary caregiver education and involvement in the procedure.

Male External Catheter Application and Removal

PURPOSES

To apply an external catheter to a male patient for urine collection; to remove the catheter without injury to the patient.

STAFF RESPONSIBLE

EQUIPMENT

Choice of External Appliance and Fixative

See local/national manufacturers for available appliances and fixatives.

For All Appliances

1. Soap, water, and towel.
2. Leg bag for night drainage.
3. Drainage bag.
4. Extension tubing.
5. Nonsterile gloves.

GENERAL CONSIDERATIONS

1. It is recommended that an external catheter is changed at least once every 24 hours until patient tolerance has developed. With proper supervision, some external catheters have been worn safely for longer periods of time. The catheter should be left off to allow the skin to air for an hour or so between changes.
2. External catheters can be removed at night for patients who are prone to skin problems. A urinal may be positioned in place with the rim padded. The care plan should indicate this intervention and include frequent skin checks. If urinal positioning is not possible because of increased tone, incontinence briefs or pads can be used instead.

3. A check on patients who are dependent in application or who require supervision at least once a shift ensures that the external catheter is not applied too tightly or becomes too tight over time. Patients who are independent are taught to perform self-checks.
4. External catheters are *not* to be applied over red or broken skin areas. If possible, the catheter is to be applied distal to the open area. A Crixiline strip may be applied over the open area to provide a waterproof barrier and to assist in healing, and the external catheter can be applied over this strip. If neither option is available, the external catheter is not worn. A pad or incontinence briefs with proper skin care can be used to manage the incontinence.
5. If applied to an erect penis, external catheters should not be applied tightly. Clipping the ring that forms at the top of the condom will prevent a tourniquet effect if the patient experiences frequent or prolonged erections.
6. A foreskin that is not pulled forward over the glans penis may act as a tourniquet when the patient has an erection.
7. Decisions regarding the type of external catheter and fixative are to be made by the nurse, and directions must be written in the nursing care plan. Sample options are shown in Tables 3-3 and 3-4. The following assessments are to be made before this decision:

    - cost of the external catheter and fixative, considering reusability;
    - frequency of removal (i.e., for intermittent catheterizations);
    - ease of application and construction for the person who will usually apply the device;
    - penis size (flaccid and erect);
    - reaction to a skin patch test with fixatives before routine use to rule out sensitivity;
    - degree of sensation;
    - patient's cognitive status;
    - frequency and duration of erections;
    - activity level, including positions assumed throughout the day;
    - previous use, success, and problems;
    - availability of the external catheter when the patient is outside the hospital; and
    - type of drainage tubing and bag to be used.
8. Different fixatives may be combined. Try fixatives, one at a time, starting with the simplest and least expensive first. The patient should be monitored at least every shift each time the type of external catheter or fixative is altered until tolerance and appropriateness are determined. No addi-

Table 3-3 Sample Product Options for Male External Catheters

Type of External Catheter	Sizes	Considerations
Bardic Urosheath	Small, medium, and large	Rigid; no expansion; reusable; very durable; firm base that prevents twisting. Clean by washing with soap and water and rinsing thoroughly.
Condom with Latex tubing	One size	Disposable; parts can be reused with a new condom. Tubing can be cut to custom length for drainage. Be sure that a drainage hole is made in condom. (See Figure 3-2.)
Condom with Texas or similar adaptor	One size	Disposable; parts can be reused with a new condom. Be sure that a drainage hole is made in condom.
Gizmo	Standard and small	Reusable with Crixiline tape or Posey strap. Bulb at base prevents twisting.
Hollister self-adhesive catheter and other devices	Standard, medium, pediatric, geriatric	Disposable; design prevents kinking and twisting; sheath contains nonirritating adhesive inside; long wear time. Retracted penis pouch and reusable external device are available.
Mentor Freedom	Medium and standard	No adhesive required because fixative is already applied to sheath. Recommended for use with retractable penis. A protective skin dressing can be used before application provided that it is allowed to dry completely. Not recommended if external catheter needs to be changed more than twice a day.
Texas prepackaged	One size	Disposable; parts should be saved and reused with a new condom to reduce cost.
Uri-Drain	Standard, pediatric, and geriatric	Reusable if used with Crixiline strips or Posey strap. Firm base prevents twisting.
Urosan	Standard and small	Disposable; one-time use only. Do not use if external catheter is removed more than once a day. Use only with Urosan adhesive tape.

Note: These are sample products that are now available. New products are continually being developed.

Table 3-4 Product Options for Fixatives

Fixative	Considerations
Nonadhesive sheath holder Posey sheath holder	Reusable; washable. If holder gets wet with urine or from washing, be sure that it dries completely before putting it back on. Monitor at frequent intervals for development of pressure areas on shaft of penis. Holder can also be adapted by occupational therapist for patients with limited hand function.
Latex sheath holder	Not recommended. Tendency to cause pressure areas.
Single-sided adhesives applied over sheath Elastic tape	Same as above. Expands if applied with spiral or tab technique (Figure 3-3). Use 1-inch tape. Use new external catheter with each change because tape will tear catheter when removing.
Double-sided adhesives applied between penile shaft and sheath Uriliner, Urofoam, Crixiline strips, Uristrips	Same as above. All brands are applied to penis with spiral technique; external catheter is applied over adhesive. Difficult to apply with limited hand function. These double-sided adhesives should not be used on patients who need to remove catheter more than once or twice a day. *Crixiline:* Available in 1-inch × 6-inch strips. Strips are not water soluble and turn to gel at body temperature. Allows for expansion and contraction. Can be placed over small pressure areas to aid healing. Wash off with soap and water. Must be removed and new strips applied every 24 hours. *Uristrips:* Cannot be purchased separately; packaged with Urosan external catheter and a Skin Prep swab.
Liquid adhesives Tincture of benzoin	May be used alone or with one-sided adhesive or sheath holder. Container lid can be adapted by occupational therapist for patients with limited hand function.
Skin Bond cement	Do not use if external catheter must be removed more than once a day. Remove with adhesive remover only. Adhesive remover must be followed with soap and water wash.
Protective skin barriers Skin Prep (spray or wipes) Bard protective barrier film (spray or wipes)	All are protective skin dressings. They are used with other fixatives. Remove with soap and water.
Incontinence protective barrier film (low-alcohol formula, spray only)	Use with patients with sensitive skin.

Note: These are sample products that are now available. New products are continually being developed.

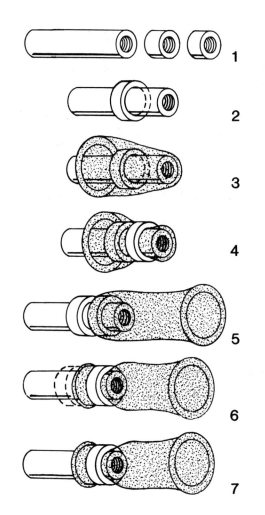

1. Take rubber tubing and cut two small pieces from tubing 1/8 inch long making a ring.

2. Roll one ring over long piece of rubber tubing one inch from end of tubing.

3. Unroll condom 2 or 3 rolls. With cuff on the inside, place condom over long rubber tubing.

4. Take second ring of tubing and roll over condom to fasten it securely on long rubber tubing.

5. Puncture condom at end of tubing to allow urine to drain.

6. Holding on to condom and tubing, roll back first ring over second ring and condom.

7. Condom now ready to be applied to penis.

Figure 3-2 Assembly for Condom with Latex Tubing.

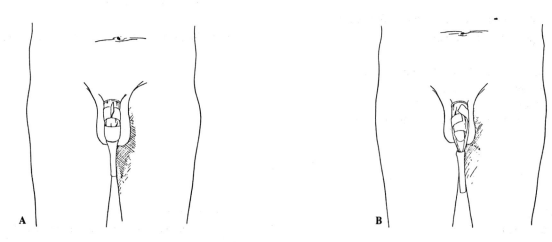

Figure 3-3 Application of Male External Catheter. (**A**) Applied with Elastic Tape Tabbed; (**B**) Applied with Elastic Tape Spiraled. *Source:* From *Rehabilitation Guide* (p. 39) by R.B. King, M. Boyink, and M. Keenan, 1977, Chicago, IL: Rehabilitation Institute of Chicago. Copyright 1977 by Rehabilitation Institute of Chicago. Reprinted by permission.

tional fixatives should be used with strapless or self-adhesive external catheters such as Freedom.

9. Patients or primary caregivers are to be taught external catheter application and removal.
10. The nurse should periodically document progress or tolerance to the external catheter.
11. Follow any and all infection control guidelines, and always discard used equipment in the appropriate manner.
12. Durable external appliances are available. The patient is fitted for the appliance by the manufacturer's representative. Additional fixatives are not necessary.

PROCEDURE: APPLYING AND REMOVING AN EXTERNAL CATHETER WITH ADHESIVES OR SKIN BARRIER

This method of application can be used for all types of external catheters except the Freedom Mentor catheter.

PATIENT AND FAMILY EDUCATION

1. Education should include the purpose of male external catheter application, its removal, and the proper techniques involved.
2. Include the patient and caregiver in decision making with regard to the type of external catheter and its method of application. Also instruct as to potential complications associated with these devices and how to observe for, prevent, and alleviate complications.
3. Whenever possible, involve the patient and family in the procedure.

Steps	*Additional Information*
Application	
1. Collect necessary equipment.	
2. Wash hands with soap and water.	Apply nonsterile gloves.
3. Provide for patient's privacy.	
4. Perform groin care (if foreskin is present, clean beneath it and pull it forward and down to original position).	
5. Check skin for any reddened or open areas.	
6. Trim or shave any pubic hairs if they will become entangled in external catheter.	
7. Apply the following if being used:	
• Skin barrier;	Apply to shaft of penis. When it becomes tacky, apply external catheter. A fenestrated, disposable washcloth may be used as a shield to keep from spraying pubic hairs.
• Crixiline strip (in spiral fashion on shaft of penis);	
• Benzoin spray (to shaft of penis); and	Put on external catheter *before* spray dries completely.
• Skin Bond cement.	
8. Position catheter 1 inch below head of penis.	
9. Roll catheter up shaft of penis.	
10. Connect to drainage equipment (either directly to drainage bag or to adaptor with extension tubing).	
Removal	
1. Provide privacy.	Put on nonsterile gloves.
2. Loosen tape or remove adhesive.	*Caution:* Do not cut external catheter to remove. Always peel gently to roll off.

Steps	*Additional Information*

3. To remove adhesive:
   - apply adhesive remover per product directions, and
   - wash penis with soap and water, rinse, and dry thoroughly.
4. Inspect skin on penis.
5. Clean reusable external catheter with soap and water; dry before reusing.

PROCEDURE: APPLYING AND REMOVING AN EXTERNAL CATHETER WITH ELASTIC TAPE OR POSEY SHEATH HOLDER

Caution: When frequent erections occur, the potential for pressure sore development exists. To test the tension of the Posey holder or tape, apply it to fingers held together of a size similar to that of the penis and place the fingers in a dependent position. Simulate the erection size with the fingers, and check the circulation in the nailbeds.

Steps	*Additional Information*

Application

Steps	Additional Information
1. Follow steps 1 through 6, applying and removing an external catheter, above.	
2. Cut a strip of Elastic tape equal to 1⅓ times circumference of penis shaft.	
3. Position external catheter 1 inch below head of penis, and roll it up shaft of penis.	
4. Secure Elastic tape or Posey sheath holder below penoscrotal junction:	
• If Elastic tape is applied, see Figure 3-3.	Apply in spiral or tabbed manner. Spiral fashion allows for even pressure to be applied.
• If Posey sheath holder is applied, place blue surface against external catheter. Overlap fabric ends on anterior surface of penis. Put a finger under sheath holder while securing Velcro closure. Press Velcro in place with wrinkling (allowing for erection or voiding). Do not use Posey holder if it overlaps over half or more of circumference of penis. Check 2 hours after application and once a shift.	

Removal

Steps	Additional Information
1. Loosen tape or Posey sheath. Gently peel and roll it off.	Put on nonsterile gloves. Provide privacy. *Caution:* Do not cut external catheter to remove.
2. Inspect skin on penis.	
3. Perform groin care.	
4. Clean reusable external catheter and Posey sheath holder with soap and water.	

PROCEDURE: APPLYING AND REMOVING A MENTOR FREEDOM EXTERNAL CATHETER

Use of a skin barrier spray or pads is not necessary, but they can be used provided that the barrier dries completely before the external catheter is applied.

Steps	*Additional Information*
Application	
1. Perform steps 1 through 6, applying and removing an external catheter, above.	
2. Place cone end of rolled sheath next to head of penis.	
3. Slowly unroll sheath all the way up length of penis.	If the penis recedes, grasp penis with one hand while rolling sheath on with other hand. Penis will retract again without sheath being pushed off.
4. Squeeze sheath all around penis to seal.	If there are many wrinkles in sheath, use a smaller external catheter. If patient has frequent erections, clip ring at top of external sheath to prevent tourniquet effect.
5. Connect to drainage equipment (either directly to drainage bag or to adaptor with extension tubing).	
6. Report skin tolerance, success, or problems to nurse in charge.	
Removal	
1. Remove by grasping end of sheath at base of penis and gently rolling toward glans penis.	Apply nonsterile gloves.
2. Inspect skin on penis, and perform groin care.	
3. Clean reusable external catheter with soap and water.	

DOCUMENTATION

1. Document the type of appliance and fixative and the method of application, frequency of penile skin check, wearing times, and degree of assistance or supervision needed.

2. Document the patient's skin tolerance, degree of satisfaction, and any problems or complications.

3. Document patient and family teaching (success and problems).

External Urinary Collection Device for Women

PURPOSE

To apply an external catheter to a female patient for urine collection.

STAFF RESPONSIBLE

EQUIPMENT

Systems are available from local/national manufacturers. Examples are:

1. Misstique (Bivona, Inc.).
2. Hollister Female Urinary Device.

GENERAL CONSIDERATIONS

1. An adjustment period is recommended when beginning use of this method. See specific instructions from the manufac-

turer. Beginning on the seventh day, wearing time can be extended to as much as tolerated.

2. It is suggested that the device be removed, cleaned, and reapplied every 24 hours.
3. When cleaning the device, wash it with mild soap, rinse it, soak it in hot water, and allow it to dry.
4. Meticulous cleansing and visual inspection of the perineal area should be carried out at least daily.
5. Provide for patient's privacy throughout the procedure.

PATIENT AND FAMILY EDUCATION

1. Decisions to use this system should be made between the patient and the nurse after having assessed the cost, ease of application, degree of sensation, cognitive status, and so forth.
2. Education should include the purpose of this device and the proper techniques for its application, removal, and care.

Also include any potential complications, such as local irritation, and how to observe for, prevent, and alleviate them.

3. Whenever possible, involve the patient and family in the procedure.

PROCEDURE

See manufacturer's instructional guidelines for specific steps.

DOCUMENTATION

1. Document success, problems, degree of assistance needed, patient and family education, wearing tolerance, and any complications or unusual circumstances.

Overview: Selection and Care of the Indwelling Catheter

PURPOSES

To determine the most appropriate choice of an indwelling catheter; to prevent complications associated with indwelling catheterization.

STAFF RESPONSIBLE

GENERAL CONSIDERATIONS

1. Although it is desirable to eliminate the use of an indwelling catheter, its use cannot be avoided in some situations. Other methods of urinary elimination that may be considered are intermittent catheterization, external catheters, timed voiding schedules, and methods to stimulate voiding.
2. The presence of a catheter carries numerous complications, the most important of which is infection. Every effort must be made to avoid introduction of bacteria into the urinary system.
3. Other commonly occurring complications, such as penoscrotal fistulas, urethritis, and urinary tract calculi, can be avoided with proper preventive care.
4. Provide for patient's privacy throughout any urinary procedures.

PATIENT AND FAMILY EDUCATION

1. Education should include the purpose and proper technique for the care of the indwelling catheter as well as how to prevent and observe for potential complications, such as urinary tract infection.
2. Whenever possible, involve the patient and family in the procedure.

PROCEDURE

Steps	*Additional Information*
1. Choose catheter least likely to result in complications. Assess the following characteristics:	
• size—the smallest possible size should be used to decrease urethral irritation. A #16 catheter with a 5-mL balloon can be used by most adults.	Leaking around catheter is not an indication to use a larger catheter.
• balloon size—the smallest amount necessary to keep catheter in bladder, usually 8 mL, is advised. Small balloon helps maintain empty bladder.	Overfilling the balloon or using large balloons increases foreign body surface in bladder and may increase calculus formation.
• catheter material—because rubber and Latex catheters are irritating to urethral mucosa, Teflon or pure silicone catheters are preferred for long-term use.	Teflon and silicone catheters may decrease incidence of calculus formation. They also provide smooth surface that may minimize irritation. Silicone catheters kink more easily than Teflon.
2. Maintain good urine flow in drainage system:	
• Monitor catheter for the following signs indicating catheter change needed: —drainage is sluggish or absent. —significant grit has accumulated in the catheter.	To test for grit, roll catheter between fingers and feel for any particles in catheter lumen.
• Check for plugging. If plugging occurs frequently, the cause should be investigated. Specific irrigation solutions may be ordered by physician to unplug and help prevent encrustations. Irrigations are not used routinely, however.	Oral fluid intake that ensures urinary output of 2,500 mL is best method of irrigation. See catheter irrigation procedure for more information.
• Always keep drainage bag below level of bladder to prevent backflow of urine into bladder.	Empty drainage bag before any transfer or turn during which bag may not stay well below level of bladder.

Steps	Additional Information
• Empty drainage bag at least every 8 hours or whenever large amount of urine is in bag.	Be sure to empty bag before patient leaves unit for a significant length of time. See procedure on attaching drainage device, below.
• Do not allow tubing to kink or to form dependent loop below level of the bag.	
3. Tape catheter to thigh or abdomen to prevent trauma caused by tension on catheter and to prevent penoscrotal fistulas in males.	See procedures on taping a catheter, below.
4. Prevent contamination of urinary drainage system:	
• Always wash hands and wear gloves for any contact with urine or urinary equipment.	
• Minimize opening of drainage system as much as possible. Use leg bag only on patients who are upright and active.	Try to time irrigations and other procedures with change of drainage device. Each opening of urinary drainage system significantly increases risk of urinary tract infection.
• If drainage device is found to be disconnected from catheter, replace with new, sterile device and tubing.	
• Twice daily, gently cleanse meatal area and catheter with soap and water. Rinse and dry.	See procedures for Routine Urinary Meatal Hygiene for Patients with Indwelling Catheters, below. Always wash from urinary meatus down catheter.
• Never allow drainage bag or tubing to touch floor.	
• Try to separate patients with indwelling catheters as much as possible (i.e., place them in separate rooms), especially if a patient has urinary tract infection.	Monitor patients for symptoms of urinary tract infections (i.e., cloudy urine, strong odor, complaint of burning or pain in area of catheter).

DOCUMENTATION

1. Document all urinary procedures and any problems or complications noted.
2. Document any signs or symptoms of urinary tract infection.
3. Document any participation in the procedure by the patient or primary caregiver.
4. Document patient and family education.

Routine Urinary Meatal Hygiene for Patients with Indwelling Catheters

PURPOSES

To minimize the potential for migration of bacteria into the urinary tract; to maintain skin integrity.

STAFF RESPONSIBLE

EQUIPMENT

1. Washcloths (two or more) and towel.
2. Basin with soap and water.
3. 3% Hydrogen peroxide (optional).
4. Nonsterile gloves.

GENERAL CONSIDERATIONS

1. Some controversy exists with regard to routine catheter care because catheter manipulation itself may lead to an increased chance of infection. The current recommendation is for gentle washing with soap and water to remove any obvious debris or encrustations (Brunner and Suddarth, 1984).

PATIENT AND FAMILY EDUCATION

1. Education should include the purpose and proper technique for routine meatal hygiene as well as how to prevent and observe for potential complications such as urinary tract infection or local irritation.
2. Whenever possible, involve the patient and family in the procedure.

PROCEDURE

Steps	Additional Information
1. Gather equipment.	
2. Provide for privacy.	
3. Wash hands.	
4. Explain procedure and rationale to patient.	
5. Position patient supine, if possible, and undress genital area.	Supine position allows for best visualization of genital area. If patient cannot be supine, extra care must be taken to ensure proper visualization.
6. Don gloves.	
7. Retract foreskin of noncircumcised males. Separate outer labia of females.	
8. Observe meatus for any ulceration, discharge, or crusting.	If ulceration or broken skin is evident, note size and characteristics of discharge present and amount, color, odor, and consistency. Notify physician.
9. Males: gently cleanse patient with soap and water in spiral motion from meatus to base of penis; cleanse underneath foreskin if uncircumcised; cleanse scrotum. Females: gently cleanse perineum with soap and water from symphysis pubis to rectum (front to back).	
10. Rinse and dry well.	
11. If encrustations still remain on catheter, cleanse catheter from meatus to distal end with another cloth and 3% hydrogen peroxide, removing any encrusted drainage. Rinse off peroxide solution thoroughly.	
12. Proceed with any further urinary care.	

DOCUMENTATION

1. Document routine procedure and the use of hydrogen peroxide.
2. Record any observations of redness, open skin areas, swelling, drainage, or crusting.
3. Document patient and primary caregiver education and involvement in the procedure.

Attaching a Drainage Device to an Indwelling or External Catheter

PURPOSE

To provide a sterile collecting device for patients with an indwelling or external catheter.

STAFF RESPONSIBLE

EQUIPMENT

1. Urinary drainage bag (bedside or leg).
2. Extension tubing with 5-inch adaptors.
3. Adapted clamps.
4. Leg bag straps (adapted straps optional).
5. Tape.
6. Alcohol wipes.
7. Plastic bags.
8. Nonsterile gloves.

GENERAL CONSIDERATIONS

1. A closed urinary drainage system should be used for those patients who remain in bed. For those who are up, dressed, and active, a leg bag should be worn during the day when the patient is in a wheelchair.

2. If an open drainage system is used, be sure that the bedside drainage system is changed at least every 24 hours or whenever contamination is suspected.
3. The bedside urinary drainage bag is to be used whenever a patient with an indwelling catheter will be supine for any length of time.
4. Meatal hygiene and catheter care should be performed before the changing of drainage devices.
5. If a bladder irrigation is to be done, it should be performed when the drainage devices are changed. This minimizes the need to disconnect the catheter an additional time.
6. Whenever a catheter is disconnected, there is an opportunity for contamination of the urinary tract. Therefore, aseptic technique should be maintained throughout the procedure in regard to exposed ports and lumens.
7. Nonsterile gloves are recommended when handling urine or urinary equipment of any patient, but they are especially important when handling urinary equipment of patients who are on urinary precautions or blood and body fluid precautions. Used drainage devices and tubing are discarded according to infection control procedures.
8. Catheter or drainage tube ports are not to be touched. They are considered sterile.
9. Empty all urine from the existing drainage device before disconnection.
10. At home, a 2-quart or larger bottle can be substituted for bedside drainage bags.

11. The following considerations refer to leg bag use:
    - The leg bag is used while the patient is up in the wheelchair.
    - Extension tubing is used for patients who prefer to wear the leg bag on the calf and for patients using external catheters.
    - To facilitate independent management of drainage devices, the occupational therapist can adapt leg bag straps and provide special clamps.
    - The leg bag should be applied to the right and left legs on alternating days. Straps should be loose so as not to compromise circulation or to cause pressure.
    - Location of the leg bag on the leg is based on patient preference.

PATIENT AND FAMILY EDUCATION

1. Education should include the purpose and proper technique for attaching a drainage device and how to prevent and observe for potential complications such as infection or obstructed drainage.
2. Whenever possible, involve the patient and family in the procedure.

PROCEDURE

Steps	*Additional Information*
1. Wash hands.	
2. Explain procedure, and provide for privacy.	
3. Check drainage bag.	Ensure that cover is on at end of tubing. Ensure that clamp is closed at bottom of drainage bag. If cap is not in place, discard unit and obtain a new one.

At Bedside

4. Open plastic bag for disposal of used equipment.	
5. Loosen cover from catheter adaptor of drainage bag; do not remove cap yet.	
6. Don nonsterile gloves.	
7. Clean area of connection between indwelling catheter and existing drainage device with alcohol wipe.	
8. Pinch indwelling catheter tubing, and separate catheter from present drainage device. If external catheter, allow all urine to drain into drainage device before disconnecting.	Ensure that tubing port of indwelling catheter remains sterile. Pinch is performed to prevent urine flow.
9. Remove cap of drainage bag with one hand, and connect (new) drainage bag to indwelling or external catheter.	Prevent contamination of connection site during removal or once cap has been removed.
10. Push together, then pull back slightly to ensure that connection is secure.	

Steps	Additional Information
11. Tape indwelling catheter to thigh or abdomen of patient.	Refer to procedure on taping an indwelling catheter, below.
12. Coil extra tubing length on bed. Tape excess tubing to itself.	This is to prevent kinking or formation of dependent loops that would hinder flow of urine. All tubing should be below level of bladder.
13. Suspend bag below level of bladder on bedframe with hanger provided.	Drainage bag should never be in contact with floor.
14. Dispose of used drainage bag.	Disposal is according to infection control procedures.
15. Remove gloves; wash hands.	

DOCUMENTATION

1. Document the difficulties in connecting the device or other observations of significance or change.

Deflating a Defective Indwelling Catheter Balloon

PURPOSE

To deflate, safely and effectively, an indwelling catheter balloon when this is not possible by withdrawal of the solution.

STAFF RESPONSIBLE

EQUIPMENT

1. Sterile mineral oil.
2. 10-mL Syringe (sterile).
3. Large-gauge needle (sterile).
4. Betadine swabs.
5. Sterile irrigation kit.
6. Normal saline (sterile).
7. Nonsterile gloves.
8. Equipment as per indwelling catheterization procedure (may use straight catheterization tray instead of indwelling catheterization tray if necessary).

GENERAL CONSIDERATIONS

1. A physician's order is required for this procedure.
2. Before attempting this procedure, ensure that the balloon cannot be deflated in the usual manner.
3. This procedure *cannot* be used with silicone catheters (for silicone catheters, the balloon may be deflated by the physician with a sterile stylet).

4. This procedure requires sterile technique because a foreign substance is introduced into the bladder.
5. Determine whether the defective catheter is still in the urinary bladder. One way to do this is to irrigate the catheter with 30 mL of normal saline solution. If this is done with ease and if all the solution is returned through the catheter, the balloon is considered in the bladder. If there is resistance or if solution returns from around the catheter, consider the balloon in the urethra. If it is in the urethra, notify the physician.
6. For effective dilution, use 3 to 5 mL of mineral oil (if 8 mL of water is in the balloon, use 5 mL of oil; if 5 mL of water, use 3 mL of oil).
7. Deflation of the balloon with mineral oil may take up to 30 minutes because the oil acts as a corrosive agent to Teflon or Latex balloons. Mineral oil is quite thick; once is inserted into the catheter balloon, it cannot be withdrawn.
8. If symptoms of autonomic dysreflexia occur, notify the physician and refer to the procedure on autonomic dysreflexia (Chapter 6).
9. If the instillation of mineral oil is ineffective, the balloon can be deflated by a physician with a sterile stylet.
10. Because mineral oil will remain in the bladder after the balloon is deflated, the bladder must be irrigated with sterile normal saline.
11. *Never* attempt to cut off the balloon inflation port because this will not deflate balloon and may render other methods of deflation difficult or impossible.

PATIENT AND FAMILY EDUCATION

1. This procedure is generally not taught to patients or families.

PROCEDURE

Steps	Additional Information
1. Explain procedure, and provide for privacy.	
2. Wash hands and don sterile gloves.	
3. Attempt to deflate balloon and remove catheter.	Use a 10-mL syringe or one of appropriate size to aspirate balloon. If unsuccessful, remove gloves, wash hands, and gather specified equipment (above).
4. Draw 3 to 5 mL of mineral oil into sterile 10-mL syringe.	A wide lumen needle will be necessary because of viscosity of mineral oil.
5. Don clean gloves.	
6. Clean Luer-lok port valve with Betadine, and allow it to dry.	
7. Detach needle from syringe, and inject mineral oil directly into catheter balloon through Luer-lok port.	
8. Allow 10 to 15 minutes before attempting gently to withdraw catheter. Balloon deflation may take up to 30 minutes.	Notify physician if unable to remove catheter after 30 minutes or if symptoms of autonomic dysreflexia occur.
9. Replace with new sterile indwelling catheter per procedure (Male/Female Indwelling Catheterization).	If indwelling catheter is not to be replaced, insert red rubber straight catheter.
10. Irrigate bladder through catheter to ensure that no foreign material is left in bladder.	See Catheter Irrigation procedure, below.
11. Complete catheterization procedure.	
12. Discard used equipment in appropriate manner.	Disposal is according to infection control procedures.
13. Remove gloves, and wash hands.	

DOCUMENTATION

1. Document the procedure, outcome, and any significant observations.

2. Document patient and primary caregiver education and involvement in the procedure.

Taping an Indwelling Catheter: Male

PURPOSE

To secure an indwelling catheter to prevent penoscrotal fistula or tension on the catheter.

STAFF RESPONSIBLE

EQUIPMENT

1. Tape, 1-inch width (select type of tape according to the patient's skin tolerance).
2. Nonsterile gloves.

GENERAL CONSIDERATIONS

1. Rotate sites of taping to prevent skin irritation.
2. Place the tape over clean, intact skin.
3. If excessive hair is present, clip the hair with scissors.
4. Observe the catheter for kinking at the site of taping; adjust if kinking is present.
5. Tape the catheter to the abdomen at night and whenever the patient will be lying down for a long period of time. When the patient is sitting, the catheter should be taped laterally to the upper anterior thigh.

PATIENT AND FAMILY EDUCATION

1. Education should include the purpose and proper technique for taping an indwelling catheter and how to prevent and observe for potential complications such as local irritation or tension on the catheter.
2. Whenever possible, involve the patient and family in the procedure.

PROCEDURE

Steps	Additional Information
1. Gather equipment.	
2. Provide privacy, and explain procedure to patient.	
3. Wash hands, and don gloves.	
4. Cut a 6-inch strip of 1-inch wide tape.	
5. Wrap center of tape around catheter, approximately 2 to 3 inches from catheter's distal end and proximal to bifurcation.	
6. Pinch tape to itself around catheter, allowing ends to remain free.	
7. Secure both ends of tape to abdomen below navel, lifting penis off scrotum (Figure 3-4), or to anterior thigh.	Enough slack should be left in catheter to prevent tension and to allow for erections.
8. Retape as necessary after movement, position changes, catheter irrigations, or change of drainage bags.	

DOCUMENTATION

1. Document the position of the tape and any problems or complications noted.

2. Document patient and primary caregiver education and involvement in the procedure.

Taping an Indwelling Catheter: Female

PURPOSE

To secure an indwelling catheter to prevent tension on the catheter.

STAFF RESPONSIBLE

EQUIPMENT

1. Tape, 1-inch width (select type of tape according to the patient's skin tolerance).
2. Nonsterile gloves.

GENERAL CONSIDERATIONS

1. Rotate sites of taping to prevent skin irritation.
2. Place the tape over clean, intact skin.
3. If excessive hair is present, trim the hair with scissors.
4. Observe the catheter for kinking at the site of taping; adjust if kinking is present.

PATIENT AND FAMILY EDUCATION

1. Education should include the purpose and proper technique for taping an indwelling catheter and how to prevent and observe for potential complications such as local irritation or tension on the catheter.
2. Whenever possible, involve the patient and family in the procedure.

PROCEDURE

Steps	Additional Information
1. Gather equipment.	
2. Provide privacy, and explain procedure to patient.	
3. Wash hands, and don gloves.	

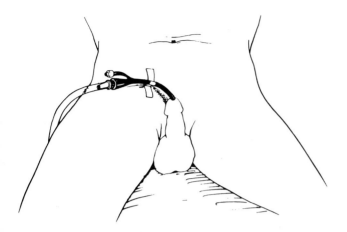

Figure 3-4 Taping an Indwelling Catheter: Male. *Source:* From *Rehabilitation Guide* (p. 48) by R.B. King, M. Boyink, and M. Keenan, 1977, Chicago, IL: Rehabilitation Institute of Chicago. Copyright 1977 by Rehabilitaton Institute of Chicago. Reprinted by permission.

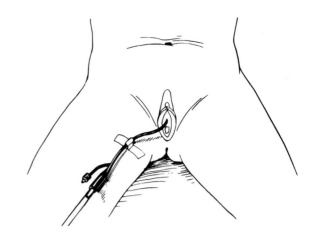

Figure 3-5 Taping an Indwelling Catheter: Female. *Source:* From *Rehabilitation Guide* (p. 49) by R.B. King, M. Boyink, and M. Keenan, 1977, Chicago, IL: Rehabilitation Institute of Chicago. Copyright 1977 by Rehabilitation Institute of Chicago. Reprinted by permission.

Steps	*Additional Information*

4. Cut 6-inch strip of 1-inch wide tape.
5. Wrap center of tape around catheter, approximately 2 to 3 inches from catheter's distal end and proximal to bifurcation.
6. Pinch tape to itself around catheter, allowing ends to remain free.
7. Secure both ends of tape to inner thigh (Figure 3-5).
8. Retape as necessary after movement, position changes, catheter irrigations, or change of drainage bags.

DOCUMENTATION

1. Document the position of the tape and any problems or complications noted.

2. Document patient and primary caregiver education and involvement in the procedure.

Catheter Irrigation

PURPOSE

To assess and/or maintain the patency of an indwelling catheter. *Note:* This procedure is no longer common practice as a routine procedure for clearing accumulation of debris in the catheter because of the risk of infection associated with a break in the closed drainage system.

STAFF RESPONSIBLE

EQUIPMENT

1. Prepackaged sterile irrigation set.
2. Sterile normal saline or other irrigating solution as ordered by physician.
3. Nonsterile gloves.
4. Alcohol prep pad.

GENERAL CONSIDERATIONS

1. Sterile ("no touch") technique is used for this procedure.
2. Attempt to coordinate this procedure with the change of the urinary drainage system to decrease the possibility of contamination. A new, sterile drainage device should be used whenever possible after opening the catheter system.
3. All irrigating solutions must be checked for loose cap, precipitate, or expiration before use.
4. Follow agency policy regarding conditions for which irrigation is indicated.
5. An oral fluid intake that ensures a daily urinary output of 2,500 mL or more is the best method of irrigation.
6. Hematuria, pain, or symptoms of autonomic dysreflexia noted during the procedure should be promptly reported to the physician.
7. Aspiration of irrigation solution is not performed routinely but only under specific conditions (if there is no return of solution or on a specific physician's order for removal of blood clots or sediment). When aspiration is necessary, force is never used, nor are large amounts of solution instilled into the bladder.
8. Common irrigation solutions (read package inserts for contraindications) include:
   - normal saline—used to check the patency of the catheter and for all irrigation procedures unless a physician's order calls for another solution;
   - acetic acid (0.25%)—may promote an acidic environment in the bladder;
   - Urologic G or Solution G—may assist in dissolving phosphatic calculi in the bladder; and
   - Renacidin—may prevent formation of calculi in the bladder (because of potential side effects, it is ordered only when other methods have been ineffective).
9. If Renacidin is used, the catheter is pinched or clamped for 10 minutes to retain the solution in the bladder. Because of potential side effects, Renacidin is instilled only once with each irrigation and normal saline is used to finish the irrigation or to flush the Renacidin from the bladder.

PATIENT AND FAMILY EDUCATION

1. Education of the patient and caregiver should include the purpose and proper technique for catheter irrigation and how to prevent and observe for potential complications such as infection or overdistended bladder.
2. Whenever possible, involve the patient and family in the procedure.

PROCEDURE

Steps	*Additional Information*
1. Prepare patient: give explanations, and provide privacy. Gather equipment.	Check solution to ensure that it is safe (sterile, without precipitate, and within date of expiration).
2. Wash hands, and don nonsterile gloves.	
3. Perform groin care and catheter care if needed at this time. If performed, wash hands and don new pair of nonsterile gloves.	
4. Open irrigation set and bottle of solution. Place waterproof pad, plastic side down, under catheter and tubing connection.	
5. Open extra sterile alcohol pad, and place it near catheter connection site.	This can be used to help prevent contamination of drainage system if it is to be reattached.
6. Lift syringe from container, and remove protective cap from tip.	
7. Pour at least 100 mL of solution into irrigation solution container, and replace syringe.	Syringe and inside of solution container must remain sterile. If they come into contact with anything, they must be replaced.
8. Swab catheter tubing junction with alcohol and allow to dry.	
9. Disconnect catheter from drainage device; place catheter in notch of sterile drainage tray.	Place so that open end of catheter does not touch anything.
10. Discard drainage device.	If reusing drainage device, place tip of tubing carefully in extra opened alcohol prep pad container or in sterile cap if provided.

Steps	*Additional Information*
11. Draw up 30 mL of irrigation solution.	
12. Hold end of catheter upward.	Do not allow open end of catheter to touch anything.
13. Set tip of syringe in catheter opening, allowing solution to enter catheter under gentle pressure.	If resistance is met, refer to procedures for changing catheter (Male/Female Indwelling Catheterization).
14. Pinch off catheter, maintaining squeeze on bulb of syringe.	This is to prevent injecting air in bladder or placing suction on bladder mucosa.
15. Disconnect catheter and syringe. Replace catheter in notch of collection tray and syringe into solution container.	
16. Observe for return of the solution; note amount and characteristics.	All solution should be returned before continuing. If not, be sure catheter is below level of bladder, gently press over bladder, and rotate patient's position.
17. If there is no return of solution and if other methods have been tried: • Instill 30 mL more solution into bladder. • Applying gentle suction, withdraw only 30 mL of solution. If solution returns readily, continue with irrigation procedures.	Do not force solution into bladder. Do not instill more solution if patient exhibits symptoms of autonomic dysreflexia. Only 30 mL of the 60 mL of solution in bladder is withdrawn to prevent trauma to bladder mucosa during aspiration. If this is not successful, refer to procedures for changing catheter (Male/Female Indwelling Catheterization).
18. Repeat instillation of 30 mL of solution twice more or until urine is clear.	A total of 90 mL or more of irrigant is used.
19. Reconnect catheter to drainage.	No touch technique is used to preserve sterility; new sterile drainage system is preferred.
20. Restore patient to comfortable position and appropriate dress.	Retape catheter to thigh or abdomen as appropriate.
21. Remove gloves, and discard used equipment in appropriate manner.	Disposal is according to infection control procedures.
22. Wash hands.	
23. Document as below.	

DOCUMENTATION

1. Document the procedure, the characteristics and amount of returned solution, and any unusual circumstances during the irrigation.

2. Document patient and primary caregiver education and involvement in the procedure.

Male Straight Catheterization

PURPOSE

To empty the bladder of urine or to measure the amount of urine remaining in the bladder immediately after voiding (residual urine).

STAFF RESPONSIBLE

EQUIPMENT

1. Prepackaged sterile catheterization tray with straight catheter.
2. Washcloth, towel, soap, and water.
3. Nonsterile gloves.
4. Bag for disposal.
5. Additional lubricant (optional).
6. Urinal (if attempting to stimulate void).
7. Coudé tip catheter if needed.
8. Benzylchonium chloride prepackaged sterile catheterization tray (if patient is allergic to Betadine).

GENERAL CONSIDERATIONS

1. A physician's order is required for catheterization.
2. Maintain privacy for the patient throughout the procedure.
3. If the patient is allergic to Betadine, order benzylchonium chloride solution in a prepackaged sterile catheterization tray. Indicate "Allergy To" per agency protocol.
4. If the foreskin is present, retract it over the head of the penis during catheterization. During groin care, wash the penis with the foreskin down, and then with it retracted. After catheterization, perform this procedure in reverse.
5. When introducing the catheter, sometimes resistance is met. If resistance is suspected to be due to sphincter tone, try one or more of the following techniques:
   - Have the patient take a deep breath or use the incentive spirometer. As the patient exhales, gently advance the catheter.
   - Use ROM to the lower extremities before catheter insertion.
   - Position the patient with his hips externally rotated and knees flexed (frog-leg position).
   - Position the patient on his side with his hips and knees flexed.
   - Try anal stretch (see methods to stimulate voiding and to empty the bladder, above).
   - If continued resistance is met, notify the physician.
6. If resistance is thought to be due to a stricture, consult the physician about the possible use of a coudé tip catheter, and document the decision.
7. For patients with spinal cord injury at T-6 or above, autonomic dysreflexia may be experienced during catheter insertion. Anesthetic lubricant may help in these patients.

PATIENT AND FAMILY EDUCATION

1. Education should include the purpose and proper technique for catheterization. Also instruct on how to observe for and prevent potential complications such as infection, incomplete emptying of bladder, and difficulty in introduction of the catheter.
2. Whenever possible, involve the patient and family in the procedure.

PROCEDURE

Steps	Additional Information
1. Prepare patient, give explanations, and provide privacy.	If residual urine is ordered, stimulate void as directed in care plan or physician's orders.
2. Wash hands; don nonsterile gloves.	
3. Perform groin care.	
4. Remove gloves, and wash hands.	
5. Open kit, and establish sterile field.	Establish clean, uncluttered area.
6. Remove top drape, and place under patient's penis.	
7. Remove second fenestrated drape, and place over patient's penis.	

Steps	*Additional Information*
8. Apply sterile gloves.	
9. Open and pour Betadine over cotton balls.	
10. Open lubricant, and lubricate catheter from tip to near distal end.	Additional lubricant may be necessary. Return catheter to tray.
11. With nondominant hand, grasp penis and hold upward at 60 to 90° angle to body.	If foreskin is present, keep retracted throughout procedure.
12. Using forceps, cleanse head of penis with cotton balls in circular motion, starting at urinary meatus and continuing downward on penis.	Cleanse once with each cotton ball, and discard each cotton ball after use.
13. Place tray on drape. Pick up catheter with dominant hand, and hold it about 4 inches from tip.	Be sure distal end of catheter remains in tray.
14. Gently insert well-lubricated catheter to 1 or 2 inches beyond point where urine begins to flow.	Continue holding penis at 60° to 90° angle. If resistance is met, apply relaxation techniques or consult physician about possible use of coudé tip catheter. Check for signs and symptoms of autonomic dysreflexia.
15. Holding catheter firmly in place, allow urine to drain completely. Then withdraw catheter a slight amount, and observe for any further urine return.	If more than 500 mL of urine is in bladder, pinch catheter for 5 to 10 minutes before allowing remaining urine to drain, or remove catheter and repeat catheterization procedure from step 5 in 5 to 10 minutes.
16. Remove catheter and perform groin care.	
17. Dispose of used equipment in appropriate manner.	Disposal is according to infection control procedures.
18. Wash hands.	
19. Restore patient to comfortable position and appropriate dress.	

DOCUMENTATION

1. Record the procedure, the amount of urine, any attempts to stimulate void and voided amounts of urine, and any complications or unusual observations.

2. Record any participation by the patient or primary caregiver in the procedure.

Female Straight Catheterization

PURPOSE

To empty the bladder of urine or to measure the amount of urine remaining immediately after voiding (residual urine).

STAFF RESPONSIBLE

EQUIPMENT

1. Prepackaged sterile catheterization tray with straight catheter.
2. Washcloth, towel, soap, and water.
3. Nonsterile gloves.

4. Bag for disposal.
5. Urine container (if attempting to stimulate void).
6. Flashlight (optional).
7. Sheet or bath blanket.
8. Coudé tip catheter if needed.
9. Benzylchonium chloride prepackaged sterile catheterization tray (if patient is allergic to Betadine).

GENERAL CONSIDERATIONS

1. A physician's order is required for catheterization.
2. Assistance may be needed to carry out the procedure if the patient's lower extremities are severely spastic, if the patient is unable to cooperate, or if adequate lighting is only available by flashlight.
3. Maintain privacy for the patient throughout the procedure.

4. If the patient is allergic to Betadine, order benzylchonium chloride solution in a prepackaged sterile catheterization tray. Indicate "Allergy To" per agency protocol.
5. If a spasm occurs during insertion of the catheter, stop and wait for it to subside. If continued resistance is met, do not use force. Stop and notify the physician.
6. For patients with spinal cord injury at T-6 or above, autonomic dysreflexia may be experienced during catheter insertion. Anesthetic lubricant may help these patients.

PATIENT AND FAMILY EDUCATION

1. Education should include the purpose and proper technique for catheterization. Also instruct on how to observe for and prevent potential complications such as infection and incomplete emptying of bladder.
2. Whenever possible, involve the patient and family in the procedure.

PROCEDURE

Steps	*Additional Information*
1. Prepare patient in supine position with knees flexed and hips abducted. Drape with sheet or bath blanket to allow for exposure from suprapubic area to knees.	If patient has loss of motor control in lower extremities, position may be better maintained with ankles crossed. If residual urine is ordered, stimulate void as directed in care plan or physician's orders.
2. Explain procedure to patient and caregiver.	
3. Ensure adequate lighting.	A flashlight may be necessary.
4. Wash hands; don nonsterile gloves.	
5. Cleanse perineal area with soap and water.	Cleanse from clitoris toward anus.
6. Remove gloves, and wash hands.	
7. Open kit, and establish sterile field.	Have clean, uncluttered area.
8. Position moisture-proof drape under patient's buttocks.	Maintain sterility of exposed surface of drape.
9. Apply sterile gloves.	
10. Open and pour Betadine over cotton balls.	
11. Open lubricant, and lubricate catheter.	Lubricate from tip to several inches down on catheter.
12. Move equipment to between patient's legs.	
13. Separate labia minora with your nondominant hand so that urinary meatus is well visualized; maintain this separation until catheterization is completed.	This hand is now contaminated.
14. Pick up cotton balls with forceps, and cleanse around urinary meatus.	Cleanse with one downward stroke from clitoris toward anus for each cotton ball and then discard cotton ball; use all cotton balls. Cleanse both sides of meatus before cleaning meatus itself.
15. Place tray on drape close to, but not touching, perineal area.	
16. Pick up catheter with dominant hand, holding it about 4 inches from tip with open end in tray.	Sterile catheter and gloved hand must not touch labia or pubic hair.
17. Insert lubricated catheter slowly to 1 to 2 inches beyond point where urine begins to flow.	Observe for signs and symptoms of autonomic dysreflexia. If urine does not immediately flow, exert gentle pressure over bladder, or ask patient to cough or deep breathe.
18. Holding catheter firmly in place, allow urine to drain completely. Then withdraw catheter a slight amount, and observe for any further urine return.	If more than 500 mL of urine is in the bladder, pinch catheter for 5 to 10 minutes before allowing remaining urine to drain, or remove catheter and repeat procedure from step 7 in 5 to 10 minutes.
19. Remove catheter, and cleanse perineal area.	
20. Dispose of equipment in appropriate manner.	Disposal is according to infection control procedures.
21. Remove gloves.	
22. Restore patient to comfortable position and appropriate dress.	
23. Wash hands.	

DOCUMENTATION

1. Record the procedure, the amount of urine, any attempts to stimulate void and voided amount of urine, and any complications or unusual observations.

2. Record any participation by the patient or primary caregiver in the procedure.

Male Indwelling Catheterization

PURPOSE

To establish urinary drainage or to facilitate certain diagnostic procedures and assessments.

STAFF RESPONSIBLE

5. If the foreskin is present, retract it over the head of the penis. If this is not possible or if the foreskin will not remain in position, notify the physician. While performing groin care, wash the penis with the foreskin down and then with the foreskin retracted. Be sure to repeat this procedure in reverse when performing groin care after indwelling catheterization.
6. When introducing the catheter, sometimes resistance is met. If resistance is suspected to be due to sphincter tone, try one or more of the following techniques:

EQUIPMENT

1. Prepackaged sterile catheterization tray with appropriate size and type of indwelling catheter.
2. Washcloths, towels, soap, and water.
3. Sterile leg bag or bedside drainage bag.
4. 10-mL Syringe (if removing indwelling catheter).
5. Nonsterile gloves and bag for disposal.
6. Additional lubricant.
7. Additional equipment for high-risk patients:
   - irrigation set,
   - bottle of sterile normal saline solution, and
   - measuring tape.
8. Special indwelling catheters if needed (coudé tip, balloons with greater than 10-mL capacity).
9. Benzylchonium chloride prepackaged sterile catheterization trays (for patients who are allergic to Betadine solution).

GENERAL CONSIDERATIONS

1. A physician's order is required for catheterization.
2. Before the initial insertion or change of an indwelling catheter of a male patient, assessment of the patient's risk of developing urinary complications during catheterization (Exhibit 3-2) must be determined and documented in the progress notes or admission form.
3. Maintain privacy for the patient throughout the procedure.
4. If the patient is allergic to Betadine solution, order benzylchonium chloride solution in a prepackaged sterile catheterization tray. Indicate "Allergy To" per agency protocol.

Exhibit 3-2 Assessment To Determine Risk of Urinary Complications in Males During Indwelling Catheter Insertion

Before inserting or changing an indwelling catheter in a male for the first time, ask the patient or primary caregiver the following questions (check the medical record if the patient or primary caregiver is unreliable or unavailable).

1. Have you ever had an indwelling catheter, one that stays in your body?
   YES ☐ (continue with rest of questions)
   NO ☐ (skip question 2)
2. Have you ever had bleeding from your penis during or after an indwelling catheter has been put in?
   YES ☐   NO ☐
   If YES, describe _____
3. Have you or anyone else ever had problems putting a catheter in you?
   YES ☐   NO ☐
   If YES, describe _____
4. Have you ever been told how to perform, or noticed others performing, an anal stretch or using a coudé tip catheter when putting a catheter in you?
   YES ☐   NO ☐
   If YES, describe _____
5. Have you ever had surgery on your bladder, such as a sphincterotomy, cystoscopy, transurethral resection, or urethral dilation?
   YES ☐   NO ☐
   If YES, describe _____
6. Have you ever had any injury or trauma to your bladder, penis, or urethra?
   YES ☐   NO ☐
   If YES, describe _____
7. Have you ever been told that you have a urethral stricture, enlarged prostate, or spastic bladder?
   YES ☐   NO ☐
   If YES, describe _____

Rating: If the answer was "no" to questions 2 through 7, consider the patient a normal risk. If the answer was "yes" to any question 2 through 7, consider the patient at high risk for urinary complications.

- Have the patient take a deep breath or use the incentive spirometer. When the patient exhales, gently advance the catheter.
- Try ROM to the lower extremities before catheter insertion.
- Position the patient's legs in external rotation of the hips with flexed knees (frog-leg position).
- Position the patient on his side with his hips and knees flexed.
- Try anal stretch (see methods to stimulate voiding and to empty the bladder, above).

If none of these techniques works, stop and notify the physician.

7. If resistance is thought to be the result of stricture, the nurse should consult the physician with regard to the use of a coudé tip catheter. This should be noted in the progress notes.
8. The standard balloon size is 5 mL. Balloons should be inflated to 8 to 10 mL. Otherwise, the balloon may be expelled through the sphincter and into the urethra. Larger balloon sizes are not recommended for use in males unless ordered by the physician.
9. Follow these steps to assess for proper placement of the catheter:
   - Pressure exerted to inflate the balloon during testing should be equal to the pressure exerted to inflate the balloon after insertion. If pressure is greater after insertion, the balloon may be in the urethra.
   - After balloon insertion, if gentle withdrawal of the catheter does not produce movement, the balloon may be in the urethra.
   - Nonresolving symptoms of autonomic dysreflexia in patients with spinal cord injury above the level of T-6 may indicate that the balloon is in the urethra.
   - Irrigate the catheter with 30 mL of normal saline solution. If the irrigation instills with ease and if all the solution returns through the lumen of the catheter, the balloon can be considered in the bladder. If there is resistance to instillation or if the solution returns from around the catheter, consider the balloon in the urethra.

10. If at any time an incident of tautness or pulling on the catheter occurs, placement should be reevaluated by means of any of the measures above.
11. If the balloon is considered in the urethra, deflate immediately. The catheter should be repositioned and assessed, or removed and a new catheter inserted. If the patient has had a sphincterotomy and if an indwelling catheter is needed, monitor for signs of balloon placement in the urethra. This is not an uncommon occurrence.
12. If there is no urine return after ensuring proper balloon placement, perform Credé maneuver on the patient's bladder, push fluids, and continue to observe for urine return.
13. If hemorrhage occurs during or after the catheterization, institute emergency measures and contact the physician immediately.
14. For patients with spinal cord injury at T-6 or above, autonomic dysreflexia may occur during insertion.
15. An anesthetic lubricant may be used for chronic autonomic dysreflexia or for discomfort associated with catheterizations (allergies should be considered).

PATIENT AND FAMILY EDUCATION

1. Education should include the purpose and proper technique for catheterization. Also instruct on how to observe for potential complications such as infection, incomplete emptying of the bladder, difficulty in introduction of the catheter, or inflation of the balloon in the urethra.
2. Whenever possible, involve the patient and family in the procedure.

PROCEDURE

Steps	Additional Information
1. Check current catheter size, type, and measured length exposed.	Measured length is attained by measuring distance from tip of penis to end of catheter.
2. Prepare patient: Explain procedure and provide privacy. Gather equipment, and wash hands.	If high-risk patient, have additional equipment on hand and conveniently placed (see equipment, 7).
3. Don nonsterile gloves.	
4. Completely deflate balloon of current catheter.	Use 10-mL syringe or one of appropriate size (see Deflating a Defective Indwelling Catheter Balloon procedure, if balloon does not deflate).
5. Gently remove catheter.	Observe and feel tip for stones or grit.
6. Perform groin care. Remove gloves. Wash hands.	
7. Determine optimum position of both patient and yourself. Open catheter tray, and establish sterile field.	Establish clean, uncluttered area. Provide bag for disposal.
8. Remove top drape, and place under patient's penis.	Place shiny side down against bed, and touch only edges.
9. Remove second fenestrated drape, and place over patient's penis.	

Steps	*Additional Information*
10. Apply sterile gloves.	
11. To test balloon, attach sterile water-filled syringe to balloon lumen and slowly inflate and deflate balloon completely.	Note amount of pressure required to inflate balloon. Discard catheter if it does not inflate and deflate easily.
12. Leave syringe attached to balloon lumen.	This will facilitate easy inflation of balloon later.
13. Open and pour Betadine over cotton balls.	
14. Open lubricant, and lubricate catheter to bifurcation near end.	Additional lubricant may be necessary.
15. Place equipment to between patient's legs or, if patient is side lying, next to upper thighs or lower abdomen.	
16. Use nondominant hand to grasp penis firmly and hold upward at 60° to 90° angle to body.	This hand is now contaminated.
17. Cleanse head of penis with cotton balls (held in forceps) in circular motion, starting at urinary meatus.	
18. Pick up catheter with dominant hand, holding it about 4 inches from tip with open end in collecting device.	
19. Slowly insert well-lubricated catheter, noting when urine begins to flow.	If more than 500 mL of urine is in bladder, pinch catheter for 5 to 10 minutes before allowing remaining urine to drain.
20. Insert catheter 2 inches beyond point where flow of urine starts or up to bifurcation of catheter.	Evaluate to determine whether catheter is in bladder. If patient has erection, wait for it to resolve. If erection does not readily resolve, consult physician.
21. Inflate balloon with 8 to 10 mL of sterile water. Amount of pressure should be same as when testing balloon. Hold catheter firmly in place until balloon is inflated.	If amount of pressure is increased, evaluate placement; balloon may be in urethra. Evaluate and monitor patient for complications.
22. Gently withdraw catheter until balloon rests against bladder neck.	If patient has had a sphincterotomy, do not pull back on catheter.
23. Measure length of catheter exposed.	Length should be the same as or less than measured length at beginning of procedure.
24. Attach catheter to sterile drainage system.	
25. Tape catheter to abdomen or upper anterior thigh.	
26. Perform groin care.	
27. Discard used equipment in appropriate manner.	Disposal is according to infection control procedures.
28. Remove gloves, and wash hands.	
29. Restore patient to comfortable position and appropriate dress.	

DOCUMENTATION

1. Document your assessment of risk factors in the progress notes (see Exhibit 3-2).
2. Document in the care plan and patient record the size and type of catheter, size of the balloon, length of catheter exposed, the date of change, any special instructions, and the level of staff to perform the procedure.
3. Document any complications or significant observations, and notify the physician.
4. Record any participation by the patient or the primary caregiver in the procedure.

Female Indwelling Catheterization

PURPOSE

To establish urinary drainage or to facilitate certain diagnostic procedures and assessments.

STAFF RESPONSIBLE

EQUIPMENT

1. Prepackaged sterile catheterization tray with appropriate size and type of indwelling catheter.
2. Nonsterile gloves.
3. Bag for disposal.
4. Washcloths, towels, soap, and water.
5. Sterile leg bag or bedside drainage bag.
6. 10-mL Syringe (if removing catheter).
7. Sheet or bath blanket.
8. Optional: flashlight, irrigation set, and normal saline solution.
9. Special indwelling catheters if needed (coudé tip, special size catheter or balloon).
10. Benzylchonium chloride prepackaged sterile catheterization tray (for patients who are allergic to Betadine).

GENERAL CONSIDERATIONS

1. A physician's order is required for catheterization.
2. Assistance may be needed to perform this procedure if the patient's lower extremities are severely spastic, if the patient is unable to cooperate, or if adequate lighting is available only by flashlight.
3. Maintain privacy for the patient throughout the procedure.
4. If the patient is allergic to Betadine solution, order benzylchonium chloride. Indicate ''Allergy To'' per agency protocol.
5. The standard balloon size is 5 mL. Balloons are to be inflated to a volume of 8 to 10 mL. Otherwise, the balloon may be expelled through the sphincter into the urethra.
6. If a spasm occurs during insertion of the catheter, stop and wait until it subsides. If continued resistance is met, do not use force. Stop and notify the physician.
7. Follow these steps to assess for proper placement of the catheter:
   - Pressure exerted to inflate the balloon during testing should be approximately equal to the pressure exerted to inflate the balloon after insertion. If the pressure is greater after insertion, the balloon may be in the urethra.
   - After balloon insertion, if gentle withdrawal of the catheter does not produce movement, the balloon may be in the urethra.
   - Nonresolving symptoms of autonomic dysreflexia in patients with spinal cord injury may indicate that the balloon is in the urethra.
   - Irrigate the catheter with 30 mL of normal saline solution. If the irrigation instills with ease and if all the solution returns through the lumen of the catheter, the balloon can be considered in the bladder. If there is resistance to instillation or if the solution returns from around the catheter, consider the balloon in the urethra.
8. If at any time an incident of taughtness or pulling on the catheter occurs, placement should be reevaluated by means of any of the measures above.
9. If the balloon is considered in the urethra, it should immediately be deflated. The catheter should be repositioned and reassessment made, or the catheter should be removed and a new catheter inserted.
10. If there is no urine return after ensuring proper placement, perform Credé maneuver on the patient's bladder, push fluids, and observe for urine return.
11. If hemorrhage occurs during or after the catheterization, institute emergency measures and contact the physician immediately.
12. For patients with spinal cord injury at T-6 or above, autonomic dysreflexia may occur during catheter insertion.
13. An anesthetic lubricant may be used for chronic autonomic dysreflexia or for severe discomfort associated with catheterizations (allergies should be considered).

PATIENT AND FAMILY EDUCATION

1. Education should include the purpose and proper technique for catheterization. Also instruct on how to observe for and prevent potential complications such as infection, incomplete emptying of the bladder, and inflation of the balloon in the urethra.
2. Whenever possible, involve the patient and/or family in the procedure.

PROCEDURE

Steps	Additional Information
1. Prepare patient in supine position with knees flexed and hips abducted. Drape with sheet or bath blanket to allow for exposure from suprapubic area to knees. Explain procedure to patient or caregiver.	If patient has loss of motor control in lower extremities, position may be better maintained with ankles crossed and legs supported with pillows.
2. Ensure adequate lighting.	A flashlight may be necessary.
3. Wash hands, and don nonsterile gloves.	

Steps	*Additional Information*
4. Completely deflate balloon of current catheter.	Use 10-mL syringe or one of appropriate size (see Deflating a Defective Indwelling Catheter Balloon procedure, if balloon does not deflate).
5. Gently remove catheter, and dispose of appropriately.	Observe and feel tip for stones or grit.
6. Cleanse perineal area with soap and water. Remove gloves, and wash hands.	Cleanse from clitoris toward anus.
7. Open catheterization tray, and establish sterile field.	Have clean, uncluttered area.
8. Position moisture-proof drape under patient's buttocks.	Maintain sterility of exposed surface of drape.
9. Apply sterile gloves.	
10. To test balloon, attach sterile water-filled syringe to balloon lumen, and slowly inflate and deflate balloon.	Discard catheter if it does not inflate and deflate easily. Note amount of pressure required to inflate balloon. Leave syringe attached to balloon lumen.
11. Open and pour Betadine over cotton balls.	Use benzylchonium chloride if patient is allergic to Betadine.
12. Open lubricant, and lubricate catheter from tip to several inches down.	
13. Move equipment to between patient's legs.	
14. Separate labia minora with your nondominant hand so that meatus is well visualized; maintain this separation until catheterization is completed.	This hand is now contaminated.
15. With forceps holding cotton ball, cleanse meatus and urethral opening.	Cleanse with one downward stroke from clitoris toward anus for each cotton ball and then discard cotton ball; use all cotton balls. Cleanse along both sides of meatus before cleansing meatus itself.
16. Place tray on drape close to but not touching perineal area.	
17. Pick up catheter with dominant hand, holding it about 4 inches from tip with open end in collecting device.	Sterile catheter or gloved hand must not touch labia or pubic hair.
18. Insert lubricated catheter slowly, noting when urine begins to flow.	If more than 500 mL of urine is in bladder, pinch catheter for 5 to 10 minutes before allowing remaining urine to drain.
19. Insert catheter 2 inches beyond point where flow of urine starts. Hold catheter firmly in place until balloon is inflated.	Evaluate to determine whether catheter is placed in bladder.
20. If urine does not immediately flow, exert gentle pressure over bladder, or ask patient to cough or deep breathe.	Catheter may need to be reinserted slightly in case it has been expelled a bit before inflation of balloon.
21. Inflate balloon with 8 to 10 mL of sterile water. Amount of pressure should be same as when testing balloon.	If amount of pressure is increased, evaluate placement; balloon may be in urethra. Evaluate and monitor patient for complications.
22. Gently withdraw catheter until balloon rests against bladder neck.	If patient has had a sphincterotomy, do not pull back on catheter.
23. Attach catheter to sterile drainage system.	
24. Tape catheter to upper inner thigh.	
25. Perform perineal care.	
26. Discard used equipment in appropriate manner.	Disposal is according to infection control guidelines.
27. Remove gloves, and wash hands.	
28. Restore patient to comfortable position and appropriate dress.	

DOCUMENTATION

1. Document in the care plan and patient record the size and type of catheter, the size of the balloon, the date of change, any special instructions, and the level of staff to perform the procedure.

2. Document any complications or significant observations, and notify the physician.

3. Record any participation by the patient or primary caregiver in the procedure.

Suprapubic Cystostomy Catheterization

PURPOSES

To establish urinary drainage through a suprapubic cystostomy; to avoid the disadvantages and complications of a urethral indwelling catheter.

STAFF RESPONSIBLE

EQUIPMENT

1. Prepackaged sterile catheterization tray (without catheter).
2. Indwelling catheter (size indicated by physician).
3. 30-mL Syringe with approximately 22-gauge needle.
4. Another 30-mL syringe (if changing catheter).
5. Sterile water vial.
6. Nonsterile gloves.
7. Washcloths, soap, and water.
8. Plastic bags.
9. Sheet or bath blanket.
10. Sterile leg bag or bedside drainage bag.
11. Tape.
12. Two 4 × 4 fenestrated gauze pads.

GENERAL CONSIDERATIONS

1. The physician's order for catheterization must include the type and size of catheter and balloon and the amount of solution needed to inflate the balloon.
2. This procedure must be performed with sterile technique.
3. Assistance may be needed to carry out the procedure if the patient is severely spastic or unable to cooperate.
4. Maintain privacy throughout the procedure.
5. If the patient is allergic to Betadine, order benzylchonium chloride solution. Indicate ''Allergy To'' per agency protocol.

PATIENT AND FAMILY EDUCATION

1. Education should include the purpose and proper technique for catheterization as well as how to observe for and prevent complications such as infection.
2. Whenever possible, involve the patient and family in the procedure.

PROCEDURE

Steps	Additional Information
1. Prepare patient for procedure: explain procedure, and provide privacy. Gather equipment, and adjust lighting.	
2. Place patient in supine position with legs extended.	If patient is severely spastic, you may need assistance to perform catheterization.
3. Wash hands, and don nonsterile gloves.	
4. Remove dressing from stoma site.	Note any redness, drainage, and the like.
5. Pull existing catheter gently until resistance is met. Note catheter size and type and balloon size; measure length exposed.	Measure with measuring tape or ruler from stoma site to end of catheter.
6. Aspirate fluid from balloon with 30-mL syringe, and remove catheter.	See Deflating a Defective Indwelling Catheter Balloon procedure, if balloon does not deflate.
7. Gently remove catheter.	Observe catheter for calculi, grit, or clots. Roll tip of catheter between fingers to note grit.
8. Dispose of catheter and draining bag appropriately.	Disposal is according to infection control procedures.
9. Cleanse suprapubic stoma site with soap and water. Remove gloves, and wash hands.	
10. Fill sterile 30-mL syringe with prescribed amount of sterile water.	Place filled syringe next to sterile field.
11. Open catheterization tray, and establish sterile field. Open catheter package, and place on sterile field.	Provide bag for disposal. Avoid contamination of catheter and sterile field.
12. Place top drape on or next to patient's abdomen or symphysis pubis.	
13. Place second drape over suprapubic stoma site.	

Steps	*Additional Information*
14. Put on sterile gloves.	
15. Pour Betadine over cotton balls, and lubricate catheter.	Lubricate from tip to approximate length as measured before.
16. To test balloon, hold sterile water-filled syringe with nondominant hand, attach to balloon lumen, and slowly inflate and deflate.	Discard catheter if balloon does not inflate or deflate easily. Nondominant hand is now contaminated.
17. Position nondominant hand lightly over stoma.	This acts as anchor during cleansing and catheter insertion.
18. Cleanse stoma with Betadine-soaked cotton balls held in forceps.	Cleansing motion should start at center of stoma and continue in spiral motion away from center. Discard each cotton ball after one use.
19. Pick up catheter with dominant hand, holding it about 4 inches from tip with open end in sterile collecting tray.	
20. Gently insert well-lubricated catheter into stoma 1 to 2 inches beyond previously estimated length.	If resistance is felt, direct tip of catheter toward symphysis pubis. Notify physician if resistance continues.
21. If urine does not immediately flow, exert gentle pressure over bladder, or ask patient to deep breathe.	If more than 500 mL of urine is in bladder, pinch catheter for 5 to 10 minutes before allowing remaining urine to drain.
22. Using prefilled syringe, inflate balloon with prescribed amount of sterile water.	
23. Gently withdraw catheter until resistance is met.	
24. Connect catheter to sterile drainage system.	
25. Dress stoma with fenestrated 4 × 4 gauze pads. Tape securely.	Preserves skin integrity around stoma.
26. Discard used equipment in appropriate manner.	Disposal is according to infection control procedures.
27. Remove gloves.	
28. Tape catheter to abdomen.	This prevents pulling or pressure on catheter.
29. Restore patient to comfortable position and appropriate dress.	
30. Wash hands.	

DOCUMENTATION

1. Document in the care plan and patient record the size and type of catheter, the size of the balloon, the length of catheter exposed, the date of change, any special instructions, and the level of staff to perform the procedure.

2. Document any complications or significant observations, and notify the physician.

3. Record any participation by the patient or primary caregiver in the procedure.

Male Sterile Intermittent Catheterization: Touchless

PURPOSE

To provide periodic drainage of urine from the bladder.

STAFF RESPONSIBLE

EQUIPMENT

1. Touchless sterile catheter kit.
2. Nonsterile gloves (2 pairs).
3. Washcloth, soap, and water.

GENERAL CONSIDERATIONS

1. A physician's order is required for catheterization.
2. Assistance may be needed to carry out the procedure if the patient's legs are severely spastic or if he is unable to cooperate.

3. Sterile technique must be used with this procedure.
4. Maintain privacy for the patient throughout the procedure.
5. If the foreskin is present, retract it over the head of the penis. If this is not possible or if the foreskin will not remain in position, notify the physician. While performing groin care, wash the penis with the foreskin down and then with the foreskin retracted.
6. When introducing the catheter, sometimes resistance is met. If resistance is suspected to be due to sphincter tone, try one or more of the following techniques:

- Have the patient take a deep breath or use the incentive spirometer. When the patient exhales, gently advance the catheter.
- Try ROM to the lower extremities before catheter insertion.
- Position the patient's legs with his hips externally rotated and his knees flexed (frog-leg position).
- Position the patient on his side with his hips and knees flexed.

- Try anal stretch (see methods to stimulate voiding and to empty the bladder).

If none of these techniques works, stop and notify the physician.

7. If resistance is thought to be the result of stricture, consult the physician regarding the use of a coudé tip catheter.
8. For patients with spinal cord injury at T-6 or above, autonomic dysreflexia may occur during catheter insertion. Anesthetic lubricant may be used if this is a chronic problem.

PATIENT AND FAMILY EDUCATION

1. Education should include the purpose and proper technique for catheterization. Also instruct on how to observe for and prevent potential complications such as infection, incomplete emptying of the bladder, and difficulty in introduction of the catheter.
2. Whenever possible, involve the patient and family in the procedure.

PROCEDURE

Steps	*Additional Information*
1. Prepare patient: Explain procedure, and provide privacy. Gather equipment.	
2. Wash hands, and don nonsterile gloves.	
3. Perform groin care. Remove gloves, and wash hands.	
4. Don nonsterile gloves.	
5. Open catheterization kit, and remove contents.	Save outer package.
6. Open lubricant package, and hold it between fingers.	
7. Pick up catheter sheath, and remove plastic cover at top. Do not let anything touch top of cuff.	Top edge and inside of cuff must remain sterile.
8. Push on sides of cuff to form a round opening.	
9. Squeeze lubricant into bottom of cuff chamber.	Do not let lubricant package touch inside portion of cuff.
10. Push catheter up through clear plastic guide to lubricate it. Then slide catheter down below tip of catheter guide.	
11. Place catheter sheath carefully across outer package.	This will keep top edge of cuff from touching anything.
12. Open package of Betadine swabs.	If patient is allergic to Betadine, benzylchonium chloride may be used.
13. Using nondominant hand, hold penis upward at 60° to 90° angle to body.	If foreskin is present, it should be retracted and held in place during procedure.
14. Cleanse urinary meatus once with each swab. Cleanse in a circular motion, starting at meatus and working away from it.	Cleanse entire head of penis and distal area of shaft.
15. Still holding penis at 60° to 90° angle, pick up catheter sheath near cuff.	Do not touch top edge or inside of cuff.
16. Place cuff over head of penis, and hold in place with nondominant hand. Position so that urinary opening is against catheter guide.	
17. Using dominant hand, push catheter up through catheter guide, and gently insert catheter into urinary opening.	Use nondominant hand to hold penis and catheter guide and dominant hand to push catheter. Thumb and finger of nondominant hand can pinch catheter through guide so that you can readjust fingers on catheter while advancing it.
18. Insert catheter until you note a urine flow; advance catheter slightly beyond this point.	If resistance is met, use suggested methods to overcome it. If resistance continues, stop and notify physician.

Steps	Additional Information
19. Holding catheter firmly in place, allow urine to flow until bladder is empty or bag is full.	If more than 500 mL of urine is in bladder, pinch or remove catheter for 5 to 10 minutes, and then continue draining bladder.
20. When flow stops, retract catheter slightly, and observe for more urine flow.	May need to perform gentle Credé maneuver to empty bladder completely.
21. Withdraw catheter. Note volume of urine collected, and empty urine into toilet.	
22. Perform groin care.	
23. Dispose of used equipment appropriately.	Disposal is according to infection control procedures.
24. Remove gloves, wash hands.	
25. Restore patient to comfortable position and appropriate dress.	

DOCUMENTATION

1. Document the amount of urine and the time of the procedure.
2. Document any complications or significant observations, and notify the physician.
3. Document patient and primary caregiver education and involvement in the procedure.

Female Sterile Intermittent Catheterization: Touchless

PURPOSE

To perform periodic drainage of urine from the bladder.

STAFF RESPONSIBLE

EQUIPMENT

1. Touchless sterile catheterization kit.
2. Nonsterile gloves (2 pairs).
3. Washcloth, soap, and water.
4. Flashlight (optional).

GENERAL CONSIDERATIONS

1. A physician's order is required for catheterization.
2. Assistance may be needed to carry out the procedure if the patient's legs are severely spastic, if she is unable to cooperate, or if lighting is poor.
3. Sterile technique must be used with this procedure.
4. Maintain privacy for the patient throughout the procedure.
5. For patients with spinal cord injury at T-6 or above, autonomic dysreflexia may occur during catheter insertion. Anesthetic lubricant may be used if this is a chronic problem.

PATIENT AND FAMILY EDUCATION

1. Education should include the purpose and proper technique for catheterization as well as how to observe for and prevent complications such as infection or incomplete emptying of the bladder.
2. Whenever possible, involve the patient and family in the procedure.

PROCEDURE

Steps	Additional Information
1. Prepare patient: Explain procedure, and provide privacy. Gather equipment.	
2. Wash hands. Don nonsterile gloves.	
3. Perform perineal care. Remove gloves, and wash hands.	
4. Don nonsterile gloves.	
5. Open catheter kit, and remove contents.	Save outer package.

Steps	Additional Information
6. Open lubricant package, and hold it between fingers.	
7. Pick up catheter sheath, and remove plastic cover at top.	Do not allow anything to touch catheter guide.
8. Squeeze lubricant into catheter guide.	Do not touch lubricant package to catheter guide.
9. Advance catheter ½ to 1 inch above catheter guide to lubricate. Then slide catheter back below tip of catheter guide.	
10. Open package of Betadine swabs.	If patient is allergic to Betadine, benzylchonium chloride may be used.
11. Place catheter sheath across outer package so that catheter guide does not touch anything.	
12. Using nondominant hand, hold labia minora apart so that urinary meatus is well visualized.	Ensure adequate lighting.
13. Cleanse urinary meatus once with each swab.	Cleanse downward once with each swab from clitoral area to vagina. Cleanse both sides of meatus before cleansing meatus itself.
14. Pick up catheter sheath with dominant hand, holding catheter through catheter guide. Advance tip of catheter slightly beyond tip of catheter guide.	Continue holding labia open with nondominant hand.
15. Insert catheter tip into meatus.	
16. Hold soft, top end of catheter guide gently but firmly against meatus.	
17. Move nondominant hand to catheter guide and dominant hand to bag, holding catheter 1 inch below guide.	Be sure to maintain gentle pressure of catheter guide against meatus.
18. Gently advance catheter with dominant hand.	
19. Stabilize catheter through catheter guide with nondominant hand, and return dominant hand to below catheter guide.	
20. Continue in this manner until urine starts to flow. Advance catheter slightly beyond this point.	If resistance is met, ask patient to deep breathe, and advance catheter on exhalation. If resistance continues, stop and notify physician.
21. Holding catheter firmly in place, allow urine to flow until bladder is empty or bag is full.	If more than 500 mL of urine is in bladder, pinch or remove catheter for 5 to 10 minutes, and then continue draining bladder.
22. When flow stops, retract catheter slightly, and observe for more urine return.	May perform gentle Credé maneuver to empty bladder completely.
23. Withdraw catheter. Note volume of urine collected, and empty urine into toilet.	
24. Perform perineal care.	
25. Dispose of used equipment appropriately.	Disposal is according to infection control procedures.
26. Remove gloves. Wash hands.	
27. Restore patient to comfortable position and appropriate dress.	

DOCUMENTATION

1. Document the amount of urine and the time of the procedure.

2. Document any complications or significant observations, and notify the physician.

3. Document patient and primary caregiver education and involvement in the procedure.

Preparation of Normal Saline Solution for Home Use

PURPOSE

To teach patients and families how to prepare sterile normal saline solution for home use.

STAFF RESPONSIBLE

EQUIPMENT

1. Table salt, two level teaspoons.
2. Distilled water, 1 qt.

3. Deep pan or kettle with tight lid.
4. Clean glass jar or wide-mouth bottle (1-qt size) with lid.

GENERAL CONSIDERATIONS

1. Two level teaspoons of table salt in one quart of distilled water is the formula commonly used to approximate normal saline solution.
2. The procedure should be taught to patients and families who will be performing procedures after discharge requiring normal saline solution and is not meant to be used as a routine in the hospital. It is much less costly than purchasing the solution at a pharmacy.
3. If distilled water is not available, boiled tap water may be used.
4. Allow the solution to cool or warm to room temperature before use.
5. The solution is good for 1 week (kept in the refrigerator) once the glass container has been opened.

PROCEDURE

Steps	*Additional Information*
1. Assemble supplies needed to prepare solution.	
2. Pour two level teaspoons of table salt into glass quart-size jar or bottle.	
3. Add distilled water to jar to make 1 qt of solution.	If distilled water is not available, boil needed amount of tap water for 5 minutes before use. Allow any sediment to settle to bottom before pouring into solution container.
4. Tighten lid, and mix well.	
5. Loosen lid, and place jar or bottle into deep pan or kettle.	A loosened lid allows for expansion during heating process.
6. Add water to pan or kettle to depth of 4 to 6 inches.	
7. Put lid on pan or kettle, and boil for 20 minutes.	
8. Allow to cool, and tighten lid on glass container.	
9. Label container with type of solution and date prepared.	

DOCUMENTATION

1. Document the teaching done, progress, and patient and family outcomes of being able to prepare the solution.

Disinfecting Urinary Drainage Equipment for Home Use

PURPOSE

To teach patients and families how to disinfect urinary drainage equipment at home.

STAFF RESPONSIBLE

EQUIPMENT

1. Leg bag or bedside drainage bag.
2. Tubing and cap.
3. Bulb syringe or turkey baster.
4. Bleach solution.
5. Two quarts of tap water (or more).
6. Cotton-tipped applicator (Q-Tips), toothpick, or small bottle cleaner.
7. Soap and running water.
8. Basin (dish pan or bath basin).

GENERAL CONSIDERATIONS

1. This procedure is utilized for patient education purposes and is not meant to be used as a routine in the hospital.
2. Patients with a resistant infection are not to clean their used equipment. Equipment is discarded after use for these patients.
3. As many leg bags as can be totally submerged in the bleach solution can be disinfected at the same time (an average basin holds three to five leg bags).

PATIENT AND FAMILY EDUCATION

Education should include the purpose and proper technique for disinfecting urinary drainage equipment as well as how to observe for and prevent potential complications such as infection and skin irritation from contact with bleach solution.

PROCEDURE

Steps	Additional Information
1. Disconnect rubber tubing from leg bag to be disinfected.	
2. Wash bag and tubing in hot, soapy water.	Wash cap if disinfecting night drainage bag.
3. Force soapy solution through top valve of bag with syringe. Clean out any material adherent to inside of leg adaptor with cotton-tipped applicator.	
4. Turn leg bag upside-down when filled with soapy solution to test flutter valve at top.	If water runs out, throw bag away.
5. Hold bag and tubing under faucet to rinse.	
6. Mix bleach and water solution in basin.	For leg bags, concentration of mixture should be 5 mL of bleach to 1 qt of water. Night drainage bags require 1 tbsp of bleach to 1 gal of water.
7. Fill bag half full with bleach solution, then submerge bag and tubing in basin.	Use bulb syringe to fill. Solution should be in contact with entire inner surface of bag.
8. Soak bags for 1 hour.	One hour is minimum time. They may also be left overnight; cover basin if left overnight.
9. To remove, drain enough solution from basin so that you can pick up bag and tubing without putting your hand in solution.	Allow solution to drain completely out of bag and tubing.
10. Attach hose to adaptors on top and bottom of bag without touching adaptors.	Use cap to cover adaptor or night drainage bag.
11. Store in clean, dry place until ready for use.	Recommended places include a cabinet or drawer.

DOCUMENTATION

1. Documentation should include patient and family education, any unusual circumstances or problems noted, and the ability of the patient and family to carry out the procedure safely.

Disinfecting Reusable Urinary Irrigation Syringe for Home Use

PURPOSE

To teach patients and families how to disinfect a reusable urinary irrigation syringe (Asepto bulb syringe) at home.

STAFF RESPONSIBLE

EQUIPMENT

1. Asepto bulb syringe.
2. Small jar.
3. Soap and water.
4. Pan with lid.

GENERAL CONSIDERATIONS

1. This procedure is utilized for patient education purposes and is not meant to be used as a routine in the hospital.
2. A supply of Asepto syringes and jars may be made available in the hospital for patient education purposes. If a patient is to use this procedure in the hospital for reinforcement of learning, an Asepto bulb syringe for the individual patient must be ordered. In addition, this patient or family should bring a small jar from home for the irrigation solution.
3. Patients with resistant infection are not to disinfect used urinary equipment. Equipment is discarded after use for these patients.

PATIENT AND FAMILY EDUCATION

Education should include the purpose and proper technique for disinfection of the syringe as well as how to observe for and prevent potential complications such as infection.

PROCEDURE

Steps	*Additional Information*
1. Wash bulb, glass syringe, jar, pan, and lid with soapy water, and rinse.	
2. Place glass syringe, rubber bulb, and jar for solution in pan, and cover with water.	
3. Boil 15 minutes (covered) at rolling boil.	
4. Allow water and equipment to cool.	
5. Pour off water (keep cover over pan while pouring).	
6. Store equipment in pan (covered) until ready to use.	
7. When ready to use, remove jar and then syringe and bulb (squirt water out of bulb).	

DOCUMENTATION

1. Documentation should include patient and family education, any unusual circumstances or problems noted, and the ability of the patient and family to carry out the procedure safely.

BIBLIOGRAPHY

Broadwell, D., & Jackson, B. (1982). *Principles of ostomy care*. St. Louis, MO: Mosby.

Brunner, L.S., & Suddarth, D.S. (1984). *Textbook of medical surgical nursing*. Philadelphia: Lippincott.

Burkitt, D.P., & Meisner, P. (1979). How to manage constipation with high fiber diet. *Geriatrics, 33*, 33–38.

Cannon, B. (1981). Bowel function. In N. Martin, N.B. Holt, & D. Hicks (Eds.), *Comprehensive rehabilitation nursing* (pp. 223-241). New York: McGraw-Hill.

Cardenas, D.D., Kelly, E., & Mayo, M.E. (1985). Manual stimulation of reflex voiding after spinal cord injury. *Archives of Physical Medicine and Rehabilitation, 66*, 459–462.

Johnson, J. (1980). Rehabilitative aspects of neurologic bladder dysfunction: Symposium on Rehabilitation Nursing. *Nursing Clinics of North America, 15*, 293–308.

King, R.B., Boyink, M., & Keenan, M. (1977). *Rehabilitation guide*. Chicago: Rehabilitation Institute of Chicago.

Matthews, P. (1987). Elimination. In P. Matthews, C. Carlson, & N. Holt (Eds.), *Spinal cord injury: A guide to rehabilitation nursing*. Rockville, MD: Aspen.

McConnell, E.A., & Zimmerman, M.F. (1983). *Care of patients with urologic problems*. Philadelphia: Lippincott.

McCormick, K.A., Scheve, A.S., & Leahy, E. (1988). Nursing management of urinary incontinence in geriatric inpatients. *Nursing Clinics of North America, 23*, 231–363.

Newman, E., Price, M., & Magney, J. (1986). *Care of the disabled urinary tract*. Springfield, IL: Thomas.

O'Brien, M.T., & Pallett, P.J. (1978). *Total care of the stroke patient*. Boston: Little, Brown.

Pallett, P.J., & O'Brien, M.T. (1985). *Textbook of neurosurgical nursing*. Boston: Little, Brown.

Shields, L. (1981). Urinary function. In N. Martin, N. Holt, & D. Hicks (Eds.), *Comprehensive rehabilitation nursing* (pp. 186–222). New York: McGraw-Hill.

Stass, W.E., & DeNault, P.M. (1973). Bowel control. *American Family Physician, 7*, 90–100.

Wu, Y. (1983). Total bladder care for the spinal cord injured patient. *Annals of the Academy of Medicine (Singapore), 12*, 391.

Wu, Y., Nanninga, J.B., & Hamilton, B.B. (1986). Inhibition of the external urethral sphincter and sacral reflex by anal stretch in spinal cord injured patients. *Archives of Physical Medicine and Rehabilitation, 67*, 135–136.

chapter 4

Procedures To Maintain and Restore Tissue Integrity

INTRODUCTION

The emphasis of this chapter is prevention and management of pressure sores. Pressure sores are a source of morbidity and mortality for individuals with chronic illness and disability and can create tremendous financial, personal, and social costs. Pressure sores are a particular risk in conditions resulting in motor or sensory deficits or debilitation and among elderly persons with acute or chronic illness. It has been estimated that 5% to 10% (50,000 to 100,000) of patients hospitalized in the United States each year develop pressure sores (Shanon, 1982). The incidence of pressure sores varies widely according to the population studied, but several studies have demonstrated a high incidence in elderly patients (Norton, McLaren, & Exton-Smith, 1962; Barbenel, Jordan, Nicol, & Clark, 1977) and persons with neurologic disorders.

A pressure sore is an area of soft tissue necrosis, generally found over bony prominences, that results from interruption of blood supply to the tissue. Although pressure is considered the primary factor in the development of pressure sores, the amount and duration required to produce tissue necrosis appear to vary. Multiple intrinsic factors such as body temperature and metabolic status and extrinsic factors such as friction and shear contribute to tissue necrosis. Therefore, assessment of factors that increase risk for pressure sores and interfere with wound healing is a critical nursing function. In recent years, nurse authors have suggested that the incidence of pressure sores can be decreased through improved assessment of risk and rigorous application of preventive measures for those at risk (King, 1981; Braden & Bergstrom, 1987; Gosnell, 1987). Several scales that systemize risk assessment have been developed (Norton et al, 1962; Bergstrom,

Demuth, & Braden, 1987; Gosnell, 1973). The scales have not been included in this chapter, but nurses are encouraged to evaluate these instruments for clinical application in a specific setting. Most scales employ the criteria of mobility, continence, nutrition, and mental alertness.

Over the years, a large variety of treatments have been proposed to aid healing of pressure sores. Until recent years, few treatments were based on controlled studies of wound healing. The nurse, in collaboration with the physician, should evaluate the merit of a potential treatment and should assess its effectiveness for an individual patient. Interventions to promote healing should be based on the classification of severity of breakdown and on the presence or absence of exudate and eschar. To assist in decision making in the choice of dressing, a procedure describes options for dressings on the basis of grade and characteristics of the pressure sore. A specific dressing procedure representing each option category is included.

Claims are made frequently for the pressure relief effectiveness of numerous support devices, but again, many claims are not based on research. Before selecting a support surface for institution-wide or individual patient use, it is wise to seek evidence of effectiveness in laboratory or clinical settings. Recent interest in the evaluation of support systems has resulted in the publication of a number of studies that provide a basis for decision making about special mattresses, beds, and cushions (Lilla, Friedrichs, & Vistnes, 1975; Wells & Geden, 1984; Krouskop, Williams, Krebs, Herszkowicz, & Garber, 1985; Maklebust, Mondoux, & Sieggreen, 1986).

Patient and family education is a primary consideration in prevention and management of pressure sores for individuals with chronic risk factors. Specific skin procedures for home care are available elsewhere and are not included in this manual (King, Boyink, & Keenan, 1977). The clinical discipline responsible for some aspects of patient education related to skin care varies from agency to agency. For example, an occupational therapist, physical therapist, or nurse may select wheelchair cushions and teach pressure relief behavior. Nevertheless, nursing generally has primary responsibility for skin care education and is always responsible for reinforcing all aspects of skin care and for ensuring the correct use of equipment.

Decisions regarding preventive measures as well as procedures to manage existing sores are based on thorough assessment of the patient, environment, and activities. Socioemotional factors also influence patient and family education about skin care and decisions affecting postdischarge care and are a consideration for assessment.

An attempt has been made to be objective in describing wound care options and support surfaces. Inclusion of a product does not represent endorsement or recommendation for use.

Assessment and Management of Pressure Sore Risk Factors

PURPOSES

To prevent pressure sores; to minimize risk factors; to prevent further damage; to promote healing.

STAFF RESPONSIBLE

GENERAL CONSIDERATIONS

1. A patient's individual skin care plan should reflect the following considerations:
   - risk factors,
   - economics,
   - feasibility,
   - compatibility with activities of daily living (ADLs), and
   - patient goals.
2. Intrinsic (person-related) risk factors that appear to be most predictive of risk for pressure sores are:
   - mental status,
   - mobility,
   - nutrition,
   - decreased sensation,
   - elevated temperature, and
   - low diastolic blood pressure.
3. Extrinsic factors that contribute to the development of pressure sores are:
   - pressure in excess of capillary pressure that is sustained for long periods,
   - shear forces,
   - friction,
   - local moisture (incontinence, perspiration, or humidity), and
   - local temperature (elevated local temperature from contact with a surface).
4. The literature on pressure sores indicates that elderly patients (Norton et al., 1962; Lowthian, 1979) and individuals with spinal cord injuries (Young & Burns, 1981) have a high incidence of pressure sores.
5. Involve the patient and primary caregiver in planning the skin care program as soon as possible.
6. Assess the patient's and primary caregiver's knowledge of prevention and management of skin breakdown.
7. Avoid the use of agents that can dry the skin (alcohol and excess soap), especially for older persons.
8. For dry skin problems, use emollients.
9. Do not massage over a red area as it produces friction and increased pressure.
10. Routine pressure relief with a turning schedule is required for all persons at risk for pressure sores. Increased frequency of pressure relief or special support device is advised for a patient who is at high risk (i.e., having several risk factors).
11. Inadequate nutrition contributes to the risk for pressure sore formation. Assess the patient's dietary intake and the presence of hypoproteinemia, anemia, or avitaminosis.
12. Cleanse patients after incontinence, and apply emollient lotion, if needed. Change wet clothing and bed linens immediately.
13. Mobilize patients, and perform routine range of motion (ROM) to prevent contractures. Contractures and other body deformities alter pressure loading and can result in increased risk for pressure sores.

PATIENT AND FAMILY EDUCATION

1. Educate the patient and family about actual and potential risk factors and interventions to decrease risk when the risk for pressure sore development is chronic.
2. Teach and reinforce:
   - assessment of risk factors and early signs of skin necrosis,
   - preventive skin care measures,
   - adaptation of the program to various community situations,
   - guidelines for safely upgrading skin tolerance,
   - methods to monitor skin problems, and
   - management of skin redness or breakdown.

PROCEDURE

Steps	Additional Information
1. Assess patient's risk for pressure sores. Consider patient at high risk if he or she exhibits risk factors. • Attempt to minimize those risk factors that can be reduced through nursing interventions (marked with asterisk in right column). • Reassess patient routinely for changes in risk factors. Alter plan on basis of these factors. Frequency of assessment is based on acuity and severity of risk factors.	Risk factors include: • advanced age (older than 60 years of age), • low diastolic blood pressure, • decreased mobility,* • decreased sensation, • fever or infection,* • moisture or diaphoresis,* • incontinence (bowel and bladder),* • dry skin,* • edema,* • nutritional state (anemia, hypoproteinemia, or avitaminosis),* • medication that can alter mental status,* • overweight or underweight,* • decreased muscle tone, and • decreased hydration.*
2. Minimize duration of pressure: • Change patient's position frequently. Establish tissue tolerance time for patient when lying or sitting on basis of individual's ability to tolerate pressure and risk factors. • When patient is sitting, reinforce pressure reliefs every 15 to 30 minutes. • Upgrade skin tolerance time slowly (no more than 30 minutes at a time). Assess skin carefully when attempting new tolerance time.	See procedure on Turning and Positioning (below). When patient is recumbent, attempt to incorporate as many different positions as possible (side, back, and prone lying). Small shifts in position are also advised. Patients with multiple risk factors may not tolerate repositioning every 2 hours. Turning hourly, making small shifts, and using supports that provide pressure no greater than 30 mmHg are options. See procedures on Pressure Relief Activities (below). Assess that established program is well tolerated (hyperemia resolves in 30 minutes or less) before continuing to upgrade tolerance.
3. Minimize intensity of pressure: • Use pressure relieving devices (special beds, mattress toppers, wheelchair cushions, and elbow and foot protectors). • Consider bridging bony prominences with pillows or foam blocks and using positioning techniques that distribute pressure more evenly (proning).	See procedure on choosing support surfaces (below). When choosing a device, consider its effectiveness in decreasing pressure, its cost, and whether it will alter patient's abilities (e.g., make ADLs more difficult). See procedures on Turning and Positioning (below). When bridging, check with your hand to be sure that bony prominence lies between pillows or blocks and receives no pressure.
4. Perform frequent skin checks: • after each turn and after sitting, and • at least twice a day for chronic conditions after tolerance is established. Bony prominences must be monitored more frequently than twice daily whenever there is a change in any part of skin program or in patient's risk factors or if any redness, heat, or swelling is noticed in area. If any signs of damage are noticed, ensure that area receives no pressure until signs have resolved. Then revise program to decrease possibility of recurrence.	See procedure on Skin Check (below). Patients must continue skin checks at home when risk factors persist. If any change occurs, assess skin after each turn or transfer from wheelchair until you are certain that current tolerance (length of time lying or sitting without pressure relief) is acceptable. Check site every 15 minutes. If signs of circulatory impairment do not resolve within 30 minutes, length of time sitting or lying without pressure relief must be reduced.
5. Minimize shearing forces by limiting amount of time patient sits at greater than 30° but less than 90°.	When patient sits in this position, sacrum and attached deep fascia slide downward while skin stays in same position

Steps	Additional Information
	(shearing). This action causes stretching and angulation of local blood vessels and contributes to tissue necrosis.
6. Support patient's feet against footplate or footboard to prevent sliding when sitting in bed.	
7. Minimize friction:	Friction increases potential for skin breakdown by applying mechanical forces to skin and can cause abrasion.
• Avoid sliding patient across sheets. Turning sheets should not be used routinely but only when specifically included in care plan and if proper use is demonstrated.	Turning sheet may result in less friction for repositioning heavy patients who are difficult to raise off sheet during turns.
• Avoid sliding bare skin against transfer sliding board.	
• Patients with spasticity may need careful positioning or padding to reduce friction.	

DOCUMENTATION

1. Document the assessment of the skin condition and risk factors.
2. Note the skin care program, including tolerances, pressure reliefs, skin checks, and other interventions.
3. Note patient and family teaching and their ability to carry out the program.
4. Document the patient's response to the skin care program.

Assessment of a Pressure Sore

PURPOSES

To assess accurately, to communicate, and to document skin breakdown.

STAFF RESPONSIBLE

EQUIPMENT

1. Adequate lighting (overhead or flashlight).
2. Straight-edge ruler or other measuring device.
3. Sterile probe.

GENERAL CONSIDERATIONS

1. Assessment and documentation should occur when skin breakdown or redness is initially noted. Assess a reddened area each time the person is repositioned and open areas with each dressing change.
2. Documentation includes all standard criteria applicable to pressure sore assessment. Objective terminology is used at all times.
3. If the pressure sore is not responding to treatment, the plan of care should be reevaluated.

PATIENT AND FAMILY EDUCATION

1. Patients and primary caregivers are taught to assess pressure sores before passes and if a pressure sore is present at discharge.
2. Emphasize the importance of contacting the clinical service if healing does not progress or if the sore deteriorates.

PROCEDURE

Standard Criteria	Additional Information
1. *Size:* Measure length and width of pressure sore area with ruler or commercially available plastic measuring device.	Do not contaminate sore with measurement tool. Measure largest diameter, then take another measurement perpendicular to largest diameter.

Standard Criteria	*Additional Information*
2. *Depth or tissue involved:* If tunneled or deep wound, measure with sterile probe or cotton swab, then measure probe against ruler.	For shallow wounds, assessment of tissue involved (i.e., grade) is better than pure depth. Necrotic tissue results in inaccurate assessment.
3. *Shape:* If not circular, draw scaled-down version of shape in assessment chart form.	
4. *Location:* Describe in terms of nearest anatomical landmark.	For example, right medial malleolus or sacrum.
5. *Color:* Include that of wound base edges and surrounding tissue.	Describe changes in hue in relation to person's normal color.
6. *Heat:* Note whether heat is present over site or around sore.	Compare temperature to contralateral body part if possible.
7. *Edema:* Note whether edema is present and its extent.	
8. *Edges and surrounding tissue:* Note whether edges are regular or irregular, distinct or not, rolled under, or different in color.	If surrounding tissue is affected, describe color, extent, and grade if applicable. Deeper wounds have more distinct edges.
9. *Necrotic or healthy tissue:* Describe color, extent, and location in sore.	Describe anything that is not pink, healthy tissue. Describe simply and objectively.
10. *Drainage:* Describe presence, color, opacity, and amount.	If there is no drainage, note whether sore is moist or dry. Measure soiled area on sponge or in terms of number of sponges soiled and the length of time dressing was in place.
11. *Odor:* Describe whether odor is present, strong, or recognizable.	
12. *Grading pressure sores:* See Shea (1975).	
• Grade 1. Ulcer is limited to epidermis: ill-defined area of soft tissue swelling, induration, heat, and erythema over bony prominence that is sustained for 24 hours *or* partial-thickness ulcer limited to epidermis.	All soft tissue layers involved, but there may not be a break in epidermis. Dermis may be exposed but remains intact.
• Grade 2. Shallow full-thickness ulcer that penetrates dermis, leaving subcutaneous tissue intact.	Edges are more distinct with early fibrosis and pigmentation changes, blending into broad, indistinct area of heat, erythema, and induration.
• Grade 3. Ulcer extends into subcutaneous fat; limited by deep fascia.	Extensive undermining can occur along with infection. Edges are distinct and rolled with alternating dark and light pigmentation. Muscle is intact but is distorted by swelling and inflammation.
• Grade 4. Deep fascia is penetrated with extensive soft tissue involvement; bone may be exposed.	Clinical presentation resembles grade 3 but bone may be exposed (this may not be visible because of necrotic tissue or drainage). Large amounts of drainage and necrotic tissue are usually present.
• Grade closed. Deep sinuslike ulcer that is lined by reactive fibrosis and extends to deep fascia or bone. May be closed or draining through small skin defect.	Area may be small and appear benign but is potentially serious lesion.

DOCUMENTATION

1. All standard assessment criteria are recorded each time that the pressure sore assessment is documented.
2. Frequency of documentation is based on institutional policy.
3. Document any change in nursing interventions on the basis of the assessment.

Skin Check

PURPOSES

To assess skin areas (with emphasis on bony prominences) for the presence of potential or existing skin breakdown to maintain skin integrity; to promote wound healing by providing a basis for decision making.

STAFF RESPONSIBLE

EQUIPMENT

1. Mirrors. (Two mirrors are necessary for patients with high quadriplegia to do self-inspections. A long-handled mirror is issued to all patients who will learn the skin self-check procedure.)

GENERAL CONSIDERATIONS

1. Regular, systematic skin checks are essential for patients with decreased or absent sensation or impaired motor function as well as for those individuals assessed at risk for pressure sores on the basis of other risk factors.
2. Patients who are stable and at low risk, who maintain their turning tolerances and wheelchair tolerances, and who have intact, healthy skin require skin inspection twice a day (in the morning before dressing and at night when undressing).
3. In addition to routine twice-daily skin checks, inspection should be performed in the following circumstances:

- on admission;
- until sitting and turning tolerances are established by checking after wheelchair sitting or when the patient is recumbent, after each turn, until the patient is medically stable, and until high risk for pressure sores does not exist;
- when upgrading turning tolerance (with each turn) and when upgrading wheelchair tolerance (after sitting);
- when decreasing wheelchair tolerance (after sitting) and when decreasing turning tolerance (with each turn);
- every 15 minutes up to 1 hour after the initial skin check if circulation to the skin shows signs of impairment (after 1 hour, inspect the skin after each body repositioning until redness resolves—do *not* reposition on red area);
- when changing the type of supportive (cushion or mattress) or adaptive equipment being used, when the patient is wearing new shoes (after sitting or turning, after removal of equipment, and after the patient has been wearing shoes for 1 to 2 hours); and
- after wheelchair sitting or turning if risk factors increase.

PATIENT AND FAMILY EDUCATION

1. All patients with decreased or absent sensation or motor deficits should learn to check their own skin or how to direct or assist others in checking their skin.
2. Patients who are to be independent in skin checks are taught by the nurse and then supervised for each check until they regularly do self-initiated skin checks. After this point, periodic supervision is needed.
3. Patient education includes information about method of inspection, areas to be inspected, frequency of inspections (including upgrading of tolerance), and management when signs of pressure sores are noted.

PROCEDURE

Steps	*Additional Information*
1. Remove patient's clothing, and position patient in relation to areas to be checked, mirrors, and light source.	Many patients are able to do skin self-inspection (Figure 4-1). Patient position for skin check and position of mirror for self-inspection will be dependent on patient's previous activity or position and indications on nursing care plan. When checking skin of patient with high quadriplegia, position first mirror at inspection site. Position second mirror at patient's head so that patient can check skin. Positioning of second mirror is important because patient may need to teach others and needs to direct others regarding pressure points and management of alterations in skin.
2. Identify areas of the body to be checked (Figure 4-2).	All skin surfaces are checked, at minimum, during admission, before morning dressing, and when undressing in evening.

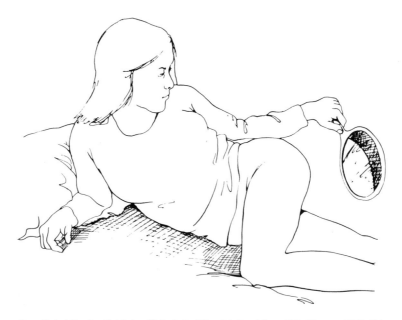

Figure 4-1 Skin Self-Check. *Source:* From *Rehabilitation Guide* (p. 63) by R.B. King, M. Boyink, and M. Keenan, 1977, Chicago, IL: Rehabilitation Institute of Chicago. Copyright 1977 by Rehabilitation Institute of Chicago. Reprinted by permission.

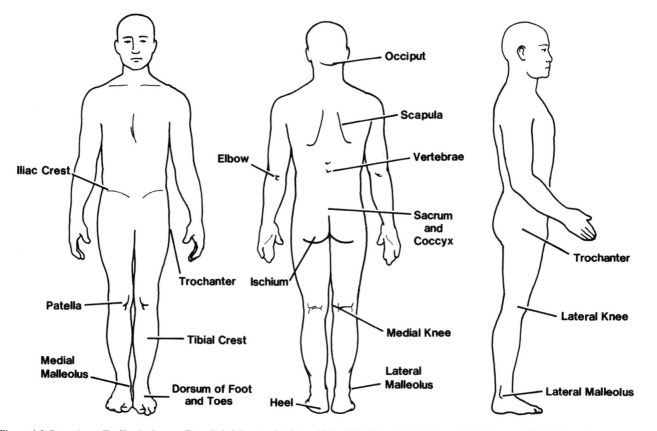

Figure 4-2 Bony Areas To Check. *Source:* From *Rehabilitation Guide* (p. 65) by R.B. King, M. Boyink, and M. Keenan, 1977, Chicago, IL: Rehabilitation Institute of Chicago. Copyright 1977 by Rehabilitation Institute of Chicago. Reprinted by permission.

Steps	*Additional Information*

3. Visually check the skin for:
  • signs of pressure (redness, blistering, open areas, areas of color or temperature changes, and rashes),
  • burns,
  • rashes,
  • excess moisture, and
  • abrasions.
Temperature changes in skin can be crudely assessed by touching area with back of fingers.
	Moisture between skin folds may result in maceration of skin. Tactile temperature checks are especially helpful if unable to detect redness in dark-skinned patients.

4. If signs of pressure sores are present (e.g., hyperemia that persists for more than 30 minutes, increased heat, swelling, or open area), position patient to relieve all pressure over area.	Refer to positioning and bridging procedures if necessary. Attempt to identify cause of damage, and take necessary action to prevent further damage to skin.
5. Reassess area in question in 15 minutes and again in 30 minutes if necessary. If redness is unresolved in 60 minutes, continue to monitor until resolution occurs.	Do not reposition patient on damaged areas. Professional nurse assesses pressure area after report of skin damage by nonprofessional staff member.
6. If signs of rash or moisture between skin folds are present, clean area with mild soap and water. Dry thoroughly, and air.	Apply medicated ointments only as directed by physician. Cornstarch may be applied to clean and dry skin fold.
7. Inform physician of skin breakdown, unresolved red areas, rashes, bruises, edema, and other skin changes.	

DOCUMENTATION

1. Document any unusual findings from the skin check (e.g., initial signs of pressure, resolution of pressure effects, rashes, edema, or any trauma to the skin).
2. Document changes in sitting and positioning tolerance, turning schedules, and local treatment of the skin area on the basis of the findings of the skin inspection.
3. Document the routine performance of the skin check according to institutional policy.

Pressure Relief Activities

PURPOSE

To prevent pressure sores by providing regular intermittent relief of pressure over bony prominences.

STAFF RESPONSIBLE

EQUIPMENT

See below under specific activities.

GENERAL CONSIDERATIONS

1. Pressure is considered the primary factor contributing to soft tissue necrosis and pressure sores.
2. Pressures greater than 32 mmHg interfere with circulation and thus with nutrition of tissues (Landis, 1930).
3. Pressure sores can be prevented by intermittent relief of pressure over bony prominences.
4. When the patient is in the recumbent position, the greatest pressures are exerted over the heels when supine and the trochanters when side lying. Therefore, these areas are at highest risk for skin breakdown. Few support surfaces reduce trochanteric and heel pressures to less than capillary pressure.
5. The greatest pressures over bony prominences occur when the patient is in the sitting position. In this position, pressure greater than 100 mmHg can be exerted over the ischia (Mooney, Einbund, Rogers, & Stauffer, 1971).
6. When mentation, sensation, and motor function are intact, persons change position in response to the discomfort of pressure. A deficit in any of these areas requires that the patient (or someone else) remember to relieve pressure.
7. When the patient is seated, pressure is relieved for a minimum of 10 seconds every 15 to 30 minutes (King, 1981; Kling, 1983). When recumbent, a change of position is usually recommended every 2 hours or more often, depending on the presence of risk factors.
8. Risk factors for the development of pressure sores may dictate more frequent pressure relief activity or the use of devices to distribute pressure evenly (see procedure on Assessment and Management of Pressure Sore Risk Factors, above).
9. Individualized assessment, goal setting, planning, reevaluation, and patient education are basic to the development of an effective pressure relief program.

PATIENT AND FAMILY EDUCATION

1. Teach the patient and primary caregiver:
   - frequency of pressure relief activities required,
   - length of pressure relief,
   - methods (includes requesting assistance),
   - the rationale for pressure relief,
   - assessment of the adequacy of pressure relief, and
   - the rationale and methods for increasing or decreasing the frequency of pressure relief.

   All these points are taught before hospital discharge. The first five are taught before a day or weekend pass, and the first three are taught when the patient initially sits for 30 minutes or longer. The presence of brain damage, aging, or anxiety associated with sitting for the first time or with transfer to a new unit can interfere with learning. Therefore, frequent assessment and reinforcement are generally required.
2. Physical therapists or occupational therapists may teach patients individualized techniques for push-ups and leans. Nevertheless, nurses provide initial instruction and evaluation of compliance when they assist the patient to sit for the first time.
3. Evaluate the patient's compliance with pressure relief activity. Attempt to assess follow through when the patient is off the unit (i.e., in therapy or on passes) as well as while he or she is on the nursing unit.

Pressure Relief Activities (continued)

Wheelchair Pressure Relief

PURPOSE

To prevent pressure sores through regular relief of pressure while the patient is seated.

STAFF RESPONSIBLE

EQUIPMENT

1. Optional equipment for patients with weak upper extremities: electric reclining wheelchair.
2. Wheelchair cushion.

GENERAL CONSIDERATIONS

1. Refer to general considerations of Pressure Relief Activities, above.
2. Patients with intact upper extremities (triceps) can do push-ups. If the upper extremities are weak, the patient can do forward or side leans, or another person can lift the patient.
3. Wheelchair cushions are necessary to redistribute pressure, but no cushion eliminates the need for regular pressure relief.
4. Wheelchair armrests and footplates must be properly adjusted for the person to promote pressure reduction.

PATIENT AND FAMILY EDUCATION

1. Method of pressure relief, frequency, and length of pressure relief are taught as soon as possible after the patient initiates sitting.
2. Teach the principles for increasing or discontinuing sitting time.

PROCEDURE

Steps	*Additional Information*

Assessment and Teaching

Steps	Additional Information
1. Assess patient knowledge about wheelchair pressure reliefs.	
2. Inform patient of frequency for pressure relief (push-ups, leans). Demonstrate method, or inform patient to request assistance every 15 to 30 minutes (depending on policy).	Do not assume that patients who are beginning to sit or those who are sitting when admitted to a unit will independently perform wheelchair push-ups or request assistance.
3. Limit sitting time to 30 minutes to 1 hour the first time that patient sits.	Sitting time depends on number and intensity of risk factors present as well as on other factors, such as fatigue and pain.
4. Examine patient's ischia, posterior trochanters, and sacral-coccygeal bony prominences for hyperemia when patient returns to bed to determine whether pressure relief activity was adequate.	Prolonged hyperemia (more than 30 minutes) is evidence of potential cellular damage. When this situation exists, time in position must be decreased or pressure reliefs must be increased (or both).
5. Gradually increase sitting time (tolerance) by 30 minutes. Maintain increased tolerance time for 2 days before increasing sitting tolerance again. Examine skin each time patient returns to bed until satisfactory sitting tolerance is reached.	Goal for sitting tolerance should be established with patient. For most persons, tolerance of several hours or longer is required to resume important life activities. Hyperemia must resolve in less than 30 minutes to increase sitting tolerance. Frequent pressure reliefs can enable patient to achieve longer sitting tolerance.

Steps	*Additional Information*
6. Regularly review with patient progress or problems in performing wheelchair pressure reliefs at prescribed intervals.	Review reinforces importance of this preventive activity and provides opportunity for mutual problem solving.
7. Remind patient to do pressure relief, or offer assistance if he or she is in your presence for 30 minutes and has not done a push-up or lean.	
8. Consult with physical therapist (if needed) regarding specific pressure relief technique that patient should be using.	

Specific Methods

1. *Push-up:* Patient places hands on both wheels or armrests and pushes up (Figure 4-3).	Intact triceps are required to perform a stable push-up. Push-ups lift patient's weight off both buttocks.
2. *Side lean:* Patient places one arm under wheelchair push handle while leaning toward opposite side of wheelchair (Figure 4-4).	

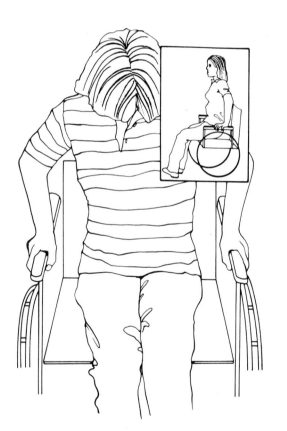

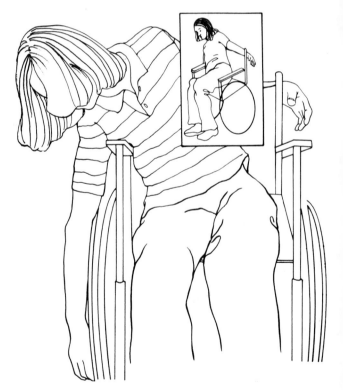

Figure 4-3 Wheelchair Push-Up. *Source:* From *Rehabilitation Guide* (p. 72) by R.B. King, M. Boyink, and M. Keenan, 1977, Chicago, IL: Rehabilitation Institute of Chicago. Copyright 1977 by Rehabilitation Institute of Chicago. Reprinted by permission.

Figure 4-4 Wheelchair Pressure Relief by Leaning to One Side. *Source:* From *Rehabilitation Guide* (p. 71) by R.B. King, M. Boyink, and M. Keenan, 1977, Chicago, IL: Rehabilitation Institute of Chicago. Copyright 1977 by Rehabilitation Institute of Chicago. Reprinted by permission.

Steps	*Additional Information*
3. *Forward lean:* Patient leans forward, resting forearms on thighs. To return to upright position, patient uses triceps or pectoral muscles to push upright. In presence of inadequate musculature, patient places one arm over wheelchair push handle while leaning forward and reaching forward with other arm. Alternatively, patient may be able to rest upper body on bed or low table.	Forward leans can be performed if trunk musculature, triceps, or strong pectoral muscles are present (Nixon, 1985). Patient safety is factor for independent forward leans. This maneuver often does not totally eliminate pressure but can decrease pressure by transferring weight to posterior thighs.
4. For individuals who are unable to perform the foregoing maneuvers, caregiver can shift weight by lifting person from behind or from front of wheelchair.	This is an impractical option for routine long-term pressure relief.
5. Motorized reclining wheelchair can be used to achieve recumbent position to decrease pressure over ischia.	This is a more realistic option for individuals who are dependent in pressure relief activity.

DOCUMENTATION

1. Document education and patient's performance of pressure relief as well as sitting tolerance.

2. Document the method of pressure relief.

Turning and Positioning

PURPOSES

To prevent pressure sores; to maintain ROM; to decrease the influence of pathologic reflexes and posturing; to prevent pooling of lung secretions through regular repositioning; to improve circulation.

STAFF RESPONSIBLE

EQUIPMENT

1. Pillows, foam blocks, or small towels.
2. Optional:
   • Proning cart.
   • Protective boots.
   • Body wedges.
   • Special mattresses or beds that reduce or alternate pressures.

GENERAL CONSIDERATIONS

1. Refer to general considerations of pressure relief activities, above.

2. Few products can reduce pressure to less than capillary pressure for all positions. Therefore, the major emphasis is relieving pressure by change of position.
3. All patients with reduced mobility or sensation need to be turned and positioned on an individualized schedule.
4. No two skin surfaces should rest together. A pillow or foam block is placed between the patient's legs so that one leg is not lying on top of the other.
5. Proper body mechanics must be practiced by the lifters during all turning and positioning procedures.
6. Patients are positioned for comfort as well as pressure relief.
7. Turning schedules are individualized according to the patient's skin tolerance. Most individuals can tolerate turning every 2 hours, but some may require more frequent repositioning. Turning or sitting time can be increased only when hyperemia over bony prominences resolves within 30 minutes after pressure relief.
8. Always increase time in one position gradually (i.e., usually no more than a half hour at a time). Evaluate a new schedule for 2 to 3 days.
9. Whenever possible, all positions are utilized. Prone, supine, side lying, and small shifts in position are encouraged.
10. The prone position assists with even distribution of weight and can promote extension of the hips and knees. Nevertheless, this position is contraindicated in certain medical conditions (breathing problems), when it

increases flexor or extensor tone, when there are limitations in ROM of hip and knee extension (elderly persons or persons with arthritis), and in the presence of increased intracranial pressure, unstable spine, or any condition in which increased intrathoracic pressure is to be prevented. Patients with sacral pressure sores utilize the prone position to mobilize themselves on a stretcher cart.

11. At times, minor rotations in position are adequate to relieve pressure and may allow increased intervals between turning and increased patient comfort.
12. Inspect the skin when repositioning the patient.
13. Firm (not hard) standard mattresses that support the body are recommended. Foam mattresses over a regular mattress aid slightly in distributing pressure.
14. For patients who must be turned more than every 2 hours because of risk of pressure sores, consider using a special bed or mattress that reduces pressures to less than capillary pressure.
15. A footboard may be used to support the patient's feet at a 90° angle. If increased spasticity occurs or if the patient moves out of position, commercial support boots or splints can be used. If spasticity continues with the foot support, remove it, increase the frequency of ROM to the ankle joint, and support the lower legs on a foam wedge or small pillows to decrease heel pressure.
16. Static positioning devices (e.g., pillows under a leg or placed to support side lying) may not stay in place if a patient is mobile.

17. Patients should be positioned so that they are able to call for assistance if needed (i.e., the call light should be within reach, or the patient should be on a monitor).
18. Caution with turning and positioning is necessary for patients with increased intracranial pressure (ICP). Evidence exists that turning from supine to side lying and proning can increase ICP. Consultation with the physician is indicated before using these positions for patients with ICP (Palmer & Wyness, 1988).
19. Nursing care plans should contain special positioning instructions if abnormal tone exists. If needed, physical and occupational therapists can be consulted regarding positioning approaches to control abnormal tone.
20. Patients should have a well-established turning tolerance before hospital discharge.

PATIENT AND FAMILY EDUCATION

1. Patients and primary caregivers are taught the following:
   - positioning techniques for all position options;
   - principles for increasing tolerances or for decreasing tolerances if risk factors increase;
   - maintenance of equipment; and
   - purchasing of equipment.
2. Include the patient and primary caregiver in carrying out the procedure as much as possible to encourage independence at the patient's level of function.

PROCEDURES

Steps	*Additional Information*
1. Gather equipment, and keep it within reach.	Support equipment needed may be pillows or foam blocks, small towels, or foam wedges.
2. Position bed at waist level with side rail closest to you in low position.	
3. Assess patient's ability to assist.	Consider patient's physiologic condition, mobility, strength and endurance, balance, understanding, and motivation.
4. Explain procedure to patient. Choose one of the following positions.	

Supine Position

1. Follow steps 1 through 4, above.	When patient is positioned supine, heels should not rest on mattress. Pad footboards, if they are used (Figure 4-5). Foam wedge or small soft pillow under legs will free heels from pressure, or special support boots can be used. Pillows and foam blocks can be used for bridging to prevent pressure over bony prominences (Figure 4-6).

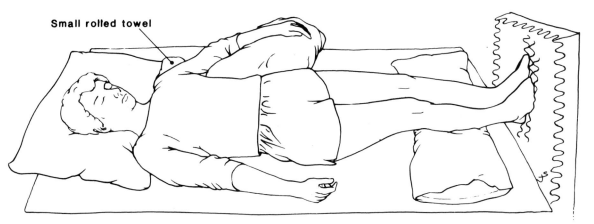

Small rolled towel

Figure 4-5 Positioning Supine. *Source:* From *Spinal Cord Injury: A Guide to Rehabilitation Nursing* (p. 211) by P.J. Matthews, C.E. Carlson, and N.B. Holt, 1987, Rockville, MD: Aspen Publishers, Inc. Copyright 1987 by Aspen Publishers, Inc.

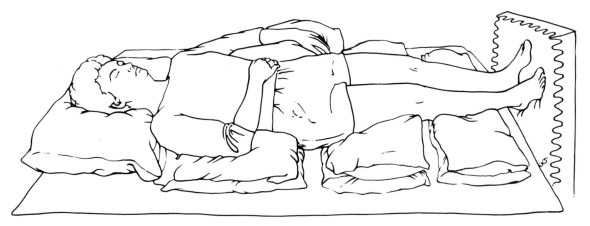

Figure 4-6 Bridging Supine. *Source:* From *Spinal Cord Injury: A Guide to Rehabilitation Nursing* (p. 211) by P.J. Matthews, C.E. Carlson, and N.B. Holt, 1987, Rockville, MD: Aspen Publishers, Inc. Copyright 1987 by Aspen Publishers, Inc.

Steps	*Additional Information*
2. Position patient on his or her back in center of bed.	You can move patient in bed by moving one-third of body at a time unless logrolling is required for spinal precautions or other condition. Extra assistance of one or two staff may be needed if patient is heavy or has complications.
3. Position patient in proper alignment.	For patient to be in correct alignment, the following should form a straight line: chin, sternal notch, and symphysis pubis. Both sides of body, including trunk, should be symmetrical, and head should be in midline.
4. Place pillow under upper and lateral borders of scapulae, shoulders, neck, and head.	This position will help prevent flexion contracture of neck. For patients with hemiplegia, it may be necessary to position small pillow or rolled towel under scapula to protract it (see Figure 4-5).
5. Place pillows or arm supports under involved upper extremities, positioning arm alongside body and forearm slightly supinated or in neutral position.	This will help prevent internal rotation of shoulder and flexion of elbow as well as edema formation.

Steps	*Additional Information*
6. Place trochanter roll alongside involved hip and upper half of thigh, if external rotation of hip is problematic.	Placement of small pillow or roll under distal thigh producing slight knee flexion can reduce extensor spasticity, which is commonly seen in presence of hemiplegia. Roll must not exert any pressure on popliteal space. Such pressure interferes with circulation and compresses nerves.
7. Position to maintain dorsiflexion of foot and to prevent pressure on heel. Place firm foam block between legs to prevent hip adduction and internal rotation when potential for these problems exists.	Generally, footboard is only used when extremities are flaccid (refer to general considerations, 15). Use foam block between legs when spasticity is present.
8. Apply equipment (e.g., casts or splints) as directed by care plan.	
9. Place call light within reach. Put up side rails.	

Side-Lying Position

1. Follow steps 1 through 4, above.	When patient is positioned on his or her side (Figure 4-7), ankles should be free of pressure. Do not rest one leg on top of the other. You can bridge trochanter, side of knee, and ankle. Angle of positioning can be altered slightly to change pressure. Alternate sides in side lying unless one side is contraindicated.
2. Pull patient to edge of bed closest to you.	
3. Position patient's arms at sides or on chest.	

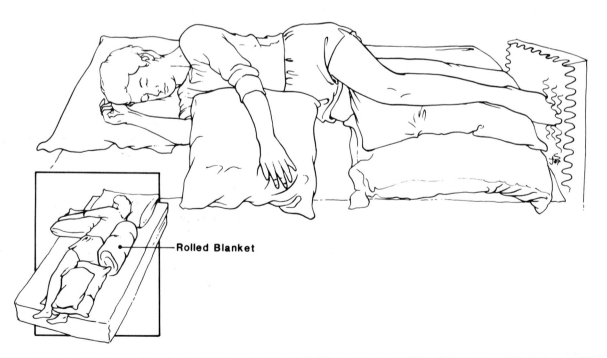

—Rolled Blanket

Figure 4-7 Side-Lying Position. *Source:* From *Spinal Cord Injury: A Guide to Rehabilitation Nursing* (p. 212) by P.J. Matthews, C.E. Carlson, and N.B. Holt, 1987, Rockville, MD: Aspen Publishers, Inc. Copyright 1987 by Aspen Publishers, Inc.

Steps	*Additional Information*
4. Cross leg closest to you over the other in direction to which patient will turn. Check contraindications before carrying out this step.	This step will help turn part of patient's body over to side.
5. Put one hand on patient's shoulder closest to you and other hand on trochanter.	
6. Roll patient away from you.	Keep patient from rolling prone by keeping your hand on patient's shoulder and trochanter until pillows are placed.
7. Place pillow behind patient's back.	This will help prevent patient from rolling onto his or her back.
8. Place upper leg in flexed position away from bottom leg (hip flexed 55° to 60° and knee flexed 80°), or position upper leg behind body with 30° flexion at hip and 35° at knee.	Positioning upper leg behind body reduces trochanteric pressure (Garber, Campion, & Krouskop, 1982). Pillows between legs and attention to placing top leg in front of or behind bottom leg ensures that two skin surfaces are not in contact with each other and avoids excess pressure.
9. Position one or two pillows under top leg to support it from groin to foot.	Do this to prevent internal rotation and adduction of hip and to maintain horizontal plane in line with hip, preventing pull on hip joint.
10. Position upper arm on pillows to provide support for joints and to prevent edema.	
11. Apply equipment as directed by nursing care plan (e.g., casts or splints).	
12. Put call light within reach. Put up side rails.	

Prone Position

1. Follow steps 1 through 4, above.	When positioning prone, protect iliac crests, patellae, dorsum of feet, and toes. Position feet between mattress and footboard if possible (Figure 4-8).

Figure 4-8 Positioning Prone. *Source:* From *Spinal Cord Injury: A Guide to Rehabilitation Nursing* (p. 213) by P.J. Matthews, C.E. Carlson, and N.B. Holt, 1987, Rockville, MD: Aspen Publishers, Inc. Copyright 1987 by Aspen Publishers, Inc.

Steps	Additional Information
2. Move patient down in bed so that feet are beyond mattress.	Discuss appropriateness of proning patients with physician if potential contraindications to proning exist (see general considerations, 10).
3. Position patient supine on one side of bed, with arm toward which patient will roll positioned overhead or extended at side (can be slightly tucked under body).	
4. When bridging, position pillows so that patient will roll onto them when rolled prone.	When bridging, pillows should be positioned to protect iliac crests, knees, and dorsum of feet as shown in Figure 4-8. If patient will not be bridged, small, flat support is placed under abdomen to prevent hyperextension of lumbar curve, and chest is supported with flat pillow. Small foam support is placed under lower legs.
5. Cross uppermost leg over body in direction to which patient will turn.	This step will help turn patient to prone position.
6. Roll patient to side toward pillows. For example, if turning patient toward right, position left leg across body. Place right arm over head or extended at side. Roll patient over on pillows.	
7. Position patient's head on pillow that provides comfortable support, and maintain neutral position without promoting flexion or extension. Patient's head can be rotated to either side if this activity is not contraindicated.	
8. Position upper extremities in comfortable position.	
9. Check for effective pressure relief, when bridging, by running your hand under iliac crests, knees, and dorsum of feet. Check that undue pressure is not exerted over genitalia of males.	
10. Arrange urinary equipment to promote effective drainage and to avoid undue pressure on skin tissue.	
11. Leave patient in this position for one half-hour initially, and remain with patient during that time.	At first, attempt prone position during the day when patient is alert. Often, patient is fearful of positioning prone. Time can be increased after patient has established comfort level. Patient's skin can often tolerate longer periods of time in prone position than in other positions because this position tends to distribute pressure evenly.
12. Apply any equipment as directed by nursing care plan (e.g., splints).	
13. Put call light within reach. Put up side rails.	

DOCUMENTATION

1. Document the time in each position and redness over a bony prominence that does not resolve within 30 minutes of resting off the site.
2. Document the effectiveness of specific positioning approaches (i.e., small rotations or bridging) to manage spasticity and to prevent excessive pressure.

3. Document any unusual occurrences during turning and positioning.
4. Document patient and family teaching and success.

Guide To Choosing Bed and Mattress Toppers

PURPOSE

To assist the nurse in selecting the appropriate support device for individual patients.

STAFF RESPONSIBLE

EQUIPMENT

1. Bed or mattress topper (Table 4-1).

GENERAL CONSIDERATIONS

1. The nurse assesses the following factors to determine the appropriate bed or mattress topper:
   - skin integrity, including site, number, and severity of pressure sores;
   - risk factors for skin breakdown;
   - cost to the patient;
   - discharge plans;
   - risk for other complications of immobility; and
   - influence on ADL independence (may decrease patient's ability to perform ADLs).
2. The nurse orders the appropriate bed or mattress topper and documents the type of support, including turning and positioning. Selection of the support surface may be done in collaboration with the physician.
3. Skin checks should be performed with each turn when using a new support device and when increasing turn tolerances. Documentation should reflect the patient's skin tolerance.
4. Beds and mattress toppers for home use should be ordered and evaluated at least 2 weeks before hospital discharge.

5. For most beds and mattress toppers (e.g., water mattress topper, modular water mattress topper, or foam toppers), using a fitted sheet can interfere with pressure reduction capacity.
6. The mean capillary pressure of skin is approximately 20 mmHg. Arteriolar pressure is estimated at 32 mmHg and venous pressure at 12 mmHg (Landis, 1930). Generally, the more intense the pressure, the less time tissue can tolerate the pressure load. Contact pressure can be increased by factors such as atrophy of soft tissue or alterations in skeletal structure such as scoliosis or joint contractures.
7. Contact pressure (the amount of pressure between the skin surface and the support surface) is in excess of capillary pressure over bony prominences while the patient is resting on most surfaces. Therefore, routine repositioning is required in most situations. Certain support surfaces reduce intensity of pressure, however, and may allow an increase in time between repositionings.
8. Professional nurses must be knowledgeable about the advantages and limitations of support devices. Inservice programs are indicated when a new device is used.
9. In general, the more expensive systems, such as air flotation and air-fluidized beds, reduce pressure over all bony prominences and should be reserved for individuals who are assessed at highest risk for pressure sores or those who cannot be repositioned at desired frequencies.
10. No one support device (cushion, mattress, or bed) can be recommended for all individuals. This is particularly true of wheelchair cushions, in which wide fluctuations in pressure occur for various individuals using a given cushion type.
11. Support devices are only an adjunct to skin care and do not substitute for continued comprehensive preventive measures.

PATIENT AND FAMILY EDUCATION

1. Patients and primary caregivers are informed of the rationale and limitations for use of a special support device.
2. If a device is ordered for home use, the patient and caregiver are instructed about its correct use, correction of problems, and vendor to contact.

Table 4-1 Beds and Mattress Toppers (Support Surfaces Are Presented in Order of Least Effective to Most Effective in Generalized Pressure Reduction Capability)

Type, Action, and Indication	Advantages	Disadvantages	Special Considerations
1. Foam mattress toppers (Bioclinic, Medfoam) • Foam provides soft support surface that conforms better than standard mattress to body's contour and aids slightly in distributing pressure over greater contact surface. Available in 2- to 4-inch heights. • Indications for use: patients at low risk for skin breakdown.	Low purchase cost compared to other options if not needed long term; lightweight and easy to transport; can be cut to fit bed, cart, car, and so forth.	If wet, can contribute to skin maceration because it tends to act as a sponge; foam will dry out and crumble with age. Trochanteric and heel pressures are consistently greater than capillary pressures with this topper. A recent study shows little advantage of 2-inch foam over standard mattress, whereas 4-inch foam is somewhat more effective (Krouskop et al., 1985). Sacral pressures have been found to be inconsistently less than capillary pressure even with use of 2-inch foam toppers (Wells & Geden, 1984).	Linen is applied loosely over topper; foam mattress topper will lose its flame-retardant ability when wet or soiled; patient may be allergic to materials. Protective plastic sheet is available for patients when indicated. Protective sheaths should be closely evaluated: they will reduce effectiveness of foam, cause local heat, and increase moisture.
2. Modular water mattress topper (Rochester) • Consists of 3-inch nonconvoluted foam sections. Water bladders are inserted into cut-out foam sections as needed to provide selected flotation. • Indications for use: patients assessed at relatively low risk for pressure sores.	Can focus on selected area of potential skin breakdown (i.e., heels and sacrum for supine position); obtains fluid pressure dispersal effect without wave effect of water bed or water mattress topper; more portable and easier to fill than full water mattress topper or water bed; can evaluate flotation by observation of water column in tubing.	If foam is wet, can cause skin maceration because it tends to act as a sponge; foam will dry out and crumble with age; water bladder will leak if punctured; maximal pressure reduction is limited to area over water bladder; requires maintenance of water bladder (daily inspection for leaks, observation of water column; does come with repair kit).	Fitted sheets should not be used; flat sheets should not be tucked in because this will reduce effectiveness of pressure relief; foam, if washed, loses its flame-retardant ability. Consider patient's weight and effectiveness of flotation on water bladder during initial trial. Patient discharge teaching should include specific directions about set up, proper filling, maintenance, and how to evaluate effectiveness.
3. Water mattress topper • Consists of plastic mattress topper filled with water. Promotes even distribution of pressure. • Indications for use: patients at relatively low risk to develop pressure sores.	Acts as cooling mattress for patients who have chronically elevated temperatures. If filled properly, reduces pressure in comparison to standard mattresses, but pressures are often greater than capillary pressure (Lilla et al., 1975).	Mattress topper is difficult to fill (start with it half full, and fill it until it is three-quarters full); heavy and bulky; if overfilled, it is too hard and flotation effect is lost; if underfilled, does not distribute pressure evenly; leaks if punctured (do not use pins or sharp objects on or near topper); patient may chill with cooling of water temperature; patients find it difficult to perform ADLs, transfers, or unsupported sitting (especially if patient has compromised motor function); pressures are not less than capillary pressure (Lilla et al., 1975).	Side lying decreases effective pressure relief, with marked increase in amount of pressure over smaller surface area; flotation and pressure distribution are not as effective as with a full water bed. Careful evaluation of heels is indicated because this part of body tends to have consistently higher pressures than other bony prominences in supine position. Fitted sheets should not be used; flat sheets should not be tucked in because this will reduce effectiveness of pressure relief. Patient and family discharge teaching should include instructions about brand to purchase, filling and maintenance, and how to evaluate effectiveness.

Table 4-1 continued

Type, Action, and Indication	Advantages	Disadvantages	Special Considerations
4. Static air mattress [Roho; gel-cell-foam topper and mattress (Akros) has pressure reduction properties similar to those of the Roho] • Air-filled rubber intercommunicating balloons on flat rubber base. • Indications for use: patients at moderate or low risk for pressure sores.	Average pressure over sacrum and scapula is less than 30 mmHg; trochanteric pressures are less than those with most other topper devices but are about 45 mmHg (Krouskop et al., 1985); may allow longer intervals between turns in supine position.	Requires daily inspection and maintenance to ensure proper filling; can be punctured with sudden loss of air.	Most useful for responsible individual who will provide maintenance; balloon filling can be adjusted for individual patient; can be purchased for home use.
5. Sof-Care (Gaymar) • Mattress is filled with air by means of inflator. System softens around body shape. • Indications for use: patients with moderate or low risk for pressure sores or patients with pressure sores who can be positioned off area.	Mattress contours to patient to provide even distribution of weight; inexpensive yet durable; average trochanteric pressures reported to be less than capillary pressure; easy to clean; may allow longer intervals between supine or prone turns.	Surface could be punctured with loss of air; average heel pressures, 52 mmHg (Maklebust et al., 1986).	Topper is inflated for individual patient first time it is used. Thereafter, daily hand check is done by placing hand under mattress to evaluate flotation. Can be purchased for home use.
6. Alternating pressure mattress (Grant, Gaymar, Lapidus) • Mattress is filled with air, which inflates and deflates certain sections over specific period of time (cycle). • Indications for use: patients who require long-term use of support device and who are at moderate or low risk for breakdown.	Has a regular cycle by minutes so that pressure at any point is alleviated for set time; lightweight; cannot be overfilled or underfilled if working properly; easily wipes clean. Need for turning continues, but frequency of turns may be decreased if no other complications contraindicate and if patient is not assessed at high risk for pressure sores.	May leak (pins may not be used on or near mattress topper); all electric (must have power source and maintenance of motor, tubing, and pump); can be noisy; patients with sensation may feel motion of mattress. Reduction of pressures varies among individuals. Trochanteric pressures exceed capillary pressure in both high and low cycles but are lower than those for foam topper. Sacral pressures are in the moderately high range (up to 60 mmHg) in high cycle but as low as 10 to 20 mmHg in low cycle (Krouskop et al., 1985).	Check all electrical parts of the system (motor, pump, and tubing) daily; check daily for leaks, and ensure that filling and cycling systems are working (takes 5 minutes to complete check); check tubing with every turn because mattress easily disconnects from power source (checking can be accomplished in less than 30 seconds). Cost is covered by Medicare, and mattress can be purchased for home use through vendors in community.
7. Low air loss (dynamic air support) [Kinair & Therapulse (Kinetic Concepts), Mediscus, Flexicair; description refers to Kinair; other beds are similar] • Mattress is composed of 23 air-filled Gore-Tex–covered cushions that are continuously inflated with air. • Indications for use: patients who need to be turned more than every 2 hours or cannot be turned; have multiple risk factors present (high risk); have one or more grade 1 or 2 sores and cannot be bridged or have a grade 3 or 4 sore; are postsurgical for repair of pressure sore.	Waterproof (but water-vapor permeable); extra-long length; head of bed can be elevated; comes with reusable underpads made of Gore-Tex that are easy to clean when soiled; beds can be moved from room to room and have adjustable side rails; sections collapse for cardiopulmonary resuscitation, transferring, and	Must measure air pressures correctly for maximum effect (requires some adjustment and daily check); frame of bed is steel and, if mattress is not properly inflated, does not provide adequate pressure relief; split side rails may present a problem if patient is confused or restless.	Can be used with patients on isolation precautions; education is needed for patient, family, and staff; expensive to purchase or rent, but some patients with long-term need and high risk may consider purchase to facilitate home care. Although turning intervals may be extended for many patients, repositioning is

Table 4-1 continued

Type, Action, and Indication	Advantages	Disadvantages	Special Considerations
	care; pressures are 15 to 30 mmHg over bony prominences (pressure greater than 30 mmHg may occur over heels); dehydration is not a problem, as it is with air-fluidized beds.		necessary to prevent other complications of immobility and to maintain low risk for pressure sores at all sites.
8. Air-fluidized bed (Clinitron, Skytron; description refers to Clinitron; Skytron is similar) • Mattress contains glass beads that are kept in continuous motion by currents of warm air. Beads are enclosed in polyester filter sheet. • Indications for use: patients with severe burns or pressure sores at more than one site; patients at high risk for pressure sores who require turning more than every 2 hours to all sides, thus interfering with rest and placing unusual demands on caregivers; after surgical repair of pressure sores; patients at high risk for pressure sores who are not transferred out of bed often.	Contact pressure is extremely low (usually approximately 15 to 30 mmHg); allows for supine positioning; no need to turn patient for skin reasons (turning is recommended to reduce hazards of immobility, however); quickly deflates for cardiopulmonary resuscitation; moisture and exudates are filtered away from patient's body; decreases friction and shear.	Bed itself weighs so much that it must be positioned in structurally sound areas in hospital; bed cannot be moved or height adjusted; patient cannot sit in bed unsupported; transfers require two- to three-person lifts; noisy; if punctured, beads leak out and can cover patient or be aspirated; dehydration can occur in a few days if multiple open skin areas exist and hydration is poor; dries out respiratory tract; dressing changes and transfers are difficult because of mechanics of bed; some patients develop a feeling of being confused or have difficulty sleeping because of noise. Contraindicated for patients who are confused or at high risk for pulmonary complications. When bed is deflated for cardiopulmonary resuscitation, rescuer must get into bed with patient.	Not recommended for patients with uncontrolled incontinence because of buildup of odor; patients with special dressings (i.e., wet to dry) may require more frequent dressing changes because wet dressings dry out quickly; not feasible for home use because of weight; patients may need aggressive measures to prevent pulmonary complications (e.g., frequent elevation of head, postural drainage, incentive spirometry, and large fluid intake).
9. Kinetic bed (Roto Rest) • Bed consists of foam-padded boards on metal frame that electrically oscillates side to side, providing continuous motion. • Indications for use: patients with increased tone, restricted ROM, or who are difficult to position to maintain or increase ROM; patients with respiratory complications or complications of immobility such as severe constipation; comatose or restless patients; patients who are immobilized for prolonged period because of neurologic lesions; patients who are difficult to move or reposition regularly.	Bed is said to reduce or prevent hazards of immobility (e.g., constipation and pneumonia); stimulates vestibular system and peristalsis. Patient may require reduction of sedatives and muscle relaxants. Bed is adjusted to fit each individual patient's need and size. Bed can be manually turned or locked in central position in case of power failure or motor malfunction.	Only relieves pressure while bed is moving because bed consists of foam-covered boards that do not provide adequate pressure relief benefits when static; shearing and friction preventive measures are necessary; inappropriate fit of positioning parts resulting in pressure or friction can contribute to pressure sores; ROM continues to be necessary; safety straps must always be used; transfers and ADL activities are difficult.	Contraindicated in cases of severe claustrophobia. Precautions need to be taken with pathologic or traumatic rib fractures (adjust rotation to avoid weight-bearing on affected side) and large cranial defects (adjust head pack accordingly to prevent pressure). Patients in extremely restless state are not appropriate and may become more restless. Others may be calmed by motion. Monitor restless patients carefully when placed on bed to ensure that they do not pull off safety straps or resist positioning. Severe, uncontrollable diarrhea may develop because bed stimulates peristalsis. Never rotate patient in sitting position or without all safety straps in place. Inservice is needed for patient, staff, and family.

Overview: Care of Pressure Sores by Severity

Grade 1 Pressure Sore

DEFINITION

An area of soft tissue swelling, ulceration, heat, and erythema sustained for 24 hours or longer, or a partial-thickness ulcer limited to the epidermis, or both. Grade 1 pressure sores can be considered reversible in that they do not cause permanent changes in the skin, as do deep grade 2, grade 3, and grade 4 sores. It is imperative to prevent further damage when the pressure sore is at a grade 1 level.

PURPOSES

To promote wound healing; to prevent development of a more severe pressure sore.

STAFF RESPONSIBLE

PROCEDURE

Steps	Additional Information
1. Assessment:	
• Assess factors precipitating skin breakdown and intervene. These include change in risk factors; damage or deterioration of support surface (cushion, bed, or mattress); recent application or use of orthosis, prosthesis, or new shoes; participation in activities that could increase pressure, shear, or friction to bony prominences; and prolonged sitting or bed positioning that exceeded established tolerance.	Change in nutritional state (decreased hemoglobin or negative nitrogen balance), altered metabolic state, elevated temperature, and drop in blood pressure are common intrinsic risk factors that can create sudden increase in vulnerability to pressure sores. Deterioration of foam surfaces that occurs with aging interferes with pressure redistribution, resulting in increased pressure.
• Assess wound site each time dressing is changed.	See procedure on Assessment of Pressure Sore (above).
2. Eliminate all pressure over pressure sore site by:	
• not turning patient to side on which pressure sore exists;	Patient can be positioned on pressure area only when using support mattresses or beds that produce pressures less than capillary pressure; see Guide To Choosing Bed and Mattress Toppers (above). If ischial sore is present, patient should not sit because there is no cushion that reduces pressure to less than capillary pressure.
• bridging pressure sore site; and	When bridging, ensure that all pressure is eliminated from pressure sore and surrounding bony prominences. Edge of foam block or pillows could create high pressures.
• positioning patient on device that eliminates pressure.	Use special support surface such as air-fluidized support bed if patient cannot be positioned off site and if other areas are vulnerable because of frequent turning to these sites. If patient has been independent in repositioning, assess ability to reposition self without causing friction or shear to pressure area.
3. Avoid friction and shear forces to pressure area.	Avoid elevation of head of bed more than 30° and less than 90° when the patient is in supine position because this will promote shearing forces.

Steps	Additional Information
4. Apply topical agents or protective dressing.	Use of topical agents for grade 1 sores is matter of professional judgment and preference. Some clinicians prefer to use topical agent or dressing to protect site from trauma when lesion is closed grade 1 sore. Open grade 1 sores are generally covered with dressing to provide protection from contamination. Skin barriers such as Stomahesive or plasticized sealants can be applied for protection of closed areas. Controversy exists about utility of ointments such as zinc and of sealants. Non-adherent dressing protects from friction and infection and will not disturb granulating tissue on open wound. Dressings that maintain moist environment facilitate healing of open wounds.

Grade 2 Pressure Sore

DEFINITION

A shallow, full-thickness ulcer that penetrates the dermis, leaving subcutaneous tissue intact.

PURPOSES

To promote wound healing; to prevent the development of a more severe pressure sore.

STAFF RESPONSIBLE

PROCEDURE

Steps	Additional Information
1. Assessment: • Assess factors precipitating skin breakdown (refer to grade 1 assessment, above). • Assess wound healing, and report delayed healing or deterioration in wound.	Depending on treatment ordered, assessments of wound itself may occur one to four times daily or as infrequently as weekly if occlusive dressing is used. Assess wound and surrounding tissue during each dressing change. Check dressing and surrounding area at least once per shift if dressing change is not done (see procedure on Assessment of a Pressure Sore, above).
2. Eliminate all pressure to pressure area (see step 2 for grade 1 pressure sores). Use caution in upgrading skin tolerance after wound healing.	Prolonged immobilization of patient on cart or in bed may be indicated when ischial or sacrococcygeal pressure sores are present. ROM activities must be maintained if paralysis exists. Strengthening exercises may be indicated for individuals with weak but preserved motor function. Full grade 2 sores result in decreased elasticity and scarring, which increase risk for future breakdown.
3. Apply dressings to grade 2 sores to prevent further contamination of wound and to promote healing. The following options can be used:	

Steps	*Additional Information*
• semipermeable dressing (Op-Site, Tegaderm);	
• occlusive dressing (Duoderm);	Use only if signs of infection are not present.
• absorptive dressing (if large amounts of drainage);	
• dry, sterile, fine-mesh dressing (if minimal amount of drainage); or	
• nonadherent dressing (if little or no drainage).	

Grade 3 Pressure Sore

DEFINITION

A soft tissue ulcer that extends into subcutaneous fat and is limited by the deep fascia, so that muscle is not exposed.

PURPOSES

To improve metabolic status; to reduce infection; to promote wound healing (conservative healing can take 3 months or longer); to eliminate necrotic tissue when present.

STAFF RESPONSIBLE

PROCEDURE

Steps	*Additional Information*
1. Assess factors precipitating onset or deterioration of pressure area, and intervene (refer to grade 1 assessment).	Interventions to restore positive nitrogen balance may have to be aggressive because patient is likely to lose more protein through grade 3 sore than through less severe sores. Infected grade 3 sores can result in febrile states, which further interfere with healing. Because of negative nitrogen balance and metabolic imbalance, increased risk for skin breakdown at other sites is present. Surgical repair is frequently treatment of choice after wound is cleaned and patient's physical condition is improved.
2. Eliminate all pressure to pressure area or areas. Use caution in upgrading tolerance after healing.	Bridging may be difficult if sore is large in diameter. Consider use of pressure-reduction devices (water bed, air support, and air-fluidized beds) because patients with grade 3 sores often are susceptible to developing other sores. Healed grade 3 sores result in fragile scar tissue that is prone to breakdown.
3. Treatment varies depending on amount of drainage and presence of necrotic tissue.	
• If minimal drainage and no necrotic tissue, options are dry, sterile, fine-mesh dressing, semipermeable dressing, or occlusive dressing.	Granulating tissue is less likely to be removed with fine-mesh gauze than other dressings. Use occlusive dressing only when wound is not infected.
• If large amount of drainage exists, use absorptive dressing, or pack wound with mesh gauze to absorb drainage.	
• If eschar is present, physician may decide to débride tissue surgically.	Portion of wound covered by eschar cannot be evaluated in terms of depth of involvement.
• If necrotic tissue is present, several options are available to aid débridement: mechanical (wet to dry dressings, wide-mesh gauze, Iodoform gauze) and chemical (enzyme ointments such as Elase, Travase, or Santyl).	Plastic surgery may be indicated to achieve healing. Mechanical débridement results in nonselective débridement.

Grade 4 Pressure Sore

DEFINITION

A soft tissue ulcer that penetrates the deep fascia. Muscle involvement is extensive, and bone may be exposed.

PURPOSES

To improve metabolic status; to eliminate necrotic tissue when present; to reduce local wound infection.

STAFF RESPONSIBLE

GENERAL CONSIDERATIONS

Patients with grade 4 pressure sores are generally quite sick, with multisystem problems or sepsis from a deep wound that usually takes many months to heal with conservative treatment. Meanwhile the patient is often immobilized or restricted from significant life activities and is at risk to develop complications of immobility. Therefore, plastic surgery is often performed.

Assessments, pressure relief activities, and wound treatments are similar to those for grade 3 pressure sore. The patient with grade 4 pressure sores, however, often is febrile, may have severe negative nitrogen balance and anemia, and may be in isolation as a result of wound infection. The major goal is generally not conservative healing but improved physical condition, including cleaning the wound in preparation for surgery and maintaining or improving socioemotional equilibrium.

Closed Wounds

DEFINITION

A deep, sinus-like ulcer lined by reactive fibrotic tissue. The ulcer resembles a grade 3 or 4 pressure sore, extending to the deep fascia, and can result in extensive bone and joint involvement. It may be closed or draining through a small skin opening.

PURPOSES

To improve metabolic status; to eliminate necrotic tissue when present; to reduce local wound infection.

STAFF RESPONSIBLE

GENERAL CONSIDERATIONS

Treatment of closed wounds is generally surgical because the sinus tract is extensive, often involving bone joints and surrounding tissue. Suspicious-looking skin areas (closed, indurated, swollen areas or small skin defects with induration or edema) should be palpated to identify a possible closed, deep wound.

DOCUMENTATION FOR ALL GRADES OF PRESSURE SORES

1. Document the grade of pressure sore and assess parameters according to agency policy.
2. Document patient and family education as appropriate.

Product Options for Wound Care

PURPOSES

To provide a comprehensive comparison of currently available product options for wound care; to increase awareness and appropriate utilization of products for patients requiring wound care.

STAFF RESPONSIBLE

EQUIPMENT

See individual dressing procedures and Table 4-2.

GENERAL CONSIDERATIONS

1. All appropriate preventive measures for pressure sores and proper skin care must be correctly implemented by nursing staff.
2. A written physician's order stating specific dressing, cleansing agent, and frequency of change is required before implementing many of the product options.
3. The nurse should assist the physician in evaluating the type of product or dressing to be used. A complete assessment of the pressure sore (refer to Assessment of a Pressure Sore, above) should be done by the nurse. Cost effectiveness of the product during hospitalization and after discharge is a consideration.
4. If the patient will be discharged to home with a dressing change, the nurse must evaluate the ability of the patient or family member to manage wound care and provide the necessary patient and family education.
5. Wound size and characteristics are documented in the appropriate record initially and at intervals specified by agency policy.
6. A moist environment favors wound healing more than a dry environment.
7. The ideal wound dressing should protect the wound from contaminants and provide a moist environment and should not disrupt epithelization when removed. Additional considerations are patient comfort, cost of the dressing, time involved in the dressing change, and ease of use.
8. Product selection is guided by the stage of the wound, the presence or absence of infection, the amount of drainage, and the presence of necrosis or eschar.
9. Generally, a physician surgically removes eschar.
10. Wounds that are clean and granulating require nonadherent dressings that will not damage granulation tissue.
11. A dressing in contact with the wound surface should contain no cotton filler, which could adhere to the wound bed.

Table 4-2 Product Options for Wound Care

Product	Uses	Action	Considerations
1. Semipermeable transparent dressings			
• Opraflex • Tegaderm • Op-Site	Grades 1 through 3, no evidence of infection, and minimal or no drainage.	Act as a barrier to fluid, stool, environmental contaminants; permeable to oxygen, and moisture vapor; keep wound base moist.	Can be left on up to 7 days or until loose; allow visualization of wound; will only adhere to dry skin; are not used in presence of large amounts of drainage. Dressings may not adhere to surrounding skin if it is moist. Cleanse and dry area with soap and water to promote adherence.
2. Absorptive dressings			
• Bard absorption dressing	Grades 2 through 4 with significant amounts of drainage and no sinusing or tunneling.	Hydrophilic flakes absorb wound exudate, cleanse wound surface, and maintain a moist wound bed.	Must be hydrated according to directions before use; may use topical ointments (e.g., enzymes) in conjunction with dressing; effective only in secreting wounds. Cover with gauze dressing, and change dressing as frequently as needed on basis of amount of drainage.
• Debrisan	Grades 2 through 4 with significant amounts of drainage and no tunneling.	Hydrophilic beads absorb wound exudate and cleanse wound surface.	Supports granulation; reduces odor; used in wounds with no necrotic tissue; does not débride; effective only in secreting wounds; can be painful to patients with sensation; can dessicate healthy tissue if used in wound without drainage; must be covered with gauze; dressing must be changed two or more times daily depending on amount of drainage.

Table 4-2 continued

Product	Uses	Action	Considerations
• Vigilon	Grades 1 through 3.	Gel dressing creates fluid environment; will absorb drainage; permeable to oxygen; cushions sores and reduces friction.	Contains no adhesive on edges; provides variable degrees of pain relief; must be changed when gel dries (one to two times daily); may be difficult to keep in place if patient is active.
• Wet to wet dressing	Wounds with eschar.	Mechanically softens necrotic tissue; absorbs and reduces drainage; creates osmotic gradient to promote migration of exudate into gauze from wound bed.	Must be covered with gauze; must be changed at least every 2 hours to keep dressing moist (if it dries it becomes wet to dry dressing); reduces eschar if used in combination with cross-hatching (done by physician); only a fair option for drainage control; may use on infected wound; may excoriate surrounding tissue because of increased moisture. Wet to wet dressing with enzyme solution can be used as débriding dressing.
• Gauze packing strip	Grades 3 and 4.	Keeps wound entry from closing before healing of underlying tissues; absorbs exudate from wound surface.	Do not pack wound too tightly because this may add pressure to healthy tissue and cause enlargement of wound. Cover with dry dressing.
3. Absorptive dressings, occlusive			
• Duoderm hydrophilic wafers (Convatec)	Grades 1 through 3 with no signs of infection; may be used if small areas of necrotic tissue or eschar are present.	Occlusive dressing that interacts with wound fluid, forming a soft, moist gel that protects wound bed; facilitates dressing removal and avoids damage to fragile, healing tissues.	Dressing is changed every 5 to 7 days; effective for adhering to sacral and intergluteal sores; has distinctive odor; not for use on infected wound or one with extensive necrotic tissue or eschar; allows passage of exudate from wound surface to dressing. Sore cannot be visualized except during dressing change. Inspect dressing once a shift to determine whether it is intact, and inspect surrounding skin. Sore sometimes looks worse (gel tends to look like necrotic material). Also, dressing may lyse damaged margin tissues when first removed; thus wound may appear larger. Dressing must extend at least 1 inch beyond perimeter of sore. When dressing leaks, it must be changed not reinforced. First time dressing is used, it may leak within 72 hours. If it continues to leak in less than 1 week after two changes, consider using different type of dressing (or consider use with Duoderm granules to absorb excess drainage).

Table 4-2 continued

Product	Uses	Action	Considerations
4. Débridement dressings (Proteolytic enzymes liquefy necrotic tissue. Enzymes are discontinued when granulation tissue is noted. Topical enzymes require a physician order. Débridement process is slow for all methods and depends on extent and depth of necrotic tissue.)			
• Enzymes			
—Elase	Grades 2 through 4 with necrotic tissue and no exposed nerve or bone.	Breaks down protein bonds in necrotic tissue; liquefies necrotic tissue.	Easy to use; may irritate surrounding healthy tissue; dry eschar must be removed or cross-hatched for Elase to be effective; deactivates after 24 hours (change dressing daily at least). Elase is deactivated by iodine products (do not use these products to cleanse wound before applying Elase, or rinse these agents off after cleansing). Apply in thin layer. Elase is available commercially as powder to make solution for wet to dry dressings for débriding.
—Travase	Grades 2 through 4 with necrotic tissue and no exposed nerve or bone.	Acts against necrotic soft tissue.	Change three to four times daily; sore must be kept wet for enzymes to be effective. Thoroughly moisten wound area before applying enzyme. Apply enzyme in thin layer over necrotic tissue extending ¼- to ½-inch beyond necrotic area. Apply loose moist dressing. Enzyme activity may be impaired by some detergents, iodine, and hexachlorophene. Cross-hatching or removal of eschar facilitates action.
—Santyl	Grades 2 through 4 with necrotic tissues and with no exposed nerve or bone.	Contains collagenase, which attacks collagen in necrotic tissue.	Most effective in environment with *p*H 6 to 8; enzymatic activity is decreased by use of detergents, hexachlorophene and heavy metal ions; peroxide, Dakins, and saline are compatible with Santyl; tissue surrounding wound may become irritated if Santyl is not kept in boundary of wound; cross-hatching or removal of eschar facilitates contact of enzyme with more necrotic tissue.
• Wet to dry dressing	Grades 2 through 4; used in necrotic infected wounds.	Layer of gauze in contact with wound dries, and necrotic debris adherent to dressing is removed.	Must use wide-mesh cotton gauze to débride effectively; can be used in conjunction with hydrotherapy. If there is excessive drainage, dressing will not dry. Dressing will not débride if hard eschar is present. Packing too tightly may cause additional necrosis.

Table 4-2 continued

Product	Uses	Action	Considerations
			Débridement is nonselective and involves loss of healthy as well as necrotic tissue. Dressing may be used with antimicrobial solutions on infected wound. Removal of necrotic tissue is painful when sensation is present. If technique must be used in presence of sensation, analgesic medication may reduce pain.
• Mesalt	Grades 2 through 4; used in necrotic, infected wounds.	Similar to wet to dry dressings (100% cotton gauze dressing containing sodium chloride in crystalline form). Dressing is hypertonic and stimulates cleansing of wound. Thin necrotic material and drainage are absorbed into the dressing.	Easy to use; provides moist environment; absorbs drainage. Do not use on wounds with only scant amount of drainage. Dressing is changed one or two times daily. Long-term treatment with wet dressings may cause irritation to surrounding tissues because of moisture.
• Wet to wet dressing	Grades 2 through 4; can be used with necrotic wounds.	Small amounts of necrotic tissue are trapped in gauze.	Change as often as necessary. If minimal debris is on dressing, change less often. If large amounts of debris, change more frequently (Rudolph & Noe, 1983, p. 14).
• Iodoform packing	Grades 3 and 4; may be used in necrotic and infected wounds.	Antiseptic action from presence of iodine; aids in mechanically débriding necrotic tissue; keeps wound entry from closing before healing of underlying tissues; absorbs exudate from wound surface.	Must be covered by sterile dressing; can be caustic to healthy tissue; packing too tightly can irritate and enlarge wound.
5. Protective dressings			
• Petrolatum-treated gauze (Adaptic, Xeroform)	Nondraining, clean grade 1 and 2 areas.	Minimizes adherence of dressing to wound; questionable moisturizing effect.	Must be covered with gauze dressing to prevent drying. Change daily. If dressing adheres to wound, moisten with normal saline before removal, and increase frequency of change to two to three times a day. If dressing continues to adhere, consider use of semipermeable dressing.
• Nonadherent gauze (Telfa)	Scantily draining or nondraining, clean grade 1 and 2 areas.	Minimizes adherence of exterior dressing to wound.	Routinely change every day. If dressing adheres to wound, use procedure as described for petrolatum-treated gauze, above.
• Gauze dressing (nonwoven gauze sponge)	Covers any other dressing for cosmetic effect; absorbs exudate; can be used as stoma dressing.	Absorbs moisture from wound surface to dressing surface.	If gauze dressing adheres, saturate with normal saline to prevent destruction of granulating tissue, and consider another type of dressing.
• Gauze or elastic rolled bandage	Keeps large or multiple dressings in place. Also used to keep standard dressings in	Provides physical barrier between tape and skin, thus preventing skin irritation.	Wrap bandages with figure-of-eight technique when used on extremity. Do not use tension

Table 4-2 continued

Product	Uses	Action	Considerations
	place for the following patients: those with diaphoresis, elderly individuals, those with tape allergies, those with fragile skin, and those who require moisturizing therapy to skin around wound (thus preventing tape from adhering to skin).		with any nonelastic gauze. If unable to get one finger width underneath bandage, it is wrapped too tightly and will impede circulation. If this occurs, rewrap bandage. Assess circulation to the area after wrapping bandage.
• Fenestrated drain sponges	Used around tubes entering body (i.e., gastrostomy, suprapubic).	Absorb drainage from tube site; protect tube entry site from contaminants; may prevent tube from being pulled out if taped appropriately.	If entry site is healed and nondraining, may want to keep area open to air and clean with soap and water every hour and as needed.
• Large absorptive dressing	Large or multiple wound areas; applied over primary dressing; also for grades 2 to 4.	Covers large or multiple wound areas; absorbs larger amounts of wound exudate than standard dressings.	Do not cover more than one wound area with single dressing if all wounds are not clean.
• Steri Strips	Surgical incision sites.	Nonallergenic porous adhesive; may be used to support sutures or to provide reinforcement for wound that requires closure after sutures are removed; helps prevent wound dehiscence.	Skin must be clean and dry before applying. A thin coat of tincture of benzoin may be applied to skin surface parallel to wound to increase strip adhesion. Steri Strips are usually allowed to remain on skin until they fall off. Assess suture site closely for redness, swelling, drainage, and signs of dehiscence.
6. Antimicrobials (see general consideration 3 in procedure on General Wound Care)			All antimicrobials listed can damage fibroblasts. If antimicrobials are used for irrigation, rinse with normal saline.
• Acetic acid	May reduce bacterial flora; sometimes used in wet to dry dressings.		
• Hydrogen peroxide	Weak germicidal action.		When used under pressure, may create subcutaneous bullae. Use only in areas from which oxygen bubbles can escape.
• Povidone-iodine (Betadine)	Effective against most organisms, but resistance may develop.		Drying agent; iodine may be absorbed into tissue and elevate serum inorganic iodide (Dunavant, 1982).
• Dakin's (sodium hypochlorite) solution	Antibacterial action; may be used in wet to dry dressings.	Releases chlorine, which is bactericidal.	Unstable: must be reconstituted daily (*Nurses Reference Library Series*, 1983). Protect surrounding skin with skin barrier.
• Silvadene cream (silver sulfadiazine)	Antibacterial action.	Can penetrate necrotic tissue.	May reduce epithelization.

Note: Some information is adapted from materials provided by the manufacturers.

General Wound Care

PURPOSES

To prevent infection of the wound; to protect adjacent skin surfaces from irritation from wound drainage; to promote wound healing.

STAFF RESPONSIBLE

EQUIPMENT

Supplies may be available in dressing packs, or items may be obtained separately, depending on institutional preference.

1. Clean examination gloves.
2. Sterile gloves.
3. Sterile dressings for cleansing wound (4 × 4 or 2 × 2).
4. Solution for cleansing wound.
5. Sterile dressing for application over wound.
6. Prescribed topical agent (optional, based on physician's order).
7. Material for irrigating or culturing wound (optional).
8. Plastic bag and tie.
9. Pouch drainage bags (optional, for fistulas).
10. Tape or alternative adherent (binder).
11. Skin barrier (optional, for use under tape).
12. Isolation set up (optional, based on isolation procedures).

GENERAL CONSIDERATIONS

1. Maintain sterile technique for dressing changes to prevent wound infection.
2. Use isolation procedures as appropriate. Precautions will generally be dictated by the amount of drainage, results of wound cultures, or the presence of a condition such as AIDS or hepatitis, which require isolation of bodily secretions.
3. In general, normal saline or a surfactant wound cleanser is used to cleanse the wound. Antibacterial solutions are preferred by some clinicians for cleansing, but precautions are indicated with the use of hydrogen peroxide 3%, acetic acid 0.5%, Dakin's 0.25%, and povidone-iodine 1% to cleanse wounds. All the above solutions in the given strengths have been found to be toxic to fibroblasts (Lineaweaver, McMorris, Soucy, & Howard, 1985). Hydrogen peroxide should not be used to irrigate a wound because when used under pressure it has been shown to contribute to the formation of subcutaneous gas (Nurses' Drug Alert, June 1987). Irrigation with antiseptic solu-

tion, when used, is followed by rinsing with normal saline.
4. Wounds should be cleansed with gentle pressure if the tissue is nonnecrotic. Firm pressure can be used in the presence of necrotic tissue. Friction or firm pressure can damage freshly granulating tissue.
5. Fine-mesh gauze is the choice rather than wide-mesh when using dry sterile dressings on an open granulating wound. There is less likelihood that granulating tissue will be pulled from the wound bed when using fine-mesh gauze.
6. Use wide-mesh gauze when the objective of wound care is mechanical débridement.
7. If a dressing adheres to the wound bed, moisten the dressing with saline to decrease the possibility of trauma when removing the dressing. Consider use of a dressing that will not adhere.
8. A moist wound base promotes epithelization. Avoid use of heat lamps or fans because they will dry the base of the wound.
9. Label solutions with the date and time opened. Discard solutions according to infection control standards.
10. Assess patient sensitivity to tape, and select tape on the basis of the assessment. Alternate patterns of taping to prevent irritation. Consider the use of a binder, Montgomery straps, or a dressing that does not require taping if irritation occurs. Adhesive tape is not used over areas with decreased tactile sensation.
11. Assess the wound and wound area each time the dressing is changed, at least every 8 hours. Document the assessment according to departmental standards. Assessment includes signs of sensitivity to topical agents. Pink granulation tissue indicates a clean, healthy wound. Refer to the procedure on Assessment of a Pressure Sore (above) for specific parameters of assessment.
12. Provide privacy for patients by drawing curtains, closing the door, and exposing only the area that is to be treated. Wash hands between caring for patients.
13. Many clinicians prefer to use a syringe fitted with an 18- or 19-gauge needle when forceful irrigation is used to loosen necrotic tissue. The needle should be removed when irrigating undermined tissue. Use high-pressure irrigation only when the purpose of irrigation is to remove debris and bacteria from heavily contaminated wounds. Generally, an Asepto syringe is used for low-pressure irrigation (Dunavant, 1982, pp. 658–686).

PATIENT AND FAMILY EDUCATION

The patient or caregiver will need to learn the wound care procedure if the patient is going on an overnight pass or if a wound is present at the time of discharge from the hospital.

PROCEDURE

Steps	*Additional Information*
1. Verify treatment order.	
2. Gather all equipment, and bring it to patient's bedside.	
3. Explain procedure to patient, elicit cooperation, and position him or her to expose wound.	Provide privacy.
4. Wash hands.	
5. Set up equipment (remove bottle caps, open dressings, set up plastic trash bag, and cut tape).	Follow infection control procedures when additional precautions are indicated.
6. Apply clean examination gloves.	
7. Remove soiled dressing with gloved hand.	Remove dressing by holding patient's skin and pulling tape toward wound to prevent stress to wound or incision. Apply sterile saline if dressing adheres.
8. Observe amount, color, and odor of drainage and condition of wound bed or incision.	See procedure on Assessment of a Pressure Sore (above). Also observe for untoward reaction to topical agent.
9. Place soiled dressing and glove in plastic bag.	
10. Apply sterile gloves.	Designate one hand as sterile, one as unsterile.
11. Use unsterile hand to pour solutions.	
12. Irrigate wound, or obtain culture if ordered (optional step).	Fistulas will require irrigation or cleansing with applicators. Deep wounds may require irrigation. Use protective underpads to protect linens. If irritating cleansing solutions are used, clean wound with sterile saline after using prescribed solution.
13. Pour wetting solution while holding dressings over plastic bag, or pour wetting solution into basin with cleansing dressing.	The plastic bag must be positioned away from sterile field.
14. Cleanse wound from center outward using spiral motion and gentle pressure.	If undermined tissue is present, irrigate or use gentle pressure to cleanse area. Scrubbing motion may be needed when necrotic tissue is present.
15. Discard cleansing dressing into plastic bag, and use fresh sterile dressing each time wound is cleansed.	
16. Follow treatment order for application of topical medication, if ordered.	Wound bed should always be cleansed before applying topical agents. Ointments may be applied with sterile tongue blade.
17. If ordered, pack wound with gauze, or apply absorbant powders or gels. Apply dressing or pouch bag as ordered.	Refer to specific procedures for application of occlusive, semi-permeable, or wet to dry dressings and packings.
18. If needed, apply an absorbant dressing over 4 × 4 or 2 × 2 dressing and adhere with tape.	
19. Remove gloves, and discard plastic bag.	Gloves must be removed before applying tape. Assess condition of skin to which tape will adhere. Do not apply tape over reddened or open skin.
20. Adhere dressing with tape.	
21. Close bag, and set it aside.	
22. Replace patient's clothing, and reposition the patient.	
23. Check that call light is accessible to patient.	
24. Replace side rails.	
25. Store wound care supplies.	
26. Wash hands.	
27. Discard solutions and soiled materials according to infection control procedures.	

DOCUMENTATION

1. Document the prescribed treatment time on the appropriate form used by the institution.
2. Document the appearance of the wound and drainage (see procedure on Assessment of a Pressure Sore).
3. Document patient and family education.

Duoderm Hydroactive Dressings

PURPOSES

To provide a protective environment for a healing wound through correct use, application, and removal of a dressing; to promote healing.

STAFF RESPONSIBLE

EQUIPMENT

1. Cleansing solution.
2. Sterile normal saline.
3. Sterile 4 × 4 gauze.
4. Tape.
5. Irrigation kit or syringe for irrigating.
6. One piece of Duoderm (two sizes: the dressing should cover at least 3 inches of healthy tissue around the open area).

GENERAL CONSIDERATIONS

1. A physician's order is required for the use of Duoderm.
2. Duoderm may be used on the following skin areas:
   - grade 1, 2, and 3 areas,
   - areas with minimal necrotic tissue,
   - areas with no tunneling, and
   - areas that are not infected.
3. Duoderm interacts with the wound fluid, forming a soft moist gel that protects the wound bed, facilitates dressing removal, and avoids damage to fragile healing tissue.
4. The dressing should be changed once a week. The wound site and covering should be observed each shift, however. If the dressing must be changed more frequently than every 4 to 5 days because of drainage, then Duoderm granules can be put in the wound to absorb excess drainage.
5. Duoderm must not be considered a padding or cushion to prevent friction or pressure over an area. Sitting and turning tolerance must be observed as well as other pressure-relief techniques (e.g., bridging, cut-outs, and the like).

PROCEDURE

Steps	Additional Information
1. Follow steps 1 to 15 in procedure on General Wound Care.	
2. Blot wound dry with sterile 4 × 4 gauze.	Do not rub. Rubbing will remove newly formed, delicate granulation cells.
3. Remove backing from dressing.	Hold edges to maintain sterility of dressing.
4. Apply dressing over area, and press it gently with palm of hand for a few seconds.	Body heat helps dressing to adhere and contour to body. Dressing should cover at least 3 inches of healthy tissue around open area.
5. For contoured areas (e.g., gluteal slit): • fold Duoderm in half, • start applying in center, • press center of dressing firmly in place, and • smooth out one side and then other.	
6. Seal all four sides with tape.	There must be air-tight seal formed around entire open area. Change tape as needed.
7. Change dressing if drainage is noted around dressing.	Bubble of fluid will form in center of dressing in a few days. This is normal and should be of no concern.
8. To contain drainage, try a larger sheet of Duoderm.	
9. Use Duoderm granules if excessive drainage becomes a problem. Sprinkle in wound just before dressing is applied.	Do not overfill beyond skin edges.
10. Discard waste according to infection control procedures.	

DOCUMENTATION

1. Document in the appropriate record; the frequency of documentation is based on agency policy.

2. Document any problems encountered.

Bard Absorption Dressing

PURPOSES

To use and apply properly the Bard absorption dressing; to promote absorption of wound drainage.

STAFF RESPONSIBLE

EQUIPMENT

1. Sterile saline.
2. Sterile specimen cup or container.
3. Two sterile wooden tongue blades.
4. Sterile gloves.
5. Garbage bag.
6. Bard absorption dressing.
7. Tape.
8. 4 × 4 Gauze sponges (12-ply are preferable to absorb drainage).
9. Clean gloves.

GENERAL CONSIDERATIONS

1. A physician's order is required for use of the Bard absorption dressing. The order should include frequency of change and cleansing solution.
2. This dressing is indicated for grade 2 through 4 wounds that have significant drainage but no tunneling or sinusing. If signs or symptoms of infection are present, verify the use with the physician and infection control nurse, and use the prescribed cleansing solution.
3. The dressing is capable of absorbing large quantities of fluid (approximately 30 times its weight). The dressing also absorbs wound exudate, bacteria, and odor.
4. This dressing should be changed at least twice daily. It should be changed more often if the wound drainage is such that the gel dries out between changes.
5. If wound drainage increases to the point where the dressing is liquefied and leaks out, notify the physician.
6. This dressing does not interfere with topical medication applied in conjunction with it.

PATIENT AND FAMILY EDUCATION

The patient or caregiver of a patient who goes on an overnight pass or is discharged from the hospital with a wound should be taught the procedure.

PROCEDURE

Steps	*Additional Information*
1. Follow steps 1 through 15 in procedure on General Wound Care.	
2. Clean wound bed, removing all absorption dressing from undermined areas.	Irrigation may be necessary to cleanse wound bed thoroughly.
3. Use 5 mL of dressing flakes per 30 mL of liquid (sterile normal saline or water). Prepare absorption dressing in sterile container.	
4. Stir mixture well with sterile tongue blade until gelled.	
5. Cover wound with gelled absorption dressing by using second tongue blade.	Begin in middle of wound. Working out, extend dressing 1 cm beyond margin of wound and to depth of at least 0.5 to 1 cm above skin surface. If dressing is not applied to sufficient depth, normal amount of drainage may cause liquefaction of gel.
6. Cover with dry gauze and adhere to tape.	
7. Dispose of waste materials and wash hands.	Discard according to infection control procedures.

DOCUMENTATION

1. Document the procedure and description of the wound in the appropriate record.
2. Document any problems encountered.
3. Document patient and family education and results.

Vigilon Dressing

PURPOSE

To promote wound healing.

STAFF RESPONSIBLE

EQUIPMENT

1. Nonsterile gloves.
2. Plastic bag.
3. Sterile gloves.
4. Gauze 4 × 4 pads.
5. Tape.
6. Vigilon.
7. Sterile field.
8. Normal saline or other cleansing agent.

GENERAL CONSIDERATIONS

1. Refer to Product Options for Wound Care.
2. A physician's order is necessary for the use of Vigilon.
3. Vigilon is available in sterile 3 × 6 inch and 4 × 4 inch and in nonsterile 4 × 4 and 13 × 24 inch sizes.
4. Topical medications can be applied underneath Vigilon.
5. Vigilon is permeable to oxygen, pliable, nonadhering, and occlusive. Vigilon promotes healing of grades 1, 2, and 3 wounds by absorbing excess drainage, preventing formation of eschar, and providing protection from friction and rubbing.
6. Vigilon should be changed each shift and as necessary.
7. Vigilon can be refrigerated 1 hour before use to enhance its analgesic properties.

PROCEDURE

Steps	*Additional Information*
1. Follow steps 1 to 15 in procedure on General Wound Care.	Use sterile field under patient if needed to prevent wound contamination. If antiseptic cleansing solutions are used, follow with cleansing with normal saline.
2. Remove transparent backing from both sides of Vigilon.	
3. Apply Vigilon to wound.	Apply topical medications if ordered by physician.
4. Place sterile gauze 4 × 4 pads over Vigilon, and secure them in place with tape.	
5. Follow steps 19 to 26 in procedure on General Wound Care.	

DOCUMENTATION

Document the treatment and description of the wound according to agency policy.

Semipermeable Dressings

PURPOSE

To provide protective environment to promote wound healing.

STAFF RESPONSIBLE

EQUIPMENT

1. Cleansing agent.
2. Sterile normal saline.
3. Sterile 4 × 4 gauze.
4. Bag for disposal.
5. Nonsterile gloves (one pair).
6. Sterile gloves (one pair).
7. Tape (optional).
8. Semipermeable dressing (Op-Site, Tegaderm, or Opraflex).

GENERAL CONSIDERATIONS

1. These dressings require a physician's order.
2. Semipermeable dressings may be used on:
   - grade 1, 2, or 3 areas,
   - areas with minimal necrotic tissue,
   - areas that are not infected, and
   - areas with no tunneling.
3. Semipermeable dressings are permeable to air and moisture vapor but keep contaminants out. They provide a moist healing environment. The wound can be visualized through this dressing.
4. These dressings will not adhere in a moist environment and are not a choice for highly draining wounds or patients with diaphoresis.
5. It is normal for some fluid to gather under the dressing, and its color may change from clear yellow to white to rust (Irrgang, 1987).
6. The dressing should be observed each shift and should be changed if the seal is broken or if there is any sign of fluid leakage. The dressing should remain in place 3 to 7 days.
7. The dressing should be removed if any signs of infection are noted or if the surrounding tissue becomes macerated. The physician should be notified and another type of dressing considered.
8. If the dressing must be changed daily or more often, the skin may become irritated, and another treatment option should be considered.
9. These dressings are available in several sizes. Select one that will provide at least a 2-inch margin around the wound.

Note: Procedure is adapted from information provided by product manufacturers.

PATIENT AND FAMILY EDUCATION

The patient or caregiver should be taught the procedure before the patient leaves on an overnight pass or is discharged from the hospital if needed.

PROCEDURE

Steps	*Additional Information*
1. Follow steps 1 through 15 in procedure on General Wound Care.	When removing old dressing, do not lift dressing straight up. Apply tension horizontally to break seal. If dressing is difficult to remove, wash with warm soapy water. Excessive hair may need to be clipped for better adherence of dressing.
2. Dry wound thoroughly.	
3. Cleanse and thoroughly dry surrounding skin.	Skin may need to be defatted with alcohol for better adherence of dressing.
4. Remove dressing from outer package.	When choosing size, be sure it will provide at least a 2-inch margin around wound.
5. Starting at corner, remove part of protective paper, and apply dressing to skin surrounding wound.	Be sure to hold dressing with only minimal tension. Do not stretch, or it will cause skin to wrinkle.
6. Peeling away protective paper diagonally, smooth dressing onto surrounding skin and over wound.	If patient has wrinkled skin, smooth skin out before applying dressing, and tape it back. If dressing wrinkles during application, flatten wrinkles out.
7. Press edges gently but firmly into place.	
8. For Op-Site, green handles may be torn off, leaving a few millimeters of handles attached. Alternatively, protective paper may be removed from handles for extra anchorage.	
9. Remove gloves, discard waste in appropriate manner, and wash hands.	Discard waste according to infection control procedures.
10. Observe dressing. Change dressing if leakage occurs, if dressing is not intact, or every 3 to 7 days.	Inspect wound site and dressing once each shift.
11. Document as below.	

DOCUMENTATION

1. Document the wound size and characteristics at intervals specified by agency policy.
2. Notify the physician of signs of infection.
3. Document the dressing change in the record specified by agency policy.
4. Document patient and family teaching and results.

Packing a Wound with Gauze

PURPOSE

To pack a wound with gauze strips or pads to facilitate wound healing.

STAFF RESPONSIBLE

EQUIPMENT

1. Gauze strip per physician's order.
2. Prescribed cleansing agents.
3. Sterile suture removal kit (use for first packing, and keep scissors as reusable item).
4. Dressing pack, including:
   - sterile gloves,
   - sterile dressings or fluffs,
   - forceps,
   - plastic bag and tie,
   - tape, and
   - folding basin.
5. Sterile field.
6. Waste bag.

GENERAL CONSIDERATIONS

1. Patients on isolation or precautions should be treated per infection control guidelines.
2. Gauze should reach the active depths of the wound but is not packed tightly. Tight packing can create additional tissue damage.
3. The distal end of the gauze strip should extend beyond the opening of the wound to allow easy removal. Use only one strip.
4. Scissors need not be sterile but must be clean for each packing procedure.
5. Label gauze bottle and solutions with name, date, and time opened.
6. Iodophorm gauze is active as long as its odor can be detected in the bottle.
7. Wound packing can be used with grades 3 and 4 pressure sores to achieve healing from the tissue depths to the skin surface and to aid in the débriding of necrotic tissue. In most situations, surgery will eventually be done to close grade 3 and 4 sores.

PATIENT AND FAMILY EDUCATION

Teach the patient and family as appropriate.

PROCEDURE

Steps	*Additional Information*
1. Refer to General Wound Care (above) for steps of routine wound care.	
2. Wash hands.	
3. Open dressing pack and scissors. Prepare sterile field.	
4. Remove old gauze while wearing sterile gloves or using forceps.	Note length of gauze or number of pads removed.
5. Observe amount, color, and odor of drainage and condition of wound tissue.	
6. Discard dressing and forceps or gloves.	
7. Don sterile gloves.	
8. Cleanse wound, working from middle to outside edges. Irrigate wound if necessary.	Deep-tunneling wounds may require irrigation to cleanse.
9. Gather amount of gauze needed into sterile gloved hand.	Amount needed can be approximated from previous packing.
10. Hold gauze taut between thumb and fingers, and cut it cleanly with scissors.	Cut close to mouth of bottle to prevent contamination.
11. Pack slowly into wound with sterile forceps held in other hand. Do not touch edges of wound.	If diameter of wound is small, wooden end of sterile cotton-tipped applicators may be used to introduce gauze.
12. Apply dressing over wound, and adhere with tape or binder.	Remove gloves before applying tape, and discard them in plastic bag.
13. Close plastic waste bag, and set it aside.	

Steps	*Additional Information*
14. Replace patient's clothing, and reposition the patient as needed.	
15. Check that call light is accessible to patient.	
16. Replace side rails.	
17. Store wound care supplies.	
18. Wash hands.	Discard waste according to infection control procedures.
19. Wash scissors with soap and water, and then clean scissors with Betadine, alcohol, or chlorine solution.	
20. Store scissors in clean, covered container such as suture kit tray.	

DOCUMENTATION

1. Document the treatment and description of the wound in the appropriate records.
2. Document any problems found in removing the old dressing and in packing the wound.
3. Document the patient's and family's ability to follow-through safely.

Wet to Dry Dressing

PURPOSE

To débride necrotic tissue from a wound through correct application of a wet to dry dressing.

STAFF RESPONSIBLE

EQUIPMENT

1. Tape.
2. Skin prep (optional).
3. Sterile normal saline.
4. Prescribed irrigation solution.
5. Plastic bags.
6. Sterile barrier drapes.
7. Gauze dressings.
8. Betadine swab stick.
9. Binder or Montgomery straps.
10. Dressing tray.
11. 4 × 4 Wide-mesh gauze.
12. 2 × 2 Gauze dressings.

GENERAL CONSIDERATIONS

1. Wet to dry dressings mechanically débride a wound of necrotic tissue. Nevertheless, the débridement is nonselective and can remove healthy granulation tissue.
2. The solutions commonly used in wet to dry dressings are normal saline, acetic acid, and povidone-iodine. See the precautions on the use of acetic acid and povidone-iodine in the general considerations of General Wound Care, above.
3. The application of wet to dry dressings is a sterile procedure.
4. The frequency of dressing change, the solution to be used, and wound cultures will be ordered by the physician. The procedure is usually ordered every 4 hours.
5. Label the solution with the date and time opened, and discard according to infection control standards.
6. Patients on isolation or precautions should be treated per infection control guidelines.
7. Removal of the dry dressing causes pain for individuals with intact sensation.

PATIENT AND FAMILY EDUCATION

Patients or caregivers should be taught the procedure before the patient goes on a day or overnight pass or is discharged from the hospital. Instructions include assessment of the wound characteristics and reporting untoward signs.

PROCEDURE

Steps	Additional Information

Preparation

1. Position patient for procedure. Drape patient, and allow for privacy.
2. Assemble necessary equipment.
3. Wash hands.
4. Explain procedure to patient.
5. Place sterile barrier drape on overbed table. Set up sterile equipment and supplies on drape.
6. Set up plastic disposal bag in close proximity.

Explanation helps decrease patient's anxiety.

Removal of Contaminated Dressing

1. Loosen tape gently, pulling toward wound.

Frequent dressing changes needed for wet to dry dressings may result in irritation from tape. Consider using binder, Montgomery straps, or Kerlex to secure dressing.

2. Remove dressing with nonsterile gloves.

Sterile gloves may be needed depending on extent or depth or wound. Be careful to touch only dressings and not wound itself when wearing nonsterile gloves.

3. Place contaminated dressing and gloves in plastic bag for disposal.

Avoid touching inside of bag.

4. Perform or assist with any special procedures (e.g., wound culture, débridement, or irrigation).

These procedures will require additional equipment and supplies.

5. Don sterile gloves.
6. Cleanse wound with single stroke by using forceps. Start at center, and cleanse outward with circular motion.

Solution to be used will be determined by physician's order and action desired.

7. Discard cleaning materials after each use, and repeat procedure as needed.

Use plastic bags for discarding materials.

8. Discard forceps, or remove gloves if forceps not used.

Application of Dressing

1. Pour or soak prescribed solution over sterile gauze.
2. Put on sterile gloves.

Sterile plastic container is provided in most dressing trays.

3. Squeeze excess solution from gauze, and unfold gauze into single layer.

Dressing should be thin enough and just damp enough to dry thoroughly between dressing changes.

4. Place moistened gauze against wound surface, gently pressing into any depressions or crevices.

Dressing must come in contact with all necrotic material in order to débride.

5. Cover with dry dressing.

Type and thickness of dry dressing will vary with extent of wound and amount of drainage.

6. Remove gloves.
7. Tape edge of gauze in place. Do not cover entire dressing with tape.

Excessive tape over the dressing will block air circulation and interfere with drying.

8. Dispose of material, and wash hands.

Dispose of waste according to infection control procedures.

DOCUMENTATION

1. Document the treatment and description of the wound in the appropriate records.

2. Document any problems encountered.
3. Document patient and family teaching and success.

BIBLIOGRAPHY

Barbenel, J., Jordan, M., Nicol, S., & Clark, M. (1977). Incidence of pressure sores in the Greater Glasgow Health Board area. *Lancet, 2*, 548–550.

Bergstrom, N., Demuth, P., & Braden, B. (1987). A clinical trial of the Braden scale for predicting pressure sore risk. *Nursing Clinics of North America, 22*, 417–428.

Braden, B., & Bergstrom, N. (1987). A conceptual scheme for the study of the etiology of pressure sores. *Rehabilitation Nursing, 12*, 8–12.

Dunavant, M.K. (1982). Wound and fistula management. In D. Broadwell & B. Jackson (Eds.), *Principles of ostomy care* (pp. 658–686). St. Louis, MO: Mosby.

Fowler, E.M. (1987). Equipment and products used in management and treatment of pressure ulcers. *Nursing Clinics of North America, 22*, 449–461.

Garber, S., Campion, L., & Krouskop, T. (1982). Trochanteric pressure in spinal cord injury. *Archives of Physical Medicine and Rehabilitation, 63*, 549–552.

Gee, Z., & Passarella, P. (1985). *Nursing care of the stroke patient: A therapeutic approach*. Pittsburgh, PA: AREN.

Gosnell, D.J. (1973). An assessment tool to identify pressure sores. *Nursing Research, 22*, 55.

Gosnell, D.J. (1987). Assessment and evaluation of pressure sores. *Nursing Clinics of North America, 22*, 399–415.

Irrgang, S. (1987). Topical treatment of pressure ulcers. *Home Care, 9*, 44–52.

King, R.B. (1981). Assessment and management of soft tissue pressure. In N. Martin, N.B. Holt, & D. Hicks (Eds.), *Comprehensive rehabilitation nursing*. New York: McGraw-Hill, 242–268.

King, R.B., Boyink, M., & Keenan, M. (1977). *Rehabilitation guide*. Chicago, IL: Rehabilitation Institute of Chicago.

Kling, C. (1983). Integumental system. In S. Benda (Ed.), *Spinal cord injury nursing education suggested content*. American Spinal Injury Association.

Krouskop, T., Williams, R., Krebs, M., Herszkowicz, I., & Garber, S. (1985). Effectiveness of mattress overlays in reducing interface pressure during recumbency. *Journal of Rehabilitation Research and Development, 22*, 7–10.

Landis, E. (1930). Studies of capillary blood pressure in human skin. *Heart, 5*, 209.

Lilla, J.A., Friedrichs, R.R., & Vistnes, L.H. (1975). Flotation mattresses for preventing and treating tissue breakdown. *Geriatrics, 30*, 71.

Lineaweaver, W., McMorris, S., Soucy, D., & Howard, R. (1985). Cellular and bacterial toxicities of topical antimicrobials. *Plastic and Reconstructive Surgery, 75*, 394–396.

Lippincott manual of nursing practice (3rd ed). (1982). Philadelphia, PA: Lippincott.

Lowthian, P. (1979). Pressure sore prevalence. *Nursing Times, 75*, 358–360.

Maklebust, J., Mondoux, L., & Sieggreen, M. (1986). Pressure relief characteristics of various support surfaces used in prevention and treatment of pressure ulcers. *Journal of Enterostomal Therapy, 14*, 85–89.

Matthews, P., Carlson, C.E., & Holt, N.B. (Eds.). (1987). *Spinal cord injury: A guide to rehabilitation nursing*. Rockville, MD: Aspen.

Mooney, V., Einbund, M., Rogers, J., & Stauffer, E. (1971, Spring). Comparison of pressure distribution qualities in seat cushions. *Bulletin of Prosthetic Research*, pp. 129–143.

Nixon, V. (1985). *Spinal cord injury: A guide to functional outcomes in physical therapy management*. Rockville, MD: Aspen.

Norton, D., McLaren, R., & Exton-Smith, A.N. (1962). *An investigation of geriatric nursing problems in hospitals*. London: National Corporation for the Care of Old People.

Nurses' Drug Alert. (1987, June). Avoid use of hydrogen peroxide and povidone-iodine in open wounds. *American Journal of Nursing, 11*, 41.

Nurses Reference Library Series: Procedures. (1983). Springhouse, PA: Intermed Communications.

Oberg, M., & Lindsey, D. (1987). Do not put hydrogen peroxide or povidone-iodine into wounds. *American Journal of Diseases of Children, 141*, 27–28.

Palmer, M., & Wyness, M. (1988). Positioning and handling: Important considerations in the care of the severely head-injured patient. *Journal of Neuroscience Nursing, 20*, 42–49.

Rudolph, R., & Noe, J.M. (1983). *Chronic problem wounds*. Boston: Little, Brown.

Schneider, D., & Hebert, L. (1987). Subcutaneous gas from hydrogen peroxide administration under pressure. *American Journal of Diseases of Children, 141*, 10–11.

Shanon, M.L. (1982). Pressure sores. In C.M. Norris (Ed.), *Concept clarification in nursing*. Rockville, MD: Aspen.

Shea, D. (1975). Pressure sores: Classification and management. *Clinical orthopedics and related research, 112*, 89–100.

Wells, P., & Geden, E. (1984). Paraplegic body-support pressures on convoluted foam, waterbed and standard mattresses. *Research in Nursing and Health, 7*, 127–133.

Young, J.S., & Burns, P.E. (1981). Pressure sores and the spinal cord injured: Part II. *SCI Digest, 3*, 11–26.

Zejdlik, C. (1983). *Management of spinal cord injury*. Monterey, CA: Wadsworth.

chapter 5

Procedures To Maintain and Restore Respiratory Function

INTRODUCTION

Approximately one of five Americans has some form of respiratory disease. A history of premorbid respiratory disease coupled with a neurologic disability, as is commonly seen in rehabilitation, can put the individual at risk for respiratory complications.

Respiration involves mechanical, neurological, and chemical controls. Respiration involves delivery of oxygen to the cells and removal of carbon dioxide. Air moves in and out of the lungs by means of a mechanical process called ventilation. Ventilation is regulated by neurologic centers in the brainstem and chemoreceptors in the vascular system. The neurologic centers and chemoreceptors regulate the rate, rhythm, and depth of inspiration. Ventilation consists of two phases: inspiration and expiration. Inspiration is an active process in which the diaphragm and intercostal muscles contract and create a negative intrapulmonary pressure that draws air into the lungs. Expiration under normal circumstances is a passive process that occurs when the intrapulmonary pressure is greater than atmospheric pressure. A forceful expiration is required to produce a cough or sneeze; this requires muscular effort from the abdominal and internal intercostal muscles (Stevens, 1987).

Injuries to the brainstem, such as might occur with stroke or head injury, can damage neuroregulatory centers and produce an irregular respiratory pattern. Damage to the cranial nerves, in particular IX (glossopharyngeal) and X (vagus), will interfere with the gag reflex and airway protection, thus putting the individual at great risk for aspiration (see also Chapter 1).

After a spinal cord injury, an impairment of respiratory function may also occur. If the damage to the cord occurs at C-3 or above, mechanical ventilation will be necessary. This may be accomplished with a mechanical ventilator or with phrenic nerve stimulators. Damage to the cervical and upper thoracic levels of the cord results in decreased vital capacities and a weak, ineffective cough.

Brain damage and spinal cord injury are disabilities commonly encountered in rehabilitation that affect respiratory function. Nursing procedures address measures to optimize respiratory function, to maintain a patent airway, to prevent potential injury, and to utilize equipment associated with respiratory function.

When discussing procedures in rehabilitation, it is important to keep in mind some basic tenets of rehabilitation:

1. Rehabilitation is goal directed, and goals are mutually set with the patient and family.
2. Mobility is encouraged, and as the patient becomes more mobile (either ambulatory or in wheelchair) special adaptations of procedures may be necessary.
3. Patient and family education is a major goal. Educating the patient and family about procedures is an ongoing process.
4. Programs for care in the home must be able to be performed safely by caregivers, and necessary equipment must be available to the patient and family.

The procedures in this chapter address these issues as they pertain to respiratory care for the patient in rehabilitation and were developed in conjunction with the respiratory therapy staff of Northwestern Memorial Hospital.

Oxygen Therapy

PURPOSES

To reverse and prevent tissue hypoxia; to treat or correct arterial hypoxemia; to decrease the work of breathing; to decrease myocardial work.

STAFF RESPONSIBLE

EQUIPMENT

1. Oxygen source with pressure regulator and flow meter.
2. "No Smoking" sign.
3. Oxygen delivery device prescribed.
4. Humidifier (if flow is greater than 4 L/min).

GENERAL CONSIDERATIONS

1. The need for oxygen therapy must always be based on sound clinical judgment aided by arterial blood gas measurement and a physician's order. Hypoxemia may elicit a compensatory increase in ventilatory and cardiac work; thus the cardiopulmonary system works harder and total oxygen requirements are increased at times (Shapiro, Harrison, & Trout, 1979).
2. All oxygen therapy orders must be written by a physician and should include delivery device flow rate and approximate concentrations and parameters for use.
3. Arterial blood gas measurements provide a clinical means of assessing and evaluating the physiologic effects of oxygen and of documenting the need for continued oxygen therapy. It is suggested that the physician order arterial blood gas measurements before initiating therapy and periodically during treatment to evaluate the effectiveness of the therapy. A recent arterial blood gas measurement will be needed to get oxygen supplied for home use.
4. Using the correct oxygen delivery device is crucial to provide proper oxygen concentrations. Oxygen delivery devices are not interchangeable. Table 5-1 lists the most common delivery devices, flow rates, and fraction of in-

spired oxygen (F_{IO_2}) concentrations provided. An F_{IO_2} of 21% is equivalent to room air oxygen concentration.
5. When oxygen is needed during transport or off-unit procedures, ensure that an adequate volume of oxygen is available to the patient (Tables 5-2A and B).
6. The respiratory therapist is responsible for initial assembly of the oxygen therapy delivery system except in emergency situations. The respiratory therapist is responsible for checking the equipment each shift, checking emergency equipment, and documenting an equipment check.
7. Patients with a documented history of chronic obstructive pulmonary disease must be regulated on low concentrations of oxygen.
8. Care should be exercised when handling equipment; refer to infection control guidelines. A good rule of thumb is to

Table 5-1 Comparison of Oxygen Delivery Devices and Flow Rates

Oxygen Delivery Device	Flow Rate (liters per minute)	F_{IO_2} (percent)	Comments
Nasal cannula[a]	1	24	No humidity is needed at rates <4 L/min.
	2	28	
	3	32	
	4	36	
	5	40	Humidity is needed.
	6	44	
Simple face mask	5	40	
	6	50	
	7	60	
High-humidity tracheostomy collar	5 to 8	28 to 30	F_{IO_2} is set on nebulizer dial.
	10	>35	Concentrations range from 35% to 100%.

[a]At times the physician will order a nasal cannula at meals to replace a mask.

Note: The equivalents are as follows:

- Simple mask, 5 L/min = cannula, 5 L/min
- Simple mask, 6 L/min = cannula, 6 L/min
- Simple mask, 7 L/min = cannula, 7 L/min
- High-humidity face mask, 35% = cannula, 4 L/min
- High-humidity face mask, 40% = cannula, 5 L/min
- High-humidity face mask, 60% = cannula, 6 L/min

Table 5-2A E Cylinder Duration*[1]

Estimated volume of oxygen duration[2] based on flow rate, gauge pressure, and cylinder type.

Flow Rate (liters per minute)	Gauge Pressure								
	2200 psi	1800 psi	1600 psi	1400 psi	1200 psi	1000 psi	800 psi	600 psi	400 psi
10	61 min	50 min	44 min	39 min	33 min	28 min	22 min	16 min	11 min
8	1 hr 17 min	63 min	56 min	49 min	42 min	35 min	28 min	21 min	14 min
6	1 hr 42 min	1 hr 24 min	1 hr 14 min	65 min	56 min	46 min	37 min	28 min	18 min
4	2 hr 34 min	2 hr 6 min	1 hr 52 min	1 hr 38 min	1 hr 24 min	1 hr 10 min	56 min	42 min	28 min
3	3 hr 25 min	2 hr 48 min	2 hr 29 min	2 hr 10 min	1 hr 52 min	1 hr 33 min	1 hr 14 min	56 min	37 min
2	5 hr 8 min	4 hr 12 min	3 hr 44 min	3 hr 16 min	2 hr 48 min	2 hr 20 min	1 hr 52 min	1 hr 24 min	56 min
1	10 hr 16 min	8 hr 24 min	7 hr 28 min	6 hr 32 min	5 hr 36 min	4 hr 40 min	3 hr 44 min	2 hr 48 min	1 hr 52 min

Table 5-2B H Cylinder Duration**[2]

Estimated volume of oxygen duration[2] based on flow rate, gauge pressure, and cylinder type.

Flow Rate (liters per minute)	Gauge Pressure								
	2200 psi	2000 psi	1800 psi	1600 psi	1400 psi	1200 psi	1000 psi	800 psi	600 psi
10	11 hours 30 minutes	10 hours 28 minutes	9 hours 25 minutes	8 hours 22 minutes	7 hours 19 minutes	6 hours 16 minutes	5 hours 14 minutes	4 hours 11 minutes	3 hours 8 minutes
8	14 hours 23 minutes	13 hours 5 minutes	11 hours 46 minutes	10 hours 28 minutes	9 hours 9 minutes	7 hours 51 minutes	6 hours 30 minutes	5 hours 14 minutes	3 hours 8 minutes
6	19 hours 10 minutes								
4	28 hours 47 minutes	26 hours 10 minutes	23 hours 33 minutes	20 hours 51 minutes	18 hours 19 minutes	15 hours 42 minutes	13 hours 5 minutes	10 hours 28 minutes	7 hours 51 minutes

Factors

[1]Commonly used approximations that any oxygen supply company can provide

[2]Duration of flow (minutes) = $\dfrac{\text{Gauge Pressure} \times \text{Factor}}{\text{Liter Flow}}$

*E Cylinder = .28 L/psi
**H Cylinder = 3.14 L/psi

keep the oxygen at least 5 feet away from a source of ignition (cigarettes, hair dryers, and the like). Consult the safety engineer regarding oxygen safety requirements at your facility.

9. Respiratory equipment including oxygen may be necessary after discharge. Planning must start early. Consult available resources for additional information about equipment ordering.

PATIENT AND FAMILY EDUCATION

1. Teach the patient and family about the type of oxygen therapy ordered, oxygen precautions, flow rate, and therapeutic value.
2. Instruct the family on how to obtain and maintain necessary equipment.
3. Teach other specific procedures as appropriate.

PROCEDURES

Steps	Additional Information
1. Check physician order for method of delivery and flow rate.	
2. Call orders to respiratory therapy department.	Respiratory therapist is responsible for initial assembly of oxygen delivery system and for checking equipment each shift.
3. Gather equipment, wash hands, and explain procedure to patient.	Anxiety can increase oxygen demand.
4. Assess patient's current respiratory status (rate, effort, pulse, color, rhythm, and endurance).	
5. Check patient room for safety:	
• All electrical equipment must be within acceptable limits as set by your agency.	
• "No Smoking" sign must be placed on door and by patient bed. Explain safety precautions to patients and visitors in room.	Do not allow smoking within 5 feet of oxygen source.
6. Use specific delivery system (detailed below).	
7. Throughout administration, periodically assess respiratory status (rate, work of breathing, endurance, color, nature of secretions, and ability to mobilize secretions).	Notify physician of significant changes.
8. Check oxygen delivery settings and oxygen volume every shift, and notify respiratory therapist of any problems.	
9. Maintain oxygen delivery system at all times as prescribed.	Evaluate patient for therapies on unit.
Notify rehabilitation therapists of need for oxygen, and ensure that adequate volume of oxygen is present and that settings are correct before transporting patient.	Notify physician if patient status changes with exercise.
10. When oxygen therapy is discontinued, notify respiratory therapist to remove oxygen equipment.	
11. Discard any disposable equipment.	Disposal is according to infection control procedures.

Nasal Cannula Oxygen Therapy

1. Check nasal patency and condition of nares. Check daily before inserting cannula.	Common hazards include obstructed nostril, nasal trauma, bleeding, tissue necrosis, and mucosal drying.
2. Check for reddened areas under nose and over ears.	
3. Provide good nose and mouth care twice daily.	Use water-soluble lubricant as needed.
4. Verify correct flow rate and adequate volumes in tank each shift. Notify respiratory therapist if volumes are low.	
5. Position cannula by inserting nasal prongs into each nostril so that curve follows natural contour of nostril.	
6. Pass cannula tubing over both ears, and position it under chin.	
7. Slide adaptor cinch to adjust fit.	

Simple Oxygen Mask

1. Check pressure points on face and over ears for redness or irritation.	

Steps	*Additional Information*
2. Wash and dry patient's face thoroughly.	Humidified air will create excess moisture on face, so that it may be necessary to dry patient's face every 1 or 2 hours.
3. Provide mouth care once per shift.	
4. Verify flow rate and adequate volumes in tank. Notify respiratory therapist if volumes are low.	
5. Replace mask, and secure it with elastic strap around patient's neck at level of tragus of ear or around head above ear.	
6. Adjust nose clip and strap so that mask fits snugly.	

High-Humidity Tracheostomy Collar

1. Check patient's skin at stoma site and posterior neck for signs of irritation or pressure.	
2. Wash and dry patient's neck thoroughly.	
3. Check nebulizer and, if necessary, attach new prefilled nebulizer container.	Nebulizers are available from respiratory therapist. Consult respiratory therapist about brand and method of attachment in your facility.
4. Plug in heater.	Always attach nebulizer to heater before plugging heater into electrical outlet. Make certain hands are dry before plugging in heater. Warm air is less irritating to tracheal-bronchial lining. Cold air can induce bronchospasm, so heater should be used as much as possible.
5. Verify prescribed settings. Check flow rate and setting on nebulizer.	Settings are prescribed by physician, and equipment is set up at prescribed flow rates by respiratory therapist. With high-humidity tracheostomy collar, prescribed FIO_2 is set on nebulizer. Flow rate from oxygen source to nebulizer is determined by standards of your respiratory therapy department.
6. Empty tubing of excess fluid.	Always drain away from patient and into appropriate receptacle. Allow adequate slack on strap to prevent pressure on neck, but keep collar in proper alignment.
7. Place collar over tracheostomy, and secure strap around patient's neck.	

DOCUMENTATION

1. Document in the appropriate record:
   - assessment of the patient's status before initiation of therapy;
   - assessment of the patient's status each shift when active respiratory problem exists; and
   - when oxygen therapy is discontinued, and the patient's response; and
   - any changes in the patient's status, tolerance to therapy, or ability to keep the device in place.
2. Note the care performed each shift.
3. Document patient and family teaching on the progress note or teaching checklist.

Liquid Oxygen Therapy

PURPOSES

To provide an individual with a portable form of supplemental oxygen; to provide oxygen as prescribed for an individual's need.

STAFF RESPONSIBLE

EQUIPMENT

1. Liberator canister (tank) (Figure 5-1B).
2. Humidifier.
3. Oxygen delivery device.
4. Plastic tubing.
5. Stroller (portable oxygen tank) (Figure 5-1C).
6. Portable cart.
7. Shoulder strap.

GENERAL CONSIDERATIONS

1. Liquid oxygen is nonflammable but will rapidly support and accelerate combustion; common sense should prevail when using liquid oxygen.

2. A good rule of thumb is to keep the oxygen at least 5 feet away from a source of ignition (cigarettes, hair dryers, and the like). Consult the safety engineer regarding oxygen safety requirements at your facility.
3. The oxygen units are designed to be stored and operated in the upright position; otherwise leaking can occur.
4. The liquid cannister should be kept in a well-ventilated area; if it is used in a car, a window should be open slightly.
5. The walls of the cannister are insulated like a Thermos to keep the oxygen on the inside at a cold temperature. This is necessary to keep it in its liquid form.
6. When the flow meter attached to the cannister is turned on, the oxygen is warmed and delivered in the form of a gas without color, odor, or taste.
7. Keep hands away from the oxygen outlets while the portable tank is filling. The liquid oxygen temperature is far below freezing and may cause skin injuries similar to a burn.
8. The stroller is lightweight (approximately 9 lbs when full). Oxygen, when delivered at 2 L/min, is estimated to last up to 8 hours.
9. The unit should be checked for volume of oxygen once per shift.

PATIENT AND FAMILY EDUCATION

Patient and family education for use at home should be arranged with the home care vendor supplying the equipment.

PROCEDURES (based on systems shown in Figure 5-1)

Steps	Additional Information
To Fill the Stroller	
1. Connectors must be free of moisture and dirt.	Moisture can cause freeze-up.
2. Turn stroller flow selector off.	
3. Attach stroller fill connection to Liberator canister connection with stroller in upright position (Figure 5-1A).	
4. Rotate stroller counterclockwise approximately 45° until connectors engage.	
5. Carefully rotate stroller back to start position, thus locking units together.	
6. With wrench, open vent valve to begin fill.	Full is indicated by ''F'' on level indicator.
7. When unit is full, use wrench to close valve tightly.	
8. Disengage by rotating stroller counterclockwise until units separate.	If units do not disengage easily, do not use force because they may be frozen. Wait until they warm up, and they should disengage easily.

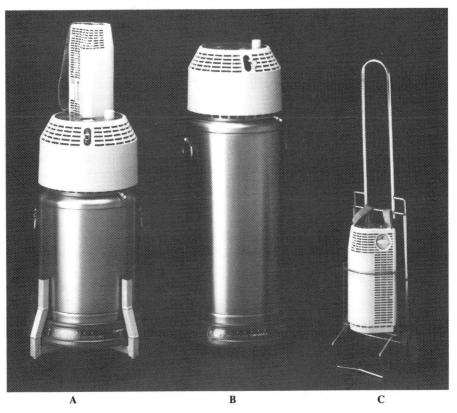

Figure 5-1 Liquid Oxygen Systems. (**A**) Filling Process, (**B**) Liberator, (**C**) Stroller. *Source:* Courtesy of Puritan-Bennett Corporation, Lenexa, KS.

Steps	*Additional Information*

Using the Stroller

1. Attach humidifier to disk connection.

   Humidification is helpful against drying effects of oxygen. If oxygen is used at 4 L/min or less, humidity is not needed because of natural lubrication of upper airway.

2. Attach prescribed oxygen delivery system (i.e., cannula, face mask, or tubing) to humidifier outlet, and adjust fit.

3. Turn dial clockwise to prescribed flow rate.

   Flow meter can be locked to ensure that patient will not exceed prescribed amount of oxygen.

4. Check amounts of oxygen available by depressing switch adjacent to contents gauge.

   Small portion of liquid oxygen will evaporate each day, so that supply will decrease even when not in use.

DOCUMENTATION

1. Document in appropriate record:
   - assessment of the patient's status before initiation of therapy;
   - use of liquid oxygen, the time when the unit was filled, and routine equipment checks; and
   - when therapy is discontinued, and the patient's response.
2. Document patient and family education in use of the equipment.

Ambu and Inflation Hold

PURPOSES

To provide a manually sustained maximal inflation in order to prophylactically loosen secretions in patients with an artificial airway; to provide manual ventilatory support and oxygenation for patients with an artificial airway.

STAFF RESPONSIBLE

EQUIPMENT

All equipment is considered emergency equipment to be kept at the bedside of any patient with an artificial airway.

1. Manual resuscitator bag (ambu bag).
2. Oxygen source.
3. Oxygen connecting tubing (may be part of ambu bag).
4. Oxygen flow meter.

GENERAL CONSIDERATIONS

1. Ambu with inflation hold is used to pre-oxygenate patients with suctioning. For patients receiving oxygen therapy or on mechanical ventilation, ambu and inflation hold must be performed with supplemental oxygen flow (10 L/min) before and after suctioning. For patients with known chronic obstructive pulmonary disease, check with the physician regarding the recommended flow rate.

2. Ambu and inflation hold should be performed prophylactically on all patients with an artificial airway at least once per shift if they are unable to perform sustained maximal inspiration on their own.
3. When ambu and inflation hold is being performed to provide manual ventilatory support for patients on mechanical ventilation, the number of breaths should be consistent with the ventilator rate or the typical respiratory rate.
4. The volume of air delivered with each breath depends on how the bag is compressed. Generally, a one-hand technique is adequate. Additional volume (two-hand technique) may be necessary for large individuals or those with significant retained secretions.
5. All patients on mechanical ventilation *must* have an ambu bag on their person at all times, and the staff assigned must be familiar with use of the bag in emergency situations.
6. Before and after the procedure, the nurse should assess the patient's respiratory status, including:
   - respiratory rate,
   - depth of respirations,
   - pattern,
   - symmetry, and
   - breath sounds.
7. Infection control measures should be followed with use of equipment. Position the ambu bag to avoid any contact with surfaces that are grossly contaminated (i.e., the floor, linen by urinary drainage devices, and the like).

PATIENT AND FAMILY EDUCATION

1. Explain the methods and actions to reduce anxiety.
2. Teach the procedure as necessary.

PROCEDURE

Steps	Additional Information
1. Check order for frequency and need for supplemental oxygen.	Physician's order for emergency equipment should be obtained with admission order for all patients with artificial airway.
2. Assemble necessary equipment.	
3. Identify patient. Introduce yourself and procedure to be performed.	
4. Wash hands. Apply gloves.	Nonsterile gloves may be used if hands are likely to come in contact with body secretions.
5. Attach connective tubing of ambu bag to flow meter. Turn oxygen on at rate of 10 L/min.	Oxygen is required for patient on supplemental oxygen therapy (more than 21%) or mechanical ventilation.
6. Verify that airway cuff is inflated.	

Steps	*Additional Information*
7. Connect adaptor of ambu bag to patient's tracheostomy tube. For cuffless tracheostomies, have patient close mouth and breathe in as you give breath and hold breath until bag is released.	If mouth is open and pattern is not synchronized, benefits of procedure may be negated by air loss through upper airway.
8. Instruct patient to breathe in as you compress bag. Hold bag in compressed position for 3 to 5 seconds, and then release.	Maximal inhalations should be synchronized with patient's own respiratory rate as much as possible.
9. Observe for any adverse reactions.	Procedure may loosen secretions.
10. Repeat steps 7, 8, and 9.	With suctioning, give three breaths before suctioning and three breaths after each pass of catheter. For prophylactic treatment, perform five repetitions.
11. Suction if necessary.	
12. Disconnect ambu bag from tracheostomy tube.	
13. Check cuff inflation orders, and set cuff accordingly.	Physician order will include cuff instructions for inflation and deflation.
14. Reconnect mechanical ventilator tubing or supplemental oxygen to tracheostomy tube as prescribed.	
15. Turn off oxygen, and return equipment to appropriate storage place.	

DOCUMENTATION

1. Document the procedure and frequency of care provided in the appropriate medical record.

2. Document any unusual findings.

Suctioning (Oral, Nasal, or Pharyngeal) in Patients without an Artificial Airway

PURPOSES

To maintain a patent airway and to provide for removal of secretions by application of negative pressure in patients without an artificial airway.

STAFF RESPONSIBLE

EQUIPMENT

1. Suction catheter kit.
2. Sterile normal saline.
3. Plastic bag.
4. Water-soluble lubricant.
5. Suction machine and tubing.
6. Ambu bag.
7. Oxygen source and tubing.
8. Oxygen flow meter.
9. Nasal airway (if appropriate).

GENERAL CONSIDERATIONS

1. Do not unnecessarily suction a patient. Attempt a cough first and, if ineffective, then suction. Suctioning is a common procedure but not without its risks. The major complications include:
   - hypoxemia,
   - cardiac dysrhythmias,
   - hypotension,
   - lung collapse, and
   - tracheal edema.
   These can be avoided by selecting the appropriate-size catheters, preoxygenating the patient, and limiting the duration of suctioning. If complications occur, terminate the procedure, administer oxygen, and notify the physician (Shapiro, Harrison, & Trout, 1979).
2. Frequent suctioning by the nasal, oral, or pharyngeal routes can be uncomfortable and irritating. Complications related to suctioning of the upper airway include tissue trauma, bleeding, and gagging. To minimize trauma to the nasal mucosa, consider the use of a nasal airway. A nasal airway may be obtained and inserted by the respiratory therapist.
3. Catheter size is based on the size of the lumen of the catheter. The common catheter size for an adult is 10 French, for a child is 6 to 8 French, and for an infant is 6 to 8 French.
4. A new catheter kit is used for each suctioning session. The same catheter may be used for an upper airway only after lower airway aspiration is completed.
5. If the patient is on oxygen therapy, preoxygenate him or her by placing on oxygen delivery device for 30 seconds before and after suctioning attempts.
6. The vacuum generator on the suction machine should be set between 80 and 120 mmHg negative pressure for adults and between 80 and 90 mmHg negative pressure for children and infants.
7. Suction bottles should be rinsed at least once per shift and emptied as needed.
8. Suctioning procedures are performed in accordance with infection control policies.

PATIENT AND FAMILY EDUCATION

1. Teach procedures and precaution to the patient and family documenting competence.

PROCEDURE

Steps	Additional Information
1. Assemble all equipment. Explain procedure to patient.	
2. Turn machine on, and test vacuum source by occluding tubing and observing manometer.	

Steps	*Additional Information*
3. Wash hands.	
4. Take baseline pulse.	Assess rate and rhythm of pulse.
5. Open bottle of sterile solution.	
6. Open suction catheter kit in aseptic manner, and position it on flat surface close to patient.	
7. Don sterile gloves.	One or two gloves may be provided, depending on manufacturer.
8. Open basin and, with nonsterile hand, pour solution into basin.	
9. With sterile hand pick up catheter, expose connector end, and attach to connecting tubing on suction machine.	Only sterile hand should be in contact with catheter.
10. Preoxygenate patient. Ask patient to take three to five deep breaths.	If patient is on oxygen, make certain that he or she breathes oxygen-rich environment.
11. Nasal route:	
• Lubricate catheter with water-soluble lubricant.	
• Check nasal passage for patency.	
• Insert catheter gently into airway following anatomical floor of airway.	
• If unable to pass catheter, pull it back, and try again in other nasal passage.	
• Insert to just above epiglottis, and apply intermittent suction as you slowly withdraw catheter.	Before inserting catheter, estimate length of tubing from nose to epiglottis. Do not apply suction for more than 10 seconds. This minimizes trauma and helps reduce contamination from upper airway.
• Release suction; do not remove catheter from nose.	
• Reapply oxygen apparatus.	
• Repeat procedure until secretions are cleared.	Listen to breath sounds to determine when secretions are cleared. Preoxygenate patient before and after each attempt.
12. Oral route:	
• Insert catheter along side of patient's tongue along oral floor.	
• Insert catheter to level of the epiglottis, and apply intermittent suction as you withdraw catheter.	Do not suction for more than 10 seconds.
• Replace oxygen device.	Preoxygenate patient before and after each attempt.
• Repeat procedure until secretions are cleared.	
13. Shut off machine.	
14. Pull glove back over catheter, and discard all materials in plastic bag.	
15. Empty suction bottle if needed.	
16. Check patient's pulse, and listen to breath sounds.	Notify physician of significant rate or rhythm changes, especially bradycardia or irregular rhythms.

DOCUMENTATION

1. Document the time, route, and frequency.
2. Document in a progress note with the initial procedure and any unusual situations on periodic basis:
   • pulse rate changes with the procedure;
   • color, amount, and consistency of secretions;
   • patient response to the procedure; and
   • effectiveness of the procedure.
3. Report any unusual circumstances to the physician and respiratory therapist.
4. Document patient and family teaching and response.

Suctioning through a Tracheostomy Tube

PURPOSE

To provide for removal of secretions by application of negative pressure to the patient's airway.

STAFF RESPONSIBLE

EQUIPMENT

The equipment needed depends on the setting.

1. Suction catheter kit.
2. Sterile normal saline.
3. Plastic bag.
4. Suction machine (portable or battery operated) and tubing.
5. Ambu bag.
6. Oxygen source and tubing.
7. Oxygen flow meter.

GENERAL CONSIDERATIONS

1. Suctioning is a routine procedure. The major complications associated with suctioning include:
   - hypoxemia,
   - cardiac dysrhythmia,
   - hypotension, and
   - lung collapse.

   These can be avoided by carefully selecting the appropriate-size suction catheter, preoxygenating the patient, and limiting the duration of suctioning. If these complications occur, terminate the procedure, administer oxygen, and notify the physician.
2. Catheter size is based on the size of the internal lumen of the inner cannula. The suction catheter should occupy no more than half the lumen of the inner cannula (Table 5-3).
3. A new catheter kit is used for each suctioning session.
4. Surface suctioning of a tracheostomy tube is done with a sterile catheter.
5. Patients on oxygen therapy or mechanical ventilation must be oxygenated by means of a manual resuscitator (ambu bag) at a flow rate of 10 L/min before and after suctioning.
6. The vacuum generator on the suction machine should be set between 80 and 120 mmHg negative pressure for adults and between 80 and 90 mmHg negative pressure for children and infants.

7. Suction bottles are emptied and rinsed at least once per shift in accordance with infection control guidelines. Never allow fluid to reach the full level.
8. Special considerations with different tracheostomy tubes are as follows:
   - *Tracheostomy buttons* (Kistner, Olympic)—suction only in case of respiratory distress and per written physician's order because damage may occur to the tracheal wall. In case of emergency, you may suction and then notify the physician.
   - *Montgomery tube*—push up on the tube to guide the catheter into the lower airway. To suction the upper airway, push down on the tube and direct the catheter upward.
   - *Fenestrated tracheostomy tube*—insert the inner cannula, and inflate the cuff. After suctioning, deflate the cuff, remove the inner cannula, and cork the tube as ordered. Rinse the inner cannula with sterile water or saline, and dry it with sterile 4 × 4 gauze. Store the cannula in a clean, dry, capped container. Send the cannula with the patient if frequent suctioning is required.
9. Suctioning procedures must be performed in accordance with infection control policies:
   - sterile technique must be used at all times except in emergency situations, and
   - sterile solutions must be properly labeled and are discarded 24 hours after opening.

PATIENT AND FAMILY EDUCATION

The nurse is responsible for teaching caregivers suctioning procedures and documenting response and competence.

Table 5-3 Catheter Sizes for Suctioning through a Tracheostomy Tube

Tracheostomy Tube Size	Catheter Size Recommended
0	4
1	5
2	6
4	8
6	10
8	10 or 12
10	14

PROCEDURE

Steps	*Additional Information*
1. Gather equipment. Wash hands.	
2. Explain procedure to patient.	
3. Take baseline pulse.	
4. Turn on suction machine, and check vacuum source by occluding tubing.	
5. Verify that cuff is inflated.	Exception: cuffless tracheostomy tubes.
6. Open sterile saline.	
7. Open catheter kit in aseptic manner, and position it on flat surface close to patient.	
8. Don sterile glove.	One or two gloves may be provided, depending on manufacturer. Two gloves are recommended. One hand is kept sterile throughout procedure.
9. Pop open basin and, with nonsterile hand, pour saline into basin.	
10. With sterile gloved hand, pick up catheter, exposing only connector end.	
11. With nonsterile hand, pick up connecting tube attached to suction machine, and attach it to connector end of catheter.	
12. Preoxygenate patient:	For patients on oxygen therapy or mechanical ventilation, method 1 must be used and ambu bag connected to oxygen at 10 L/min.
• Method 1: hand ventilate patient three to five times with ambu bag, giving inflation hold on last breath.	
• Method 2: instruct patient to take three to five quick deep breaths and to hold last breath for a few additional seconds.	
13. Disconnect ambu bag. Lubricate catheter in saline.	
14. Insert catheter with sterile hand into airway without applying suction until patient reacts or resistance is felt.	Catheter should ideally reach level of carina.
15. Withdraw catheter ½ to 1 inch before applying suction.	This is done to avoid carinal irritation. Do not apply suction for more than 10 seconds at a time.
16. Intermittently apply suction with nonsterile hand as you withdraw catheter with your sterile hand. Twirl catheter with fingers of sterile gloved hand as you withdraw it.	
17. Oxygenate patient, and rinse catheter by aspirating small amount of saline through catheter.	
18. Repeat procedure as needed. Always oxygenate before and after each pass of catheter.	Do not suction more than three times consecutively without allowing a few minutes for patient to rest.
19. Shut off machine.	
20. Pull glove back over catheter, and discard all materials in plastic bag.	
21. Empty suction bottle.	
22. Check patient's pulse.	
23. Obtain new catheter kit, and replenish saline if necessary. Place equipment with suction machine. Return manual resuscitation bag to proper storage at bedside.	

DOCUMENTATION

1. Document the time and frequency of suctioning required.
2. Document in a progress note with the initial suction procedure and when unusual situations occur during the procedure or periodically thereafter:
   • baseline pulse and any rate change;
   • color, amount, and consistency of secretions; and
   • patient's response to the procedure.
3. Report any unusual circumstances to the physician or respiratory therapist.

Tracheostomy Cleaning and Stoma Care

PURPOSES

To clean the inner cannula and stoma of accumulated secretions; to maintain a patent airway; to prevent infection; to describe hygienic care of the stoma and tracheostomy tube.

STAFF RESPONSIBLE

EQUIPMENT

1. Tracheostomy cleaning kit.
2. Hydrogen peroxide (3%).
3. Sterile normal saline.
4. Plastic bag.
5. Precut individual gauze dressings (as needed).
6. Two sterile gloves.
7. Two nonsterile gloves.
8. Shiley spare inner cannula.
9. Ambu bag.
10. Disposable inner cannula for Shiley tracheostomy tube (as needed).

GENERAL CONSIDERATIONS

1. Tubes with no inner cannula (Portex, Kamen-Wilkinson, Montgomery, and Kistner) require good humidification and routine suctioning to maintain patency. No attempt is made to clean the internal lumen of these tubes. Tracheostomy care in this instance is limited to cleaning the stoma site and changing the dressing.
2. Tracheostomy care is recommended every shift and as needed. If infection of the airway or stoma is present or if secretions are profuse, the nurse should increase the frequency of tracheostomy care until the problem is resolved.
3. With Kistner buttons, Olympic buttons, or Shiley fenestrated tracheostomy tubes that are corked 24 hours per day, routine tracheostomy care can be reduced to one or two times per day. Store the inner cannula when not in use in a dry, clean, capped container.
4. If the patient requires suctioning, do this before initiating tracheostomy care.
5. With long-term use of a tracheostomy tube, a dressing may not be required if secretions are minimal and if the stoma is clean. Factors to consider before discontinuing a dressing include:
   - amount and type of secretions,
   - condition of the stoma and surrounding skin (if irritation is present, do not discontinue the dressing), and
   - environment (does it predispose the individual to infection? Will the patient be going outdoors?).
6. When the inner cannula is removed, a spare Shiley inner cannula can be inserted to maintain the airway in patients requiring positive-pressure ventilation. This cannula can be obtained from the respiratory therapy department. Whether the temporary cannula is used or not, the inner cannula should not be removed for a period longer than 10 minutes. Secretions can collect in the outer cannula and lead to obstruction of the airway.
7. Inner cannula care requires aseptic techniques.
8. The most common complication associated with tracheostomy care is accidental decannulation while changing tracheostomy ties.

PATIENT AND FAMILY EDUCATION

1. Explain procedures and complications to the patient and family.
2. Teach the procedures as appropriate.

PROCEDURE

Steps	Additional Information
1. Gather all equipment, and prepare work surface.	
2. Wash hands.	
3. Explain procedure to patient.	
4. Position patient comfortably and so that you have access to tracheostomy tube and stoma.	Generally, supine or semi-Fowler's position is recommended. If patient has sternal occipital mandibular immobilizer brace,

Steps	*Additional Information*
	position patient supine. It may be necessary to remove chin piece to gain access to tube. Maintain spinal precautions and procedures while chin piece is off.
5. Open tracheostomy cleaning kit.	
6. Remove sterile drape by grasping outer edge, and open onto flat surface with plastic side down.	This forms sterile field.
7. Without touching inside contents, turn tray over so that contents empty onto sterile field.	
8. Place sectioned tray on work surface but not on sterile field, and pour sterile saline solution for stoma care.	You may choose to pour solution at later time.
9. Position second basin within reach but not on sterile field.	Only inside of basin is sterile.
10. Pour hydrogen peroxide in small basin and sterile normal saline in large basin.	Omit peroxide if metal tube is present.
11. Don a nonsterile glove and use gloved hand to remove soiled dressing from around tube. Discard dressing and glove.	
12. Don second nonsterile glove.	
13. Open second sterile drape on patient's chest.	This drape may be used as additional work area.
14. For patients on ventilator, disconnect oxygen source, and perform ambu with inflation hold procedure. For other patients, evaluate ability to take three deep breaths to pre-oxygenate self. If patient is unable to do so, use ambu with inflation hold procedure.	Refer to Ambu and Inflation Hold Procedure (above).
15. Stabilize neck plate with one hand, and turn inner cannula connector to unlock cannula.	
16. Remove inner cannula following natural curve of trachea, and place it in peroxide solution.	Do not touch inner cannula except at connector. Submerge cannula in solution. For patients using disposable Shiley tube, remove inner cannula and discard. Insert new sterile cannula and lock in place.
17. Insert spare Shiley inner cannula (optional).	Spare cannula must be inserted with patients on ventilator.
18. Reconnect oxygen source (ventilator).	
19. Remove contaminated gloves.	
20. Put on sterile gloves.	
21. When bubbling ceases in peroxide solution, pick up sterile brush, and clean inner surface of inner cannula.	If brush does not fit, sterile pipe cleaners can be used. For pediatric tubes use pipe cleaners.
22. Place inner cannula in saline solution to rinse off hydrogen peroxide. Do not dry cannula.	Peroxide solution is irritating to tissue and must always be rinsed off thoroughly before reinserting cannula. Moisture from saline rinse will provide lubricant to assist with insertion.
23. Disconnect oxygen source, and preoxygenate patient.	
24. Unlock spare inner cannula, and remove it (optional).	
25. With sterile gloved hand, remove inner cannula from saline, and reinsert it in outer cannula.	
26. Lock inner cannula in place by turning connector to "lock" position. Reconnect oxygen source. Remove sterile gloves, and put on nonsterile gloves (optional).	Discard used equipment in plastic bag according to infection control procedures.
27. Pick up cotton-tip applicator, and soak it in peroxide or saline solution.	A 4 × 4 gauze may be used instead of cotton-tip applicator.
28. Clean stoma, posterior tracheostomy plate, and anterior tracheostomy plate with applicator. Discard applicator.	
29. Pick up second cotton-tip applicator, and pour small amount of saline on applicator. Repeat step 28.	
30. With third applicator, dry stoma.	If there are profuse secretions, use 4 × 4 gauze to dry area. Do not touch portion of dressing that will be in contact with stoma.
31. Apply dressing under tracheostomy plate on stoma.	

Steps	*Additional Information*
32. Check twill tapes. They should be dry and should adequately secure tube. If they are soiled or frayed, they should be changed.	
33. When changing tracheostomy ties, exercise care. Hold outer cannula in place while changing ties. This can be best accomplished with two people present to complete procedure.	Method 1: Thread one end through face plate, then pull tie through, leaving 6 inches out. Pull long piece around back of patient's neck, and thread it through hole on opposite side. Bring tape to reach 6-inch piece, and tie knot to side. Use square knots to secure tube, leaving one to two finger widths under ties to prevent pressure necrosis. Method 2: Order Velcro ties.
34. Put all used equipment in plastic bag, and discard.	Discard according to infection control procedure.

DOCUMENTATION

1. Document the frequency of care and routine hygienic care.
2. Document in the progress notes in the medical record as needed:
   - progression of stoma healing;
   - observations of the stoma indicative of infection (redness, odor, or increased secretions) and the treatment plan;
   - observations of the stoma indicative of infection resolution; and
   - any unusual occurrences.
3. Document patient and family education in progress notes or appropriate chart form.

Care of the Patient with a Tracheostomy Tube

PURPOSES

To describe activities to maintain a patent airway; to prevent infection; to ensure emergency care and education of the patient and caregiver before patient discharge.

STAFF RESPONSIBLE

EQUIPMENT

1. Tracheostomy tube.
2. Emergency equipment.
3. Spare tube (same model and size).
4. Manual resuscitator bag.
5. Tracheostomy tube adaptor.
6. Anatomical mask and oral airway.

GENERAL CONSIDERATIONS

1. A tracheostomy tube is an artificial airway that is surgically placed and bypasses the upper airway and glottis. It is the most permanent and desirable of all artificial airways. For types of tracheostomy tubes refer to Table 5-4.
2. Indications for tracheostomy tube include (Shapiro, Harrison, & Trout 1979):
   - relief of upper airway obstruction,
   - protection of the airway,
   - facilitation of bronchial hygiene and suctioning, and
   - prolonged mechanical ventilation.
3. Agency policy provides direction on who can insert and remove outer cannulas. Adult tracheostomy tubes are generally changed every 6 weeks; children may have tubes changed as often as three times per week. Indications for change include the following:
   - stoma is infected;
   - different style or size is required;
   - tracheostomy is grossly dirty or damaged; or
   - cuff is damaged and no longer functional.
4. Outer cannulas may be changed in emergency situations if the stoma is more than 48 hours old. Use a spare tube. Put the obturator in the outer cannula. Inflate the cuff with 14 mL of air, and observe for any air leaks. Deflate the cuff fully, and lubricate the tube with water-soluble lubricant. Put the ties on. Gently insert the tube following the curvature of the trachea; slight pressure will be needed. Once the tube is in place, immediately remove the obturator, and insert the inner cannula. If you are unable to

Table 5-4 Types of Tracheostomy Tubes (Key: X, Available)

Name	Material	Cuffed	Noncuffed	Fenestrated	Nonfenes-trated	Inner Cannula	Obturator	Other Information
Jackson	Stainless steel	X	X	X	X	X	X	Adaptor for ventilating screws on inner cannula (some are supplied permanently attached); cuffs are not as secure as with Shiley; can be resterilized; will be cold to touch in cold temperatures. Do not clean with hydrogen peroxide.
Shiley	Plastic	X Low pressure	X Pediatric sizes are noncuffed	X	X	X	X	Adaptor for ventilating is attached to inner cannula; spare inner cannula available for short-term use; fenestrated tube has plastic cork; may be chemically disinfected for reuse; special model has disposable inner cannula; cuff must be deflated when cork is in place with fenestrated tube.
Portex	Siliconized plastic	X Low pressure	Pediatric sizes are noncuffed		X		X	May or may not have cannula, depending on model of tube; has one-way valve to prevent leak; some may be used as talking tube.
Kamen-Wilkinson	Silicone	(Self-inflating) Low pressure			X		X	When adaptor is open, cuff is up. Never push air into cuff (unless emergency seal is needed) because this turns into high-pressure cuff. When adaptor is closed, this should mean that cuff is down. If in doubt, this should be checked by kinking off tube, opening up adaptor, applying syringe, and then unkinking line, withdrawing kink tube, and closing adaptor.
Montgomery (T tube)	Plastic		X					Requires no external security (surgically inserted and changed. Held in place by T structure, which is hollow and allows use of upper airway). For arrest, plug stoma, and ventilate from above.
Kistner button	Plastic							Has flanged edge for securing, but may be loosely secured with silk thread tied around patient's neck. Suctioning is not recommended except in emergency. In arrest, plug stoma, and ventilate from above. Document number of rings exposed in progress note, and monitor every shift.
Olympic button	Plastic							Has flanged inner edge that is open when tube is corked or inner cannula is in place; has inner cannula with universal tracheostomy adaptor. Suctioning is not recommended except in emergency. In arrest, plug stoma, and ventilate from above.

Table 5-4 continued

Name	Material	Cuffed	Noncuffed	Fenestrated	Nonfenes-trated	Inner Cannula	Obturator	Other Information
Talking tracheostomy tubes:		X		X Cannot be corked				Special fenestrations allow air to pass into upper airway to produce voice. Air flow is provided by attaching side port to oxygen source. When port is occluded, vocalization can occur.
Portex		X					X	
Communi-trach		X				X	X	

reinsert the tube, cover the stoma well with a pressure dressing, and ventilate the patient through the upper airway. Notify the physician immediately to evaluate the patient. Do not let the stoma close (place a suction catheter in the stoma to keep it open).

5. The obturator and spare tube should be kept with the patient. Tape it on the wall at the bedside, or attach it to the wheelchair.

6. Inner cannulas are to remain in place at all times except during cleaning and prescribed corking schedules. For patients on a ventilator, a spare Shiley inner cannula can be inserted for a maximum of 10 minutes for cleaning procedures.

7. Inner cannulas are not interchangeable. The inner cannula is fitted to the exact length of a particular tube's outer cannula.

8. Physician's orders for patients with a tracheostomy tube should include:
   - suctioning (frequency and preoxygenation needed);
   - tracheostomy tube type and size;
   - treatment regimen (tracheostomy care and humidity);
   - duration of corking or cuffing;
   - emergency equipment to be at the bedside; and
   - precautions in therapy areas and the need for on-unit therapy.

9. For tubes used to prevent aspiration, it is recommended that the cuff be inflated during meals and for 1 hour after meals, when vomiting occurs, and at other high-risk times.

10. For resuscitation purposes, cuffed tubes must be inflated. For a fenestrated tube, insert the inner cannula, inflate the balloon, and ventilate the patient. For Kistner buttons, cuffless tubes, or Montgomery tubes, occlude the tube with the appropriate cork or cap or with your hand. Begin mouth-to-mouth breathing through the upper airway. When sufficient help is available, remove the tube, and insert a cuffed tube.

11. Whenever humidity, ventilator, ambu bag, aerosol, or oxygen therapy is prescribed, the order is transmitted to a person or department designated by the agency, who will set up and maintain the equipment. When the patient is breathing through a tracheostomy tube the air bypasses the normal humidification centers, which can lead to drying of the mucosal lining within the trachea. For this reason, breathing through an open tube for prolonged periods without humidification should be avoided. Alternative sources of humidity include an artificial nose and a high-humidity tracheostomy collar. Care must be taken to follow infection control procedures with this equipment.

12. Infection control procedures are to be followed when working with all respiratory equipment. On the unit, nurses are responsible for careful use and storage of equipment, which includes the following:
    - Manual resuscitation bags—should be stored at the bedside. Tracheostomy tube adaptor should not come in contact with grossly contaminated areas.
    - Humidification tubing—routinely, the fluid that collects in the tubing must be emptied because it can be a source of bacterial growth. The tubing should be disconnected from the humidity source and emptied into an appropriate receptacle (trash can, sink, or toilet). To drain the tubing, elevate the piece that connects with the patient, and allow the water to drain out in the opposite direction. Never drain the water back into the humidity source.
    - Spare cannulas and corks—should be stored in dry, clean, closed containers at the bedside. After use, they should be cleaned with normal saline. If secretions are present, hydrogen peroxide and saline may be needed. Then wipe them dry with a sterile 4 × 4 pad.

13. Patients with tracheostomy tubes are considered priority patients for transport and should be assessed carefully before transport. If there is a significant risk of airway obstruction, a nurse should accompany the patient and bring portable suction. Factors to consider include:
    - current respiratory status (stable or changing),
    - frequency of suctioning needed,
    - cough adequacy,

- duration of time off the unit,
- age of the patient,
- cognition,
- communication ability,
- nature of the disability, and
- patient's ability to manage his or her own tracheostomy care.

A physician's order is required for patients to be transported unescorted outside the facility.

14. Respiratory equipment for home care is ordered by nursing on the basis of a physician's prescription. Refer to your agency's procedure on durable medical equipment for process information. The respiratory therapy home care vendor is available for information about product options and patient and family teaching before weekend passes or discharge. If the family is to practice these skills on the unit, this can be arranged and should be encouraged.
15. The person responsible for extubation must be knowledgeable about airways and able to reinsert the airway if airway obstruction occurs. Common early complications associated with extubation include laryngospasm, glottic edema, and subglottic edema, and common late complications include sore throat, ulceration of the tracheal mucosa, tracheal stenosis, and vocal cord paralysis.

PATIENT AND FAMILY EDUCATION

Patient and family teaching before weekend passes or discharge should include:

- anatomy and physiology of the respiratory system,
- effects of injury on respiratory status,
- measures to maintain a patent airway,
- measures to improve vital capacity,
- tracheostomy care,
- equipment use and maintenance,
- recognition of complications, and
- emergency measures.

PROCEDURE

Steps	*Additional Information*
1. Bring suction machine and catheters to bedside.	
2. Note on admission form:	
• type and size of tube;	
• reason for tracheostomy;	
• frequency of suctioning and catheter size;	
• airway management (medications, fluids, and cough assist);	
• bronchial hygiene (ultrasonic nebulization, postural drainage techniques, chest percussion and vibration, incentive spirometry, ventilating, and humidification);	
• oxygen therapy;	
• corking program;	
• emergency equipment (present or not); and	
• breath sounds and complete respiratory assessments.	
3. Have physician write necessary orders.	See general considerations.
4. Notify appropriate person or department to supply emergency equipment and of other appropriate orders.	
5. Evaluate patient use of call system, and order alternative system if necessary.	
6. Determine method of patient communication, and document in care plan.	Verbal communication is limited with tracheostomy tube.

DOCUMENTATION

1. Document patient and family education.
2. Record the type and size of the equipment.
3. Document the care given and the outcome.

Minimal Leak Technique

PURPOSES

To prevent overinflation of the cuff; to prevent complications associated with pressure to the tracheal wall.

STAFF RESPONSIBLE

EQUIPMENT

1. 10-mL Syringe.
2. Stethoscope.
3. Tracheostomy tube.
4. Manual resuscitation bag.
5. Suction equipment.

GENERAL CONSIDERATIONS

1. The objective of minimal leak technique is to place the minimal volume of air in the cuff to allow optimal sealing of the airway. Minimal leak should be verified at least once per day with continuously inflated cuffs and with each inflation with periodic inflation. The technique may also be referred to as minimal occluding volumes (Shapiro, Harrison, & Trout, 1979).
2. This technique cannot be used on self-inflating cuffs, such as the Kamen-Wilkinson tube.
3. The technique is based on the principle that during positive-pressure ventilation the tracheal diameter is maximal on inspiration.
4. Minimal leak cannot be measured by air volumes because it can change slightly with postural changes and position changes of the tracheostomy tube.
5. Periodic cuff deflation is not necessary when the minimal leak technique is used.
6. Never inflate the cuff if the decannulation cannula (red plug) is in place.
7. The physician is to write orders for cuff inflation and deflation frequency and parameters.

PROCEDURE

Steps	Additional Information
1. Explain procedure to patient. Gather equipment. Wash hands.	
2. Suction oral pharynx.	This is to clear oral secretions that could enter lower airway when cuff is deflated.
3. Attach syringe to Luer-lok valve of cuff inflation port.	This is a one-way valve that allows air to enter but not to exit.
4. Connect ambu bag to tracheostomy tube, and give patient a deep breath.	Patient may take a deep breath rather than use ambu bag.
5. At start of expiration of this breath, deflate cuff by aspirating air with a syringe.	Expiratory flow can prevent particles above cuff from entering lower airway.
6. Position stethoscope on lateral aspect of trachea superior to thyroid cartilage.	
7. Inflate cuff until you can no longer auscultate air with stethoscope on inspiration.	If unable to hear with stethoscope, place hand over patient's nose and mouth and continue. Cuff is maximally inflated when you can no longer feel air leak. Using ambu bag to provide positive-pressure ventilation can facilitate auscultation of air leak.
8. Aspirate by 0.5-mL increments until air leak is again auscultated with stethoscope on inspiration.	If unable to hear with stethoscope, place hand over patient's nose and mouth and feel for air leak. When air leak is initially felt, you have minimal leak. For positive-pressure ventilation, listen for air leak on inspiration. Also, there should be no decrease in exhaled volume. If no minimal leak is detected or if cuff leak is present, physician should be notified.
9. Disconnect syringe, label it, and store it in clean area at bedside.	

DOCUMENTATION

1. Document the frequency of minimal leak checks.
2. Note the scheduled times for checks.
3. Note the implementation of the procedure.

Corking Fenestrated Tracheostomy Tubes

PURPOSES

To evaluate the patient's ability to breathe through the upper airway and to mobilize secretions; to protect the airway in preparation for decannulation.

STAFF RESPONSIBLE

EQUIPMENT

1. Syringe (5 to 10 mL).
2. Stethoscope.
3. Storage containers.
4. Inner cannula.
5. Decannulation cannula (red plug).

GENERAL CONSIDERATIONS

1. A fenestrated tube is a tracheostomy tube in which a window has been cut in the posterior wall of the outer cannula.
2. Customized fenestration tubes are available.
3. With long-term use, periodically check for granulation tissue, which can occlude fenestration and restrict air flow. This can be done by removing the inner cannula and shining a flashlight at the fenestration. If tissue is seen at the fenestration, notify the physician.
4. For resuscitation purposes, insert the inner cannula, and inflate the cuff.
5. To cork a cuffed tracheostomy tube, the tube must be fenestrated and the cuff deflated. *Never cork a cuffed, nonfenestrated tube*.

PATIENT AND FAMILY EDUCATION

1. Explain the procedure and its meaning. Involve the patient and family as appropriate.
2. Teach the management of the potential complications.

PROCEDURE

Steps	*Additional Information*
1. Obtain physician order.	Physician's order will indicate duration and frequency for corking procedure.
2. Explain procedure to patient.	
3. Gather equipment.	
4. Observe patient's current respiratory rate, effort, and subjective feelings.	These are used as baseline parameters.
5. Wash hands.	
6. Suction trachea, and then suction oral pharynx.	This prevents secretions that have collected on cuff from entering trachea.
7. Insert Luer-lok tip of syringe into Luer-lok valve on pilot balloon.	
8. Withdraw all air into syringe until resistance is met.	All air must be removed from balloon. Air flow through fenestration alone is not adequate. With balloon deflated, air will flow around tube as well.
9. Disconnect syringe, and aspirate air.	
10. Reconnect to pilot balloon, and attempt to withdraw additional air. If resistance is felt, disconnect syringe.	

Steps	*Additional Information*
11. Remove inner cannula.	
12. Insert decannulation cannula (red plug), and twist it to lock in place.	Hold only outer portion. Avoid touching inner lumen.
13. Observe patient closely for respiratory distress when decannulation cannula (red plug) is in place.	Distress can occur if upper airway is obstructed. If this is initial attempt, keep patient on nursing unit for observation for at least 2 hours. Notify therapist to return patient to nursing unit if respiratory distress occurs.
14. Remove decannulation cannula and insert inner cannula if respiratory distress occurs or when set time limit is achieved.	Determine duration and frequency of corking program with physician, and increase as patient's tolerance allows. Notify physician of respiratory distress episodes. Initially insert decannulation cannula during day and remove it at night, replacing it with inner cannula.
15. After each use, rinse cannula with hydrogen peroxide and normal saline. Store cannula in clean, dry, closed container at bedside.	If patient requires suctioning in therapy, send container in wheelchair bag with patient.

DOCUMENTATION

1. Document in a progress note for the initial corking:
   - initial respiratory status (rate, rhythm, effort, patient's response to corking, any changes in respiratory rate or effort, or signs of distress);
   - duration of the corking;
   - patient's ability to mobilize secretions while the tube is corked; and
   - patient's ability to speak.
2. Document the corking schedule and routine implementation.
3. Document any occurrences of respiratory distress and actions taken in a progress note in the medical record.
4. Document patient and family education.

Assistive Cough

PURPOSE

To loosen pulmonary secretions and to force them into the upper respiratory tract, where they can be expectorated or suctioned.

STAFF RESPONSIBLE

EQUIPMENT

1. Pillows.
2. Facial tissues.
3. Emesis basin.
4. Specimen cup (if culture is ordered).
5. Optional: suction equipment.

GENERAL CONSIDERATIONS

1. The cough is a reflex or voluntary action.
2. The mechanics of the cough involve:
   - deep inspiration;
   - closure of the glottis;
   - contraction of the muscles of the chest wall, abdomen, and pelvic floor, which increases intrathoracic and intra-abdominal pressure;
   - opening of the glottis; and
   - rapid expulsion of air in the exhalation phase.
3. Any disruption of the above steps in the cough mechanism may produce a need for assistive cough.
4. Several aspects of the patient's condition should be assessed:
   - energy source for the cough,
   - ciliary movement,
   - structural abnormalities in airways or lung parenchyma, and
   - neurological function.
5. An effective cough should be low pitched and deep.
6. The patient will generally be able to cough more effectively after respiratory treatments but may require assistive coughing at other times throughout the day (i.e., after a position change or after eating or drinking).
7. Assistive coughing is indicated as needed for all patients with T-6 or higher spinal cord injury or chronic lung disease and every 2 hours or more in patients with active respiratory problems or a tracheostomy. Patients with a lesion as low as T-11 may need assistive cough.
8. An abdominal binder is often issued to patients with spinal cord injury who have loss of abdominal musculature (e.g., high paraplegia and quadriplegia).
9. Exercise caution in patients with sensation.

PATIENT AND FAMILY EDUCATION

The technique and indications for assistive cough should be demonstrated and taught to patients and primary caregivers before the first weekend pass.

PROCEDURE

Steps	*Additional Information*
1. Explain procedure and rationale to patient.	
2. Position patient.	Sitting up straight or leaning forward pushes diaphragm upward and puts patient in position that facilitates exhalation. Consider each patient individually. For maximum comfort and to work with gravity, other positions may be used, including side lying, head down, and supine.
3. Hand placement: • One-handed abdominal thrust (Figure 5-2). • Lateral costal border—two-handed with hands on diaphragm and thumbs meeting at xiphoid process (Figure 5-3).	Patient may do this independently by placing wrists one on top of the other under xiphoid process. Hand placement is crucial to prevent injury to underlying organs.

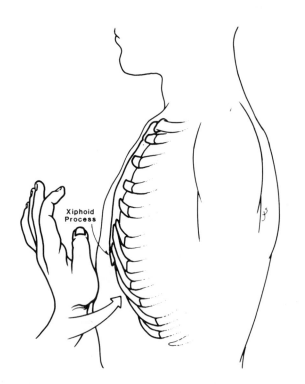

Figure 5-2 Assistive Cough: Hand Cupped over Xiphoid Process. Place hand (cupped) over xiphoid process. On exhalation, hand should move in and upward, assisting the diaphragm. *Source:* From *Spinal Cord Injury: A Guide to Rehabilitation Nursing* (p. 227) by P.J. Matthews, C.E. Carlson, and N.B. Holt, 1987, Rockville, MD: Aspen Publishers, Inc. Copyright 1987 by Aspen Publishers, Inc.

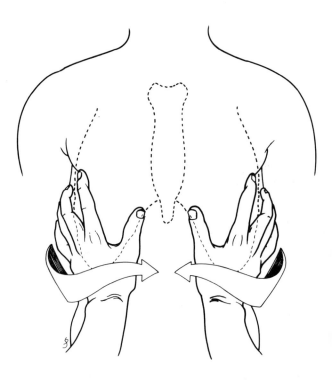

Figure 5-3 Hand Location and Movement for Assistive Cough. Hands are placed on side of rib cage. On exhalation, push inward and up following normal anatomical movement. *Source:* From *Spinal Cord Injury: A Guide to Rehabilitation Nursing* (p. 227) by P.J. Matthews, C.E. Carlson, and N.B. Holt, 1987, Rockville, MD: Aspen Publishers, Inc. Copyright 1987 by Aspen Publishers, Inc.

Steps	*Additional Information*
• If patient is side lying, place one hand along lower border of rib cage on side uppermost, or use the one-handed abdominal thrust (Figure 5-2).	
4. Instruct patient to take several deep breaths and to try to hold breath for several seconds before coughing.	Large volumes are necessary to generate high expiratory flow to dislodge obstructions.
5. Instruct patient to cough while you (or patient) push upward and inward against diaphragm.	Exception: lateral costal border cough assist, in which case hands push medially and inferiorly.
6. Steps 3 through 5 may be repeated until secretions are expelled or until patient is unable to produce secretions.	Cough may be ineffective, or patient may become exhausted or unable to exert energy necessary for cough.
7. Check patient's respiratory status (color, breathing rate, character of secretions, ability to breathe alone, and ability to phonate).	Based on assessment, plan should be instituted to discontinue assistive cough and let patient rest, to suction secretions, to request further respiratory therapy, to increase hydration, or to implement other measures to mobilize secretions.

DOCUMENTATION

1. Note the method and frequency of assistive cough and the patient's response.
2. In the progress notes, note the effectiveness of the assistive cough, the patient's tolerance of the procedure, the need for suctioning, and any unusual occurrences.
3. Document patient and family instruction or demonstration.

Postural Drainage with Chest Percussion and Vibration

PURPOSES

To prevent the accumulation of secretions and possible infection; to mobilize and drain secretions.

STAFF RESPONSIBLE

EQUIPMENT

1. Stethoscope.
2. Pillows or other positioning aids.
3. Tissues.
4. Emesis basin or sputum cup.
5. Suctioning equipment as needed.
6. Supplies for oral care.

GENERAL CONSIDERATIONS

1. Postural drainage is the use of specific positions to drain specific lung segments and bronchi by gravity. Percussion and vibration utilize tapping and vibrating the chest wall to assist in mobilizing secretions.
2. In the acutely ill or injured patient, modified positions may commonly be used because the general condition of the patient frequently will not allow for a great amount of patient manipulations. If this is the case, specific rotational positions for the particular patient should be discussed with the physician.
3. Postural drainage is indicated when there is an accumulation of secretions, which may occur with:
   - atelectasis;
   - obstructive lung disease (asthma, bronchitis, or bronchiectasis when present);
   - cystic fibrosis;
   - postoperative or bed-ridden patients with retained secretions; and
   - patients with high cervical injuries, multiple sclerosis, or cerebral palsy who are prone to aspiration.
4. Contraindications to the use of postural drainage techniques include:
   - unstable cardiovascular system,
   - fractured ribs or flail chest,
   - hemorrhagic conditions,
   - empyema,
   - increased intracranial pressure,
   - unstable spine,
   - recent skin grafts,
   - recent spinal fusion,
   - recent craniotomy,
   - untreated tension pneumothorax,
   - hemoptysis, and
   - diagnosed or suspected pulmonary embolus.
5. Respiratory therapy treatments if ordered (intermittent positive-pressure breathing aerosol or nebulizer) should precede postural drainage for maximal effectiveness.
6. The effectiveness of postural drainage is enhanced when combined with percussion and vibration. The following conditions represent situations in which consultation with the physician is advised:
   - metastatic cancer,
   - pulmonary embolus and anticoagulant therapy,
   - osteoporotic changes,
   - empyema, and
   - possible pneumothorax.
7. Areas of evaluation to be considered in decreasing the frequency of or stopping treatments include:
   - ability adequately to mobilize secretions with cough assist;
   - breath sounds;
   - activity level (if patient is up and about this may be adequate to mobilize secretions);
   - sputum production (absent, decreased in amount, or easily mobilized);
   - mental state (whether patient can follow instructions and maintain his or her own bronchial hygiene); and
   - absence of signs of respiratory infection or retained secretions (elevated temperature, elevated white blood count, and color of sputum).
8. Auscultate breath sounds before and after the procedure.
9. Do not perform the procedure for 1 to 2 hours after administering tube feeding unless an order is obtained from the physician for concurrent treatment with feedings.
10. A patient who is in pain should have treatment coordinated with pain medication.
11. In the acutely ill or injured patient, percussion and vibration must be ordered by the physician.
12. If unable to raise the front of the bed, place pillows under the patient's hip to achieve a head-down position.
13. Percussion should be done only over the rib cage. Areas on the clavicle, scapula, and vertebrae should be very gently percussed. Areas over the breasts and kidney should not be percussed.

14. Cough alone is of limited value beyond generation six or seven of the bronchial branching. Percussion and vibration move secretions from narrow passages to wider ones, where cough is effective.
15. The four basic positions with variations: right side lying, left side lying, supine, and prone with strategic placement of pillows will facilitate overall drainage of the lung and can be taught to patients who will need postural drainage at home. Six positions are taught and are as effective as more elaborate and isolated segmental postural drainage positions. (Positions used with children may vary.)

16. Generally, the technique is best done early in the morning because decreased mobility at night may increase secretion retention.
17. Work from more dependent to less dependent areas of the lung.

PATIENT AND FAMILY EDUCATION

Teach the patient and family procedures necessary as well as adaptations for home use.

PROCEDURE

Steps	*Additional Information*
1. Explain procedure to patient.	
2. Place patient in proper position for drainage (Figure 5-4).	Area of lung to be emphasized should be assessed through looking at patient's chart, making chest assessment (especially for breath sounds), examining roentgenograms, and consulting physician. If bed does not allow for Trendlenburg's position, pillows may be used to achieve head-down position. For children, procedures may be done best with lap positioning. Maintain position longer if it is productive.
3. Maintain position for at least 5 to 10 minutes. Do not leave patient in postural drainage.	
4. If ordered, perform percussion for 5 to 10 minutes to specific area being drained while patient is in position (Figure 5-5). Cup hands (finger and thumbs together), and rhythmically and alternately strike chest wall.	Cupping hands provides cushion of air between hands and chest to eliminate irritation or pain. Sound produced is muffled clap, not a slap. Use thin sheet or piece of clothing between your hand and patient.
5. If ordered, perform vibration for three to five breaths: • Ask patient to take a deep breath. • Perform vibration on exhalation only. • Keep elbows straight, and gently shake chest wall.	Pressure from vibration on inhalation will limit chest expansion. Vibration technique entails short, quick, fine jerking movements. Power comes from shoulder of person doing technique.
6. Cough and/or suction following treatment.	
7. Repeat steps 3, 4, 5, and 6 in all positions. Evaluate which positions are productive, and discontinue unproductive positions.	

DOCUMENTATION

1. Note in a progress note the effectiveness of the treatment and any unusual occurrences.

2. Document patient and caregiver instruction.

Position 1: Prone—Lying face downward with pillows under lower abdomen. Drains portion of lower lobe. (Percuss over lower lobe)*

Position 2: Supine—Lying on back with pillows under hips. Drains anterior portion of hips. (Percuss over lower ribs)*

Position 3: Right side lying—Lying on right side, pillow under lower lobe. (Percuss over lower ribs)*

Position 4: Left side lying—Lying on left side, pillow under lower abdomen. Drains right lower lobe. (Percuss over lower ribs)*

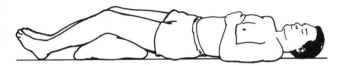

Position 5: Supine—Lying on back, slightly turned on one side. Pillow under knees. Drains anterior basal segment of lower lobe. (Percuss over lower ribs)*

Position 6: Side lying in Trendelenburg—Lying on right side, feet higher than head, pillow between hip bone and bottom ribs. Drains lingular segment. (Percuss over left nipple area)*

Figure 5-4 Postural Drainage Positions.

*Percuss if ordered by the physician.

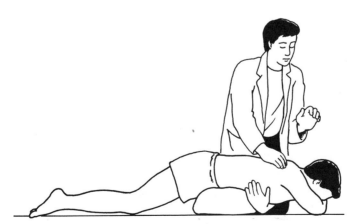

Figure 5-5 Percussion with Postural Drainage.

Self-Nebulizing Therapy

PURPOSES

To describe the method of self-administration of nebulizer therapy with a home nebulizer unit; to describe the role of the nurse in supervising patient performance.

STAFF RESPONSIBLE

EQUIPMENT

1. Bedside nebulizer unit as prescribed (Pulmo-Aide, Medi-Mist, Schuco-Mist; available from respiratory equipment vendor).
2. Prescribed medication.
3. Sterile saline (0.45% or 0.90% as prescribed).
4. Clean plastic bag.
5. Tissues.
6. Syringe.

GENERAL CONSIDERATIONS

1. The goals of aerosol (nebulizer) therapy are:
   - to aid bronchial hygiene by restoring mucous blanket continuity, by hydrating dry, retained secretions, and by promoting expectoration;
   - to humidify inspired gases; and
   - to deliver medications.
2. Equipment brought in from the home must be checked for electrical safety before use.
3. Nebulizers may run off the oxygen source or compressed air source provided by Pulmo-Aide, Medi-Mist, or Schuco-Mist bedside units.
4. Disposable nebulizers should be changed in accordance with infection control policies (usually every 24 hours).
5. A physician's order is necessary to initiate treatment and should include treatment, frequency, and prescribed medications.
6. Assess for the following symptoms:
   - shortness of breath,
   - dyspnea,
   - chest pain,
   - dizziness,
   - increased tightness in chest,
   - headache, and
   - shakiness or tremors.
   If these occur, stop the treatment, notify the physician, and resume treatment only with the physician's approval.
7. Treatments should be spaced with a minimum of 4 hours between sessions.

PATIENT AND FAMILY EDUCATION

Teach the patient and family the procedure, medication purpose and side effects, and care of the equipment prior to discharge, if appropriate.

PROCEDURE

Steps	*Additional Information*
1. Gather equipment. Verify physician's order.	
2. Explain purpose, method of treatment, and side effects of medication to patient.	This procedure will be performed by patient under supervision of nurse.
3. Wash hands.	Encourage patient to perform these steps.
4. Take baseline pulse.	Note rate and rhythm. *Do not start treatment if resting pulse is greater than 100 bpm without physician's approval.*
5. Place prescribed medication dose in nebulizer, and mix with saline (0.45% or 0.90%) as prescribed.	
6. Assist patient to comfortable position that allows for good chest expansion.	Patient's posture should be relaxed and as upright (Fowler's position) as possible.
7. Reinstruct patient in deep breathing techniques (diaphragmatic and lateral costal expansion with inspiratory pause on each breath).	
8. Turn machine on, and instruct patient to insert mouthpiece and to take slow, deep breaths.	

Steps	*Additional Information*
9. Check pulse 1 minute after procedure is initiated.	If significant change in rate or rhythm occurs, notify physician.
10. Monitor for side effects of medication. Instruct patient to report any adverse effects.	See general consideration 6.
11. Continue treatment until medication is completely dispersed.	This usually takes 10 to 15 minutes.
12. Wash nebulizer with water to remove excess medication.	
13. Dry nebulizer, and store it in clear plastic bag in well-lighted area.	
14. Take patient's pulse, and check breath sounds.	

DOCUMENTATION

1. Document in the appropriate record the medication administered, the route, and the time in the patient's record.
2. Document in the progress notes with the initial treatment and periodically throughout the patient's stay:
   - patient's response to treatment (baseline pulse and any pulse changes that occur; type, amount, and consistency of secretions; effort required to mobilize secretions; breath sounds before and after treatment; and any adverse effects of the treatment), and
   - patient's competence in performing the procedure and in taking care of the equipment.
3. Document in the progress notes any adverse effects that occur during the treatment and the actions taken to follow up.

Use of Metered-Dose Inhalers

PURPOSE

To facilitate the distribution and the effectiveness of medication administered through metered-dose inhalers.

STAFF RESPONSIBLE

EQUIPMENT

1. Inhaler.

GENERAL CONSIDERATIONS

1. The effectiveness of the inhaled medication depends on how the inhaler is used.
2. There are three types of metered-dose inhalers available:
   - Bronchodilators, including β-agonists, metaproterenol (Alupent), and albuterol (Ventolin and Proventil). Actions: produce both bronchodilation and cardiac stimulation; provide quick relief (in 5 to 15 minutes) and are used during an acute episode of breathlessness or routinely as prevention; enhance mucociliary transport. Most common side effects: tachycardia and shakiness.
   - Corticosteroids, such as beclomethasone. Actions: reduce lung inflammation; used as a preventive measure (do not provide fast relief). Most common side effects: hoarseness and dry mouth.
   - Mast cell inhibitors, such as cromolyn (Intal). Actions: prevent mast cells in the lungs from releasing histamine and slow reacting substance of anaphylaxis after exposure to specific antigens; prevent bronchospasm induced by inhalation of specific antigens or exercise; therapeutic benefit may not occur until 1 to 4 weeks after initiation of therapy; do not have direct bronchodilation, antihistamine, or anti-inflammatory effects. Most common side effects: bronchospasm, cough, nasal congestion, and wheezing.
3. The inhaler provides an exact dose of medication, so that each dose must be inhaled completely.

4. Discourage the use of any over-the-counter inhalants unless the patient checks with his or her physician. Most of these inhalants contain epinephrine, which is effective for only a short time and can cause excessive cardiac or central nervous system stimulation. In an attempt to maintain relief, the patient may use these inhalers too frequently, thereby overdosing and causing rebound bronchospasm.

PATIENT AND FAMILY EDUCATION

1. Initiate patient and family education early, and involve the patient and family in the procedure as soon as possible.
2. See procedural steps related to patient and family education.

PROCEDURES

Note: The first ten steps below are for the patient to follow.

Steps	*Additional Information*
1. Put inhaler together.	
2. Shake inhaler to mix medication and propellent.	Otherwise dosage may be inadequate.
3. Remove cap from mouthpiece.	
4. Hold canister with your index and third fingers on top and thumb on bottom.	
5. Exhale gently through your mouth.	If patient is unable to perform self-administration, cue patient to exhale gently through his or her mouth before administering medication.
6. Place mouthpiece in your mouth, keeping your tongue below the opening of the inhaler. Keep mouth open.	
7. Inhale slowly and deeply while depressing top of canister with your fingers.	
8. Close mouth.	
9. Hold breath as long as you can comfortably (10 seconds is good).	This allows medication to be absorbed into bloodstream.
10. If two puffs are prescribed, wait 1 minute before taking second one. If practical, it is optimal to take second puff 10 to 15 minutes after first.	This allows first puff to dilate airways, which will allow second puff to penetrate more deeply into bronchial tree.

Other Pertinent Information for Patient Education

11. If patient is to take bronchodilator and corticosteroid, administer bronchodilator first.	This dilates the airways so that corticosteroid can be inhaled more deeply into lungs.
12. If using beclomethasone, patient should gargle with water or mouthwash after use.	This helps prevent fungal infections in mouth and throat from medication's normal flora.
13. Most canisters contain 200 or 300 puffs of medication.	
14. Clean inhaler daily. Remove metal canister by pulling it up firmly. Rinse plastic container under warm water, and dry it thoroughly.	

DOCUMENTATION

1. On the medication record, transcribe the specific order for the metered-dose inhaler, the number of puffs to be administered, and the frequency of administration. Document accordingly.

2. In the progress notes, document the initial administration, the effectiveness of the procedure, and any adverse reactions.
3. Document patient and family education and their response.

Incentive Spirometry (Sustained Maximal Inspiratory Therapy)

PURPOSES

To optimize lung inflation; to optimize cough mechanism; to detect early acute pulmonary disease.

STAFF RESPONSIBLE

EQUIPMENT

1. Tissues.
2. Soap and water.
3. Incentive spirometer.

GENERAL CONSIDERATIONS

1. The incentive spirometer promotes sustained maximal inspiration, which is a technique used for prophylactic bronchial hygiene. Several models are available, but all work on the same principle.
2. Studies indicate that inflated alveoli remain open for at least 1 hour after the onset of hypoventilation (Shapiro, Harrison, & Trout, 1979).

3. Advantages of incentive spirometry therapy include the following:
   - incentive spirometry is an effective prophylactic technique,
   - the patient is able to do the therapy frequently without supervision once competence has been documented,
   - acute pulmonary disease is reflected in changes in performance,
   - minimal staff time is required, and
   - a physician order is required.
4. Criteria for incentive spirometry include the following:
   - the patient must be cooperative and able to take voluntary deep breaths;
   - the patient's inspiratory capacity must be greater than 12 mL/kg;
   - the patient's respiratory rate must be less than 25 per minute; and
   - the patient must be free of acute atelectasis, pneumonia, or obvious retained secretions.
5. For patients with a tracheostomy tube, a tracheostomy adaptor may be obtained from the respiratory therapist to allow them to use the spirometer attached to the tracheostomy tube.

PATIENT AND FAMILY EDUCATION

Teach the use of the spirometer and the care of the equipment to the patient and family.

PROCEDURE

Steps	Additional Information
1. Gather equipment. Explain procedure to patient.	
2. Position patient.	Semi-Fowler's position is advantageous for lung expansion. Avoid restrictive clothing or bed linens.
3. Rinse mouthpiece with warm water.	
4. Connect mouthpiece to end of tubing.	
5. Slide flow rate indicator to prescribed level.	Inspiratory goal should be twice patient's tidal volume.
6. Instruct patient to take four slow, easy breaths.	
7. After fourth inhalation, have patient let out all air until he or she can exhale no further.	
8. Position unit in upright position, and put mouthpiece into patient's mouth.	Tilting device toward patient at 30° or 45° angle can reduce amount of work required.

Steps	*Additional Information*
9. Instruct patient to make tight seal on mouthpiece.	
10. Instruct patient to take a *slow*, deep breath through spirometer.	Patient should not blow into unit. It works on inspiration, not expiration.
11. Patient should try to inhale and hold breath for 3 to 5 seconds or as tolerated.	Note how high patient raises cup or ball and length of time it is held in place.
12. Have patient exhale completely.	
13. Take a moment for patient to relax, and then resume exercise.	With rapid use, sustained maximal inspiratory effort cannot be attained and may lead to hyperventilation.
14. Repeat steps 8 to 13 as prescribed.	Generally, four to five breaths every 1 to 2 hours are done unless otherwise indicated. For patients with T-6 or higher level of injury, routine use should be at least twice a day.
15. Encourage cough and deep breathing.	
16. Clean mouthpiece with soap and warm water, and store unit in its bag.	

DOCUMENTATION

1. Document the initial use of the spirometer and changes in the patient's status in a progress note in the medical record. Information should include the following:
   - respiratory status,
   - current performance (volume and frequency),
   - position of the patient and unit, and
   - signs and symptoms of fatigue or respiratory distress.
2. Document routine use.
3. Document the patient and family teaching.

P-Flex Inspiratory Muscle Trainer

PURPOSES

To improve diaphragmatic strength and endurance through resistive training exercises with the P-Flex trainer; to protect against muscle fatigue.

STAFF RESPONSIBLE

EQUIPMENT

1. P-Flex trainer (Figure 5-6).
2. Nose clips.
3. Oxygen.
4. Oxygen adaptor.

GENERAL CONSIDERATIONS

1. Studies regarding the use of the P-Flex trainer are currently in progress. This device is most frequently used with patients with chronic obstructive pulmonary disease as part of the pulmonary rehabilitation program.
2. The P-Flex trainer is based on the principle that as the patient inhales the resistance provided by the training device makes the respiratory muscles work harder.
3. A physician's order is required to initiate treatment.
4. Documentation of the patient's current respiratory status is to include:
   - respiratory rate and effort,
   - vital capacity, and
   - pulse.
5. If the device is improperly used or if training time is not adhered to, diaphragmatic fatigue can occur. Characteristic signs of fatigue include:
   - abdominal paradoxing,
   - tachypnea,
   - intercostal retraction or use of accessory muscles, and
   - subjective complaints of increased work of breathing.
6. An oxygen adaptor port can be added between the mouthpiece and the body of the device. The oxygen adaptor

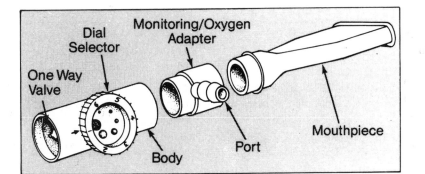

Dial Setting	1																				
Training Period	Week 1							Week 2							Week 3						
Day	1	2	3	4	5	6	7	1	2	3	4	5	6	7	1	2	3	4	5	6	7
Training Record ✓when completed each day																					
Performance Record: (walking distance, exercise tolerance, etc.)	Baseline:																				

Figure 5-6 P-Flex Inspiratory Muscle Trainer and Flow Sheet To Monitor Progress. Each patient should have a copy to track his or her progress. *Source:* Courtesy of Healthscan Products, Cedar Grove, NJ.

should be used with the flow rate of oxygen prescribed by the physician.

7. It is generally recommended that the device be used at the same time each day and no sooner than 2 hours after meals.
8. Any change in the patient's respiratory status, including increased secretions, infection, and changes in the airway, will mandate a change in the training regimen.

PATIENT AND FAMILY EDUCATION

1. Teach the patient and family how to use P-Flex trainer and document progress.
2. Instruct the patient and family on the training parameters and the actions to be taken.

PROCEDURE

Steps	Additional Information
1. Obtain physician order for P-Flex inspiratory muscle trainer.	Order should include length of training session, frequency, and initial setting. It is best to start at lowest setting.
2. Gather equipment.	
3. Rinse mouthpiece with water, and dry it before use.	
4. Explain procedure to patient.	
5. Have patient sit in position that promotes good lung expansion. Generally, Semi-Fowler's position is recommended.	
6. Assess patient's respiratory status and pulse rate before starting training session.	If physician has advised oxygen use, connect oxygen tubing to adaptor.
7. Apply nose clips provided with trainer.	This ensures maximum benefit because patient then breathes solely through device.
8. Insert mouthpiece into patient's mouth, and encourage him or her to make a tight seal on device.	

Steps	Additional Information
9. Set dial selector at 1 or prescribed setting.	
10. Instruct patient to inhale and exhale through trainer in relaxed manner.	
11. Maintain mouthpiece in place, and continue until signs of respiratory fatigue are noted, 15-minute training session is completed, or patient discomfort occurs. Then discontinue training session.	Initially, training should be limited to 15 minutes a day. Slowly increase time as tolerated by patient over course of a week, until patient can tolerate two 15-minute sessions per day.
12. Increase degree of resistance on dial selector as directed by physician.	When patient tolerates two 15-minute training sessions per day for at least 3 days, notify physician because resistance may now be increased. When resistance is increased, training time should be reduced to 15 minutes once a day, then gradually increased until patient tolerates two training sessions per day.
13. Measure patient's pulse after training.	
14. Clean device by washing it with soap. Then shake it dry, and store it in bag.	Because breath is inhaled through trainer, clean device in hot soapy water and rinse once a week. Then soak in half-strength white vinegar and water solution for ½ hour. Rinse device, and dry it.

DOCUMENTATION

1. Document the initial performance, including the patient's respiratory status before training, pulse before training, degree of resistance, length of the training session, respiratory status and pulse after training, and response to the training session, in a progress note in the medical record.
2. Indicate the training parameters (degree of resistance, length of training, and the patient's functional level).

3. Document the training session.
4. Encourage the patient to track his or her own progress on the P-Flex flow sheet provided with the training device (see Figure 5-6).

BIBLIOGRAPHY

Demus, R.R. (1982, April). Complications of endotracheal suctioning procedures. *Respiratory Care, 27,* 453–457.

Fuchs, P.L. (1984). Streamlining your suctioning techniques: Part I: Nasotracheal suctioning. *Nursing 84, 14.*

Fuchs, P.L. (1984). Streamlining your suctioning techniques: Part III: Tracheostomy suctioning. *Nursing 84, 14.*

Shapiro, B., Harrison, R., & Trout, C.A. (1979). *Clinical application of respiratory care* (2nd ed.). Chicago: Year Book Medical Publishers.

Stevens, K. (1987). Autonomic regulation and respiratory function: Section 2: Respiratory function: Alterations in airway clearance. In P. Matthews and C.E. Carlson (Eds.), *Spinal cord injury: A guide to rehabilitation nursing.* Rockville, MD: Aspen.

Procedures To Provide Safety

INTRODUCTION

Safety considerations are a common concern in nursing care of patients with neuromusculoskeletal conditions due to cognitive, sensory, and mobility changes. This chapter addresses several patient problems (seizures, confusion, agitation, and the like) that have implications for safety of the individual. Although the behavior of each individual should be assessed and specific plans developed to manage the behavior to provide safety for the patient and others, these guidelines can facilitate and direct this process.

Many nursing interventions involve designing or altering the environment to enhance patient goal achievement. For example, the guidelines for care of the agitated patient and the procedure for the Craig bed are included in this chapter because they are used to create a safe environment for the individual. Although the philosophy of the authors is to minimize the use of restraints, there are times when they are required for patient safety. Types of products available and guidelines for their use are also described.

Guidelines for Care

PURPOSES

To describe preventive safety measures that minimize the risk of injury to the patient and the staff; to identify resources available to deal with situations when a patient becomes combative; to describe nursing responsibilities in the care and treatment of the agitated patient.

STAFF RESPONSIBLE

GENERAL CONSIDERATIONS

1. Agitated or combative behavior may be the result of neurologic dysfunction (i.e., toxic encephalopathy, drug or alcohol abuse, or electrolyte imbalance) or psychiatric disturbances (paranoia).
2. Agitated or combative behaviors can occur as the patient recovers from head injury. The individual is unable to process or make sense of the stimuli around him or her, and the environment can be frightening as a consequence. Concurrently, there is an impaired ability to monitor and control emotions. The primary goals are to protect the patient from injury and to help him or her make sense of the environment.
3. Signs and symptoms to be aware of include:
   - angry facial expression;
   - rigid, defensive posture;
   - increased motor activity of extremities (often purposeless) or pacing;
   - hostile or threatening verbalizations;
   - rage;
   - suspicion of others;
   - exaggerated emotional response to stimuli;
   - persistent restlessness; and
   - primary cognitive deficits (inattention, distractibility, lack of concentration, disorientation, and poor short-term memory).

   The nurse must be aware that these deficits will limit the patient's ability to cooperate with and to understand demands placed on him or her. The environment must be externally controlled by sensitive staff.
4. Interventions to manage behavior should be discussed and communicated among all team and family members so that a consistent message of acceptable and unacceptable behaviors is communicated to the patient.
5. The use of physical restraints (jacket restraint or extremity restraints) should be minimized. Restraints usually present an additional noxious stimulus. Beds that provide a safe environment may result in reduced agitation and allow more freedom of movement than conventional restraints. Chemical restraints (medications) are used according to a physician's prescription and with the awareness that side effects may further interfere with the patient's cognitive ability and recovery.
6. A consistent caregiver is often beneficial for the patient. A consistent caregiver can provide the cues, structure, and monitored physical activity that address the cognitive deficits and emotional reactions of the patient. A physician's order is necessary for a private duty sitter. Documentation at the time of initiation should include a description of behaviors warranting one-on-one private duty staffing, the goals to be accomplished with its use, and the method of ongoing evaluation. Document behavior routinely in the medical record.

FAMILY EDUCATION

Educate the family on the nature and etiology of the behaviors and approaches to be used.

PROCEDURE

Steps	*Additional Information*

1. Assess patient on admission for high-risk behaviors and signs of same:
   • behavior history,
   • current level of activity,	

Steps	*Additional Information*

- bruises or abrasions on body,

- use of physical restraints and rationale for use,
- use of medications for behavior control and rationale for use, and
- behavioral response to change in environment.

2. Assess patient for physical problems that create noxious stimuli.

3. Identify situations or interactions that elicit high-risk behaviors and calming techniques that reduce symptoms.

4. Consider the following questions when designing an environment that will minimize risk for injury:
   - Is special bed needed?
   - Is activity in room too distracting?
   - Does patient require private room?
5. Assess current level of activity and potential for injury or elopement:
   - Is wheelchair needed?
   - Is patient ambulatory?
   - Is patient an elopement risk?
6. If patient is an elopement risk:

   - situate patient's room away from stairwells and exits;
   - place sign on wheelchair alerting staff of elopement risk and where to call or return patient;
   - make sure patient is wearing correct name band;
   - obtain photographs of patient, and distribute them to security at entrances (keep one picture in medical record);
   - consider use of one-on-one staff assignment;
   - if possible, schedule all therapies in room or on unit, and provide escort when patient is off unit; and
   - instruct patient and family about activity restrictions and need for supervision.
7. Reduce stimuli, and gradually reintroduce them at rate tolerated by patient.

8. Remove noxious stimuli (e.g., tubes, catheters, restraints) as much as possible.
9. Establish familiar routine and supportive environment:
   - place a few familiar personal objects in room;
   - establish consistent daily schedule;
   - present one activity at a time;

Additional Information column:

Physical injuries may occur from repetitive hyperactivity and impulsivity and may not be perceived by patient.

Patient may be agitated by stimuli such as nasogastric tube, indwelling catheter, injury, infection, constipation, and the like.

Patient may be unable to cope with demands for performance and approaches that are perceived as threatening or demeaning. Language and performance deficits also create frustration.

Elopement desire is a result of patient's lack of insight regarding deficits. Distraction with new activity, phone call to home, or reminder about visitor's schedule may diminish or exacerbate this behavior.

Reduced stimulation and structure are not equivalent to isolation and rigidity of approach. Patient requires various stimuli and outlets for activity presented at short intervals. Recovery, improved tolerance to stimuli, and clearing of cognitive problems require moderate challenges for success.

Steps	*Additional Information*
• give directions in a firm, soft voice using simple commands;	
• evaluate need for one-on-one staffing assignment; and	
• provide frequent positive comment on simple achievements in performance and control.	
10. For agitated behaviors:	
• move patient to quiet area away from other patients, and allow "cool down" time under close supervision;	
• avoid arguing with patient;	
• provide safe environment (Craig bed or other safety bed);	Do not try to transfer patient from wheelchair while he or she is agitated. Allow "cool down" time in wheelchair. If Craig bed is used, wheelchair may be moved inside bed if mattress is up and doors are closed around patient.
• use reassurance, calming techniques, and distraction to reduce symptoms;	
• remove potentially harmful objects from reach;	
• supervise closely until behavior subsides; and	
• note provoking cause.	
11. For violent behavior:	Have clear, well-planned approach ready to implement should this occur.
• keep your distance from patient, but keep patient in view at all times;	
• calmly notify patient of consequences that will occur in response to behavior;	This assumes that patient is able to understand consequences and to assist with control.
• position yourself with space behind or beside you with your back to the exit;	This allows you to move and avoid being trapped.
• call for help in calm, forceful voice if you are unable to handle behavior;	Security may need to be called by second person responding.
• restrain or medicate patient per physician's order to subdue behavior;	
• implement use of restraints or medication quickly and with adequate help;	Avoid negative comment or annoyance because patient may perceive this as punitive.
• keep patient under direct supervision until behavior subsides;	
• review incident briefly with patient when he or she is able; and	This reinforces patient's knowledge that behavior will be responded to with a plan.
• note provoking cause.	

DOCUMENTATION

1. Document the initial assessment, plan, and interventions and patient response in the appropriate record.
2. Document specifics in the appropriate medical record:
   • note indications for one-on-one staffing;
   • periodically document the patient's behavior, the effectiveness of the current plan, and achievement of behavioral goals; and
   • note specifics about the behavior when acute agitation or violent behavior occurs and about interventions.
3. Document the patient and family education.

Craig Bed

PURPOSES

To decrease environmental stimuli; to provide an emotionally and physically secure environment; to prevent falls; to provide an alternative method to physical restraints.

STAFF RESPONSIBLE

EQUIPMENT

1. Craig bed (Figure 6-1).
2. Two to four mattresses.
3. Sheet of plastic.
4. Two convoluted foam mattresses.
5. Two fitted sheets or one king-size fitted sheet.
6. One flat sheet.
7. Pillows.

GENERAL CONSIDERATIONS

1. The Craig bed is a specially designed bed that was initially crafted at Craig Rehabilitation Center. It consists of four 5-foot high padded walls that surround one or two mattresses placed on the floor in the center. The walls form a square that surrounds the mattresses. This bed works best if the patient is able to transfer himself or herself from the floor to the wheelchair with minimal assistance. Patients with tracheostomy or enteric feeding tubes may be difficult to manage in this type of bed. The bed works well with patients who have the potential for agitation or violent behavior because a wheelchair can be positioned in the center if mattresses are removed. This allows the patient a small, confined area with decreased stimulation as a time-out period. It works best for patients who can use a flat bed and who can pull themselves up to a standing position when they are restless. The Craig bed has been modified at the Rehabilitation Institute of Chicago to single and junior bed sizes as well. The inner surface of the bed can be used to display orientation aids or familiar objects.

2. The decision to use a Craig bed should be made by the physician and the nurse on the basis of the amount of stimulation that the patient can tolerate, the current functional level, and the current nursing care needs. Mobile, agitated patients generally are not candidates for using the Craig bed because of safety concerns. The goals and outcome during the use of the bed should be frequently reevaluated. A physician's order should be written for the desired bed.

3. Safety issues necessitating the use of the particular bed should be documented in the medical record.

4. A private room is preferred when using the large Craig bed.

5. Families should be taught how to interact with the patient in the Craig bed and when and how to secure the locks on the bed.

6. Each bed should be cleaned at regular intervals with antiseptic solution and on discontinuation of use. Notify housekeeping of the need to clean the unit.

7. When using the Craig bed with incontinent patients, it is imperative that a large plastic sheet be placed on the floor beneath the mattress.

8. Engineering should be notified to repair the beds as necessary.

9. The bed is discontinued when the goals and outcomes are achieved, when the goals and outcomes are not realized and further use is deemed unnecessary, or when adverse effects occur (e.g., agitation increases).

PATIENT AND FAMILY EDUCATION

1. The patient and family should be informed about the purpose and reasons for using the bed. The appearance of the bed may be frightening to the patient and family.

2. If its use is anticipated, orient the family to its appearance, use, and therapeutic benefits.

PROCEDURE

Steps	*Additional Information*
1. Describe bed and desired outcomes to patient and family.	
2. Obtain physician's order.	
3. Evaluate amount of stimulation that patient should receive.	
4. Notify appropriate staff of need to set up bed and determine whether additional mattresses will be needed.	Bed surface may be raised with additional mattresses stacked on top of each other.
5. Lock entrance walls when patient is unattended.	

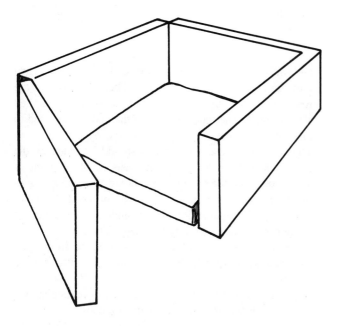

DOCUMENTATION

1. Note in a progress note when the bed is ordered, the reason for its use and the goals and outcomes to be achieved.
2. Enter the order for the bed in the patient's care plan, and chart its daily use.
3. Document in a progress note on periodic basis the achievement of goals and any limitations.

Figure 6-1 Craig Bed.

Guidelines for Use

PURPOSES

To provide guidelines for decision making regarding the appropriate use of physical restraints for patient safety; to alert staff to the importance of maintaining patient rights when using physical restraints.

STAFF RESPONSIBLE

EQUIPMENT

1. Restraints.

GENERAL CONSIDERATIONS

1. The nurse carefully assesses the need for restraint, taking into consideration the patient's:
   - age,
   - cognitive status,
   - underlying cause of agitation or confusion,
   - mobility,
   - skin status, and
   - potential for injury to self or others.
2. Behavioral management strategies are preferred. Use physical restraints only if other methods are unsuccessful. See procedure on guidelines for care of the agitated patient.
3. Jacket or belt restraints are generally used for confused or sedated patients to prevent them from climbing or falling out of bed or from sliding or getting out of a chair.

4. A physician's order is required indicating any type of restraint other than a wheelchair safety strap and the length of time that the restraint is to be used.
5. Instructions for application and removal of all types of restraints must be clearly documented in the patient's care plan.
6. Agency procedures for the initial application of restraints should be followed.
7. Padding restraints with sheepskin or other soft material is necessary if the restraint will cause friction, rubbing, or skin abrasions or if the patient has fragile skin.
8. A restrained patient must be checked frequently (at least every 30 minutes) for safety, circulatory status, and comfort needs.
9. Side rails are to be up while the patient is restrained in bed.
10. Tie knots with hitches (square knot or clove hitch) that can be released quickly. Tie the knot at a place where it can be reached easily in an emergency.
11. In an emergency, a restraint may be applied by the nurse to protect the patient and others. A physician's order is obtained immediately after this incident.
12. States and accrediting agencies have regulations influencing the use of restraints to protect patient rights.

PATIENT AND FAMILY EDUCATION

1. Explain rationale for the use of restraints to the patient and family as frequently as necessary.
2. Teach family members the appropriate use of restraints, if necessary for a pass or discharge.

DOCUMENTATION

1. Document the assessment of: (a) the need for restraints, (b) the method, (c) patient and family responses, and (d) the plan for ongoing assessment of the effectiveness and safety in the use of restraints.

Application of Elbow Restraints for Infants and Small Children

PURPOSE

To protect a child from injury.

STAFF RESPONSIBLE

EQUIPMENT

1. Elbow restraints.
2. Tongue blades.
3. Tape.

GENERAL CONSIDERATIONS

See general considerations for all types of restraints.

SPECIFIC CONSIDERATIONS

1. Elbow restraints are used to prevent infants or small children from flexing their arms. The restraint consists of material with pockets into which plastic or wood tongue depressors are inserted to provide rigidity (Figure 6-2).
2. Elbow restraints are applied to infants or small children with eczema; lesions of the neck, face, or head; or abdominal or urinary devices or tubes in place to prevent contamination or dislodging with hands or fingers.
3. Elbow restraints are removed, according to specific instructions in the care plan, at least once per shift or at meal times to inspect the skin and to give the child the opportunity to move his or her arms.

PATIENT AND FAMILY EDUCATION

1. Explain rationale for the restraints to the patient and family.
2. Instruct the family in restraint use, if appropriate for protection.

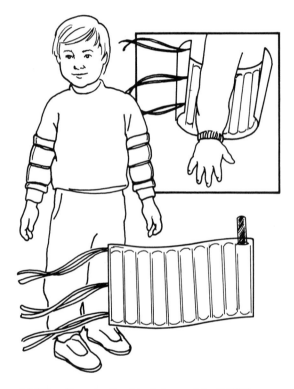

Figure 6-2 Elbow Restraints Used for Infants and Small Children.

PROCEDURE

Steps	Additional Information
1. Insert tongue blades into every or every other pocket of restraint.	Size of restraint may be modified by breaking tongue blade, taping broken edges, and then inserting blade into pockets.
2. Lay child's elbow into center of restraint.	Apply over child's shirt or gown, being sure that sleeve is as free from wrinkles as possible.
3. Wrap restraint smoothly around arm, and tie all three pairs of ties securely.	Restraint should fit securely but not occlude circulation. Tie knots on back of arm.
4. Tape upper end of restraint to gown or shirt sleeve.	This prevents it from sliding down arm.
5. Check patient and restraints as required. Remove restraint to relieve pressure or for meals.	

DOCUMENTATION

1. Document in the appropriate record the application and removal times, the type of restraint used, and the frequency of monitoring.
2. Document in a progress note when initiating or discontinuing the use of restraints and once a day thereafter. Indicate the behavior necessitating the use of the restraint, the effectiveness of the restraint, any unusual occurrences, and the response of the patient.
3. Document the patient and family teaching and their response.

Application of Cloth Extremity Restraints

PURPOSES

To protect the physical well-being of the patient or the well-being of others; to limit movement to facilitate the safe administration of a therapeutic procedure.

STAFF RESPONSIBLE

EQUIPMENT

1. Cloth extremity restraints.
2. Sheepskin (optional).

GENERAL CONSIDERATIONS

See general considerations for all restraints, above.

SPECIFIC CONSIDERATIONS

1. Soft cloth extremity restraints are used to restrain extremities and to prevent a patient from rolling out of bed, striking out, or pulling at tubes. These restraints may be applied only as follows:
   - one on the wrist and one on the opposite ankle,
   - on both wrists and one ankle, or
   - on both ankles and one wrist.
2. Restraints on both ankles only or on the wrist and ankle on the same side only are not permitted because these allow movement that could be a safety hazard to the patient.
3. One arm or leg may be restrained for therapeutic purposes if the opposite extremity has limited movement because of paralysis (e.g., in a patient with hemiplegia whose unaffected arm is restrained to prevent pulling out a catheter or other tubes).
4. Obtain a physician's order for a specific restraint.

PATIENT AND FAMILY EDUCATION

1. Explain rationale of restraint use to the patient and family.
2. Instruct family in restraint use if necessary to protect the patient and others or to facilitate the therapeutic procedure.

PROCEDURE

Steps	*Additional Information*
1. Explain necessity of restraints to patient and family.	An explanation is required for all patients.
2. Put patient in comfortable position in proper alignment.	
3. Apply restraint to wrist or ankle with soft flannel side against skin.	Be sure that arm or leg can assume normal anatomic position with restraint applied (e.g., elbow is able to flex slightly). Pad restraint with sheepskin or other soft material as necessary for fragile skin.
4. Adjust restraint to size of extremity by: • pulling one of the ties through the slotted end, • slipping tie through loop on outside of restraint, or • pulling restraint to fit snugly but allowing for adequate circulation.	

Steps	*Additional Information*
5. Secure ties to movable portion of bedframe with square knot or clove hitch (these will not tighten when pulled).	It is essential that restraint be tied to movable part of bed to prevent injury. Never secure restraint to side rails.
6. Leave patient comfortable and with call light in reach.	If both wrists are restrained, audible monitor may be used for patients to call for assistance.
7. Check restraints every 30 minutes for signs of circulatory impairment, skin excoriation, or other needs.	
8. Release restraints at least once per shift or as needed for skin tolerance, toileting, or feeding.	If patient is acutely agitated, release restraints one at a time.
9. Check skin for pressure areas.	
10. Turn and reposition patient.	
11. Reapply restraints.	

DOCUMENTATION

1. Note application and removal times, the type of restraint used, and the frequency of monitoring.
2. Note the behavior necessitating the use of the restraint.
3. Note the effectiveness of the restraint.
4. Document any unusual occurrences and the response of the patient.
5. Record patient and family education.

Application of Jacket Restraints

PURPOSE

To protect the physical well-being of the patient while he or she is in bed or up in a chair.

STAFF RESPONSIBLE

EQUIPMENT

1. Sheepskin.
2. Jacket restraint.

PROCEDURE

GENERAL CONSIDERATIONS

See general considerations for all restraints, above.

SPECIFIC CONSIDERATIONS

1. A jacket restraint is generally used for confused or sedated patients to prevent them from falling out of bed or slipping out of a wheelchair.
2. The correct jacket restraint size is important for proper application and patient comfort.
3. A physician's order is necessary before applying jacket restraints.

PATIENT AND FAMILY EDUCATION

1. Explain rationale for using a jacket restraint to protect the patient.
2. Instruct the family on its application as appropriate.

Steps	*Additional Information*
1. Explain necessity of jacket restraint to patient and family.	Give explanation even if patient appears to be confused.
2. Choose correct size.	
3. Put patient in comfortable position in proper alignment in bed or wheelchair.	If patient is in bed, position him or her so that hips are at center of bed (where hips would be located if head of bed was

Steps	*Additional Information*

| | elevated). If patient is in wheelchair, position hips at rear of seat well centered in chair. |

4. Slip jacket over patient's head with loops in front. | Jacket is placed over clothing. Adjust jacket 2 to 3 inches longer in front. |

5. Apply jacket per style instructions. | If patient is in bed, bring ties directly over sides of bed, and wrap each tie twice around movable spring frame. Then tie knot. If patient is in wheelchair, bring ties through slots at sides of seat around to back of chair. Cross ties, and secure them with knots to projections at bottom of chair and around back of chair (Figure 6-3). |

6. Leave patient in comfortable position with call light within reach.

7. Check patient every 30 minutes. Monitor patient's position, toileting needs, and application of jacket. | This may need to be done more frequently for patients with fragile skin or those who become agitated and mobile. |

8. Release jacket at least once per shift and as needed:
   - reposition patient as needed,
   - readjust jacket, and
   - retie jacket correctly.

DOCUMENTATION

1. Document in the appropriate record the application and removal times, the type of restraint used, and the frequency of monitoring.

2. Document in a progress note when initiating the use of the restraint and daily thereafter. Indicate the behavior necessitating the use of restraints, the effectiveness of the restraints, any unusual occurrences, and the response of the patient.

3. Document the patient and family education.

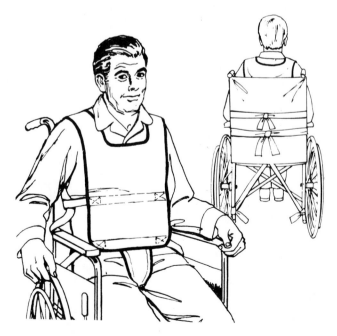

Figure 6-3 Jacket Restraint for Patient in Wheelchair. *Source:* Courtesy of Heel bo℗, Niles, IL.

HIP PRECAUTIONS

Guidelines for Hip Precautions

PURPOSE

To describe common orthopedic precautions required after hip arthroplasty surgery.

STAFF RESPONSIBLE

EQUIPMENT

1. Abductor splint.
2. Raised toilet seat.

GENERAL CONSIDERATIONS

1. Because of the nature of hip joint replacement surgery, all patients who have had a hip arthroplasty (joint replacement) are required to follow hip precautions (Exhibit 6-1) until physician orders indicate otherwise.
2. The nurse is responsible for:
   - initiating hip precautions on admission,
   - communicating the need for hip precautions to all caregivers,
   - ordering the necessary equipment, and
   - administering patient and family education.

PATIENT AND FAMILY EDUCATION

1. Teach the patient and family proper positioning and the use of the equipment.
2. Teach precautions, correct movements, movements to be avoided, signs and symptoms of complications, and long-term considerations for the reconstructed joint.

PROCEDURE

Steps	*Additional Information*
1. Initiate the above-mentioned hip precautions on admission and place an appropriate sign above bed. Note hip precautions on care plan.	Do not adduct or internally rotate affected leg because this movement can precipitate a hip dislocation. Simultaneous adduction with internal rotation presents a particularly high risk for dislocation.
2. Use abductor splint or Velcro knee straps to keep legs abducted in wheelchair.	
3. Turn to back and unaffected side only.	
4. Keep leg in neutral position during bed activities.	
5. Do not flex hip past 90° for at least 6 weeks postoperatively. This includes during transfers and while reaching for objects when sitting. Teach patients to use dressing aids or to call for assistance as needed.	
6. Order and use raised toilet seat to facilitate maintaining precautions during toilet transfers.	If not available, use raised commode chair.
7. Monitor for signs and symptoms of hip dislocation: • swelling of operated leg, • redness or discoloration of hip, • pain at operated hip (sudden or severe), and • unusual positioning of extremity.	

DOCUMENTATION

1. Document all nursing orders and interventions in the appropriate medical record.
2. Document any unusual situations, signs and symptoms of complications, and actions taken in the medical record.
3. Document the patient and family teaching of hip precautions and the patient's ability to comply.

Exhibit 6-1 Hip Precautions

WHEN? For a minimum of *6 weeks* after hip replacement surgery. All newly admitted hip surgery patients are placed on hip precautions until physician orders indicate otherwise.

Do:	**Don't:**
1. Keep legs abducted. Use abductor splint between your legs at all times. Use splint or at least two pillows between your legs when turning. Always use Velcro knee straps to keep hips abducted when you are in wheelchair.	1. Adduct legs (cross operated leg over midline).

Leg Abduction

Leg Adduction

2. Turn to back and unaffected hip only.
3. Keep operated leg in neutral position when you are in bed and during activities.
4. Use elevated toilet seat. In community, you should use handicapped toilets, which are generally raised seats.
5. Report the following to physician:
   - swelling of operated leg,
   - redness or discoloration of hip,
   - pain at hip,
   - drainage from incision line, and
   - chest pain.
6. Tell your physicians and dentists about your hip surgery.
7. Report any infections to your physician for immediate treatment.

2. Flex legs past 90° for first 6 weeks after your operation.
3. Flex hip when in side-lying position.
4. Bend forward at hip during transfers or when sitting in wheelchair, pulling pants on, or reaching for object on the floor.

Hip Flexion

5. Elevate footrests on wheelchair.
6. Sit for long periods. (You should raise up or stand for 1 to 2 minutes to relieve pressure. Every 30 minutes to 1 hour).
7. Turn onto operated side.
8. Internally rotate operated leg.

Internal Rotation

Care of the Patient with a Seizure Disorder

PURPOSES

To identify high-risk patients and to describe preventive interventions; to describe treatment interventions that promote patient safety and accurate assessment and contribute to the diagnosis of a seizure disorder.

STAFF RESPONSIBLE

EQUIPMENT

1. Cotton blankets and tape.
2. Padded side rail protectors.
3. Pillows.
4. Oral airway.
5. Unit emergency drug box.
6. Seizure precaution signs.

GENERAL CONSIDERATIONS

1. Seizures are "sudden episodes of varying severity precipitated by abnormal, excessive neuronal discharges within the brain" (Luckmann & Sorenson, 1980, p. 439). They are characterized by convulsive movements or other motor activity, sensory phenomena, or behavioral abnormalities. Seizures are the result of excessive release of electrical impulses by a group of neurons in different parts of the brain. Seizures are a symptom, not a disease.
2. Common etiological categories in which seizure activity is a symptom include:
   - cerebral injuries,
   - birth injuries,
   - infectious diseases,
   - cerebral circulatory disturbances,
   - cerebral trauma,
   - neoplasms of the brain,
   - biochemical imbalances,
   - drug or alcohol overdose,
   - medication-induced electrolyte imbalance, and
   - posttraumatic causes.
   Seizures may also be idiopathic.
3. Seizures are classified as given in Exhibit 6-2.

Exhibit 6-2 International Classification of Seizure Types

1. Partial seizures (seizures that involve or begin in one area of the brain):
   - Partial seizures with elementary symptomatology (seizures that have relatively uncomplicated symptoms; usually the person remains conscious):
     —with motor symptoms (symptoms affecting the muscles)
     —with sensory or somatosensory symptoms (symptoms affecting the senses)
     —with autonomic symptoms (symptoms affecting the internal organs)
     —compounded forms (symptoms of more than one of the above types)
   - Partial seizures with complex symptomatology (partial seizures with more complicated symptoms, usually with some loss of consciousness):
     —with impairment of consciousness only
     —with cognitive symptomatology (symptoms affecting thought)
     —with affective symptomatology (symptoms affecting mood or emotion)
     —with psychosensory symptomatology (symptoms affecting sense perception, such as illusions or hallucinations)
     —with psychomotor symptomatology (symptoms such as movement and behavior inappropriate to the situation)
     —compound forms (symptoms of more than one of the above types)
   - Partial seizures secondarily generalized (seizures that begin as partial seizures and then become generalized)
2. Generalized seizures (seizures that involve both sides of the brain):
   - Absences (brief lapses of consciousness occurring without warning and unaccompanied by prominent movements, as in petit mal)
   - Bilateral massive epileptic myoclonus (an involuntary jerking contraction of the major muscles)
   - Infantile spasms (brief muscle spasms in young children)
   - Clonic seizures (seizures consisting of jerking movements of the muscles)
   - Tonic seizures (seizures in which the muscles are rigid)
   - Tonic-clonic seizures (seizures that begin with muscle rigidity and progress to jerking muscular movement; commonly known as grand mal seizures)
   - Atonic seizures (seizures in which there is a loss of muscle tone and the person falls to the ground)
   - Akinetic seizures (seizures in which there is a loss of muscle movement)
3. Unilateral seizures (seizures involving one hemisphere, or half, of the brain and consequently affecting one side of the body)
4. Unclassified epileptic seizures (seizures that, because of incomplete information, cannot be put in a category)

Source: From "Clinical and Electroencephalographical Classification of Epileptic Seizures" by H. Gestaut, 1970, *Epilepsia, 11,* p. 102. Copyright 1970 by Raven Press. Reprinted by permission.

4. Status epilepticus is a medical emergency in which a series of seizures occurs in rapid succession and in which the patient is unable to regain consciousness between the seizures, thus increasing the risk of cerebral anoxia or pulmonary aspiration. When status epilepticus occurs, interventions are directed to:

- establish and maintain a patent airway;

- provide oxygenation:
  —apply oxygen, and
  —contact respiratory therapist;

- prevent cardiovascular collapse;

- prevent injury to the patient;

- control seizure activity with IV medications:
  —prepare patient for IV insertion (IV medications commonly used include diazepam, phenytoin, and phenobarbital and should be available in the emergency drug box or crash cart; normal saline IV fluid is required when phenytoin is given), and
  —monitor and maintain ventilation, hydration, electrolyte balance, and urine output after the medication is given because medications may precipitate respiratory depression or hypotension.

5. The nurse is responsible for:

- obtaining a seizure history and documenting it on the admission form;

- administering anticonvulsant medications per physician's order and notifying the physician when problems with administration or schedule disruption occur;

- recognizing patients at risk for seizures and instituting safety measures.

PATIENT AND FAMILY EDUCATION

Instruct the patient and family about:

- the nature of the seizure disorder,

- signs and symptoms of seizure activity, precautions, actions to take,
  —treatment, medication regime including common side effects of medications,

- common precipitating factors (alcohol, caffeine, fever, anxiety, fatigue, and stress),

- activity limitations (safety needs, use of machinery, and driving restrictions), and

- medical follow up after discharge.

Identification and Preventive Safety Measures for Patients on Seizure Precautions

Steps	Additional Information
1. Gather seizure history if possible from patient and family or from referral material. Information to be included: • length of known seizure history, • date of last seizure (type and duration), • common symptoms experienced, • presence of aura and type, • known precipitating factors, • current medications, and • patient and family knowledge.	
2. Initiate seizure precautions.	This communicates need for seizure precautions to all caregivers and therapists.
3. Initiate safety measures. Place sign for "Seizure Precautions" at patient's bedside and on wheelchair. Tape oral airway to head of bed and back of wheelchair as appropriate.	Include patient's name and room number and phone number of appropriate nurses' station. Oral airway is preferred and is used primarily if status epilepticus occurs. Never attempt to insert airway into patient's mouth during seizure or with jaw clenched.
4. Pad side rails of bed with cotton blankets or pads as judged necessary.	This may be necessary for patients with known, generalized, grand mal seizures.
5. Notify therapist if protective helmet is needed for patients with skull defect.	Physician's order is necessary. Once surgical plate is inserted, helmet may be discontinued.
6. Inform caregivers that electronic thermometer is necessary to take patient's temperature. If glass thermometer must be used, then temperature must be taken through *rectal or axillary route only*.	
7. Obtain suction machine for bedside as judged necessary.	Consider this for patients with difficulty with airway protection or at risk for status epilepticus.

DOCUMENTATION

1. Document assessment and seizure history on appropriate medical record(s).
2. Document preventive safety measures to be implemented as seizure precautions.

3. Document patient and family education on appropriate medical record.

Identification and Treatment of Seizures

Steps	Additional Information
1. At onset of symptoms, stay with patient, and call for help. Notify physician. Provide for patient's safety.	See general consideration 1 under Care of the Patient with a Seizure Disorder.
2. Turn patient's head to side, and flex it slightly to facilitate drainage of oral secretions.	Major actions: protect patient from injury, and maintain patent airway.
3. Place pillow or blanket under patient's head.	In absence of pillow, place patient's head on your lap.
4. If possible, turn patient on his or her side.	If patient is in wheelchair, tilt chair back, remove belt, and slide chair from underneath patient, thus lowering patient to floor without lifting.
5. Loosen restrictive clothing.	If patient has skull defect, turn him or her to opposite side. Remove harmful objects from reach, or pad surfaces that might injure patient. If patient falls, logroll him or her if possible.
6. Allow freedom of movement of extremities.	
7. Suction patient as needed.	This helps reduce risk of aspiration.
8. If patient is receiving tube feeding, *stop feeding*.	
9. Observe and note pattern of seizure, progression, changes in pupils or gaze, presence of incontinence, duration of seizure activity, and respiratory involvement.	
10. Monitor vital signs every 15 minutes (pulse, respiratory rate, and blood pressure).	If fall occurred, institute spinal precautions until directed otherwise by physician.
11. Once seizure has subsided, carefully move patient, take vital signs, and monitor every ½ hour.	
12. Allow patient time to sleep.	
13. Observe for presence and duration of postictal symptoms: • paralysis, • somnolence, • aphasia, • headache, and • incontinence.	
14. Monitor for recurrence of seizure activity.	
15. When patient wakes, provide orientation and reassurance.	Amnesia and disorientation are common.

DOCUMENTATION

In the appropriate medical record, note:
  • onset of symptoms (time, pattern, and duration),
  • patient's activity at the time of onset,
  • general description,
  • pupil or gaze changes,
  • any injuries,
  • postictal symptoms, and
  • notification of physician.

Protocol for Prevention, Identification, and Treatment

PURPOSES

To prevent acute episodes of autonomic dysreflexia in patients at risk; to describe methods to treat safely occurrences of dysreflexia.

STAFF RESPONSIBLE

EQUIPMENT

1. Sphygmomanometer.
2. Stethoscope.
3. Nonsterile gloves.
4. Irrigation kit.
5. Normal saline irrigation solution.
6. Straight or indwelling catheterization kit.
7. Water-soluble lubricant.
8. Protective underpads.
9. Urinal.
10. Nupercainal ointment and applicator.
11. 1% Xylocaine jelly.

GENERAL CONSIDERATIONS

1. Autonomic dysreflexia is an emergency condition that can occur in patients who have spinal cord lesions at or above the T-6 level. Lesions may be complete or incomplete. The onset of dysreflexia requires prompt recognition and treatment of the etiological factors to prevent further exacerbation of symptoms, which could ultimately result in a cerebrovascular accident, seizures, and cardiac complications if left untreated.
2. A noxious stimulus, most often visceral stretching, below the level of the lesion sends impulses up the spinal cord to the level of sympathetic outflow, thus initiating a generalized sympathetic response below the level of the injury. Vasoconstriction occurs below the level of the injury as a result of a loss of intact inhibitory fibers; vasodilation occurs above the level of the lesion (Erickson, 1982). The patient will experience sudden hypertension that will intensify until the noxious stimulus is removed. Failure to alleviate the cause may lead to neurologic or cardiac complications as a result of prolonged sympathetic excitation.

3. Signs and symptoms of autonomic dysreflexia most often include:
   - headache ranging from mild to severe and often focused over the occipital area,
   - hypertension (mild to severe),
   - diaphoresis or flushing above the level of the injury,
   - piloerection above the level of the injury,
   - bradycardia or tachycardia,
   - nasal congestion,
   - altered level of consciousness,
   - blurred vision,
   - hiccoughs,
   - penile erection,
   - increased muscle tone or spasticity,
   - Horner's syndrome (eyelid lag, pupil constriction, and unilateral facial sweating),
   - pupil changes,
   - chills,
   - dizziness,
   - warm feeling,
   - hot flashes,
   - tinnitus or loss of hearing,
   - anxiety,
   - nausea,
   - weakness,
   - nose bleeds,
   - metallic taste in the mouth,
   - numbness or tingling in the extremities,
   - chest pain, and
   - urge to void or defecate.
4. Etiological factors include the following:
   - urinary—distention, stones, infection, bladder spasticity, micturition, catheterization, and invasive testing;
   - bowel—impaction, distention, digital stimulation, suppository insertion, enema administration, evacuation, and invasive testing;
   - integumentary—pressure sores, ingrown toenail, burns, and blisters;
   - vascular—venous thrombosis and external constriction (too tight clothing or shoes, and the like);
   - reproductive—sexual intercourse, manual examination, menstruation, and uterine contractions;

- acute medical problems—abdominal trauma or pathology; and
- dental procedures—extraction or abscess.

5. If symptoms persist after nursing interventions, immediately contact physician for further treatment. Routinely, occurrences of autonomic dysreflexia and the treatment administered are reported to the physician according to policy.

PATIENT AND FAMILY EDUCATION

1. The nurse is responsible for teaching the patient and family about the following:

- what is autonomic dysreflexia,
- the consequences of dysreflexia,
- signs and symptoms,
- common etiological factors,
- treatment measures for acute and chronic episodes, and
- preventive measures to be followed.

2. This teaching should be completed before the patient's first pass or trip and should be documented on the teaching checklist or in the progress notes of the medical record.

3. The patient should be taught the common signs early in his or her hospital stay so that he or she can request assistance early if they occur.

Identification and Treatment of an Acute Episode of Dysreflexia

Steps	Additional Information
1. Assess patient for signs and symptoms.	See general considerations 3 and 4.
2. Sit patient up, and position his or her legs in dependent position.	This facilitates venous pooling and lowers venous return to heart, thus lowering blood pressure.
3. Check patient's blood pressure.	Monitor blood pressure every 5 minutes during and after treatment for 15 minutes and then every 15 minutes for first hour after treatment.
4. If indwelling catheter is present, check for full leg bag. If it is full, empty it. Check blood pressure and patient for relief of symptoms. If bag is empty, check for kinks in catheter tubing, and reposition tubing to allow free flow of urine. Check patient and blood pressure for relief of symptoms. If bag is upside down, reposition it correctly, check for urine drainage, and check patient and blood pressure for relief of symptoms.	An overfilled leg bag may result in bladder distention. An empty leg bag indicates that catheter is plugged, that tubing is kinked, or that leg bag is improperly positioned.
5. Check to determine whether balloon has deflated and whether catheter is out of position. Gently tug on catheter.	If catheter is in urethra, urine outflow will be blocked and can result in bladder distention.
6. Irrigate catheter with 30 mL of sterile saline to check patency. Check patient and blood pressure for relief of symptoms.	If catheter is plugged, irrigation will be impossible or may dislodge obstructing clot, resulting in urine emptying. Never drain more than 500 mL at one time because rebound hypotension can occur. Clamp catheter for 10 to 15 minutes before draining more urine.
7. Change indwelling catheter if plugged.	Check for relief of symptoms.
8. If patient is on toileting or intermittent catheterization program, check for bladder distention, palpate suprapubic area, and catheterize if distention is suspected. Xylocaine jelly may be used on catheter to avoid further irritation of sphincter.	Empty only 500 mL at one time. Clamp catheter for 10 to 15 minutes, then drain up to 500 mL more urine. Repeat.
9. If urinary distention is not present, suspect bowel impaction. Palpate patient's abdomen for distention, insert anesthetic ointment into rectum, and wait 2 to 3 minutes. Insert lubricated, gloved finger into rectum, gently check for stool, and gently disimpact if able to do so.	Nupercainal is a local anesthetic that anesthetizes area and minimizes further insult, which could occur with rectal check and disimpaction.
10. If rectal check is negative and if symptoms are not relieved, notify physician. Monitor patient's blood pressure every 5 minutes. Inspect for other etiological factors (skin, clothing, and so forth).	See general consideration 4.
11. Prepare for administration of medications to reduce blood pressure.	Medications used include Nitropaste, atropine, Hyperstat, and other antihypertensive agents.

DOCUMENTATION

1. Document in the appropriate record:
   - signs and symptoms noted,
   - vital signs and treatment measures employed,
   - etiological factor precipitating the episode,
   - plan to prevent further occurrence, and
   - physician notification.
2. Document the patient and family teaching in the appropriate medical record.

Prevention of Autonomic Dysreflexia Episodes

Steps	*Additional Information*
1. Assess patient for risk of dysreflexia.	See general consideration 1.
2. Teach patient and family to follow urinary management program to prevent distention, infection, and stones. If patient experiences symptoms with routine catheterizations, notify physician, and obtain order for 1% Xylocaine jelly to use with catheterization.	
3. Teach patient and family to follow bowel management program. If patient experiences symptoms routinely with bowel procedures, request physician order for use of Nupercainal ointment with program.	Patients at risk should have bowel program that results in bowel movement *at least every other day*.
4. Teach patient and family to follow skin care programs to prevent pressure sores; to check skin twice each day, including toenails; and to check for vascular changes in lower extremities.	
5. Teach patient and family about acute medical conditions and procedures that may precipitate acute episodes and to seek medical intervention should they occur.	Patients should inform community physicians that invasive bladder and bowel procedures may induce acute episode and that premedication may be warranted. Consider issuing wallet cards that contain information about dysreflexia causes and treatment. Such a card is particularly useful for emergency episodes that occur while patient is in community.
6. Counsel patients regarding sexual responses after spinal cord injury and preventive measures to minimize risks of dysreflexia. Female patients should be advised that dysreflexia can occur during delivery and that premedication may be necessary.	
7. Evaluate patient and family understanding of dysreflexia and of programs to prevent occurrence.	

DOCUMENTATION

Document the patient and family teaching in the appropriate record.

BIBLIOGRAPHY

Chui, L., & Bhatt, K. (1983). Autonomic dysreflexia. *Rehabilitation Nursing, 8,* 16–19.

Erickson, R.P. (1982). Autonomic hyperreflexia: Pathophysiology and medical management. *Archives of Physical Medicine and Rehabilitation, 61,* 431–440.

Friedman, D. (1988). Taking the scare out of caring for seizure patients. *Nursing 88, 18,* 52–59.

Fuestel, D. (1976). Autonomic dysreflexia. *American Journal of Nursing, 76,* 228–230.

Guttman, L., & Whitteridge, D. (1947). Effects of bladder retention on autonomic mechanisms after spinal cord injuries. *Brain, 70,* 361–404.

Head, H., & Riddoch, G. (1971). The autonomic bladder, excessive sweating and some other reflex conditions in gross injuries of the spinal cord. *Brain, 40,* 188–263.

Kerlinger, F.N. (1986). *Foundations of behavioral research.* New York: Holt, Rinehart & Winston.

Kewalramani, L.S. (1980). Autonomic dysreflexia in traumatic myelopathy. *American Journal of Physical Medicine, 59,* 1–19.

King, R.B., & Dudas, S. (1980). Rehabilitation of the patient with spinal cord injury. *Nursing Clinics of North America, 15*, 225–243.

Kurnick, N.B. (1956). Autonomic hyperreflexia and its control in patients with spinal cord lesions. *Annals of Internal Medicine, 44*, 678–686.

Lazure, L. (1980). Autonomic dysreflexia. *Nursing, 10*, 52–53.

Lindan, R. (1980). Incidence and clinical features of autonomic dysreflexia in patients with spinal cord injury. *Paraplegia, 18*, 285–292.

Luckmann, J., & Sorenson, K. (1980). *Medical-surgical nursing: A psychophysiologic approach* (2nd ed.). Philadelphia: W.B. Saunders.

Mathias, C.J. (1976). Plasma catecholamines during paroxysmal neurogenic hypertension in quadriplegic man. *Circulation Research, 39*, 204–209.

Monson, R. (1981). Autonomic dysreflexia: A nursing challenge. *Rehabilitation Nursing, 6*, 18–23.

Naftchi, N.E. (1978). Hypertensive crisis in quadriplegic patients. *Circulation, 57*, 336–341.

Polit, D., & Hungler, B. (1983). *Nursing research* (2nd ed.). Philadelphia: Lippincott.

Roy, S.C. (1984). *Introduction to nursing: An adaptation model* (2nd ed.). Englewood Cliffs, NJ: Prentice-Hall.

Schumacher, G.A., & Guthrie, T.C. (1951). Studies on headache. *AMA Archives of Neurology and Psychiatry, 56*, 568–580.

Taylor, A.G. (1974). Autonomic dysreflexia in spinal cord injury. *Nursing Clinics of North America, 9*, 717–724.

Index